THE POWER OF NEWS

JULIUS REUTER, 1861

THE
POWER OF
NEWS

THE HISTORY OF
REUTERS
1849–1989

DONALD READ

OXFORD UNIVERSITY PRESS
1992

Oxford University Press, Walton Street, Oxford OX2 6DP
Oxford New York Toronto
Delhi Bombay Calcutta Madras Karachi
Kuala Lumpur Singapore Hong Kong Tokyo
Nairobi Dar es Salaam Cape Town
Melbourne Auckland Madrid
and associated companies in
Berlin Ibadan

Oxford is a trade mark of Oxford University Press

Published in the United States
by Oxford University Press Inc., New York

British Library Cataloguing in Publication Data
Data available

Library of Congress Cataloging in Publication Data
Read, Donald.
The power of news: the history of Reuters, 1849–1989 /
Donald Read.
Includes index.
1. Reuters, Ltd.   I. Title.
PN5111.R4R43   1992.   070.4'35–dc20   92–27585
ISBN 0–19–820459–0 (Pbk)

Printed in Great Britain by
Butler and Tanner Ltd., Frome, Somerset

VATICAN CITY, SEPT I (1978), REUTER—POPE JOHN PAUL
SAID TODAY THAT IF THE EARLY CHRISTIAN DISCIPLE ST
PAUL RETURNED TO THE WORLD HE WOULD HEAD
REUTERS, THE INTERNATIONAL NEWS AGENCY . . .

I sing of one no Pow'r has trounced,
  Whose place in every strife is neuter,
Whose name is sometimes mispronounced
  As Reuter.

How oft, as through the news we go,
  When breakfast leaves an hour to loiter,
We quite forget the thanks we owe
  To Reuter.

His web around the globe is spun,
  He is, indeed, the world's exploiter:
'Neath ocean, e'en, the whispers run
  Of Reuter.

(*St James's Gazette*, quoted in
H. M. Collins, *From Pigeon Post to Wireless*,
1925, p. 32.)

PREFACE

THE Reuter Trust Agreement, first drawn up in 1941 and still in force, proclaims that the first objective of the company is 'to maintain in every event its position as the leading world news agency'.

The present book is not, however, a piece of promotional literature written in pursuit of this grand objective, even though what follows is an authorized history commissioned by Reuters. The text has been prepared with complete independence. I have been left entirely free to write as I please; and I have been given unrestricted use of the company's archives, except for personal records relating to living staff and pensioners. I have not had access to the records of the Newspaper Publishers Association.

Responsibility for what I have written therefore remains mine alone; but I have received much help from many people, both within Reuters and outside. I owe a particular debt to David Chipp, who has made available his experience as a distinguished journalist, first with Reuters and then with the Press Association. The news chapters in particular owe much to his detailed and enthusiastic research. Another old Reuter hand, Dennis Savage, has provided invaluable indexes and analyses, dug out of the archives with great patience and accuracy. They have saved me much time, and will help other researchers in the future.

I have benefited greatly from the good order of the Reuter Archive, and from the good humour of the archive and record staff. During the late 1980s John Entwisle, the corporate records manager, brought together a lively group of archivists. Piers Cain, the company archivist 1988–91, combined care for listing and preservation with eagerness to make the archives available for use. He himself researched enthusiastically into the early history. Ivy Stych, now retired, knew more about the records than anyone, and was ever ready to help. Overseas, Gerry Suckley has undertaken valuable research in South Africa, and the late Ingo Hertel did the same in Germany during the last months of his life. Jack Henry's 'Reuters Chronology' has proved indispensable for reference.

The voluminous papers of Sir Roderick Jones were secured for the Reuter Archive by Lord Briggs, and most usefully listed by his son Daniel. I am very grateful to Donald Haley for supplying extracts from his father's diary, and to Sir Richard Storey for access to his father's papers. Lady Hamilton kindly deposited her husband's Reuter papers in the archive.

Justine Taylor, a qualified archivist and my research assistant, has undertaken the detailed organization of the project. Her careful work has discovered much new evidence, and she has also been responsible for researching the illustrations. The book owes a great deal to her. I am also indebted to many others for help. A list of their names appears at the end of the book.

Forty years ago Graham Storey wrote *Reuters' Century*, the first official history. It still reads well, but much new material has been accumulated since 1951. The present account has been written as a middle-length, one-volume introduction. It is complete in itself. But the intention is to continue with two further volumes which will consider the history more fully—not simply by going into greater detail, but also by moving the focus away from head office and from the United Kingdom. In particular, the role of Reuters as the news agency of the British Empire deserves further attention, as does comparison between the major agencies. Constraints of space have necessarily limited the coverage possible in the present volume. This has meant for example, that the most recent news chapter, which deals with a theme well worth a book in itself, has had to be confined to a selection of episodes.

The news chapters go forward to 1989, an exciting year for general-news reporting. The company history of Reuters and of its management is taken to 1984, the year of the public flotation and a significant point of structural change.

D.R.

CONTENTS

x   *Contents*

LIST OF PLATES

Julius Reuter, 1861 *frontispiece*

Between pages 144 and 145 and pages 272 and 273

LIST OF FIGURES

LIST OF TABLES

NOTE ON THE COMPANY NAME

There are two versions of the company name: Reuters and Reuter.

Reuters is used exclusively as the company title. It is the version used in the company logotype. For all other purposes the word *Reuter* is used. To indicate possession, *Reuter* is used as an adjective: never *Reuters'*, *Reuters's,* or *Reuter's* (unless referring to Julius Reuter).

INTRODUCTION

THE name 'Reuter' appears daily in thousands of newspapers and upon thousands of screens all over the world. Enduring and universal awareness of the name has earned it a place in the language as well as in history. The 1982 supplement to the *Oxford English Dictionary* added to its roll the words 'Reuter' and 'Reuters', complete with quotations by way of illustration. The success of Reuters over almost a century and a half has provided an institutional demonstration of the power of news. News informs, news warns, news motivates. Julius Reuter made his fortune by recognizing this power.

For over a hundred years, from its foundation in 1851, Reuters was a national and imperial institution, the news agency of the British Empire. Paradoxically Reuter had been born a German Jew. In the mid-twentieth century the British Empire faded away, and Reuters might have faded with it. Instead, the old news agency saved itself by making a bold new start. During the past thirty years it has transformed itself from a national into an international institution, even though its headquarters remain in London. This transformation has been linked to the revolution in communications technology made possible by the transistor and the microchip. Computerized economic news and information—prices, trade figures, reports—are supplied on screen to business people working increasingly within a global economy. Thanks especially to the success of Reuters in providing such economic news, the company's profits have grown dramatically during the 1980s. In 1980 pre-tax profits were £3.9 million: in 1989 they were £283.1 million. This very large increase made possible a heavy investment in expansion. As part of the process, the numbers of Reuters staff worldwide grew from 2,894 in 1980 to more than 10,000 in 1989.

By that year over 90 per cent of current revenue was coming from products designed for the financial community. In a sense, the wheel had turned full circle, for in 1850 Reuter used carrier pigeons to forward stock-market and commodity prices from Brussels, where the Belgian telegraph line ended, to Aachen, where the German line began. In 1851 he moved to London, the financial centre of the Victorian world, and there launched his telegraph agency. By the end of the 1850s he had found success by establishing a standard for news gathering and distribution. Reuter had set out to be 'first with the news', and often was. But above speed he placed accuracy, and alongside accuracy he set impartiality in news distribution. He was to be less clearly successful in achieving objectivity in news reporting.

The leading theme within the present book will therefore be the working (or otherwise) of this Reuter news tradition. How did it begin? How and why did it survive? Has it always operated? Did it operate when the British Empire was at war? Was there always some unconscious bias in news selection or presentation? And how well does the Reuter tradition survive within the transformed company of the second half of the twentieth century?

Certainly, the present-day company knows that worldwide recognition of its independence in management and reporting, regardless of governmental or other pressures, is vital for its continuing progress as an international organization. In this knowledge Glen Renfrew, managing director 1981–91, said firmly: 'in an international company the Reuter people leave their patriotism at home. The longer they work abroad the more they begin to appreciate all the countries they work in.' The 1988 edition of the *Reuter International Style Guide*, produced for internal circulation, spelt out the old tradition to the latest generation of Reuter journalists. It reiterated the continuing need for accuracy, speed, and objectivity. 'Reuters does not comment on the merit of events . . . one man's terrorist is another man's freedom-fighter.'

Speed with the news, as part of the Reuter tradition, has required the ready use of the latest communications technology by the company throughout its history. The Reuter story which began with pigeons and telegraphy has now reached the age of satellites. Here is a second theme for the present book to follow, a theme full of interest in its own right. The history of any successful organization owes much to the personalities who have shaped it. Julius Reuter, and his chief assistant, Sigismund Engländer—a revolutionary of 1848—were only the first in a succession of strong or colourful Reuter personalities.

Tradition, technology, people—even this diversity does not encompass the full range of the Reuter story. The very raw material of the Reuter business—general and economic news and information—has been the stuff of history. Here is an extra dimension, exclusive to news history. The invention of plate glass or the development of man-made fibres obviously became important to mankind. But accounts of such innovations may or may not be interesting in themselves to readers in retrospect. How the world heard about the dropping of the first atomic bomb on Hiroshima in 1945 is a different story, and one reported by Reuters.

ONE

'Mr Reuter's Office'
1816–1865

I

FOR well over a hundred years the name 'Reuter' has appeared in the world's press more often than any other. News from Reuters reaches everywhere. When the founder of the news agency, Paul Julius Reuter, died in 1899, *Punch* commented in verse on 8 March:

> They need full epitaph, whose fame
> Were else oblivion's easy prey;
> 'Tis here unneeded, when each day
> A myriad prints bear Reuter's name.

Yet Julius Reuter was never primarily himself a reporter. He was a great news entrepreneur. During the second and third quarters of the nineteenth century news was becoming an opportunity commodity. If Reuter had lived two generations earlier, in late eighteenth-century England, he might well have dealt in cotton, the opportunity commodity of the industrial revolution. If he had been in business in the early twentieth century, he might well have become an oil-man. He chose news as his interest because in his day it was becoming marketable as never before. On the one hand, the public demand for news was growing fast. On the other, technology was advancing to meet and encourage that demand.

II

Paul Julius Reuter opened an office in London in October 1851. But before that date he had made several false starts on the continent of Europe. Evidence about these early ventures is patchy and sometimes contradictory. One certain fact is that, before Reuter at last founded his successful telegraph agency, he had first found himself a fresh surname. He was not born with the name which he was to send round the world.

The future Julius Reuter was born at Cassel, near the centre of

Germany, into a Jewish family on 21 July 1816. He was the third and youngest son of Samuel Levi Josaphat, and was given the names 'Israel Beer'. The Josaphats were a well-educated and well-respected family. Reuter's obituary in the *Jewish Chronicle* of 3 March 1899 remembered that his grandfather, Loeb Witzenhausen, had been judicial rabbinical adviser to the local Jewish community at Witzenhausen, and had been influential with the Government of Hesse-Cassel. However, the years before the final defeat of Napoleon in 1815 had brought great disturbance to the area, and led Reuter's father, Samuel, to move his family from Witzenhausen to Cassel. At the time of his son's birth, Samuel was acting chief rabbi of Cassel. His eldest son, Gerson, was also to become a rabbi and a notable Talmud scholar. Two of Reuter's cousins became university professors.

Reuter's father died in 1829; but his mother, Betty, about whom little is known except that she came from Cassel, survived until 1858. His attachment to her, and indeed to his whole family, was recalled by the *Jewish Chronicle* as 'one of the many excellent traits of his character'. Reuter was to help several of his relations financially in the years of his prosperity. At the start of his career, however, it was his family that helped him. His father had died leaving little money; and the boy was sent from Cassel to join the bank of his uncle Benfey at Göttingen.

During the second quarter of the nineteenth century Reuter's many relatives were thus dividing their interests between religion, scholarship, and business. Opportunities for Jews outside their own communities were opening up—witness the success of the Rothschilds. Prejudice, although never entirely removed, was diminishing. Some of Reuter's family remained strict in their practice of the Jewish faith; others became more relaxed.

Young Reuter stayed in the Göttingen bank for several years. Göttingen is a university town, and during the 1830s Professor Karl Friedrich Gauss, known as the founder of modern mathematics, was conducting pioneering experiments in sending electric signals by wire. One story, told in later years, described how Reuter had collected a bag of 30 louis d'or from Gauss at home to be credited to his account at the bank. On his way to the bank Reuter found that Gauss had mistakenly given him double louis d'or (in other words twice the amount). He rushed back to point out the professor's mistake. The master mathematician took some convincing, but was eventually persuaded of his error. Struck by Reuter's honesty and intelligence, Gauss then befriended the young man, and initiated him into the mysteries of electric telegraphy. Another later story claimed that Gauss himself had been little interested in the practical application of his discoveries about magnetism. Young Reuter, on the other hand—who attended Gauss's lectures, and may have acted as his unpaid assistant—realized that a system of telegraphy would transform world communications. Reuter foresaw that men would soon be exchanging messages at the speed of electricity, without any need for physical proximity.

The world's first telegraphic patent was taken out by Cooke and Wheatstone in England in 1837. Three years later Samuel Morse in the United States patented his dot-and-dash code for telegraphic use. The first commercial application of telegraphy was to pass train information along railway lines. On 6 August 1844 the first news received by tele-graph appeared in the British press: a telegram from Windsor Castle announced the birth of Queen Victoria's second son. News need no longer be delivered at the speed of the horse, or even the new railway—and perhaps not even at the speed of the new steamships. For in 1846 Wheatstone suggested that a submarine telegraph cable could be laid from Dover to Calais.

The news of Napoleon's defeat at Waterloo in 1815 had taken four days to reach London; the news of his death at St Helena six years later had taken two months to reach England by sea. From the 1840s such delay was ceasing to be necessary, as telegraph lines started to spread across the British Isles, Europe, and the United States. By 1862 the world's telegraph system was approaching 150,000 miles in length—some 15,000 miles in the British Isles, 80,000 on the Continent, 48,000 in North America.

Telegraphy was soon big business, in the hands either of Governments or of major companies. In England the Electric Telegraph Company was formed in 1846, and the English (later British) and Irish Magnetic Telegraph Company in 1852. The grand new offices of the latter com-pany, opened in Threadneedle Street in 1859 with the names of the con-tinents spelt out on the frontage, reflected the contemporary sense of space and time being conquered by telegraphy (see Plate 6).

Reuter was destined to become a major domestic customer of the British telegraph companies during the 1850s and 1860s. Twenty years earlier, however, he was still trying to make his way in Germany. After Göttingen, he seems to have moved through a succession of jobs in vari-ous German cities, but the evidence is confused. He was clearly unsettled, and this may well have been a factor in his decision to give up both his Jewish surname and his Jewish faith. He was never to be ashamed of his

Jewish origins, but he saw no reason why his career should be restricted by his Jewishness. Many other Jews were coming to the same conclusion.

At the same time he got married—apparently twice over—to Ida Maria Elisabeth Clementina Magnus, the daughter of a Prussian bureaucrat. The couple seem to have been first married in Berlin on 25 October 1845. They then travelled to London: 'Julius Josaphat' was recorded as entering England on 29 October. On 16 November he was baptized in the name of 'Paul Julius Reuter' at St George's German Lutheran Chapel, Whitechapel, London. On 23 November, at the same chapel, he again went through a ceremony of marriage with Ida. Perhaps the couple thought it prudent to do so in view of their change of surname.

Why choose the name 'Reuter'? Traditional explanations of a pun on *Ritter* ('rider' or 'messenger') are unconvincing: in 1845 Reuter was not in the news business. Perhaps he chose the name of a friend in England. The London directory for that year listed just one person with the surname—Simon Reuter, a wool merchant, and later a subscriber to his namesake's news service. Julius may indeed have been involved in the wool trade in 1845, for some of his family had connections with it. The certificate of aliens described him as a *Kaufmann* ('merchant'). On the other hand, Julius may have chosen the name Reuter simply because it was a common German surname, and he wanted to be accepted as entirely German. If so, it was ironic that he made it so familiar to the world only after he had become a British subject.

On this first occasion, however, the Reuters did not remain long in England. Whatever Julius's current business may have been, it did not prosper in London, and the young couple returned to the Continent. Their marriage was set to bring them lasting happiness. Julius and Ida were largely opposites, both in physique and temperament. While Julius was small, dark, keen of eye, succinct in conversation, Ida was buxom, blonde, sensitive, and discursive. But both were energetic and good with people. Ida's day-to-day involvement in the business was to be essential to her husband during the struggles of the next few years. Their first child, a daughter born in July 1846 and baptized a Christian, lived for only three weeks. No other children have been recorded until a son, Herbert, was born in London in 1852. Two daughters and one further son followed.

In 1847, using money from his wife, Reuter bought a share in an established Berlin bookshop. His partner, Joseph Stargardt, contributed the necessary book-trade experience. Early in 1848 the partners extended their activities into publishing. This was 'the year of revolutions', and there was a demand for political pamphlets. But only a handful of titles seem to have been published under the Reuter and Stargardt imprint. Reuter's motivation was probably more commercial than political. The known titles were radical but not violent in tone. One was Julius Froebel's *Kingship and the Sovereignty of the People: or is there a Democratic Monarchy?*

Such publications must have been noticed by the Prussian authorities, and fear for his safety may have led Reuter suddenly to abandon his shop and his partner. The story, told by Stargardt's widow after her husband's death in 1885, was that Reuter decamped with the proceeds of the 1848 Leipzig Easter book fair, a total of 600 thalers (£90); this was equivalent to a whole year's wages for an English artisan. Stargardt suffered a nervous breakdown as a result. When Reuter became successful in London, so the story continued, he offered to repay the money but Stargardt refused to accept it. This story, if true, is difficult to reconcile with Reuter's otherwise unchallenged reputation as an honest businessman. Perhaps he regarded the 600 thalers as simply part of his share in the firm, which he felt entitled to withdraw in an emergency.

Reuter may have next found a job in the office of the Havas news agency in Paris. France in 1848 was adding to its revolutionary tradition. The atmosphere in Paris was exciting, and news of what was happening there was in demand throughout Europe. This included both political and economic news. Paris Bourse prices, for example, influenced prices in all other stock markets. Such was the context within which Julius Reuter, already in his thirties, entered the world of journalism.

Reuter may have been a replacement on the Havas staff for Bernhard Wolff, who in 1849 was to launch his own successful agency in Berlin. The Havas agency was the world's first. Like Reuter, Charles Havas and Wolff were Jews. Havas had started in a small way in the early 1830s, but by 1848 he was well established in France and beyond. One of the Havas staff was a lively young Austrian Jew, who was to become a lifelong friend of Julius Reuter and to claim to be the co-founder of Reuter's agency.

This was Sigismund Engländer (1823–1902). Engländer was to lead a long and colourful life, moving about Europe for fifty years in search of adventure or news or both. He was a man of wide culture and revolutionary politics, his conversation fascinating on both counts. He was a Proudhonist ('Property is theft'), and the author of books in French and English. The last of these was entitled *The Abolition of the State* (1873). He stood to the left of Marx and Engels, who knew him within the German revolutionary movement and disliked him. All three were in exile in London during the 1850s.

Engländer had first come to prominence in Vienna during the revolution of 1848. His obituary in the *Jewish Chronicle* of 19 December 1902 said that he was one of the hostages demanded by the military when the Viennese rising was put down. It did not say that he was sentenced to death, but this was often claimed later. He was tipped off and escaped, eventually reaching Paris. But there too his revolutionary activities led him into trouble. He was imprisoned for several months before being deported. He apparently chose to be sent to England, 'the land of the free' as he called it, which he had never visited.

Meanwhile, Reuter was impatient to be his own master. Early in 1849 he started publishing his own news-sheet in Paris. Taxes upon newspapers had been abolished in France and Belgium in 1848. A vivid account of Reuter's under-capitalized venture was published nearly twenty years later by one of his assistants, Max Gritzner. This was the very first of all Reuter news offices. It was located in a shabby top-floor room on the Rue Jean-Jacques Rousseau. Its windows were dirty, its curtains tattered, its furnishings rickety. The enthusiasm of Reuter nevertheless made light of these shortcomings. All, he insisted, would come right. Translating and copying from French into German was done by his wife, 'with her faultlessly neat handwriting'. News was collected by Gritzner, and by an unnamed colleague who may have been Engländer, returned from London. Reuter himself was both editor and printer. His lithographed daily sheet contained news of all sorts, gossip, accounts of proceedings in the national assembly, Paris Bourse prices and reports, extracts from the Parisian press, and even original articles. This 'correspondence' was sent to subscribers in Germany, drummed up perhaps through Reuter's contacts in Jewish commercial circles there. The office stood opposite the main Paris post office, thus allowing the news-sheet to be printed just before the last post of the day at five o'clock. Bourse closing prices, of vital interest to subscribers, could therefore be included.

Unfortunately, revenue from subscriptions never equalled expenses, even after the staff had taken wage cuts. One day in the late summer of 1849 Gritzner came in and found that the office had been deprived of its vital printing-press, seized by creditors. 'The rickety table and chairs were still there as they were not worth the bother of taking.'

Reuter, ever resilient, seems to have decided that he had failed not because he was unsuited to journalism, but because he was working from the wrong place. He returned to Germany. Eventually he opened another office, which he called an 'Institute for the Promotion of Tele-graphic Dispatches', in Aachen on the border between Germany, Belgium, and The Netherlands. Aachen had stood at an important cross-roads since medieval times; and now Reuter had come to realize that the town could be given a brief extra importance as a European communica-tions centre.

The Frankfurt Parliament had encouraged greater press freedom in Germany; and even though in some states the press remained controlled, the time was right for Reuter to offer his news service. Right not only because of political, but also because of technological progress. The Prussian State telegraph line from Berlin to Aachen was opened on 1 October 1849. At the Berlin end Wolff had already started his agency, but there was still room at Aachen, where even before the opening of the telegraph Reuter may have been receiving political and economic news from Wolff by mail, for circulation to merchants and bankers in the Rhineland. He could also collect news by mail from Paris and other cen-tres. Anecdotes later circulated of how Reuter had enforced absolute equality among his Aachen subscribers. To ensure that all got market-moving news at the same time, they were locked in his office when stock-market or commodity news was expected, and all were handed the same news at the same moment. Whether Reuter enforced this system as soon as the Berlin telegraph reached Aachen is not clear. Or did he wait until the next year, when he had devised a system for getting news quickly from Paris?

The French Government did not open its Brussels telegraph line for public use until 15 April 1851. Before then, Paris–Brussels news went by train. To the east there was a telegraph gap of 76 miles between Brussels and Aachen. Were Reuter telegrams between these two cities bound to be delivered by rail? No, said Reuter. The answer was to use pigeons. They would take only two hours to Aachen. From there the telegrams could be transmitted by telegraph to Berlin.

Reuter could claim originality in spotting this opportunity; but he was never to claim that his Aachen arrangement made him the first person to employ pigeons for circulating news or commercial information. He knew that Havas had already used pigeons regularly, as had the Rothschilds and others. Their example no doubt reassured him. The Aachen pigeon-fanciers had themselves sent and received occasional mes-sages, but Reuter wanted to establish a regular pigeon service.

On 24 April 1850 Reuter made an agreement with Heinrich Geller, an Aachen brewer, baker, and pigeon-breeder, to supply a total of forty-five trained birds to maintain a service between Brussels and Aachen. Twelve birds were always to be available at Brussels. These were to be kept in the charge of Reuter's Brussels agent, Wilhelm Steffen, a former Prussian army officer and another left-wing politician. The pigeon service started on 28 April. The birds were sent each day by rail to Brussels, to fly back next day. The arrangement with Geller obviously worked well, for it was extended under a new contract dated 26 July 1850. Geller now agreed to devote all his available pigeons (more than 200) to the service.

This second contract revealed how keen Reuter was about secrecy at the Aachen end. The messages, tied under the wings of the birds, were to be opened only by Geller himself, upon their landing in his pigeon-loft at Pontstrasse 19. He was to place the papers in a sealed box, to be sent to Reuter's office without delay. The pigeon messages were taken to Reuter either by Geller's son or by another boy, F. A. Bacciocco, who was destined to become a well-respected journalist. Fifty years later Bacciocco recollected how he had hurried to the house with the brass nameplate 'Bureau Reuter'. Reuter was to be found inside with two clerks, smoking cigars and reading the papers. On receiving the pigeon messages all three sprang into action. Within seconds 'the small quick hands were writing'. Other boys would then run on to the telegraph office with the news for Berlin. Reuter met all the costs of operating this hectic service, and paid Geller 40 thalers (£6) per month. The first pigeons flew at dawn. As security against loss of a bird or delay, three birds carrying identical messages were sent up each time. While Bacciocco was running back to Geller's, he might meet the other boy bringing more pigeon messages to Reuter: 'On passing by he shouted at me "two" or "three" or "all". From this I knew whether I had to go up on the roof again watching out, or whether my morning's work was finished.'

Geller seems to have acted with considerable generosity towards Reuter. He first lodged Julius and Ida at his home, and then acted as guarantor when they took rooms at a local hotel, near the station and telegraph office.

Reuter's earliest big newspaper subscribers were the *Kölnische Zeitung* of Cologne and *L'Indépendence Belge* of Brussels. Reuter supplied the German paper with news from France and Belgium, and the Belgian paper with news from Germany and Austria. Henri-Edouard Perrot, the enterprising proprietor of *L'Indépendence Belge*, was later credited with first recommending Reuter to set up in Aachen at the end of the new telegraph line from Berlin. Perrot's paper of 27 March 1850 reported the establishment of 'a general correspondence bureau' in Aachen; Reuter was not named, but this was surely his bureau. It was said to be offering 'at a moderate charge, important news and stock-market prices' to the press and finance houses of Belgium, France, and England. This news was being delivered to Aachen by telegraph. Such systematic use of telegraphy, explained the article, distinguished the Aachen bureau from the many correspondence bureaux to be found in Paris, Berlin, and elsewhere. The emphasis of *L'Indépendence Belge* was upon the novelty of using telegraphy for news collection, not upon the use of pigeons, which were not mentioned.

Reuter must have realized all along that the telegraph gap would soon be bridged, and that he would have to develop his business upon a more lasting basis, or make yet another new start. On 2 October 1850 the telegraph line between Aachen and Verviers was completed. Reuter opened offices as the telegraph advanced, ending up near Quiévrain on the French border. On 15 March 1851 the Belgian telegraph network was completed, and linked at the same time to the Prussian system. When the French telegraph reached Valenciennes, the two telegraph systems were only five miles apart. Reuter now used relays of horses instead of pigeons. Then on 16 April 1851 the gap was finally closed. The telegraph companies were ready to handle the profitable business of news circulation for themselves, without need for an intermediary such as Reuter.

Reuter briefly hoped that he might find another intermediary role. His thoughts were again turning towards England. At the end of November 1850 he wrote from Verviers to Mowbray Morris, manager of *The Times* of London, the world's leading newspaper. Reuter's letter has not survived, but a copy of Morris's answer has. Reuter had boldly proposed 'to receive and forward to England all despatches which may be telegraphed to Verviers for *The Times*'. Morris replied with a polite evasion. *The Times* had its own news network, and did not need the services of the obscure 'Mons. Reuter'.

On 14 June 1851 he arrived in London with his wife. He had seen a chance to move his business to England: efforts were being made to lay a submarine cable across the English Channel between Dover and Calais. After failures in 1847 and again in 1850, success finally came on 13 November 1851, when the first messages were sent. The sea no longer presented a barrier to telegraphy. The North Channel between Scotland and Ireland, and the North Sea to Holland, were both crossed two years later.

THE NEW SIAMESE TWINS.

FIG. 1. *Punch*, November 1851: The laying of the Dover–Calais cable

III

London in 1851 constituted the focal point of the rapidly developing international economy. Industrial Britain was 'the workshop of the world'. The City of London, centred upon the Bank of England and the Royal and Baltic Exchanges, provided services for the commerce and industry not just of Britain and her empire, but of the whole globe. The Great Exhibition of the Works of Industry of All Nations, held triumphantly in London's Hyde Park during the summer of 1851, had illustrated Britain's centrality and predominance. Julius Reuter was to add significantly to that centrality by making London the news centre of the world.

The economic basis for Britain's success was freedom of trade. This had become an article of faith for most Britons, to be set alongside religious freedom and freedom of political expression. Vital for this last was a free press. Direct censorship had long since disappeared; but advertise-

ment duty, the stamp duty on newspapers, and the paper duty had produced continuing censorship through price. These 'taxes on knowledge',
as they were known, were finally to be abolished in 1853, 1855, and 1861
respectively. The price of daily newspapers then came down from as
much as 5*d.* to 1*d.*

Into this increasingly free business atmosphere came Julius Reuter.
Immigrants and Jews had benefited from a growing tolerance within
British society, which though not complete was sufficient. The Jews Act
of 1858 at last gave practising Jews the right to sit in parliament. The
measure had been strongly supported by Benjamin Disraeli, himself a Jew
by birth, who had converted to Anglicanism and who early in 1852
became chancellor of the exchequer; in 1868 he was to become prime
minister. Jews were acceptable, and Reuter was to do business during the
next few years with many members of the German Jewish community in
London. Yet he never became part of that community. He now regarded
himself—and wished others to regard him—as a Christian.

The Reuters took up residence at 23 Finsbury Square, not with a
Jewish family but with the family of a rising London Welsh doctor,
Herbert Davies. The long-remembered story in the Davies family was
that the friendship grew from a chance meeting in a railway carriage on
the Continent. This story claimed that Herbert Davies suggested to
Reuter that he should try his luck in London; more likely, London was
already Reuter's destination. Either way, Davies (who was known for his
kindness) offered Reuter room in his own house. Reuter's son Herbert, a
future managing director of the news agency, was born there on 10
March 1852; the baby was obviously named after the doctor. When the
Reuters left their host's house, they moved only a few doors away to 41
Finsbury Square and later to No. 19. And when in 1857 Reuter was naturalized a British subject, Herbert Davies, with his doctor brother Henry
and two other Finsbury Square medical practitioners, vouched for
Reuter. Arthur Davies, Herbert's second son, was to become medical
officer for Reuters during the later years of the century.

Finsbury Square was within walking-distance of the Royal Exchange.
Reuter opened his 'Submarine Telegraph' office at 1 Royal Exchange
Buildings on Tuesday, 10 October 1851. This was just a month before
the opening of the Channel cable. The office comprised two rooms, one
more than the Paris office of 1848. At first the staff consisted of just one
eleven-year-old office boy, Fred Griffiths.

F. J. Griffiths (1840–1915) was destined to serve Reuters in various
capacities for over sixty years. The boy had been forced to leave the

Merchant Taylors' School very early because his father's linen drapery shop in the Strand had fallen on hard times. Reuter liked to tell the story of how on one occasion in these early years, when he had gone to a chop-house nearby, his young assistant rushed in to say that 'a foreign-looking sort of gentleman' had called to see Reuter. He asked the boy why he had let the man go. 'Please, sir, I didn't,' was the answer. 'He is still at the office. I've locked him in.' Thus was one of Reuter's first subscribers secured.

In his later years such daring was not to be repeated by Griffiths. He settled for dedication and thoroughness as company secretary from 1865 to 1890, and as a director thereafter until 1912. His brother George became one of the first Reuter messenger boys in the 1850s, before going to work for the new *Daily Telegraph*. Another brother, John, was traffic superintendent from 1888 to 1915, when he was succeeded by his son F. J. Griffiths, jun.

In 1851 Reuter seems to have possessed sufficient capital to run his business successfully. He brought with him his old contacts in European financial centres and gradually began to build up a reputation. He contracted with the London Stock Exchange to provide the earliest quotations from continental exchanges, and he was given access to London Stock Exchange information. Twice a day, in return for a fixed-term payment, Reuter provided London and Paris brokers and merchants, via the new cable, with opening and closing prices in both capitals.

He was soon also busy supplying information about grain markets and prospects in Russia and the Danube basin to Greek merchants and others. The grain market had opened up after repeal of the British Corn Laws in 1846, and Russia was to be Britain's chief source of grain imports throughout the third quarter of the century. Grain supplies and prices were uncertain, at the mercy of climate or war; good weather and abundant supplies could be as disturbing to markets as bad weather and shortage. Reuter had spotted an important market for news, which he was glad to supply.

The earliest surviving telegram books, for August to October 1852, reveal Reuter's strong interest in the European grain market. The contents are mostly short messages on behalf of London firms; these gave instructions about commodity deals, provided price information, sent instructions to buy, and the like. Recipients were sometimes European branches of the same firm, sometimes partners, sometimes other firms. The main destinations were Antwerp, Hamburg, Trieste, Stettin (Szczecin), Odessa, Danzig (Gdańsk). Charges were occasionally recorded —sixty words to Trieste cost as much as £4. 17s. 6d.

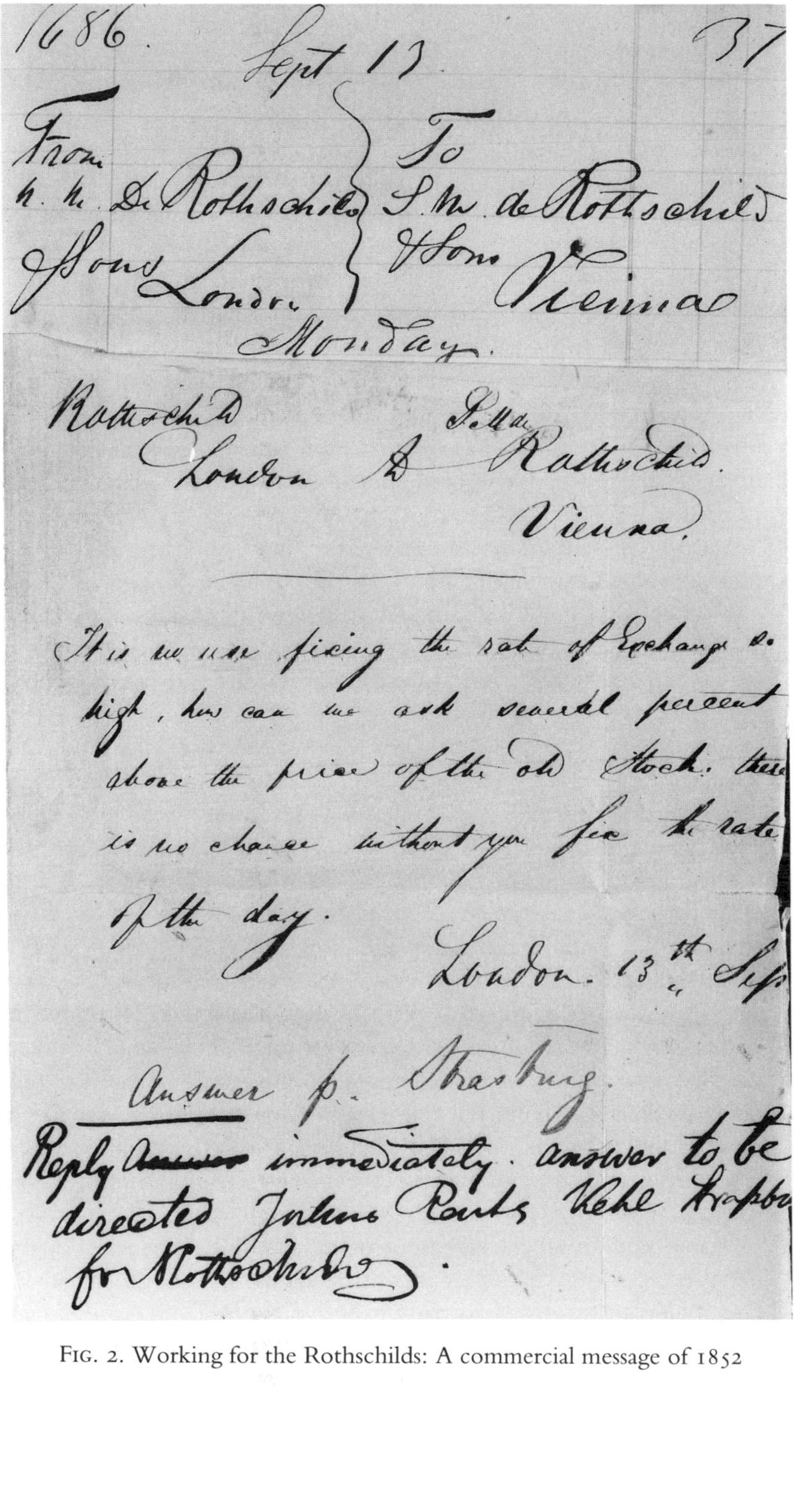

1686.   Sept 13.   37

From   To
h. m. De Rothschild   S. M. de Rothschild
& Sons London   & Sons Vienna
              Monday.

Rothschild   Pella
        London   &   Rothschild.
                        Vienna.

_____

It is no use fixing the rate of Exchange so
high, how can we ask several percent
above the price of the old Stock. there
is no chance without you fix the rate
of the day.
                        London. 13th Sep

        Answer p. Strasburg.

Reply answer immediately. answer to be
directed Julius Reuter Kehl Strasburg
for Rothschild.

FIG. 2. Working for the Rothschilds: A commercial message of 1852

Rothschilds' first use of the Reuter service read as follows (see Fig. 2):

It is no use fixing the rate of Exchange so high, how can we ask several percent above the price of the old stock; there is no chance without you fix the rate of the day.

London. 13th Sep.

Answer p. Strasburg
Reply immediately. Answer to be directed Julius Reuter Kehl Strassbu[rg] for Rothschild.

Why could firms such as Rothschilds not send messages for themselves? The answer was that the telegraphic services were still primitive and expensive, and it paid to employ an expert intermediary. The telegraph forms for the 'Submarine Telegraph' pasted in the Reuter telegram books declared plainly and comprehensively that the company accepted no responsibility for non-transmission or non-delivery of any message, 'whether repeated or unrepeated'. No International Telegraph Convention had yet set standards, and the transfer of telegrams from one line to another could produce delays and errors. Reuter agents at Calais and elsewhere were kept busy looking out for mishaps and retransmitting messages by telegraph, mail, steamship, pigeon, or by any combination necessary.

Reuter was obviously ranging far beyond the Calais end of the Channel cable; and significantly he changed the name of his office from 'Submarine Telegraph' to 'Continental Telegraph' about 1853. His stationery was now headed 'Continental Telegraph, under the direction of Mr. Julius Reuter'.

Evidence about Reuter's European contracts has survived in two instances. He was a ready traveller, and in August 1857 went to St Petersburg. He seems to have known no one there, but he had written to a local newspaper editor, N. I. Grech. Grech said that he did not understand news agencies and passed Reuter on to Paul Usoff, who was starting the first telegraph news co-operative in Russia. Reuter contracted with Usoff to deliver commercial telegrams to St Petersburg every day except Sunday for three years from 1 October 1857. Information was to be taken from all the main European centres. The subscription was 3,000 roubles (about £375) per month.

The text of another agreement of quite a different kind has survived from the previous year. This was made with Parisian bankers A. Prost et Cie. The plan was to start a daily paper of political and commercial news based upon the telegraph, and 'much quicker than the other papers'. The paper does not seem to have appeared.

Reuter might thus have become a newspaper proprietor. He was prepared to seek success in the news business in more than one direction, and was certainly not content to supply commercial news only. He kept trying to find outlets for political and general news, which his network of agents and contacts were well placed to collect. Already he included major political news as part of his commercial service, when it was likely to affect markets. Thus George Griffiths remembered in old age how as a Reuter messenger boy he one day took a message to a Stock Exchange member, and how the good news set the Exchange in uproar: 'they took me and placed me on a stool, and I was much satisfied when I was released with about fifteen shillings in my pocket.' The news was probably of a British victory in the Crimean War, perhaps of the fall of Sebastopol in September 1855.

For several years Reuter could not make the breakthrough into supplying news to the British press. The telegraph companies were offering a news service of sorts: the coverage was poor and the reports were not always correct, but newspaper editors were slow to realize that Reuter could provide a more dependable service, not only in commercial but also in political and other news.

Among the London dailies of the early 1850s, *The Times* was predominant. It sold over 50,000 copies each day, more than all the other London dailies put together. Only *The Times* possessed its own network of correspondents and 'stringers' throughout Europe, the Near East, India, China, and the United States. When at the end of 1851 Reuter offered *The Times* his service, Mowbray Morris was even more dismissive than he had been a year earlier: 'the Proprietors of *The Times* are not prepared to enter into any arrangement with you.' Three months later Morris was refusing an offer 'to furnish *The Times* with the exchanges of Brussels, Amsterdam, and Bremen at a rate of eight guineas per month'. In May 1853 Reuter was bluntly told that 'his telegraphic summaries of foreign intelligence will not be used by *The Times*'. This may have been an offer of more than commercial news. In August 1853, however, Reuter did make a small breakthrough, when Morris reluctantly accepted an arrangement whereby the Austrian office of Lloyd's began sending its Trieste news via Reuter for *The Times*.

The repeal of the newspaper stamp duty in 1855 encouraged a rapid transformation in the British newspaper scene. Penny daily papers now appeared, led by the new *Daily Telegraph*. It was selling 141,700 copies daily by 1861, leaving *The Times* far behind. In the provinces, old titles such as the *Manchester Guardian* and new titles such as the *Birmingham Post* began to appear as dailies. Both the newspaper space for news and the number of newspaper readers were extending rapidly. The 'latest telegrams', credited sometimes to correspondents and more often to the telegraph companies, were now appearing in the newspapers every day.

Up to 1858, however, the name of Reuter did not feature. Yet he was still hopeful. He knew that only *The Times* was prepared to bear the expense of employing numerous regular correspondents abroad. As late as 1914 even the *Daily Telegraph* kept permanent correspondents only in Paris, Berlin, St Petersburg, and New York. By accepting common use of Reuter's network, the new and old dailies would be able to increase their news cover at minimum cost. But how could Reuter persuade the editors to accept this mutually advantageous truth?

One way was to demonstrate that he could provide a better news service than the telegraph companies in even competition with them. In 1857 he won from Lord Clarendon, the foreign secretary, the privilege of receiving copies of Foreign Office telegrams from India, a concession already made to the telegraph companies. He told Clarendon that his agency was supplying all the leading continental newspapers with London news and official dispatches; so Reuter was apparently now dealing successfully in political news out of London. But he wanted also to direct the world's news into London: such, he knew, was the way to fortune, and towards the creation of a world news agency.

IV

There is a gap in the correspondence between Reuter and Mowbray Morris of *The Times* for five years after 1853. Then in 1858 Reuter tried again. He offered to supply Morris with a daily American money-markets service. This proposal was dependent upon the successful working of the new transatlantic cable, which was completed in mid-August. Reuter wrote to Usoff in St Petersburg on 4 September that he had made a deal with the Atlantic Telegraph Company for communication of American news. He was offering this news to subscribers at half the ordinary cable rate. But he offered Usoff the alternative of investing money in an American news-collection network. He detailed his proposal to Usoff five days later:

> the number of orders I have received from all sides for American despatches has prompted me to set up a central bureau in New York with subsidiaries in all the main cities of the United States, Central and South America. On top of the £5,000 sterling which I am contracted to pay

annually to the Atlantic Telegraph Company, this enterprise of mine will require significant capital, not less than £15,000 or £20,000 sterling . . . a large part of which I already have at my disposal. . . . I most respectfully propose to you to put £3,000 sterling into this venture on terms whereby I will send you American despatches free of charge. Your capital of £3,000 will remain your property, and instead of interest on it, I undertake to send you free of charge every day one telegram with American news. One telegram costs £2.10s, so 360 despatches amounts to £900 sterling, or 30% on capital of £3,000 sterling. You can withdraw your capital on one year's notice, and I will also offer you alternative security.

Here was a tempting offer in return for long-term commitment. Reuter was showing characteristic financial ingenuity allied to characteristic vision.

Reuter's offer of news of American money markets was also very tempting to Morris of *The Times*. This time he did not refuse: *The Times* agreed to pay 5s. per word for messages supplied by Reuter, reduced to 2s. 6d. if published with Reuter credits. The large saving seemed to be well worth making for a supply of merely routine news, even if shared with other papers. Moreover, the accuracy of Reuter's service could be subsequently checked by mail.

Alas, these schemes came to nothing. They were to be significant only in showing Reuter's businesslike readiness to 'follow the cable', as he had done in 1851 and as he was to do again. The 1858 transatlantic cable carried only a few messages before it began to break down. Hopes of repair lingered for several weeks. But no regular service of news for Reuter was ever started.

Reuter must have been greatly disappointed. Yet frustration with regard to America only led him to make a new attempt to sell his news from Europe to the London newspapers. He first approached *The Times*, and was rebuffed by Morris in letters of 5 and 6 October 1858. As an inducement, Reuter even seems to have offered Morris direct delivery of telegrams from abroad. This would presumably have given *The Times* a start over rival papers which took the news via Reuter's office.

Reuter now decided to approach these rivals. He went first to James Grant, editor of the *Morning Advertiser*. Grant's recollections of this crucial meeting were given in his *History of the Newspaper Press*, published in 1871:

In October, in the year 1858, one morning, a gentleman called on me. His accent, though he spoke English well, at once indicated his German nationality. . . . 'I am a Prussian; and have been employed for many years as a Courier to several of the Courts of Europe, from the Government of

Berlin; and in that capacity have formed personal intimacies with gentlemen connected with most of the European Governments. It has occurred to me that I might, therefore, be able to supply, by telegraph, the daily press of London with earlier and more accurate intelligence of importance, and, at the same time, at a cheaper rate, than the morning journals are now paying for their telegraphic communications from the Continent.'

Reuter explained that he had first approached *The Times*, but had been told 'that they could do their own business better than anyone else'. He was now therefore trying the other London dailies. Reuter offered to deliver 'earlier, more ample, more accurate, and more important information from the Continent' for £30 per month. This was £10 less than the *Advertiser* was paying for its own telegrams. Reuter temptingly proposed a fortnight's free trial of his service. Grant accepted. Reuter told him that he would not have tried any further if the *Advertiser* had said no. In the absence of *The Times*, the support of all the other leading papers was necessary to make the scheme profitable. Their editors agreed, like Grant, to a trial run. All were impressed by the service, and soon all had taken out subscriptions. The first telegram in the earliest book of collected Reuter general-news telegrams was received at 'Mr. Reuter's Office' on 8 October. This was perhaps the very first of the trial telegrams.

The Times now began to change its attitude. Mowbray Morris had lost the initiative. In his diary for 13 October, only a week after his last rebuff to Reuter, Morris noted: 'Saw Reuter about telegrams of foreign news. He agreed to send all to us and to charge us only for what we publish, for 2/6 for 20 words if his name is quoted, and 5/- if not quoted.' Between 13 October and the end of the year Reuter sent at least 140 telegrams to *The Times*. The first such telegram was published on 20 October, without attribution. Thereafter unattributed telegrams appeared on most days. Then on 8 December came the first telegram in *The Times* with a Reuter credit. It was prominently placed at the top right-hand corner of the leader page.

By naming Reuter, *The Times* was of course cutting its payments by half. Yet the paper seems to have remained reluctant to accept that Reuter telegrams must now be accepted as regular features. Understandably, it wanted to exploit its extensive network of correspondents as much as possible.

At this very period, Reuter was beaten by *The Times* on a major story. The paper's Paris correspondent telegraphed instantly some threatening diplomatic language used by Napoleon III at a reception on New Year's Day 1859. Napoleon's words reached London just in time to appear in the paper of 3 January, albeit in reported speech: 'the Emperor told the Austrian Minister, M. Hübner, that he regretted their relations were so bad, but his personal sentiments for the Emperor of Austria were the same as ever.' Reuter was a day behind with this news, and then sent only a second-hand account. The Reuter telegram, dated 4 January, simply provided a translation (plus the original French) of Napoleon's words as published in the *Constitutionnel* of that morning: 'I regret that our relations with your Government are not so good as they were, but I request you to tell the Emperor that my personal feelings for him have not changed.' Paradoxically, in its obituary of Julius Reuter forty years later *The Times* (27 February 1899), forgetful of its own columns, repeated the story, by then generally accepted, that this had been Reuter's first big scoop.

That first scoop was indeed to come only a few days later. The Reuter telegram in question appeared in *The Times*, duly attributed, on 10 January 1859. It summarized the important speech of the King of Sardinia at the opening of his parliament. The speech was important because, like Napoleon III's remarks earlier, it formed part of the build-up to war between France and Sardinia on the one hand, and Austria on the other, in the cause of Italian unification. The king's words had been delivered on the morning of 10 January, and Reuter in London had contrived to receive a telegraphed summary from Turin by 1.30 p.m. (see Fig. 3). The Reuter telegram was immediately published in the third edition of *The Times*, and was republished the next day. It was then accompanied by an editorial which did not question the accuracy of the Reuter summary. The full text of the speech, 'from our own correspondent', did not appear in *The Times* until 14 January.

Reuter had now demonstrated the speed and usefulness of his service, even to *The Times*, and still more to other London and provincial newspapers with few or no foreign correspondents. The leading provincial daily was the *Manchester Guardian*. It seems to have been taking unattributed Reuter telegrams from early October 1858, perhaps even ahead of the Reuter telegram of 8 October. Until January 1859, however, only the two telegraph companies, 'Electric' and 'Magnetic', were credited by the *Manchester Guardian* as sources. Then on 5 January several telegrams were published with Reuter credits alone. For a few days, though, the novelty of admitting entire dependence upon Reuter obviously caused the paper unease. So the *Manchester Guardian* played safe by sometimes giving a double credit: 'The following telegram, received by Mr. Reuter, is communicated by the Electric Telegraph Company.' From 11 January, however, Reuter alone was given credit for his telegrams. The next day the

REUTER'S TELEGRAMS.

The following Telegram was received at Mr. REUTER's Office, January 10th, 1859, 1.30 PM.

TURIN, Monday, January 10th.

OPENING OF THE SARDINIAN CHAMBERS.

The following is a summary of the Royal speech.

The King thanks the Chambers for the assistance afforded him during the last session, which consolidated the national policy and the progress of Piedmont. He announces that Government will bring in Bills for judicial administrative and municipal reform. He regrets that the financial crisis and the scarcety of Silk crops prevented a balance in the national Exchequer.

His Majesty says, that the political horizon is not clear, but that the future must be awaited with firmness. The future cannot fail to be fortunate, because the policy of Piedmont is based on justice and love of its country's liberty. Piedmont is small, but great in the councils of Europe, on account of the principles it represents, and the sympathies it inspires. It respects treaties, but is not insensible to Italy's cry of anguish.

The King concludes with the words: "Let us reso-"lutely await the decrees of Providence."

Prolonged acclamations of *Vive le Roi!* followed the conclusion of the speech.

Printed at Mr. REUTER's Office,
1, Royal Exchange Buildings, City

FIG. 3. The first scoop, 10 January 1859

newspaper carried the Sardinian scoop under a column-width headline. Here was a bold splash by the standards of the time. Reuter was now trusted.

In this same month the 'Electric' and 'Magnetic' telegraph companies jointly arranged with Reuter to supply his telegrams to all towns in the United Kingdom. He was paid £800 per annum, and retained the right to supply commercial and shipping news to private subscribers within 15 miles of London.

Within a month of the Sardinian coup, which had provided an immediate summary of a royal speech, Reuter was to do even better. He now telegraphed to London the full text of Napoleon III's speech at the opening of the French chambers on 7 February—and he did so *as the speech was being delivered*. This unprecedented scoop required Reuter to stretch his still small organization in Paris and London to the full. He needed an advance copy of the speech, and also a clear telegraph line to London. Someone (was it Reuter himself or was it Engländer?) persuaded the French Government to provide the advance copy, probably through Napoleon III's private secretary. Here was perhaps the earliest instance of news being issued to an agency under a transmission embargo. Someone persuaded the Submarine Telegraph Company to sell exclusive use of its line for one hour. At noon Reuter's agent opened a sealed envelope containing the full speech, and transmission to London began even as Napoleon III was starting to speak. His words were urgently awaited: they were likely to decide peace or war between France and Austria. By one o'clock, despite a short delay on the cable, the Emperor's whole speech had been received. It was instantly translated. And by two o'clock special editions of the London papers were on sale. The speech ran to a full column of closely printed text, 930 words in all. 'Peace, I hope, will not be disturbed,' exclaimed Napoleon in the Reuter translation—which meant, in diplomatic language, that war was near.

Morris of *The Times* tried and failed to spoil Reuter's triumph. He immediately complained to Reuter that a key passage had been omitted from the report of the speech. This was incorrect, as was admitted by the paper when on 10 February it published the full French text: 'there were one or two slight errors, not in the language, but in its division into paragraphs and sentences.'

Down the years Morris remained ever ready to complain: 'Your telegrams do not often contain any important news' (21 October 1859); 'frivolous and desultory . . . utterly worthless' (24 November 1862). Yet, complain or not, *The Times* now paid highly to receive Reuter telegrams.

The earliest surviving Reuter cash-book for 1862 showed *The Times* sub-scription at £100 per month. The *Morning Herald* and *Morning Chronicle* were paying £83. 6s. 8d., the *Daily News* £75, and the *Daily Telegraph* and *Morning Advertiser* £66. 13s. 4d. If these were payments for identical services, Reuter had perhaps contrived to make *The Times* unknowingly pay extra for its long resistance and continued grumbling.

V

The impact made by Reuter's coup with Napoleon III's speech was noticed two years later in a magazine article. This article, by Andrew Wynter, appeared in *Once A Week* on 23 February 1861; it was entitled 'Who is Mr. Reuter?' It contained an outline, regrettably sketchy, of his career from the days of the Aachen pigeons. Its questioning title indicated how widely Reuter's name was now being mentioned every day in the newspapers. The *Birmingham Journal's* London correspondent had already answered the same question on 13 October 1860: 'Reuter is not only the man of the time, but the master of Time.' Short articles in the antiquarian journal *Notes and Queries*, also took up the quest. The first, on 3 November, by 'An Octogenarian Journalist', asked who was 'this myste-rious person'. The second, on 29 December, by 'J.T.', answered that Reuter was of German birth but naturalized British. He had collected correspondents all over Europe, and also worldwide: 'intelligence is regu-larly telegraphed, or otherwise expedited, from all India, China, and the East, from North and South America, and from the Cape.' In the London office, the article continued, incoming messages were checked, transcribed by clerks, and then delivered by messengers to the newspaper offices. 'Within the last three years this office has acquired considerable importance.'

The *Birmingham Journal* writer had still not been sure whether Reuter's news was trustworthy. British readers were more interested, he claimed, in immediacy and excitement than truth—news 'piping hot, and plenty of it'. Another doubter was Karl Marx, then living in exile in London; he does not seem to have known Reuter personally. In a letter of 12 April 1860 Marx gave Engels a garbled account of Reuter's career:

> who do you think is factotum to this grammatically illiterate Jew Reuter?—Siegmund Engländer, who was expelled from Paris because, although a spy in the pay of France (600 frs. per month), he was discov-ered to be a 'secret' *Russian* spy. This same Reuter, together with Engländer, Horfel and *Schlesinger*, was a partner in a Bonapartist litho-graphic news agency in Paris . . . they fell out, etc. *Mr Bernhard Wolff* . . . is

hand-in-purse (partners) with S. *Engländer*, who is at present editing world history in Reuter's name.

The immediate occasion for this outburst was Reuter's presentation at the Court of Queen Victoria on 28 March. He was presented by the prime minister himself, Lord Palmerston. Here was a striking reflection of Reuter's new 'respectability' and good connections. Marx suggested that there were political reasons behind the presentation. 'Russia has now joined the "Austro-German Telegraphic Union" and *pour encourager les autres*, has got Pam [Palmerston] to present her Reuter to the QUEEN.' Marx seems to have been implying that Reuter was favourably regarded by the Russian as well as by the British Government, perhaps through his connection with Usoff.

Clearly Reuter was now fully established in society. The progress of his social confidence was reflected in the birth certificates of his children. On Herbert's certificate in 1852 Reuter called himself a 'gentleman'. This was a sign not of prosperity but of aspiration. On the birth certificates of his two daughters he called himself 'merchant'. This was a sign of increasing confidence in his chosen career. Finally, at the birth of his youngest son, George, in 1863 he reverted to the style of 'gentleman'. The news agency was flourishing: at last he really was a 'gentleman'.

Wynter's 'Who is Mr. Reuter?' article included the first published like-ness of Julius Reuter (see the frontispiece). This was a head-and-shoulders engraving from a photograph. It showed a man who looked what he was—'foreign' in his features, purposeful yet pleasant of aspect. His nose was prominent. A receding hairline was balanced by fashionable mutton-chop whiskers with curls over the ears. Reuter's eyes looked out alertly but genially through small glasses. His jacket was of good quality and good fit. Here was a man who obviously cared for his appearance, who took pains, who through energy, method, and persistence had already created an inter-national business.

Eleven years later Reuter was gently caricatured by *Vanity Fair* of 14 December 1872 in its celebrated 'Men of the Day' series. By now the hair had receded even further, and the whiskers were perhaps worn even fuller. Reuter's air of calm alertness, befitting a man in daily pursuit of the news, was emphasized by the artist. Reuter's influence and trustworthi-ness were described in the accompanying article: 'he who has command of telegrams has the command of public opinion on foreign affairs.'

There remained one question about Reuter—how to pronounce his name. The British public was, as ever, awkward about saying a foreign

name. One rhyme in *Punch* on 22 May 1869 made fun of such mispro-
nunciation:

On the Eminent Telegraphist

England believes his telegrams,
    Whether they please or fright her:
Other electric sparks are right,
    But he is always *right-er*

As early as 1861 the Wynter article was asking: 'is this Mr. Reuter an
institution or a myth?' Reuter was not a myth. But his agency was indeed
about to emerge as an imperial institution—as an unofficial but important
part of the worldwide machinery of the British Empire.

TWO

'Electric News'

1858–1865

I

THE Crimean War (1854–6) was one which Julius Reuter seemingly did not report. He would have liked to have done so. The telegraph had reached the Black Sea, and a service of short war telegrams could have been organized. But Reuter had not yet contrived to sell political and general news to the British press. War news was therefore available only as part of the Reuter commercial service, and was limited to news of big market-moving events such as the fall of Sebastopol. *The Times*, not Reuter, dominated reporting on the Crimean War. It published the graphic pioneering dispatches of William Howard Russell, which were sent off not by telegraph but by sea.

By the end of 1858 Reuter's position was very different. He had at last collected a sufficient number of London newspaper subscribers. And to serve them, his network of agents was providing speedy coverage of most of Europe, and slower but regular contact with much of the rest of the world. Reuter's Marseilles agent telegraphed to London political and commercial news from the East, a week or a month old; Trieste telegraphed Austrian Lloyd's messages received by ship from India, China, and Japan, up to six weeks old; and Lisbon telegraphed the news from South America, nearly three weeks old.

These earliest Reuter agents were not journalists. They collected official pronouncements and passed on newspaper reports of events:

ELECTRIC NEWS

The following Telegram was received at Mr REUTER'S Office, October 18th. [1858]

Marseilles, Oct 18.

The 'Bombay Times' contains the following:

Since the 1st September the native army in the Punyaub, whose conduct had become suspicious, has been gradually disbanded by
Government.

Twenty soldiers a day, from every regiment, are sent to their homes.

Two regiments, fearing they would be massacred in small parties,
revolted at Moultan: 1400 of the mutineers have been killed.

The same paper deplores this fatality, and asserts that the state of affairs
in Oude is still bad, and that the insurgents are strong, but thinks their
chiefs are divided.

The situation in Gwalior grows worse. The Government of the Rajah
alone is faithful, the population being very much excited by the emissaries
of Nana Sahib, four of whom have been taken and executed by blowing
them from cannons.

Tantia and the fugitives from Gwalior have surprised and captured the
town of Patun. The Rajah of Patun is in flight, his troops having revolted
and possessed themselves of considerable treasure and 40 guns.

The same journal pretends that the difficulties in Central India are only
commencing.

Ceylon has been connected to India by a Submarine Telegraph.

News of the construction of the Suez Canal as a faster route to India
and the east was to hold the public interest throughout the 1860s.
Significantly, the name of the canal's builder, Ferdinand de Lesseps, was
regarded by Reuter as needing no explanation, as were the names of
other heroes of the time—Garibaldi, Livingstone, Gordon. Such background to the news was taken for granted.

For whom, then, was the agency writing? British readers of Reuter
telegrams were taken to be men (not women) of middle-class liberal
opinions. They were assumed to be supporters of constitutional movements overseas, hence the interest in Garibaldi; but they were regarded as
royalists rather than republicans, hence much reporting of the doings of
kings and queens. They were assumed to be supporters of the British
imperial idea, hence regular reporting from all the main colonies and
from 'darkest Africa'. And they were treated as practising Christians.
Finally, they were credited with some classical education and with some
awareness of contemporary literature, music, and science.

Liberal-minded Victorians valued accuracy and honesty. Poor telegraph
lines, or incompetent operators, sometimes caused telegrams to be garbled.
Reuter always drew attention to cases where a telegram might contain
transmission errors. And although his agents often protected themselves by
quoting their sources, Reuter insisted upon ready correction of mistakes.
The first recorded correction appeared on 3 November 1858:

RECTIFICATION

It appears that the vessel, having Lord Stratford de Redcliffe on board, which ran aground near Smyrna, was not the Caradoc, but the frigate Curacao.

The Caradoc only took his lordship to the Curacao.

Napoleon III was continuously in the news during 1859. He was preparing to fight his bloody but brief and successful war with Austria in the cause of Italian unification. On 3 May Reuter's Paris office telegraphed the text of Napoleon's 550-word declaration in support of Sardinia. Earliest news of the pre-emptive Austrian advance, which started the fighting, came from the Reuter agent in Berne.

Several London newspapers had correspondents filing from forward headquarters, and Reuter left reporting in detail to them. Instead, he developed what was to become the Reuter speciality, publishing a flash or an outline before anyone else. In time of war this meant plain news of retreat or advance, victory or defeat. Such news moved markets.

Reuter placed correspondents on both sides in the war. This ensured full coverage, and also gained him credit for objectivity. Nevertheless, what won Reuter most advantage was the efficiency of his operations not at the front but in the two capitals, Paris and Vienna, where much official and unofficial information was to be gleaned. Thus the first news of the battle of Magenta broke in Paris. Reuter's telegram announced that the French were claiming a 'victory': its Vienna telegram, on the other hand, reported the Austrians as admitting only that 'the combat was undecided'.

Three weeks later the first news of the decisive battle of Solferino was carried by Reuter:

> The following most important telegram was received at Mr. REUTER'S Office, Saturday, June 25th, 8.30 a.m.
>
> PARIS, Saturday, June 25th, 7.45 a.m.
>
> The Emperor to the Empress
>
> CAVRIANA, Friday evening.—Great Battle. Great victory. The whole Austrian army formed the line of battle, which extended five leagues in length. We have taken all their positions, and captured many cannon, flags, and prisoners.
>
> The Battle lasted from four o'clock in the morning till eight o'clock in the evening.

The next day Reuter's correspondent at Austrian headquarters in Verona sent the first account from the defeated side:

VERONA, June 25th.
(Via Vienna)

The day before yesterday our right wing occupied Pozzolengo, Solferino and Cavriano, and the left wing pressed forward yesterday as far as Guidizoffo and Castellgoffredo, driving back the enemy. The collision of the two entire armies took place yesterday at 10 a.m. Our left wing under General Wimpfen advanced nearly as far as the Chiese. In the afternoon, a concentrated assault of the enemy was made upon the heroically defended town of Solferino. Our right wing repulsed the Piedmontese, but on the other hand the order of our centre could not be restored. Losses extraordinarily heavy, a violent thunderstorm, the development of powerful masses of the enemy against our left wing, and the advance of his main body against Volta, caused our retreat, which began late in the evening.

(The above is official)

Reuter's two scoops during the run-up to war—the King of Sardinia's speech in January, followed by Napoleon III's speech a month later—had established the good name of the agency. Reuter's fast and accurate reporting of the course of the war confirmed that good name.

II

During 1859–60, although European news continued to predominate in the Reuter file, intelligence from the wider world began to increase. In October 1859 Reuter had started a 'Special India and China Service'. Even so, news of the surrender of Peking to British and French troops on 13 October 1860 still took nearly two months to reach London. The report of the sacking of the summer palace—condemned by history as an act of vandalism—was brief and matter-of-fact: 'The Emperor's summer palace was taken and looted on the 6th of October. The quantity of spoil was enormous.'

By 1861 Reuter was publishing telegrams from over a hundred datelines. News from Australia, New Zealand, and South Africa now began to feature regularly. A lengthy mailed dispatch arrived in Plymouth from Cape Town on 28 September 1861, carried by a Royal Mail steamer which had taken five weeks in passage. 'Shortly after midnight her mails were landed and sent on to London by special train at about two o'clock a.m.' Thus Reuter circulated the news in good time for the London evening papers. The Cape Town dispatch included an account of Zulu unrest, news of Dr Livingstone in the African interior, and a report of an injunction 'granted Mr. Charles Dickens against the Eastern Province Herald publishing his "Great Expectations".'

During 1861–5 the main story came from across the Atlantic—news of the hard-fought American Civil War. Reuters was the prime supplier of war news to the press of both Britain and continental Europe. The war was grimly interesting. It was also significant because of its increasingly explicit moral dimension, for and against black slavery; and it became important for its damaging economic effects upon the United Kingdom. Cotton supplies from the Confederate southern states were cut off, and the resulting 'cotton famine' brought the Lancashire cotton trade, one of Britain's greatest industries, almost to a halt.

News from North America was supplied to Reuter by the Associated Press of New York (AP). In addition, Reuter's New York agent, James McLean, probably did some news gathering himself, primarily by gutting the American press for war and other news. Reuter signed a four-year news-exchange agreement with AP with effect from the start of 1862; this was probably an expansion of an existing arrangement. AP contracted to send exclusive political, commercial, and other news by every mail steamer out of New York. Each news summary was to fill two printed columns. Late news was to be telegraphed by AP agents in abstract form for putting on board outgoing vessels at 'remote ports' such as St Johns, Portland (Maine), Halifax, Farther Point, or Cape Race. An accompanying 'brief abstract' was to be sent for telegraphing to London from the British port of arrival. The abstracts were to total not less than 2,000 words per week. Reuter agreed to pay $100 per week for these. Otherwise, the agreement was for a straight news swap.

Reuter, for his part, promised to send a news summary from London to New York, enough to fill one and a half printed columns, 'of all important intelligence which may reach him from any part of Great Britain, Ireland, the Continent of Europe, India, China, Australia, New Zealand, Japan, or from any other place'. He also agreed to send a 'brief abstract' with every summary, and to telegraph abstracts of late news to his agents at the Irish ports of Queenstown, Galway, and Londonderry for steamers calling there before making the Atlantic crossing.

On 16 October 1859 John Brown led an attack on Harper's Ferry, an event that was a prelude to the American Civil War. The news took twelve days to reach England. As was the custom at that time, even such important news was given no particular prominence in a telegram first containing other items of general and commercial news:

A fearful insurrection is reported today at Harper's Ferry. The negroes have seized the United States Arsenal and were sending carloads of muskets into Maryland and elsewhere. . . . The object of the outbreak is unknown, and details very confused. . . . Later dated despatches say—All railway trains stopped. the insurrectionists number 500 to 700. Great excitement prevails.

The news of the election of Abraham Lincoln as President of the United States was published by Reuter on 18 November 1860. It had been telegraphed to London from Queenstown, where it was taken off the steamship *Asia*, which had sailed from New York eleven days earlier. The failure of the 1858 transatlantic cable meant that all news was still crossing the Atlantic at the speed of steamships. Although brief urgent news, such as that of Lincoln's election, could be dropped off as vessels passed the northern or southern Irish coasts, the news in full had to await arrival at Southampton, Liverpool, or Plymouth. Reuter had agents in all three ports. These first telegraphed to London the 'brief extracts' supplied by AP, and then forwarded by mail the full dispatches. Big American stories were therefore likely to break in stages, often over a number of days: a single fact first, more facts later, and background later still.

The Civil War started with the attack on Fort Sumter on 12 April 1861. An unconfirmed report from Portland (Maine) was brought by the *Nova Scotian* to Londonderry. The Reuter agent there telegraphed the news to London, where it was published on 25 April. Confirmation next day included news of the effect of the outbreak of war on New York financial and commodity markets.

The arrival of every mail steamer was eagerly awaited—for accounts of battles lost and won, for news of cotton supplies and prices, for information about American grain and other commodities, and for New York money- and stock-market quotations. Reuter circulated this news not only to the British press and business subscribers, but also to his European allies, Havas and Wolff, and to his agents and subscribers overseas. Cotton news carried by steamer was of great interest in India, where merchants were poised to make fortunes by selling local-grown cotton to Lancashire to compensate for the American shortfall.

Reuter's agents in Southampton, Liverpool, Plymouth, Londonderry, and Queenstown were in competition with representatives of the London newspapers, even though the same papers were subscribers to the Reuter service: they liked to publish exclusive news from their own sources alongside Reuter news. The newspapers started chartering boats to meet the incoming mail steamers, and a company called Telegraphic

Despatch began to meet steamers at Roche's Point, off Queenstown. It then telegraphed its extra-early news from Cork to London: Reuter was being beaten by several hours. Never reluctant to think big, he saw a way not merely to match this competition, but to overwhelm it. Four or five hours would be gained if steamers could be intercepted further west.

So in 1863 Reuter obtained permission to build a telegraph line from Cork to Crookhaven in the extreme south-west of Ireland, a distance of over 80 miles. He formed the South Western of Ireland Telegraph Company Ltd. to construct and operate the line. The telegraph pioneer Charles William Siemens, one of his partners, probably contributed technical advice. Local opinion was divided over the merits of the project: the *Cork Examiner* of 23 July 1863 denounced Reuter as a 'clever foreign speculator' intent on 'monopolising the American news'; but the *West Carbery Eagle* of 25 July 1863 reported strong local support for 'this telegraph king' who offered hope for development in an area which had suffered severely in the potato famine of the 1840s. By June 1864 Reuter had sold his interest in the Irish company, although his agency continued to use its facilities.

The line was in operation from early December 1863. The first ship to be met by the Reuter steam-tender *Marseilles* was the *Persia*. Messages for delivery by this new route were placed in special canisters. These were thrown into the sea from each passing mail steamer, and were picked up in nets fixed on long poles. At night the canisters were lit by phosphorus. In rough seas the work could be hazardous, and canisters were occasionally lost. While the *Marseilles* was returning to harbour, Reuter clerks below deck busily sorted the various messages. *The Times* seems to have shared in the venture, for one clerk recorded years later that reports from its New York correspondent were carried in the same canisters. This would explain how Reuters and *The Times* could each publish their own versions of the very first news story sent by this route. Both were described as 'per *Persia* via Crookhaven', and yet were written in quite different language.

News of the first big battle of the war—Bull Run on 21 July 1861—had reached London via Boston and Queenstown, with later material added 'by Telegraph to Halifax'. The Reuter report may have been written up by McLean from AP material: the story is obviously told from a northern angle. But no doubt was left about the heavy Federal defeat:

NEW YORK, JULY 23 (MORNING).
(Per Canada *via* Boston and Queenstown.)

The Federal army, under General McDowell, has sustained a disastrous defeat.

Early on the morning of the 21st, the whole of the Federal army advanced on the Confederate batteries at Bull's Run, three miles from Manassas Junction.

Great bravery was displayed by the Federal troops, and after nine hours fighting they succeeded in capturing three of the Confederate batteries, but with heavy loss on both sides. At this time General Beauregard is reported to have been reinforced by General Johnstone with 25,000 men. The Confederates then attacked the Union army, and drove them in disorder from the field. A panic from some cause seized the Federal troops, and the whole army fled in open disorder towards Washington. General McDowell endeavoured to rally his troops at Centreville and Fairfax Court-house, but found it impossible to check their retreat.

The road from Centreville to Alexandria was strewn with men wounded or fallen from exhaustion.

The Confederates pursued as far as Fairfax.

The whole of the Federal artillery of rifled cannon, and the Rhode Island battery, with large quantities of arms, stores, and small arms, were captured by the Confederates.

The Federal loss is estimated at from 500 to 2,000 men. Many colonels and officers of all grades were killed. The Confederate loss is also stated to be heavy.

The Confederate army at Manassas Junction is reported to number 90,000 men. The whole of the Federal army has fallen back on Alexandria.

The defences round Washington have been reinforced, and are stated to be strong enough to resist any attack by the Confederates. Reinforcements from all parts of the country have been telegraphed for from Washington.

The repulse has created a profound sensation.

Much Reuter war news consisted of lengthy quotations from newspapers of both the North and the South. From time to time direct reports came from the South. 'The press in the South is at liberty to discuss public matters freely. Never were a people more cordially united than the citizens of the Confederate States.' This even-handed approach led some in the North to accuse Reuter of favouring the Confederacy. In 1863 the United States Embassy in London even spread a rumour that Reuter was in the pay of the South. No evidence was produced, and Reuter fairly replied that he had agents collecting news from both sides.

Reuter's Southampton agent, Joseph Sharpe, provided the earliest first-person report to appear on the Reuter file. The Confederate ship *Nashville* had intercepted and sunk a Federal steamer, after first saving its crew. The men were landed by the *Nashville* at Southampton. 'I immediately went on board,' wrote Sharpe. He interviewed the captain and some of the passengers, and collected comments about the state of affairs in the South.

A few days later Sharpe was handling the first news of the *Trent* affair. The Confederates had appointed two envoys to Europe—James Mason to London, and John Slidell to Paris. Reuter had reported in mid-October 1861 that they had run the Federal blockade and reached Havana. They sailed for Europe on a British vessel, the *Trent*. It was stopped by a Federal warship and the male passengers, including the two Confederate commissioners, were kidnapped. Sharpe got the whole story at Southampton from the mail steamer, *La Plata*, fresh from the West Indies. Reuter personally took the story to Lord Palmerston, who, on the strength of Reuter's report alone, called an emergency Cabinet meeting.

British public opinion was outraged at this breach of sovereignty and Palmerston was not disposed to calm matters. War with the North became a serious possibility. Palmerston drafted a strongly worded dispatch. Prince Albert, already fatally ill, rewrote the draft so that, although still firm, it left room for the Americans to climb down without too much loss of face. During the crisis Reuter reported the reactions of both the Northern and Southern press, and sent summaries of British press opinion to the United States. On 20 December the New York office reported that the British note had arrived in Washington, and added: 'if the demands of the British Government for the surrender of Messrs Mason and Slidell are couched in moderate language they will be complied with.'

Reports of Washington's decision to release the commissioners were first carried in a Reuter dispatch from Paris on 7 January, quoting two French papers. The following day Reuter distributed a long report from the United States which included news of the release of the two men; the story was credited to AP. On 11 January a further Reuter report, published in *The Times*, gave a partial text of the letters between London and Washington. The full text arrived next day, a Sunday. Palmerston had not yet seen the American answer in full, and Reuter again personally delivered important news to the prime minister.

In common with others, Reuter's American file missed the significance of a speech on 19 November 1863 which was to become enduringly famous. In the middle of a long dispatch on the war—with news from Mexico and other less important events—appeared the following bare paragraph: 'Mr Lincoln, Mr Seward, and the corps diplomatique were present at the dedication of the Gettysburg cemetery. Edward Everett made an oration.' Lincoln's words on that occasion in praise of 'government of the people, by the people, and for the people' were recorded by someone. But not by Reuter.

III

The year 1860 had seen the first two recorded sports stories carried by Reuter. On 15 May a report stated that 'the New York papers teem with accounts of the fight between Heenan and Sayers'. This was the last bare-knuckle fight in England. Heenan was the American and Sayers the English champion; they fought a draw. In September came the result of a match between, to later eyes, unexpected contestants: 'the cricket match at Montreal between Canada and the United States resulted in favour of the latter in one innings.' On 9 April 1862 Reuter reported ten weeks after the event the arrival of the first English cricket team to tour Australia: 'the English eleven landed at Sydney on the 27th of January, and were to commence their match on the following day.'

Science, literature, and religion were given regular notice. One of the earliest general-news telegrams had reported in May 1859 the funeral of 'the Nestor of German science, the immortal Alexander von Humboldt'. In July 1862 Lisbon felt it worth while to announce that Victor Hugo's latest work, *Les Misérables*, was selling well in Portugal. Reuter assumed that his subscribers would know the work, and would be interested to be told later that it had been placed on the Roman Catholic Index. The future Cardinal Manning's visits to Rome were reported as news items of general interest, as were Bishop Colenso's disputes with the Anglican authorities at the Cape.

In the spring of 1865 James Heckscher, one of Reuter's most trusted journalists, was sent to New York to improve the file out of America. The war was ending just as he arrived; but he was quickly to become involved in covering the most startling American story of this period, news of the assassination of President Abraham Lincoln. How Reuters reported this dramatic story became itself a story much dramatized in the telling.

About 9.45 on the morning of 26 April the news of the assassination was taken ashore from SS *Nova Scotian* to the telegraph station at Green-castle, near Londonderry, in the north of Ireland. By 11.30 a message datelined New York, 15 April, 9 a.m., reached the offices of the London newspapers: 'President Lincoln was shot by an assassin last night, and died this morning. An attempt was likewise made to assassinate Mr Seward, and he is not expected to live.' Simultaneously, the news was distributed to Reuter commercial clients. It was from one of these—Peabody and

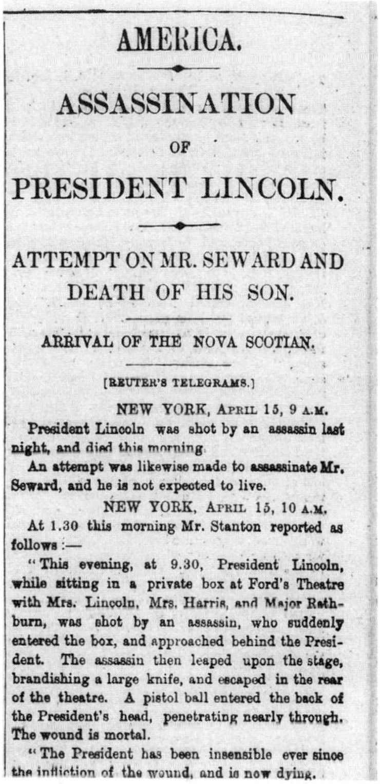

FIG. 4. Reuter report of the assassination of
Abraham Lincoln, published in the *Morning
Advertiser*, 27 April 1865

AMERICA.

ASSASSINATION

OF

PRESIDENT LINCOLN.

ATTEMPT ON MR. SEWARD AND
DEATH OF HIS SON.

ARRIVAL OF THE NOVA SCOTIAN.

[REUTER'S TELEGRAMS.]

NEW YORK, APRIL 15, 9 A.M.
President Lincoln was shot by an assassin last
night, and died this morning.

An attempt was likewise made to assassinate Mr.
Seward, and he is not expected to live.

NEW YORK, APRIL 15, 10 A.M.
At 1.30 this morning Mr. Stanton reported as
follows :—

"This evening, at 9.30, President Lincoln,
while sitting in a private box at Ford's Theatre
with Mrs. Lincoln, Mrs. Harris, and Major Rath-
burn, was shot by an assassin, who suddenly
entered the box, and approached behind the President. The assassin then leaped upon the stage,
brandishing a large knife, and escaped in the rear
of the theatre. A pistol ball entered the back of
the President's head, penetrating nearly through.
The wound is mortal.

"The President has been insensible ever since
the infliction of the wound, and is now dying.

Co., the American bankers in London—that the news first reached the wider public. The news soon got to the Bank of England, and from there quickly spread throughout the City. Initially, many believed the story to be a hoax started by Stock Exchange speculators, until it was confirmed by a dispatch received nearly two hours later. The news provoked a scuffle between opponents and supporters of the Confederacy in the Liverpool Stock Exchange, and there was consternation throughout the United Kingdom. Later myth was to extend the creditable Reuter beat of two hours into an incredible beat of several days.

A few weeks earlier, in February 1865, 'Mr Reuter's office' had become the office of Reuter's Telegram Company Limited. A private business was now a public company. And thereafter the familiar end credit 'Reuter' gradually became the normal usage.

THREE

An Imperial Institution

1865–1914

Beginnings 1865–1878

I

DURING the last forty years of the nineteenth century Reuters news agency functioned increasingly as an institution of the British Empire. This was a great status for a private company to achieve. It was the more remarkable for a firm started by a German-born Jew who had not even begun to live in England until the age of thirty-four. Yet during the 1860s and early 1870s Reuter had aspired to achieve even more than this. He had wanted to make Reuters into the world's predominant news agency. To this end, he pursued a succession of initiatives, each important in itself but each still more important as part of his grand design:

1. He sought to establish a major presence in Germany, with offices there linked to England by his own Norderney cable laid across the North Sea in 1866. He hoped to use Germany as a springboard for expansion eastwards.

2. He became joint sponsor of the French Atlantic cable opened in 1869, and intended to secure for Reuters a preferential link with North America.

3. He sought to gain control of the news agencies of continental Europe, including the two most important, the Havas and Wolff agencies in France and Germany.

4. He opened offices and appointed agents in numerous Asian, African, and Australasian outposts of the formal and informal British Empire. Eventually this imperial initiative was to be vigorously pursued for its own sake. At first it had been simply one part of his grand design.

II

For these high purposes Reuter needed not only his own great energy and business sense, but also a dedicated and efficient staff both in London and overseas. Over some twenty years, he carefully recruited and organized such a staff. At the senior level, only about a dozen men were involved in running the agency under his supervision until his retirement in 1878.

Sigismund Engländer has already been mentioned. He was chief of the London editorial department. He travelled widely through Europe to maintain contacts and to negotiate deals. His knowledge of Continental politics and culture, coupled with his engaging even if Bohemian personality, opened many doors. He told Baron Herbert de Reuter on 19 October 1886 that Reuter journalists ought not to act as mere reporters: they must be 'hommes politiques'.

Engländer's private life was untidy. Women found him attractive. His English-born colleagues thought that his lack of Victorian 'respectability' damaged the good name of the agency. F. W. Dickinson, a later chief editor, summed up Engländer as 'a viveur sans peur and with plenty of reproche . . . I detested him.' Even Engländer's friendship with Julius Reuter was frequently strained by clashes. Nevertheless, Reuter obviously felt a strong sense of obligation towards his old friend. Engländer was a great gatherer of news and opinion, whereas Reuter had been the organizer. What he thought of Engländer's repeated claim in old age to have been the co-founder of the agency is not known. When Reuter's wife refused to receive one of Engländer's mistresses, he married the woman. A son was born and was named Julius, but the marriage did not last.

When war broke out between Russia and Turkey in 1877, Engländer assigned himself to Constantinople as chief correspondent. His news sense had rightly told him that, with war between Britain and Russia a possibility, Reuters ought to be strongly represented in the Turkish capital. He quickly began to move in high diplomatic and military circles, and sent back a steady flow of inside news.

In 1888 he transferred to Paris to participate in the important negotiations about the renewal of contracts with Havas and Wolff. He continued as 'general representative' for Reuters until his retirement in 1894. He was then given a generous pension of £600 per annum, half salary. He had served Reuters long and well.

Engländer was only the first of a group of German Jews whom Julius Reuter gradually brought into his employment during the early years.

One of the first recruits was James Heckscher (1834–1909), who joined Reuter in September 1858. In 1864 he was sent to start an office in Brussels, but was soon transferred to New York to improve the coverage of the American Civil War. After the war Heckscher returned to Europe, where he set up an important office in his native Hamburg. In 1871 he became chief parliamentary correspondent at the House of Commons for Reuters. In this role he won a high reputation for the objectivity and discrimination of his reporting of British political news for continental subscribers. Heckscher was said to be very 'German', 'the Bismarck of the Press Gallery'; but he was widely liked, being both cultured and sociable. He retired from Reuters in 1905.

Another German Jewish member of staff was Emil Wolff (1849–1926). Wolff first worked for Heckscher in the Hamburg office, before joining the London staff in 1870. Reuter paid Wolff a starting salary of £120 a year, and told him: 'you will find lifelong employment.' He did. Wolff served as chief accountant from 1888 until his retirement in 1916.

Julius Reuter made all the early appointments personally. And while welcoming Jews into his business, he took care to avoid giving an impression of exclusivity. Quite soon, Jews were being outnumbered by British-born senior staff. Henry Collins (1844–1928) had taught Reuter's son Herbert at preparatory school. He asked for a job, and was given one after polishing up his French and German. In the event, he was to work chiefly in the English-speaking British Empire, where he became one of the first of a long line of Reuter managers. Collins and his successors—sometimes sent out, as he was, while still in their twenties—set up news networks and organized business over vast territories. He was posted to Bombay in 1866, and from 1878 until his retirement in 1909 he was general manager in Australia.

G. Douglas Williams (1839–1910) joined the editorial staff in 1861. His upright character, fluent command of French, Italian, and Spanish, and general culture and intelligence quickly recommended him for a major role in Reuter's expansion plans. In 1865 he was sent to Florence, the capital of newly united Italy and a centre of major news interest. In 1870 he transferred to Paris, just in time for the outbreak of the Franco-Prussian War. In 1875 he was appointed deputy to Engländer 'for the conduct, supervision, and control of the outward and homeward political services'. Williams succeeded Engländer as chief editor two years later. He retired in 1902.

Walter F. Bradshaw (1850–1932) joined in 1874. With a good command of Spanish and Portuguese, Bradshaw was immediately dispatched to Chile to help establish a new South American service. He returned five years later, and became in time a portly figure of more dignity than imagination who succeeded Griffiths as secretary in 1890. At the very end of his career in 1915 he served briefly as general manager.

Another recruit in 1874 was Frederic W. Dickinson (1856–1922), who succeeded Williams as chief editor in 1902. Dickinson set a high technical standard for Reuter telegrams. Well informed, observant, sensible, humorous—he was an active mentor for young Reuter journalists.

The commitment of these early recruits to Reuters was indicated by their long and dedicated service. It was also reflected in their readiness to introduce members of their own families into the agency. About the turn of the century Griffiths, Wolff, Collins, Williams, Bradshaw, and Dickinson all had brothers and/or sons or sons-in-law working for Reuters.

III

Office accommodation was extended to allow for expansion of the business. The original two rooms at Royal Exchange Buildings remained in use until 1866. Headquarters then moved to 5 Lothbury nearby. For several years a separate night office had been maintained in a house backing on to Julius Reuter's garden in Finsbury Square.

News reached London at irregular intervals throughout the twenty-four hours. Editorial staff worked a series of shifts, the long night shift running from 6 p.m. each evening until 10 a.m. next morning. Beds were provided so that staff could sleep when no news was coming in. Young Williams was on duty at the night office in July 1861 when news of the battle of Bull Run arrived by telegraph. He was roused by the office boy, who gave him the message. But Williams then dozed off again, message in hand. He slept untroubled until, as his son later recorded, 'in the grey light of dawn he was aroused by the spectacle of his employer in his dressing gown and slippers standing over his bed and shaking the fateful message in his face'. Julius Reuter, as was his custom, had come across his garden to see what news had arrived overnight. Young Williams was forgiven his lapse, which could have cost him his job.

Transfer to the Lothbury offices in 1866 allowed the new Reuter's Telegram Company to concentrate departments there; but the accommodation was remembered by Wolff as 'disconnected and very uncommodious'. In 1871 a further move was therefore made to a Georgian house at 24 Old Jewry, still in the City of London. Old Jewry was destined to be the main Reuter address for over fifty years. Within a few years adjacent houses at Numbers 23 and 25 were also taken.

Although rebuilding was discussed at intervals, these three old houses remained unchanged externally throughout their long occupation by Reuters. The original dining-room at Number 24 provided the board-room; former bedrooms served as editorial rooms. Williams had a small back room on the first floor; and Engländer (in Wolff's recollection) 'had stuffed the larger backroom on the second floor with a complete set of Hansard's *Parliamentary Debates* of nearly seventy sessions and a crop of socialist and democratic literature'.

The atmosphere was relaxed: open fires blazed all day and night; pots of beer stood on desks; papers were strewn about the floors; and large books of press cuttings, compiled continuously since the early days of the agency, were kept ready to hand for reference.

An article in the *Strand Magazine* for July 1895 described how news was handled at Old Jewry. The moment a telegram came in from the cable offices or elsewhere, it was registered in a book by the timekeeper. The message was then passed to the senior editor on duty. He had to decide whether to circulate the item, and to which subscribers. In the 1860s there were already direct telegraph wires from Reuters into the offices of the main London newspapers; but the printing machinery was very slow in use, and suitable only for sending short messages. From 1883 column-printers were put into these offices to receive longer messages direct. The column-printer had a type-wheel which printed words and figures on a roll; these were tapped out on a 'piano transmitter' at Old Jewry by Reuter operators. At the same time duplicate copies were made on two machines in the Reuter office; these were torn off and the mes-sages summarized—and if necessary translated—for transmission overseas. The column-printer was a major innovation in communications technol-ogy, which greatly accelerated the work of news agencies and newspaper offices.

All outgoing Reuter messages were written down by clerks called manifolders. At first this manifolding was done manually by stylus upon thin paper interleaved with black oiled sheets. An expert could make up to thirty-two copies at one writing. Then from the 1880s a typewriter was used. Each London newspaper was sent duplicates of all messages already communicated by wire. These 'flimsies' were delivered by Reuter messengers.

By the 1890s about sixty-five messenger boys were being employed. They were recruited in their early teens, and most left at eighteen. Their grey—later blue—uniforms had become familiar sights on the streets of London. From the 1890s some messengers used bicycles. Girl messengers were introduced in 1901 for daytime deliveries. 'A Woman of Experience' complained to *The Times* on 15 November about the moral danger of Reuter girls running through the streets, and about the damage to domestic service of alternative female employment.

By the late 1860s Reuters was insisting upon charging all newspapers equally for equal services. The subscription for the London dailies settled at £1,600 per annum. This was a high price, but the agency now held the initiative. No paper could afford to be without Reuter telegrams when its rivals had them. Editors at least had the consolation of knowing that, so long as they paid the price, Reuter telegrams would never be withheld from them. Impartiality in distribution was the rule: no paper was allowed to buy Reuter news exclusively. This requirement was carefully written into Julius Reuter's contract with the new Reuter's Telegram Company in 1865: 'it shall be the duty of the Managing Director to communicate the telegraphic intelligence equally and impartially to all the Subscribers . . . without giving priority to any one over any other.' This high moral line paid in terms of reputation, and it probably also paid in terms of revenue.

Reuter news for the provincial press was distributed from 1868 by the newly formed Press Association (PA). This co-operative had been started by the leading provincial newspapers, exasperated at the unreliable news service offered by the telegraph companies. The PA entered into a close relationship with Reuters, exchanging its British news for Reuter foreign news and paying a differential. This was fixed at £3,000 in 1868, increased to £8,000 from 1881. Because of this connection, Reuters never tried to operate as a British domestic news agency.

Reuter charges rose during the 1860s, in part because of the increasing volume of news. The first successful transatlantic cable was at last completed in July 1866. This had been the fifth attempt. By 1880 nine cable routes were crossing the Atlantic, and by the 1890s the world cable network was essentially in place. Thereafter came duplication and refinement, notably the completion before 1914 of an 'all-red route' encircling the globe with British-owned cables. About 60 per cent of all cables were British. This predominance helped to make Reuters in London the clearing-house for world news, even for news without interest to the British public.

The main British possessions in Asia and Africa were linked by cable to London during the 1860s and 1870s. The first line between India and

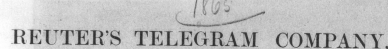

1865

REUTER'S TELEGRAM COMPANY,

L I M I T E D.

Incorporated under the Joint Stock Companies' Act, 1862.

CAPITAL £250,000, IN 10,000 SHARES OF £25 EACH.

FIRST ISSUE 4,000 SHARES.

OF WHICH MORE THAN 2,000 SHARES HAVE BEEN ALREADY SUBSCRIBED.

Payment on Application £1, and on Allotment £4 per Share; it is not intended to call up more than £20 per Share. At least Two Months to intervene between each Call.

DIRECTORS.

JOHN DENT, Esq., 35, Grosvenor Square.
SIR JOHN DALRYMPLE HAY, Bart., M.P., F.R.S.
Col. JAMES HOLLAND, Deputy Chairman London and South African Bank.
JAMES SYDNEY STOPFORD, Esq., Director of the Agra and Masterman's Bank.
JULIUS REUTER, Esq., Managing Director.

SOLICITORS.

Messrs. BISCHOFF COXE & BOMPAS, 19, Coleman Street.

BANKERS.

THE AGRA & MASTERMAN'S BANK, LIMITED, 35, Nicholas Lane.

BROKERS.

Messrs. P. CAZENOVE & Co., 52, Threadneedle Street.

SECRETARY (PRO TEM).

Mr. FREDERICK J. GRIFFITHS.

OFFICES:

1, ROYAL EXCHANGE BUILDINGS, LONDON.

This Company is established to provide capital for the purchase and extension of the well-known Telegraphic business of Mr. Julius Reuter.

FIG. 5. The original company prospectus, 1865

Europe opened in January 1865, routed via Turkey; it proved to be unsatisfactory in use. Julius Reuter complained in a letter to *The Times* on 24 December 1866 that messages took eight to fourteen days to and from India, and that they were often unintelligible on receipt because the telegraph clerks en route did not understand English. Two other cables to India were to prove more satisfactory, one overland across Russia (January 1870), the other undersea via Alexandria and Aden (June 1870). Hong Kong was reached from India in 1871, Shanghai and Tokyo by 1873. Australia was linked with India in 1872.

IV

On 20 February 1865 Julius Reuter restructured his business. It now ceased to belong to him personally, and became instead 'Reuters'. The private firm which had functioned since 1851 was transformed into Reuter's Telegram Company, a limited company under the terms of the 1862 Companies Act.

This new company offered a good investment prospect. Its work was well known and it was prospering. An auditors' report revealed the profit for 1864 as £8,630. The company was incorporated with a nominal capital of £250,000 (10,000 shares at £25 each); £80,000 capital was paid up. Reuter received £65,000 in cash for his old business, a figure which for fifty years was to be treated as the value of the company's goodwill. Reuter was appointed managing director at a handsome salary of £1,500 per annum, raised to £2,500 in years when a 10 per cent dividend was paid.

The prospectus announced that the company was being formed 'for the purchase and extension of the well-known Telegraphic business of Mr Julius Reuter'. 'Mr Reuter will continue to have the exclusive management of the Telegraphic Department, which will be conducted as heretofore, with the utmost secrecy, fidelity, and impartiality.'

The prospectus did not mention that Reuter's immediate objective in going public was to raise capital to pay for a cable across the North Sea from England to the island of Norderney off the north German coast. The necessary concession for this bold initiative was confirmed by the King of Hanover on 15 November 1865. Reuter had told his board on 28 September that the benefit to the company would be incalculable, 'because irrespective of increased speed and saving of expense, the messages of the Company would then take precedence of all others'. This would be 'the first step towards the development of a very extensive business on the continent of Europe'.

There was never any risk that the new Reuter board would refuse to back its managing director. His contract specifically gave him 'the sole and entire management' of the telegraph business, 'and no other Director or Shareholder shall be entitled to interfere'. So Julius Reuter, and his son Herbert after him, were almost obliged to play a dominating part. To make this dominance still easier, Reuter seems to have been careful to find suitably well-connected mediocrities as his fellow directors.

The board came to comprise just four members, including Reuter himself. Colonel James Holland emerged as the first regular chairman of Reuters, although not given the title until 1868. He had fought in the Crimean War. So had another foundation director, Admiral Sir John Dalrymple-Hay. Hay sat as a 'Liberal Conservative' Member of Parliament between 1862 and 1885. He was a Scottish landowner, like his wife's father, Lord Napier. His wife's nephew, Mark Napier, was to join the Reuter board when Hay succeeded Holland as chairman in 1888. Hay did not retire from the chairmanship until 1910, by which time he was sinking into senility. The fourth original director was James S. Stopford, an East India Merchant.

The first general meeting of Reuter's Telegram Company Limited was held on 24 July 1865. The shareholders were chiefly professional men with mainly London addresses—solicitors, bankers, merchants, naval and military officers, medical practitioners. The 1865 dividend was fixed at 8 per cent, free of tax; the directors announced that they were moving carefully at first. Thereafter 10 per cent became customary until the mid-1870s. The best early year for net profits was 1868, with £31,939. By 1874, however, profits had slumped to £6,329. The 1875 dividend was therefore cut to 7.5 per cent. This became the norm into the 1880s. The net profit for 1878 was only £5,627. Expenditure upon 'telegrams and agencies' grew from £27,371 in 1866 to £59,805 in 1878. Revenue grew from £49,715 to £79,414 during the same period.

V

Throughout these years Julius Reuter was pursuing his grand design of making Reuters into the predominant world news agency. The Norderney scheme was intended to play a key part in the overall plan. Reuter was now seeing himself as a cable owner as well as a cable user. Although he came to be remembered for 'following the cable' round the world, this had not been his whole ambition. He had originally aspired to build and own important parts of the cable system which he was following.

The Norderney cable was about a year in the making and was ready by the end of 1866. In a letter to *The Times* on 15 December Reuter explained that this was not just another line: it had been laid 'to introduce a new system in telegraphic communication—that, namely, of international through [direct] telegraphy'. A new direct line, explained Reuter, was expected to reduce delay by taking four wires into north Germany, one of which would reach Berlin.

Reuter's letter made no mention of his hopes of expansion within Germany, and of using it as a springboard for still further growth eastwards. These plans were in danger of being disappointed even before the line became operational. The Kingdom of Hanover, on the losing side in the Austro-Prussian War, had been absorbed into Prussia. Reuter's letter to *The Times* was written to emphasize that, contrary to rumour, the Prussians had confirmed the Norderney concession. So they had—but upon restrictive terms which were intended to prevent Reuters from gaining a strong position in Germany. The new agreement denied the agency an office in Hanover, and also the right to an exclusive line. The 1867 annual general meeting was told that this renegotiation had required 'considerable personal exertions at Berlin' by Reuter. Indirectly, he was dealing with Bismarck.

Financially, the line was a great success. Traffic was good, reaching a level of between 13,000 and 14,000 messages sent and received per month. During 1868 Norderney revenue totalled £29,744, 'or 19 per cent on the capital invested in the cable and land lines'. The entire cost had been £153,000. But Bismarck was never going to let Reuters into Germany to compete on equal terms with the Wolff bureau. This was now secretly subsidized by the Prussian Government, after being reconstituted in 1865 as the Continental Telegraph Company. Significantly, the CTC's chairman was Gerson von Bleichröder, Bismarck's banker.

Reuters might have kept ownership of the Norderney line simply as a small profit-making venture. Instead, early in 1870 the line was sold off at great gain to Reuters; the generous buyer was the British Government. Successive British ministers had pursued fluctuating policies with regard to the promotion of overland and undersea telegraphy. By the late 1860s the policy was not to invest in 'ocean telegraphy', but simply to provide assistance in marine surveying and to help private projectors in their dealings with foreign Governments. With regard to telegraphy inside the United Kingdom, however, and for 'submarine telegraphy' between the United Kingdom and the Continent, the British Government had belatedly decided that the national interest required it to take control. The

Telegraph Purchase Act of 1868 gave the Postmaster-General power to acquire, work, and maintain telegraphs. £8 million was provided for the nationalization of all private inland telegraph companies in the United Kingdom, along with the telegraphic business of the railway companies.

Reuters had petitioned against this measure, and had been represented by counsel before a House of Commons committee. This seems to have been only a stratagem to ensure rather than prevent compulsory purchase. The Government was at first not expecting to have to acquire the Norderney cable at all; but Reuters contrived to show that interlocking agreements with the Electric Telegraph Company—which the Government intended to buy out, and which provided the land link for Norderney between London and Lowestoft—made purchase of the Reuter cable unavoidable. And such a purchase was bound to include payment of compensation for rights granted by Reuters to the Indo-European Telegraph Company: one of the Norderney lines was scheduled to serve as the first leg of the Indo-European's projected route to Teheran.

Having persuaded the Government to accept these commitments, Reuters withdrew its petition. How much would the Government pay? The matter went to arbitration. The ruling was that Reuters should be given a price based upon twenty years' profits. This meant that it received £726,000 for an enterprise which had cost £153,000. Julius Reuter had been active in the negotiations with the British Government. His German dream was already fading. But at least he had contrived to obtain a very large financial consolation prize. The size of the official payment even encouraged circulation of a report that Reuters had sold its entire news agency business to the British Government.

Unfortunately for the future, the Reuter board fell into a state of euphoria at this windfall. A substantial reserve fund could have been created, but was not. Reuter himself was given £5,000; the other directors shared £4,000. Senior staff divided £7,000. £693,000 was distributed to shareholders. Only £7,000 was retained. The agency's capitalization was reduced to £72,000, with £65,000 credited to goodwill. Late Victorian Reuters was destined to operate worldwide upon a remarkably narrow capital base.

VI

As part of the drive into Europe, the board voted £20,000 on 18 September 1867 to establish new offices on the Continent. A branch had already been started in Amsterdam from 1 January 1866. Reuters had bought out the existing telegraph bureau of Alexander Delamar, and had installed him as manager for Reuters. In Brussels Alexander's brother, Herman, was made manager of a joint office opened with Havas.

The Low Countries were a key area, but Reuter wanted to break into Germany and beyond. He made most progress in Hamburg, with its tradition of trading freedom and its distrust of Prussia. Most of Germany's overseas trade flowed through Hamburg, and this gave it a great interest in commercial news. Heckscher's Hamburg branch, opened in 1867, began to supply a service to local merchants, and also to two of the five Hamburg newspapers. The breakthrough came when Heckscher negotiated a lucrative contract of 4,000 thalers (£600) per annum to supply a full service of news to the Neue Börsenhalle. This was described by Emil Wolff as 'a sort of Commercial Club and Reading Room within the Exchange Buildings'. The Börsenhalle agreed to give Reuters full credit for messages exhibited in its rooms, or when they appeared in its newspapers.

The range of news to be supplied was described in detail: world political news collected by telegraph or otherwise; fund quotations from the ten leading world exchanges (New York to St Petersburg); corn and flour reports from twenty places; cotton reports from fourteen places; colonial-product reports from seventeen places; metal reports from eight places; the rate of exchange for bills and discount reports from seventeen places; news of arrival of transatlantic mails, and of transatlantic specie; freight news; wool reports; petroleum reports. The range of news now available from Reuters was thus impressive, both for content and place of origin. It came from as far away as China and South America. Neither Havas nor Wolff could match Reuters for news from outside Europe.

Reuter offices were also opened in Berlin, Frankfurt, and Vienna. The Frankfurt and Vienna managers were brothers, Reuter's nephews Robert and Eugen Salinger. Unfortunately, the Prussian Government ensured that business in Berlin and Frankfurt did not prosper. The authorities covertly favoured the Wolff Bureau by treating its telegrams as priority official correspondence. According to Emil Wolff, 'democratic' newspapers in Prussia did take the Reuter service; but they could not afford to pay full rates because they were in competition with the subsidized Bismarckian press. On 15 June 1870 the Reuter board studied agency profit-and-loss figures for the first half of the year. The German losses were heavy (see Table 3.1).

When did Julius Reuter reopen his Paris office? At the time of his London start in 1851 he must have employed at least one agent in Paris

TABLE 3.1 Profit-and-loss figures for Reuter offices during the first half of 1870

	Credits			Debits		
	£	s.	d.	£	s.	d.
Indian Agencies	1,000	0	0			
Brussels	240	0	0			
Dutch	216	6	10			
Constantinople	163	9	11			
Alexandria	43	14	10			
Head Office				675	8	9
Berlin Agency				512	9	3
Frankfurt				375	7	2
Hamburg				203	6	7

to send Bourse prices via the Channel cable. By the period of his scoop with Napoleon III's speech in 1859, he was clearly running a full office in the French capital. His telegrams were reporting French official news almost daily. In 1871 Grant's history of the press included an account of the Paris office in the Palais Royal 'some years ago'. Its chief, wrote Grant, was 'a gentleman alike in manners and education', whose especial duty was to call upon leading officials, headed by Napoleon III's secretary. A second staff member ran the office; a third searched through the continental press for news; a fourth prepared the telegrams; and a fifth took them to the telegraph office.

At the other end of Europe lay Constantinople, a centre of dangerous great-power rivalry as the Turkish Empire slowly disintegrated. The profit-and-loss account for 1870 listed 'preliminary expenses at Constantinople' of £766. It became an important office, especially while it was conducted by Engländer.

In the late 1860s an expansive Reuter had been looking west as well as east. He entered into a second cable-ownership venture, this time across the Atlantic. The first Anglo-American cable had been opened in 1866, and to encourage its construction Reuter had apparently given an assurance that the agency would spend at least £5,000 per year on telegrams. But he became shocked by the exorbitant charges levied by the Anglo-American Company. On 25 September 1867 the Reuter board alarmedly compared costs for its American service before and after the opening of the cable. During the first half of 1865 American costs had averaged only £67 per month, whereas for the first half of 1867 they averaged £424.

In July 1868 Reuter and Baron Emil d'Erlanger, of the German Jewish banking family, secured from the French Government the right to float a French Atlantic cable company, to be called La Société du Cable

Transatlantique Française. The cable was to run from Brest on the French coast across the Atlantic to the French islands of St Pierre and Miquelon, off Newfoundland, and from there to Cape Cod. Funds were raised by sale of stock to banking houses.

Reuter had embarked upon this second cable scheme—as upon the Norderney scheme—as a prospective user as well as owner. The launching of the French Atlantic company brought a reduction by the Anglo-American Company from £5 to £1. 10s. per message of ten words even before the French cable opened in August 1869. The French Atlantic then adopted the same reduced tariff, announcing that it would better its rival not through further cuts but by quicker delivery of messages. Reuters now began to use the French Atlantic for many of its American telegrams, although not for all. Once again, however, Julius Reuter's enterprise was destined to be frustrated by the Prussian Government, albeit this time indirectly. After the French defeat in the Franco-Prussian War, the French Atlantic company was absorbed in 1873 by its Anglo-American rival to help meet French war-reparation payments.

VII

The three main early European news agencies—Reuters, Havas, and Wolff—were to be known for the imperious way in which they divided news control of the world between themselves. They operated a cartel which restricted competition. Sometimes it was called the 'ring combination'. Reuters was the most important member of this combination. Its reserved territories were the most extensive, and its network of offices and agencies, correspondents, and stringers the most numerous. It contributed the most news to the pool. All this activity, assisted by British predominance along the cables, made Old Jewry the world clearing-centre for news.

Nevertheless, when Reuter entered into the basic agreement in 1870 he was conceding a sort of defeat. He was admitting that Reuters could neither do without Havas and Wolff nor do away with them. Havas was to remain a strong force not only in western Europe, but also in French Africa and South America. Wolff was entrenched in central and eastern Europe. And later, various American news agencies were to begin striking out from their strong home bases in the United States.

Reuter seems to have made his first agreement with Havas (and probably also with Wolff) in 1856. It was for an exchange of market prices and quotations. No contract has survived, and perhaps the arrangement was verbal. The first tripartite written agreement was a record in French, dated 18 July 1859, of a discussion in Paris between Reuter, Auguste Havas (son of Charles), and Wolff. This was the time when the Reuter service of political and general news was beginning to flourish. The agreement covered all news, not just commercial. Indeed, Havas seems to have been already providing Reuter with his full service, for Havas agreed to send Wolff his telegrams without commission, 'as he is already doing to M. Reuter'. The three men also agreed to deliver telegrams exclusively to each other in their home countries. St Petersburg was made Wolff territory, at the price of 100 francs paid each month to both Reuter and Havas. Any new services were to be promoted at joint expense. In general, the aim of the trio was 'to prevent attempts at competition, and to increase the services according to the needs of the public and the development of the telegraph lines'. Reuter was obviously still the junior partner at this date, and Havas the senior. The Havas network in western Europe and through the Mediterranean was mentioned, as was Wolff's network in Germany, Scandinavia, and eastern Europe. No Reuter network was described.

The 1859 agreement was given no time limit. Yet within three years Reuter was already acting against its spirit. The agreement said that the three parties would 'maintain their services in the status quo in which they are at present'. Nothing had been said about other news agencies in other countries. And in 1862 Reuter tried to buy out Stefani, the Italian agency: the bid failed only because he was offering too little. Italy had been named in 1859 as Havas territory. Similarly, during 1867–8 Reuter tried to absorb the Ritzau agency of Copenhagen, even though Scandinavia had been named as Wolff territory.

By 1865 the agreement of 1859 had clearly lapsed, and a series of new interrelated contracts was now signed. On 23 June Reuter and Havas agreed to exchange their news for five years. Havas was to pay £500 annually to cover the extraordinary expenses of the American service. He was given a free hand in France, Italy, Spain, and Portugal; Reuter in England and Holland. The parties were not to enter into deals with rival news agencies, accepting 'all the duties of an offensive and defensive treaty of alliance'. But Wolff was to be allowed to join the alliance, 'particularly in Europe'.

Wolff duly joined. On 28 December Reuter agreed to supply him with New York news for one year. However, after the transatlantic cable had been opened in July 1866 the German agency refused to share the high transmission costs. Instead, Wolff made an exchange deal with the

Western Associated Press, a rival to the Associated Press of New York. Reuter was forced to counter with an improved service to AP. WAP soon settled with AP to take this improved Reuter service, and gave up the Wolff service. So Reuters kept its position in America; but its vulnerability to competition from Wolff or Havas even outside Europe had been demonstrated.

Reuter's response was characteristically bold: he became even more eager to take over his rivals, large or small. The details of Reuter's manœuvres in 1869 to buy the Wolff bureau are not known; the outcome was clear enough, however. Bismarck ensured that Reuter did not succeed. A letter has survived from Bismarck to Hay, the Reuter director, dated 23 November 1869. Bismarck contrived to be both disingenuous in his first paragraph and decisive in his last:

> In answer to your letter of 26th October I beg respectfully to say that the Continental Telegraph Company (Wolff's Bureau of Berlin) is a private institution. I have therefore to give no permission to sell it to Reuter's Telegram Company and must leave it to the latter to treat directly with the said Continental Telegraph Company.
>
> Neither can I hold out any hopes to influence the Continental Telegraph Company with regard to the sale of their business, as former experience has shown us that it is more expedient to have a North German Telegraph Office which is beyond Foreign influence.

This rebuff left Reuter with no choice but to do a deal. He had now to recognize that the Wolff bureau was not for sale. He had also to accept that he could not at present challenge its position within Germany, or hope to compete within its sphere of European interest. But Reuter took care to accept these realities only on terms which were likely to prevent Wolff making any further progress elsewhere.

Havas and Wolff had already concluded a deal in 1867 which spelt out their spheres of interest. This agreement then provided a geographical model for the contract signed in Paris on 17 January 1870 between Reuters, Havas, and Wolff, just two months after Bismarck's rebuff to Hay. This was no ordinary contract; the 1870 arrangement was destined to form the basis of the international news order until the 1930s. It created a ring for news collection and exchange on terms highly favourable to the three agencies. And it was binding in the first instance for the long period of twenty years.

Most news was to be exchanged between the three parties without charge. But the Wolff Bureau agreed to pay Reuters and Havas 25 per

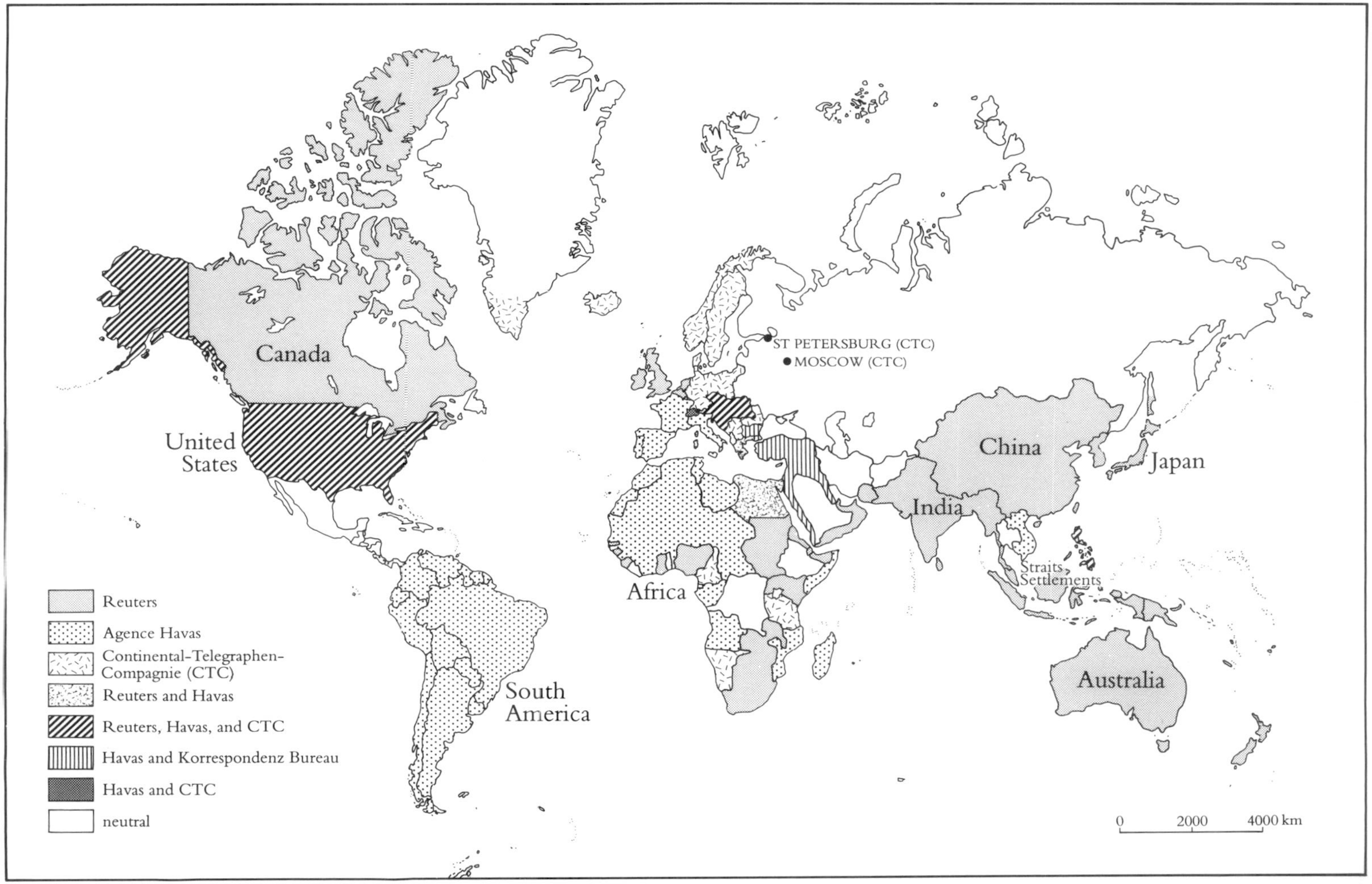
Canada
United States
South America
Africa
ST PETERSBURG (CTC)
MOSCOW (CTC)
China
India
Japan
Straits Settlements
Australia
Reuters
Agence Havas
Continental-Telegraphen-Compagnie (CTC)
Reuters and Havas
Reuters, Havas, and CTC
Havas and Korrespondenz Bureau
Havas and CTC
neutral
0 2000 4000 km

FIG. 6. Territories of international agencies, 1900

cent of its annual profits in return for American news, and also for the abandonment by Reuters of all operations in Wolff territories. Reuters agreed to close all its German and Austrian offices, except Hamburg. Wolff was given exclusive collection and distribution rights in Germany, Central Europe, Scandinavia, and Russia.

Reuters was given the news monopoly of the British Empire and the Far East. Havas was given the French Empire and the Latin countries of the Mediterranean. Provision was made for several shared territories, some of them important for news or revenue—Belgium, Egypt, Greece, Turkey, South America. The three principals were to contract with any national agencies inside their respective spheres for exchange of news with the combination. But the Austrian Telegraphen-Korrespondenz Bureau was allowed to negotiate directly with Reuters, Havas, and Wolff.

Yet the 1870 Reuter annual general meeting was told very little about this important contract: only that arrangements had been made 'to avoid expensive competition'. The directors considered it 'unadvisable in the interests of all parties to enter more fully into details'. The circulation of news throughout Europe and the world was now organized as never before. Interestingly, Havas and Wolff telegraphed their news to London in French or German; but Reuter news was translated from English before being sent to Paris or Berlin.

A fourteen-point informal statement in French of 'Rules for Common Action' supplemented the formal contract. The three parties agreed to keep secret the very existence of their ring. They recognized, however, that there might be need sometimes to reveal to Governments how their interests were linked. Governments were to be asked to give the three agencies priority in telegraphing their dispatches. An enlarged service was to be provided at times of crisis. Agents were to be discouraged from merely taking news from newspapers. There was to be no duplication of coverage. The market for commercial news and information was to be urgently studied.

In the case of the Reuter–Havas relationship collaboration had already gone further. On 4 November 1869 the two agencies had agreed to introduce 'joint-purse' working from January 1870. This meant that the total profits of the two agencies were to be shared equally. This was an important development, but Reuter would have preferred an even closer connection. In June 1869 he had signed a provisional agreement for a full merger, but difficulties with English law prevented its implementation. Even so, the wide extent of Reuter's ambition was clear. During 1869 he had sought both to merge with Havas and to buy out Wolff.

The disruption caused by the Franco-Prussian War shook the position of Havas, and Reuter persuaded his board to try again to capture the French agency. In July 1872 he offered on behalf of the company to purchase the entire Havas business for 3 million francs (£90,000), on the condition that Havas agreed to accept shares for any purchase money not subscribed by Reuter shareholders or by the public. The offer was declined. Further negotiations none the less followed, conducted in Paris by Engländer. The offer was raised to £120,000, or shares at par. Havas showed interest, but opposition was aroused in France. Engländer told Griffiths on 8 April 1873 that the Reuter bid had been reduced to an offer to buy the Havas foreign telegraph business, and 'not to acquire the French portion of their agency on account of the hostile attitude of the French papers'.

These further negotiations also failed, and the Reuter board finally decided to seek no more than a continuation of the joint-purse arrangement. But friction over finance and over joint operations in South America was already beginning to sour the relationship. And joint-purse working with Havas was ended by mutual consent in 1876.

Until the close of the century the American news agencies were not treated as equals by Reuters, Havas, and Wolff. In 1870 AP of New York had contracted for a reciprocal news service between Europe and America, with payment of an annual differential of £2,400 by AP. The assumption was that Europe's news was of more interest to America than vice versa. When this agreement was renewed in 1875, AP agreed with Reuters 'to undertake the Company's agency at New York for political and commercial news free of commission'. Reuter's agent was therefore withdrawn from New York—with satisfaction at the expense saved, and with no sense that Reuters ought to retain any direct coverage of the American scene.

VIII

The European manœuvres of Julius Reuter during the 1860s and early 1870s had been accompanied by a steady effort to draw the whole British Empire into the Reuter network. This was part of Reuter's grand world-wide design, and it was the part which worked best. It made Reuters into an imperial institution.

The prestige of Reuters—and also its profitability—came to depend heavily upon the presence of its managers and correspondents as members of the white governing and trading communities throughout the British

Empire. By 1871 that empire included some 235 million people, spread over five continents. During the rest of the century the Empire expanded until it covered about a quarter of the globe. Reuters was to report with increasing fullness the many colonial wars and confrontations which accompanied that growth.

In his agreement with Havas and Wolff of 1859 Reuter had not been credited with any areas of special interest outside Europe. Nevertheless, his telegrams for the year show that he already employed agents at the Cape, in India, and in the Far East. McLean, later to be agent in New York, was appointed in that year to visit Ceylon 'and divers other places in the East, for the purpose of conducting or managing the telegraphic business'. By the time of Reuter's agreement with AP in 1861 he was claiming agents at the principal ports of India, China, Japan, Australia, New Zealand, and at the intermediate ports of Point de Galle (Ceylon), Alexandria, and Malta.

Alexandria was a port of call *en route* to India, and also an important marketing centre for Egyptian cotton. The Suez Canal was not completed until 1869; but Suez achieved earlier importance as the end-point of the telegraph line from Europe. Egypt was becoming a focal point for news, trade, and transport. Not surprisingly, therefore, towards the end of 1865 Reuters opened an office at Alexandria. The man sent to Egypt was Edward Virnard. He seems to have been an experienced journalist specially recruited rather than a man taken from the London editorial office.

Virnard's career with Reuters began well, but ended in acrimony. He successfully launched the main office in Alexandria, and then opened a branch in Cairo. News about Egyptian cotton prices and supplies was in demand both in England and India. Conversely, incoming Reuter news was wanted in Egypt. News was published directly from the two offices in the form of bulletins in English and French, delivered by hand. Reuter bulletins were to remain a feature of the Egyptian scene until far into the twentieth century. Virnard was dismissed in 1870, and was sued by the company for a £630 deficiency in his account. He counter-claimed for wrongful dismissal and libel. Both suits were eventually successful, with the lawyers the only clear winners.

The next man sent east was Collins, aged only twenty-two. He sailed in February 1866 for Bombay, 'where the Directors have reason to believe there is a large field for the profitable extension of the system so successfully inaugurated by Mr. Reuter'. As Collins recollected in old age, Bombay possessed 'not a single European hotel, properly so called'. The

Reuter Service Bulletin of July 1920 described how he leased a tent on the Esplanade, and began business from there:

> It was in his private tent that at about 1 a.m. he received his first (specimen) message from the Head Office in London, giving the latest quotations of Cotton, &c., at Liverpool and Manchester, and Mr. Collins sat up the whole of that night reproducing over 100 'flimsy' copies which, in the absence of his one clerk and one messenger—who were asleep in their beds—he distributed personally to Reuters potential subscribers, by dropping the envelopes (somewhat furtively perhaps) into the letter boxes of the Banks, the principal mercantile firms and others whose support it was desired to secure for the twice-a-day commercial service.

For nearly a century India was destined to play a central part in the Reuter empire within the British Empire. Reuters soon came to dominate the supply of news not only to and from India, but also within the country for both the English-language and vernacular press. By the time of the 1868 annual general meeting offices were reported 'in full activity' at Bombay, Calcutta, Madras, Karachi, Colombo, and Point de Galle. 'Our business in the East', explained Griffiths to Havas on 27 October 1873, 'differs but little from that in London. We send political and commercial summaries daily, the former for the press and the latter for private subscribers; in addition to which we forward private telegrams. The high tariff explains the largeness of the totals shown in our accounts.'

Good relations were soon established with the Government of India at Calcutta. Collins remembered with pride the day when he was first received by the governor-general, Lord Lawrence. This may well have been the first semi-official meeting—the first of many—between a Reuter representative and a ruler of empire. By an agreement in May 1867 the Reuter agent at Karachi was commissioned to deliver telegrams, sent for the Indian press, for circulation also among Government officials. The subscription was fixed at 600 rupees (£60) monthly.

An office had been opened at Point de Galle on the southern tip of Ceylon. This was the end of the cable connection with London. From Galle Reuters supervised its service of messages carried by steamer to and from the Malay Straits, China, Japan, and Australia. The summaries sent to Australia were of only 100 words, which led to complaints from the Australian papers. As the cable extended eastwards from Ceylon, Collins set out in person to organize offices and agencies *en route*. In 1871 Shanghai became the headquarters of the growing Reuter presence in the Far East.

Collins left India in 1872. After an interlude in Persia, he went in 1878 to Melbourne as the first general manager for Australia and New Zealand. Despite his efforts, the position of Reuters in Australia was never to match that in India. Most profit was to come from supplying market prices and from running a private-telegram service. The Australian newspaper proprietors, rough with each other, were never going to be easy customers for Reuter news.

A cable and telegraph link through Darwin and across Australia to the south was working by October 1872, although often broken. By that date the *Melbourne Argus* and the *Sydney Morning Herald*, the main Australian dailies, had reluctantly agreed to take Reuter news. They paid £4,000 annually, plus telegraph charges. They feared, probably rightly, that Reuters aspired to gain the same dominance over the press in Australia as in India. Lachlan MacKinnon, part-owner of the *Argus*, had initially hoped to rally the Indian and Chinese papers into an anti-Reuter alliance which would telegraph its own news from London. This attempt failed. MacKinnon also wanted to form an Australian Press Association. 'Without a strong association,' he had told the manager of the *Argus* in a letter from Scotland, dated 19 May 1870, 'we shall be all of us in Reutters [*sic*] power.' In the end MacKinnon wrote (16 June 1871) that he was sufficiently satisfied by the terms agreed with 'the sneaking little Jew'. 'I do not believe that a year ago any reasonable amount of money would have induced Reutter to make the concession he has now made.'

For commercial reasons, Reuters had proved willing to be remarkably self-effacing in Australia. The new service was to be known as the Australian Associated Press service, not as a service from Reuters. Also, it was to be handled by Australian editors in London, who were to make their own selections for transmission. There was good financial reason for such self-selection, quite apart from the Australian desire for independence. The cable rate was ten shillings per word, and until charges were reduced the daily file rarely exceeded fifty words. Every word transmitted had to be what Australian readers wanted.

By 1873 John Fairfax of the *Sydney Morning Herald* was grumbling about 'Reuter and all that tremendous expense', and wondering whether to break the contract. Instead, it was renegotiated. In 1874 the subscription of £4,000 was maintained for a further year, but was cut to £3,000 for the next year, and to £2,000 for subsequent years. From November 1877 the news service from Reuters was put on offer to the whole Australian and New Zealand press. The New Zealand Press Association (NZPA), formed in 1878, followed the Australian lead and placed its own editor at Old Jewry. Relations with the New Zealanders were usually easy, but not so with the Australians. Crises over Australian newspaper subscriptions were to recur at intervals. In 1890 the Australian newspapers set up a cable service of their own from London, deliberately reducing their dependence upon Reuters.

In economic terms, South America was part of the informal British Empire in the nineteenth century. Reuters might consequently have expected to do well there, but did not. After the laying of the new cable across the South Atlantic, Reuters and Havas established joint offices in Brazil, Argentina, and Uruguay in 1874. Preliminary expenses for the year totalled as much as £4,250. The Reuter half-share of this cost was one reason for the drop in the 1874 annual dividend. The South American press always felt a greater interest in news from Havas, a Latin agency, than in Reuter news.

During the 1870s the transmission of private telegrams, either for business firms or for individuals, became a major Reuter activity. A telegram service linking New York and South America via Jamaica was started as part of the 1874 drive. A Reuter office for private telegrams was opened in New York. Unfortunately, the initiative was ruined by managerial incompetence, and it had to be abandoned with loss of money and face.

Much more satisfactory was the 'Eastern Private Telegram' service. This was used regularly by merchants and shipowners in India and beyond. Between 3,000 and 4,000 eastern telegrams per month were passing by 1875. The secret of success lay in the substitution of code-words for phrases commonly used in business or family life. These codes saved many words, and made it worthwhile to employ Reuters as an intermediary. For regular users, one word (it might be 'lion') could be chosen to cover a whole long address, or even the two addresses of both a regular sender and a regular recipient. By 1914 Reuters had 2,000–3,000 of such registered clients. Single words were used for phrases such as 'market rising' or 'market falling'. Sometimes a fourteen-word message could be compressed into as little as three words, and then 'packed' with other messages into one telegram to some far-away and telegraphically expensive place. Large identical code-books became prominent features in Reuter offices throughout the world, and staff had to be expert in their use (see Plate 29).

The credit for introducing the private-telegram business to Asia belonged to Collins. He inaugurated the service between India and London at the end of 1871. It soon also became important to and from Australia, and later with South Africa. Offices were opened in Manchester, Liverpool, and Glasgow to serve provincial 'home' customers.

The private-telegram service became known as 'traffic', to distinguish it from the news side.

IX

To what extent did the involvement of Reuters with the running of the British Empire bring the agency under the influence, or even the control, of the British Government? Reuters always claimed to be entirely independent of official direction, unlike Havas or Wolff, which received secret subsidies from their respective Governments. The Reuter board expressed dismay on 14 December 1870 when Havas—its partner in the joint-purse arrangement—was charged with having received subsidies from the former Government of Napoleon III and from the Turkish Government. Havas denied 'emphatically' that it had received a subsidy from Napoleon III, and explained that the Turkish 'payment' was a normal business arrangement.

For Reuters, as for Havas, the test question became 'When was an official payment simply a subscription, and when was it a subsidy?' A subscription at the going rate for an existing or special service was as readily acceptable from a Government as from a private firm. A Government subsidy, on the other hand, implied some degree of dependence by the agency, and influence by the Government. Would the service in question have been undertaken without government money? Was the existence of the service public knowledge? If known, was the service understood to be subsidized? Was it equally available to all?

The example of the relationship of Reuters with the Government of India illustrated how the word 'subsidy' could creep into contracts. The 1867 telegram agreement spoke of 'Government subscriptions'; but its renewal in 1873 introduced the word 'subsidy'. And when in 1876 F. J. Griffiths asked the Viceroy for an increase, the Reuter letter itself used the word 'subsidy'. Three years later the board minutes of 18 June 1879 noted with satisfaction that 'the subsidy granted to the Company' had been doubled.

Perhaps this was merely slackness in use of language. But in later years Reuters began to realize the risk to its good name of being seen to accept payments called 'subsidies' from the British or other Governments. By the end of the century printed agreement forms were employed for supplying Reuter news to officials in the smaller British colonies; the word 'subsidy' did not appear. 'The frequency and extent of the service', ran one 1897 Sierra Leone agreement, 'shall depend on the amount of the joint contributions of the West African Colonies.'

Reuters was unlikely to be influenced by the annual 'contribution' of £75 from the Crown Agents in London on behalf of Sierra Leone. But what about the position in Egypt? Looking back from 1923, Gerald C. Delany, the general manager, admitted that the whole Reuter operation there had long depended upon the 'subscription' from the Egyptian Government. This had varied down the years to 1920 between £1,000 and £2,000. The Egyptian press was too weak to sustain the Reuter presence upon the basis of newspaper subscriptions alone. The official payment had been made since at least 1868: 'we took up the role of a news agency in this country', noted Delany, 'on condition that the Government would support us in various ways, principally as a subscriber to our telegrams, and the existence of our organisation in this country depends upon the continuance of that support.' The Egyptian Government had sometimes cut the subscription for reasons of economy; but up to 1923, said Delany, it had never tried to exercise any influence over Reuter news or business because of its payment.

How much, then, did total dependence upon official money as in Egypt, or upon the regular receipt of large sums as in India, affect the reputation of Reuters for independence and objectivity? Foreign Governments simply assumed that Reuters was a semi-official body, and felt little need to prove the truth of their assumption. In Britain the perception was more confused. It was accepted that Reuters was a national and imperial institution with implied obligations towards the British Government; but Reuters was not thought to be contradictory in regularly proclaiming its independence of all Governments.

The agency acquired a good reputation early, and took care to protect it. By 1861 Julius Reuter was being praised in *Once A Week* for 'the impartiality and accuracy' of his telegrams. His care for impartiality in news distribution has already been noticed. Impartiality in the sense of standing apart from British party political differences was another early concern. On 18 October 1871 the Reuter board was alarmed to find Engländer being named in the press as a left-wing political activist. Rather implausibly, Engländer denied that he was involved in politics. The board formally required him to abstain from such involvement in future, 'inasmuch as our character for impartiality on which we mainly depend for success would be seriously imperilled by any suspicion of political partisanship'.

The possibility of bias or censorship colouring foreign news supplied to

Reuters through the ring combination was sometimes noticed. Henry Labouchere, a radical Member of Parliament and journalist, complained to Moberly Bell of *The Times* in 1892 of 'Reuter "exchanges" with Havas and Wolff, both of which receive subsidies from their respective Govts.'

The limit to Reuter objectivity in news reporting was most clearly shown in its coverage of wars, large or small, in which Britain was involved or interested. Reuter reporting strove always to be accurate, and usually was. Defeats in war were reported as truthfully as victories—notably during the Boer War of 1899–1902, which began with a series of disasters. But the British cause was always assumed (even if tacitly) to be 'right' and British troops 'ours'.

This meant that Reuters normally enjoyed the goodwill of civil and military officials. Reuter reporters were usually accepted as trustworthy, even in their reporting of bad news. And they could be relied upon occasionally not to report at all. Collins proudly gave an instance of this in his reminiscences. Just before the outbreak of the Boer War Reuters discovered that a large consignment of cartridges had been delivered to the Boer Orange Free State. It had been allowed through the British Cape Colony under the terms of a commercial convention with the Boers. Was this taking diplomatic correctness too far? Collins asked for confirmation of the story, and was told that it was true. But he was also told that publication 'would probably have a most disturbing effect in England'. He was left free to decide whether to publish. 'I had no difficulty in doing so. The news was suppressed.' At the end of the war Collins was officially thanked by the imperial secretary in South Africa for showing 'the greatest readiness to render any service to the Government'.

Representations from the British Government were likely to be heard sympathetically by Reuters. But how sympathetic was the agency towards foreign Governments? In this connection Julius Reuter exhibited considerable astuteness in his handling of Bismarck during the Franco-Prussian War. Bismarck wanted worldwide publicity for German war news: Reuter wanted to show the world that he controlled the best news organization. The two men did a deal.

Early in January 1871 Reuter proposed to Bismarck that war telegrams should be sent direct to London from the German headquarters at Versailles. He offered to distribute them not only in Britain, but also to America, India, Australia, Holland, Belgium, Spain, and Portugal. In return, he offered to supply to German headquarters 'for your assistance' all Reuter telegrams out of unoccupied France. Bismarck immediately accepted this proposal. Reuter explained on 11 January that he always took 'great care' not to use French or Belgian telegrams 'which obviously distort facts'. By way of example, he sent Bismarck a copy of a telegram from Marseilles which he had suppressed. This telegram, dated 6 January, reported that a letter had been sent by Germans long resident in Marseilles protesting to the King of Prussia against 'the cruel and barbarous war being waged on the French nation'.

Was Reuter sacrificing the independence of the news agency by making this deal? He believed the Marseilles protest to have been a French propaganda ploy. The telegram had been suppressed before the Bismarck deal had been concluded. Of course, in drawing Bismarck's attention to this action, Reuter was leaving the Germans free to draw the conclusion that he was inclined to favour them. And some historians have drawn the same conclusion by misreading the word *Orientierung* in the German of Reuter's letter of 11 January. They have translated it as meaning not 'for your assistance', but 'for authorization'. Could Reuter really have been proposing to delay publication of all his telegrams out of France while the Germans vetted them at Versailles?

X

Queen Victoria was paying nearly £20 in 1865 for a six-month supply of Reuter telegrams. Reuter, she wrote to Disraeli in 1878, was one 'who generally knows'.

In 1871 Victoria's brother-in-law, Duke Ernst II, had made Julius Reuter Baron de Reuter of Saxe-Coburg-Gotha. The title had been awarded in recognition of Reuter's services to the public. This was entirely proper; but in a sense Reuter bought his title. The duke needed the money, and it cost Reuter 10,000 florins (about £800) to obtain the necessary landed qualification in Coburg. Appropriately, he chose as his motto the words 'per mare et terram' ('by land and sea'). His arms showed a terrestrial globe between four flashes of lightning.

The energetic Reuter was not yet ready for retirement. On the contrary, he next ventured upon a project which, if it had succeeded, would have matched his achievement in creating a world news agency. In 1872 he secured a seventy-year concession from the Shah of Persia to take over and develop almost the whole economy of the country. Contemporaries were amazed. The scale of the venture was a further demonstration of Reuter's ambition, and of his confidence in his own powers as an entrepreneur.

Reuter was required to build a railway; to lay down tramways; to construct roads, bridges, and telegraphs; to work all mines except the gold and silver ones, to undertake irrigation works; to establish a national bank; and to manage the customs. He was authorized to raise £6 million on the London market, with the Persian Government guaranteeing 5 per cent interest. As an earnest of good faith, Reuter had to deposit £40,000 in caution money with the Bank of England.

The project was probably doomed from the start. There was voluble opposition from Persian religious leaders. The Russian Government was also strongly hostile, while the British and Indian Governments were cool, unwilling to give Reuter any official support. The story of Reuter's struggle—first to succeed, and then to secure compensation when he was prevented from succeeding—is not part of the history of Reuters. Suffice it to say that it took many years of intermittent negotiation by Reuter, sometimes guardedly helped by successive British Governments, before a settlement was reached. In 1889 he was given permission to establish a national bank, the Imperial Bank of Persia, in place of his original concession.

This Persian involvement drew Reuter's attention away from the news agency. The stress may also have undermined his health. The staff at Old Jewry now saw less of him, although Dickinson, who did not join until 1874, recalled the parties given at his home. Reuter now lived in a mansion at 18 Kensington Palace Gardens, a fashionable London address. There were musical evenings at which leading singers such as Adelina Patti performed. And there were innocently boisterous parties, much enjoyed by the unstuffy baron. 'No more comical scene abides in the memory', remembered Dickinson, 'than the spectacle of this Brother Cheryble leading a game of follow-my-leader up and down the stairs and through the spacious rooms of this great house.'

In May 1878 Reuter retired as managing director 'in consequence of failing health'. He was sixty-one. He remained on the board of Reuters, and regularly attended its meetings into the 1890s. He died at his house in Nice—the Villa Reuter, 97 Promenade des Anglais—on 25 February 1899, aged eighty-two. He left estate with a gross value of £262,603 (£117,653 net). Julius Reuter therefore died a rich man by the standards of his time, but not a very rich man. He had certainly deserved his success and his fortune.

FIG. 7. Contemporary map showing the telegraph network in the 1880s

Heyday 1878–1914

I

By the time of Julius Reuter's retirement in 1878 the news agency which he had created was an established institution within the British Empire. It was to remain so until the middle of the twentieth century. G. B. Dibblee's short popular book on *The Newspaper*, published in 1913, assumed that its readers would hardly need telling about Reuters: 'Reuter is so much a household word that an explanation of the function of Reuter's Telegram Company is quite unnecessary.'

Reuters was well known; but its managing director during these years, Baron Herbert de Reuter (1852–1915), was never a public figure like his father. Baron Herbert was educated at Harrow and Balliol College, Oxford, and was thoroughly 'English' in his view of the world. He did not appear to be Jewish, for his complexion was fresh and his eyes blue. He dressed in his early days in an artistic manner, befitting a young man whose ambition had been to become a professional musician. He was appointed 'Assistant Manager without salary' in November 1875, but he seems to have been working at Old Jewry for some time before that. At first he had not given his mind to Reuters. Then one day, as Dickinson recollected, a sudden change occurred. Baron Herbert had fallen deeply in love, and wanted to get married. 'The mop of fair curly hair which he had hitherto worn disappeared, and from that moment he set himself to steady work.'

Baron Herbert soon acquired a thorough knowledge of the world of Reuters. Although less shrewd than his father on the business side, he came to understand and oversee the editorial side with a steady affection. He succeeded his father as managing director in May 1878 at the age of twenty-six, and retained the post until his death nearly thirty-seven years later. Although at first the board tacitly placed him under the guidance of Griffiths, the company secretary, Baron Herbert was immediately allowed the same 'sole and entire management' as his father. His salary was increasingly generous—£1,000 plus commission in 1878, £4,000 plus commission by 1912.

Baron Herbert's commitment to Reuters was total. Nothing of importance transpired at home or overseas without his knowledge. He gave luncheon at the City Liberal Club to all managers or correspondents going overseas; he gave them lunch again on their return. In this way they were courteously briefed and debriefed. He himself never travelled outside Europe, but wide reading had provided him with an encyclopaedic knowledge of places and subjects. He corresponded regularly and fully with his overseas general managers, calling them his 'proconsuls'. Always quick with praise, he could none the less be a firm disciplinarian when necessary. Baron Herbert was a man of wide reading. He was particularly interested in mathematics and music, and liked to spend much time solving problems and reading scores. He read so much because he slept so little. He suffered from eczema, and could bear to spend only a few hours each night in the warmth of a bed. Each morning he sought vigorous exercise on foot or on bicycle, while he pondered the reading of the night before. Unlike his father, he did not entertain at home. Nor did he go out into society, not even to concerts, despite his love of music. He was, in Dickinson's phrase, a 'sociable recluse'.

II

The Old Jewry offices remained the headquarters of Reuters throughout Baron Herbert's time. At intervals, new technology was introduced into the old rooms. The telephone seems to have been installed in 1881, and typewriters came into use about the same time. Electric lighting replaced gas in 1890. From 1891 a direct telephone line was connected to Paris, placed in a special room because messages could be heard only faintly.

In 1919, as part of a history of the agency never published, Charles Marriott of the editorial staff described 'A Day at Reuters'. The routine had become more hectic than in the early days, but the work remained essentially the same. There was now much more news coming in. The twenty-four hours were covered by four shifts of editors and subeditors, with supporting tube operators, manifolders, and messenger boys. Editorial duty rotated so that each man took an equal share of day, evening, night, and early-morning duty; but the day, evening, and night editors-in-charge were more or less permanent:

> The first impression through the door of the Main Editorial Room is that of machinery; the most prominent objects being the brass tubes through which, by motor suction, telegrams and letters are passed all over the building, and the tape machines. Turn to the right and you are in a low-ceiled room with a lurching floor divided into three alley-ways by two rows of double desks. At right angles to them, under a window, is the more roomy desk of the Editor-in-Charge; its position aptly indicating his only slight detachment from the rest of the staff.

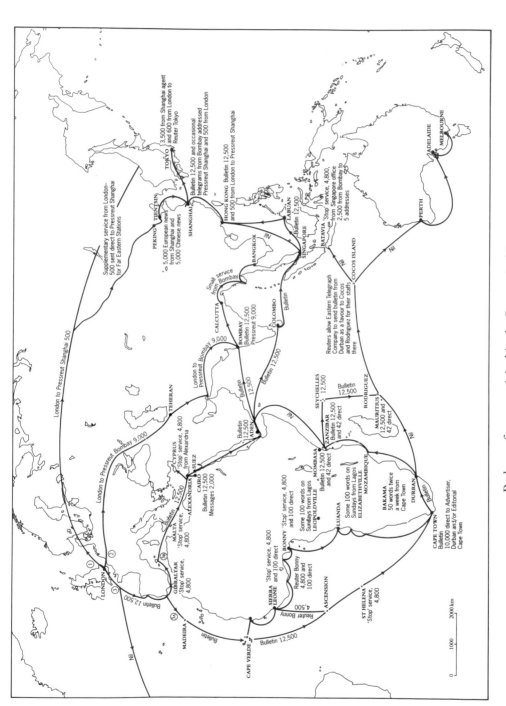

Redrawn from an original in the Reuter Archive

Fig. 8. Outward services, May 1914 (figures indicate the number of words telegraphed every month via the three routes)

In 1914 this editorial work in Old Jewry was shared between European, American, Asiatic, and Dominion rooms. Offices overseas fed news to London, and received in return items of world news selected to suit local requirements. 'For tens of thousands of scattered Englishmen and Englishwomen', explained Marriott, 'Reuters is the link with home and the only means of learning what is going on in the greater world.'

A chart of outward services in May 1914 (Fig. 8) indicated three main Reuter channels for news directed beyond Europe, other than news to North America handled by AP and to South America handled by Havas:

1. London to Pressreut Bombay—9,000 words per month for India, with a 'small service' on to Rangoon and Bangkok;
2. a Bulletin of 12,500 words per month, sent (1) through the Mediterranean to Cairo, Aden, Ceylon, Singapore, Hong Kong, and (2) to Cape Town, Durban, Mombassa, Zanzibar, the Seychelles, and Mauritius
3. a 500-words-per-month Pressreut service direct through Russia to Shanghai for Far Eastern stations.

This wordage, in tight cablese and sometimes coded, was expanded into a much greater number of words in the newspapers.

III

Everything depended upon the skill and willingness of staff at home and overseas. Staff were the main Reuter resource; in 1914 they numbered about 150 in London. Conditions of service were quite good for the period. But staff were not expected to grumble, and no trade unions functioned within Reuters. Marriott wrote of 'the invariable cheerfulness with which extra duty is undertaken in exceptional circumstances'. What he really meant was that management invariably assumed such cheerfulness to exist. London editorial staff could normally expect a day and a half off per week. A senior sub-editor's salary was typically £400 a year, while a specialist reporter might receive £700. Overall salary and wage costs were rising sharply about the turn of the century. Totals were approximately £31,135 for 1895, and £45,006 for 1902.

In 1881 a life-insurance scheme was introduced for senior staff, with policies paid by the company. In 1893 a superannuation scheme was started, with retirement at sixty-five. Senior staff contributed 2.5 per cent of salary matched by an equal company contribution. By 1910 the scheme involved 182 members and was described as 'a strong attraction to capable men'.

Good conditions of employment did not exclude recourse to redundancies at times of financial difficulty. Such difficulty persisted through the 1880s and early 1890s, and it was returning during the last months of peace in 1914. A 10 per cent dividend was paid in 1881, but never again for thirty years. The norm now became 5 per cent, and in three years (1882, 1884, and 1888) the reserves had to be raided to pay even this. Shareholders were told that these difficulties resulted from the high costs of war reporting in Egypt and elsewhere. Such costs were to become not exceptional but usual in most years. No dividend at all was paid for 1885, the year of the failure of the Gordon relief expedition to Khartoum.

The demand by more people for more news was bringing about a transformation of the British press during these years. In 1860 there had been fifteen morning and evening papers in London, and sixteen morning dailies in the provinces. By the end of the century about 150 papers, London and provincial, were being published. The cheapest were selling at only a halfpenny, thanks especially to a steady fall in newsprint prices. Alfred Harmsworth's new *Daily Mail* of 1896—'a penny newspaper for a halfpenny'—was the most notable product of the new popular journalism with a lighter touch. From the start, the *Mail* took the Reuter 'general service'. The printed contract spelt out the continuing commitment of Reuters to impartiality in news distribution, 'without preference or priority'.

Sales of the *Daily Mail* reached about one million copies per day at the height of Boer War excitement. The total number of British daily newspaper readers has been estimated to have doubled between 1896 and 1906, and to have doubled again by 1914. Yet despite this great growth Reuters found it hard to make money out of its news services. The newspapers were reluctant to pay enough to cover the costs of the improved services which they none the less expected. Dickinson, the chief editor, told Roderick Jones on 15 February 1908 that in the previous year the editorial department 'spent about six or seven hundred pounds more than we gained. The consequence is that economy in every direction is the order of the day.' Such cutbacks recurred at intervals, but spending upon news collection and distribution rose almost continuously: 1880, £61,137; 1890, £68,958; 1900, £160,993 (at the height of the Boer War); 1910, £145,192.

The year 1893 saw Reuters falling into the red for the first time, with a net loss of £2,766. Heavy expenditure upon war reporting and 'the fall in the Eastern Exchanges' were blamed. No dividend was paid for that year, or the next. By the turn of the century the situation had improved, although the dividend was prudently kept at 5 per cent. In December 1904 Baron Herbert drew the board's attention to the contrast with ten years earlier. Revenue had grown from £104,000 to £203,000. Reserves had risen from only £6,500 to £50,000. By 1912 reserves had trebled again to £152,000, with revenue at £257,000. The dividend paid for that year was 10 per cent, as for 1911. All seemed well. But within two years this complacency was to be severely shaken.

IV

The international community was lurching towards the First World War. The chairman complained to the 1909 annual general meeting of 'the incessant and growing demands of the news department . . . the day appears to have passed by when it was possible to recoup in quiet times for heavy expenditure during periods of political activity.' This reality was reflected in expenditure upon news collection and distribution for the immediate pre-war years: 1910, £145,192; 1911, £153,018; 1912, £162,158; 1913, £160,953. To cover news costs Baron Herbert had enthusiastically launched a succession of sideline activities down the years. None was given the status of the news service, but all were begun in the hope that they would make money. One did. But the last and most ambitious venture, the bank scheme, was the chief cause of the financial crisis of 1914–15.

The successful venture was the transmission of financial remittances. This was started in 1891. It was an extension of the private-telegram business, and was run alongside it by the traffic department. Jones accurately described this department in his reminiscences as 'the servants' hall' of Reuters. It 'produced the cash which the Editorial Department cheerfully spent'. Reuter customers in (say) London, or Sydney, or Cape Town, or Calcutta were able to pay sums of money through Reuter offices to relatives, friends, or firms in other parts of the world. The Reuter offices handled this traffic as readily as news. Indeed, traffic was the more noticeable activity. The business of private telegrams and remittances kept staff busy all day dealing with customers at the counters, whereas the news side was invisible to outsiders. Reuters found that its world network could conduct financial transfers much more cheaply than the banks, and still make a profit. Improved codes, introduced from 1905, added further to the profitability of the remittance business. For the period 1 March 1913 to 31 July 1914 gross revenue from private telegrams and remittances together amounted to over £36,000 to and from Australia, £15,000 to and from India, and almost £8,500 to and from South Africa. Overall profit was £6,542.

The land boom in Australia during the early 1890s had given the business an initial boost there. The local banks became unsafe, and the common instruction was to 'remit everything through Reuters'. Reuters was an imperial institution, and so could be trusted. During 1893 £1,500,000 sterling passed through the Australian offices of Reuters. In South Africa Indian sugar workers usually remitted their earnings home through Reuters.

Another venture, started soon after the remittance business, was for the daily publication of the British parliamentary debates. Hansard, the long-standing publisher, had given up the work as unremunerative. Reuters quickly found the same; but not until money had been spent upon reporters and printers. Only the debates for 1892 were published under the Reuter imprint.

At this same period Reuters also ventured deeply into advertising. Havas had long found it profitable, and the French example was an influence upon Reuters down the years. In the early 1860s the agency's contracts with newspapers often allowed part-payment of subscriptions through allocation of newspaper advertising space to the agency. Julius Reuter then sought to sell this space. But he seems to have encountered difficulty in finding enough advertisers, and the practice was abandoned when the new company was formed in 1865.

A proposal from Engländer in 1876 that Reuters should undertake advertising had been rejected by the board on 22 March as tending to 'lower the Telegraphic Service in the eyes of the press'. Engländer had to wait for another fourteen years. The late nineteenth-century expansion of trade and industry was increasing the need for publicity through press advertising. The chairman of Reuters remarked at a special general meeting on 6 December 1890 that the idea of venturing into advertising had 'long been entertained by our Managing Director':

> this Company has exceptional means of establishing an International Advertising business on a large scale, with, we believe, immense advantage to our subscribers. We, in fact, seek to create a new business for the newspapers as well as for ourselves.'

The first idea in 1890 had been to work through a subsidiary company formed with Havas; but the Reuter board soon decided that only direct commitment by Reuters itself would attract sufficient capital. So an arrangement was made to work with a firm of commission and general agents—Gower, Dodson and Company. Profits were to be shared equally. An advertisement department was opened at 25 Old Jewry. This separate address was chosen in order to make plain that advertisers were not to be allowed to influence the news side of Reuters.

The advertising venture never looked like prospering. Trade depression was blamed; but the management was reckless. Business was undertaken far beyond the placing of advertisements in newspapers, including advertising inside and on the exterior of tramcars in provincial towns. Prospectuses were printed for companies which failed to start, or to pay their bills. Reuters believed that it had secured the European monopoly for the circulation of the guidebook to the 1893 Chicago Exposition. Advertisers sued when they found that no such monopoly existed, and that only 2,000 copies were distributed by Reuters, not the 100,000 promised.

An attempt in 1894 to transfer the venture to a new company, Reuter's International Agency Limited, failed. Reuters had lost over £27,000 in three years because of these diversions, and tarnished its reputation for sound judgement. No dividend was paid for 1893 and 1894. A small advertising department survived, working with branches overseas.

V

The biggest flop resulting from Baron Herbert's search for alternative sources of revenue and profit was the venture into banking. This was not necessarily a bad idea in itself, but it was bad in the way that it was conducted. 'He believed that he thoroughly understood finance', wrote Dickinson in retrospect, 'and that he was a shrewd business man. In both respects he was mistaken.'

The idea had been in Baron Herbert's mind for many years. In 1903 the articles of association had been extended to allow Reuters to engage upon financial business unconnected with telegraphy. In 1908 the articles were again revised. The company was now specifically authorized 'to act as Bankers'. Finally, in 1910 a 'banking department' was opened.

This new department was described by the chairman at the 1911 annual general meeting as 'purely subsidiary . . . this business will not be carried on with the slightest risk to the stability and maintenance of the old tradition'. The banking manager was Arnold J. Hajduska. He was a Hungarian who had come to Reuters from the Jewish Banking Corporation upon the recommendation of Wolff, the chief accountant. Hajduska was said to be an expert in foreign-exchange dealing.

In 1912 the capital of Reuter's Telegram Company Limited was increased from £100,000 to £500,000. At the annual general meeting the chairman emphasized how disheartening it was for 'a keen man of business', such as Hajduska, to miss good openings because of lack of capital. An increase in capital would also assist the remittance traffic by allowing transfer of accumulated funds at remunerative rates. There was a good response to the Reuter share offer, and all seemed set fair. On 1 July 1913 Reuter's Bank Limited opened its doors. Nominal capital was £1 million, of which half was issued in fully paid £10 shares—49,795 to Reuter's Telegram Company, fifty each to the four Reuter main board directors (who constituted the board of the bank), one each to five senior Reuter staff. No other shares were issued: Reuters thus retained control. The first address of the bank was at 25 Old Jewry, but eventually it moved to 43 Coleman Street.

Reuter's Bank attracted very few private deposit customers. It engaged chiefly in foreign-exchange dealing, and in negotiating foreign loans. Baron Herbert trusted Hajduska totally. The sceptical Dickinson even began to wonder if Baron Herbert was grooming the bank manager as his successor. Dickinson wrote to Jones on 4 April 1913 about a Chinese loan which had thankfully fallen through. Unfortunately, a risky Mexican loan was undertaken. 'Imagine Reuter lending 25 million sterling to the Chinese Government. It is a bit too strong for me . . . The poor Baron! who has so many projects which very nearly succeed, and produce thousands of pounds, and then just fail, with a loss of some hundreds in preliminaries.'

The first annual general meeting of Reuter's Bank Limited was held on 20 May 1914. Given the restricted nature of the share ownership, it was a formality. Profit for 1913 was announced as a 'satisfactory' £20,257, and 6.25 per cent dividend was paid. Had Dickinson been wrong in sensing eventual trouble? At the annual general meeting of Reuter's Telegram Company, held just a week after the bank general meeting, an experienced London stockbroker, Gerald Williams, voiced doubts from the floor about the running of the bank. He asked for an Englishman to be appointed to the staff, 'who will keep you in touch with the banking sentiment of London'. Here was a coded warning.

These first serious doubts about the bank to be uttered in public were expressed at a time when other episodes had already damaged the good name of Reuters. In 1913 a financial publicity department had been started. In October its manager, W. T. Hedges, sent out a circular to subscribing newspapers which suggested that advertisements placed through

Reuters 'would enable us to make representations for extended editorial reference to your interests'. *The Times* led a press campaign of protest at the suggestion that British newspapers could be thus influenced. It announced that it would refuse all advertising placed by news agencies. Baron Herbert had to repudiate the circulars, and the publicity department was closed down. Hedges, who clearly had no idea about Reuter standards, was sacked. In June 1914 he committed suicide.

By 1914 two established sources of Reuter revenue were under threat. The private-telegram business was falling off, and the British newspapers were beginning to press for reduced subscriptions. Early in the year both the *Daily Mirror* and the *Daily Graphic* secured a cut of one half in their payments. The *Mirror* now paid only £800. But in a desperate attempt to maintain the appearance of equal contributions by morning papers, the *Graphic* was persuaded to continue paying £1,600 in return for a firm commitment from Reuters to supply £800 worth of advertisements.

Then there was the Pooley affair. Andrew Pooley, the Reuter correspondent in Tokyo, had bought stolen documents which revealed that Japanese naval officers and officials had been bribed over shipbuilding contracts with several foreign firms. Foremost among these were Siemens and Vickers, German and British respectively. Siemens was desperate to get the documents back, and Pooley eventually returned them unpublished, after making a profit of several thousand pounds for himself. He gave Baron Herbert a very different account of the affair in a letter of 4 December 1913, implying that it was the Japanese Government which wanted the papers:

After discussing the matter with the British Ambassador, I decided not to publish the papers and the same have now been restored to the owners on the following terms:-

1) A subscription of £250 to our general service.
2) Payment of all expenses.
3) Support from the government for our commercial service, when ready.
4) An undertaking not to interfere any further with either our inward or outward services.

Pooley added that full reports had been sent to the British Admiralty and to the Foreign Office. 'We have dealt the Germans a very hard blow and done Great Britain a very good turn, as the Ambassador has written me.'

Although Baron Herbert expressed satisfaction that the British Embassy knew about the affair, he became uncomfortable over the financial aspect, and on 29 December he told Pooley to refund the £250 that had supposedly been paid by the Japanese Government. 'I feel we must forego it because it constitutes part of a bargain which, otherwise unexceptionable, invests it with a flavour of blood money.' Dickinson commented to Jones on 7 February 1914: 'It is to be hoped that this part of the business won't come out.'

It did all come out. Press reports were telegraphed from Germany to Tokyo about the trial in Berlin of the Siemens clerk who had first stolen the documents and sold them to Pooley. Pooley was arrested on charges of possessing stolen goods and blackmail. George Blundell, the financial agent at Yokohama for Reuters, was also arrested, along with two Siemens employees and two Japanese newspaper reporters. Pooley's wife attempted to commit suicide, and one of the Siemens employees succeeded in doing so while in prison. The scandal was noticed extensively by the press in Japan. There was rioting in the streets. Suspicion centred upon the prime minister, Admiral Yamamoto, head of the Satsuma (or naval) clan which dominated the Japanese cabinet. Yamamoto's Government had already been in difficulties, and it fell on 24 March.

Pooley received a two-year prison sentence in July 1914. The other defendants received suspended sentences. The affair was described as the biggest case of bribery ever tried in a Japanese court. Anglo-Japanese relations were damaged. The British ambassador, Conyngham Greene, had commented on 13 May:

> I cannot but regret the severance, by the official retirement of these distinguished officers, of the friendly ties which have united them to His Majesty's Embassy, and I regret it all the more because their downfall appears to have been largely brought about thro the mischievous activity of a British journalist here, who has thereby not only helped to drag the navy of our ally through the mire, but to injure the reputation of British firms doing business with the imperial government.

Reuters tried to distance itself from Pooley by explaining that he had been acting on his own account and not in its name. He jumped bail in August and fled to England.

VI

The 1870 ring combination of news agencies continued to operate until 1914, and beyond. But there was prolonged uncertainty and much plotting before the first renewal of the ring contract in 1890. Reuters was unsure about the intentions of Havas.

Given this uncertainty, Reuters felt bound to explore alternatives. Abandoning Havas would mean doing some sort of new deal with Wolff, probably in association with the Italian and Austrian agencies. In 1887 the Italian Government had joined with Germany and Austria to form the triple alliance. Bismarck was trying to attract the British Government into this diplomatic web. And as part of these manœuvres, he and Crispi, the Italian prime minister—a personal friend of Engländer—set out to draw Reuters into a parallel news-agency alliance.

Richard Wentzel, the director of the Wolff bureau, visited London, where he met both Baron Herbert and his father. The fact that the old Baron came out of retirement reflected the strength of his concern about the future. The outcome of the visit was an 'offensive–defensive' alliance with Wolff, signed in February 1887, providing for joint action if the 1870 agreement were not renewed.

But after protracted negotiations, mainly conducted for Reuters by Engländer, the ring combination was continued for another ten years from 1890. It was to be twice further renewed before 1914. Havas gained South America as its exclusive territory, and also Indo-China, which had come under French rule. In return, it gave up its share in Egypt to Reuters. Belgium and Central America were confirmed as shared territories.

North America was more difficult. In the early 1890s Reuters became unavoidably caught up in struggles between rival American news agencies. In the expectation of doing a news-exchange deal jointly with two new agencies, the United Press (UP) and the Associated Press of Illinois, Reuters broke with the Associated Press of New York. Then in March 1893 Reuters signed a long-term agreement with Associated Press of Illinois alone. Reuters had preferred the Illinois organization upon the advice of S. Levy Lawson, the Reuter New York agent. In angry response William Laffan of UP repudiated an interim agreement under which UP news was being supplied to Reuters. The other company was not yet ready with its service, and Lawson had hurriedly to open a temporary news office for Reuters in New York—a reminder that at this period no such office existed. When Associated Press of Illinois finally took over in October 1893, Lawson reverted, in his own words, to merely 'supervising the service'. In 1900 Associated Press of Illinois was replaced by the present-day Associated Press (AP), with headquarters in New York.

The 1893 agreement with Associated Press of Illinois made it a member of the ring combination. It was given exclusive rights to distribute news from Reuters, Havas, and Wolff throughout the United States, Canada, Alaska, and the Hawaiian Islands. This news was to be supplied to agents of the American company in London, Paris, and Berlin, who were entitled to receive all telegrams supplied to local newspapers. In return, 'all American or other news' was to be supplied exclusively to the agents of Reuters, Havas, and Wolff in New York. A yearly differential of £3,500 was payable by Associated Press of Illinois, a measure of its still junior status.

When the 1893 agreement was renewed ten years later important changes were made in favour of the Americans. The differential was reduced to £2,400. Central America, Cuba, and the Philippines were added to the American sphere. And the news-delivery arrangements for Reuters in New York were now put upon the same basis as for AP in London. Under the 1893 agreement the Americans had undertaken to conduct and make the whole service of news for delivery to the Reuter agent in New York. Now the news was going to need editing by Reuters itself. AP agreed to pay $225 per month to meet the cost of extra staff. The Reuter presence in North America once more began to grow.

AP remained part of the ring combination on these terms up to 1914 and after. However, in 1911 the possibility of switching to UP was discussed by the European agencies. During these discussions the head of the Wolff Bureau, Dr Heinrich Mantler, reminded Baron Herbert on 2 September 1911 that one day the Americans would break free: 'all Americans desire to make themselves as independent of Europe as possible. This is the same as regards the United Press as the Associated Press.'

VII

The predominance of Reuters within the formal and informal British Empire was destined to be challenged by the Americans during the inter-war years. But the last years of the nineteenth century and the first of the twentieth were the heyday of that predominance. Baron Herbert wrote regularly to his general managers in India, Australia, the Far East, and South Africa. He told Jones in South Africa on 29 April 1908 that 'it was a principle of the Company to leave its pro-consuls on the spot practically a free hand to safeguard its local interests, and it was only on questions of principle and policy that the Head Office was consulted'. This meant, of course, that Baron Herbert played an active part in explaining and enforcing such policy.

Not all managers proved to be competent, or even trustworthy. They were often in charge of large sums of money. In 1871 E. A. Perkins was charged with misappropriation in Egypt of nearly £1,100; but as with his predecessor, Virnard, legal action achieved little. The Reuter board decided in 1875 that present and future agents should enter into 'substantial' guarantees, and that large cash balances should be remitted to London monthly. Revenue figures by territory showed where Reuters was strongest:

TABLE 3.2 Revenue figures by territory 1898–1918. (£)

	Total	Revenue from largest territories					Net profit
	revenue all sources	UK	Europe	India	Far East	N. America	after tax
1898	142,000	54,800	36,155	11,500	5,100	1,200	6,000
1908	196,500	44,700	29,500	18,400	9,300	600	14,200
1918	266,300	49,400	31,600	35,200	16,200	800	4,600

India was the most profitable part of the British Empire for Reuters. It constituted a great market for political and commercial news, both incoming and outgoing. Whole pages of the Indian newspapers were filled with Reuter telegrams. Conversely, news from India, the jewel of the Empire, was in steady demand in England. Edward Buck (1862–1948), who became the Reuter representative with the Government of India in 1897, reported the doings of the Viceroy and other officials. 'Buckie' was readily accepted as a member of the Anglo-Indian community, sharing fully in the round of entertainments, shooting-parties, and gossip. Each year he joined in the summer migration to Simla. He concealed his shrewdness as a journalist under a genial manner. As well as filing official news and supplying colourful accounts of frontier wars, Buck reported the everyday India of the soldiers and the merchants. He secured a steady number of beats, notably his on-the-spot account of the attempted assassination of the Viceroy in 1913. In 1929 his contribution was recognized by the award of an Indian knighthood. He retired in 1933.

The Reuter view of what constituted important news out of India did not exclude the reporting of nationalist activity. A Reuter circular to British newspapers in 1910 announced that a special correspondent was being sent to the Indian National Congress meeting at Allahabad. 'Late events in India tend to impart special interest to this gathering . . . and to emphasize the need of an independent and impartial record of the discussions.' Newspapers were charged an extra six guineas for the service.

Egypt continued to be another important centre for news during these years. Reuter headquarters were moved from Alexandria to Cairo in 1879, when Dr Joseph Schnitzler was manager. Schnitzler served through a turbulent period, which included the bombardment of Alexandria by the British in 1882. He kept in touch with London from the cable ship offshore with the British fleet. News of the bombardment was the first important story to be communicated by telephone to the PA from Old Jewry.

The next manager for Reuters in Egypt was David Rees, who remained in charge from 1884 until 1914. He was in Cairo at the time of the abortive Gordon relief expedition to Khartoum in 1885. Rees spent much time humouring Egyptian politicians, whose goodwill was necessary to ensure payment of the vital Egyptian Government subscription. He also successfully cultivated Lord Cromer, the powerful British agent, and Sir Herbert Kitchener, the sirdar of the Egyptian army. Cromer was particularly well disposed towards Reuters. His important two-hour farewell speech in 1907 was telegraphed in full, sentence by sentence. The next annual general meeting was told that this was the longest telegraph message ever received at Old Jewry. The episode strikingly illustrated Reuters in action as the busy servant of the British imperial idea.

Egypt was at least half within the formal British Empire; whereas China—or, more accurately, a few cities of eastern China—constituted an important part of the informal Empire. Shanghai, where Reuters had its headquarters, was the centre of British commercial interest. Chinese and other Far Eastern traders were coming to depend heavily and without question upon the accuracy of Reuter commodity prices and stock-market news from around the world. The best years for Reuters in the Far East in terms of revenue were to come between the wars; but successive annual general meetings from 1901 onwards were told of the desirability of increasing the Reuter presence in China.

Japan too was awakening, and much more quickly than China. In 1894 Engländer was instrumental in negotiating an agreement with the Japanese minister in London whereby Reuters exclusively received all official news issued by the Japanese Government, 'publication of which will be useful to a better understanding of Japan'. In return, Reuters supplied its telegrams to the Japanese Government, and agreed to act 'as the intermediaries for the financial and commercial requirements of Japan'. The subscription was set at £600 per annum. It is not known how long this intriguing arrangement lasted. It may well have been Engländer's last flash of imagination for Reuters.

Reuters expanded comparatively late on a large scale in South Africa. During the last quarter of the nineteenth century the area was transformed from a backwater into an important market for political and commercial news, both incoming and outgoing. This transformation resulted from the gold and diamond discoveries on the Rand. These brought rapid prosperity, but also political tension between Britons and Boers, leading to two wars in 1880–1 and 1899–1902. British settlers controlled Cape Colony and Natal; the Boers held the republics of the Transvaal and the Orange Free State. The first full-time Reuter agent, Walter H. Croom, 'of the head office staff', was sent to Cape Town in 1876. There had been a local representative there since about 1859. The east-coast cable reached Durban in 1879, and Cape Town in 1887. Cape Town remained the headquarters of Reuters throughout the period; but in 1895 an office was opened in Johannesburg, the new mining city on the Rand. There was already an office at Pretoria, the Transvaal capital. Reuters was taking care, in other words, to be fully represented on both sides of the British–Boer divide.

Montalt J. M. Bellasyse, an Irishman, became manager for South Africa at the Cape in 1887. He was unfairly dismissed in 1899 soon after the outbreak of war. Reuters had been charged by the *Daily Mail* in London with being in the pay of the Boers. This was ridiculous. Reuters was simply receiving a normal news subscription of £300 per annum from the Transvaal Government. Nevertheless, Reuter telegrams were said by the *Mail* to have shown a pro-Boer bias for several years. Baron Herbert was at first reluctant to give way to such pressure. Bellasyse was eventually sacrificed when Baron Herbert found that H. A. Gwynne—who had been sent out as chief correspondent for the Boer War—could not work with a manager who saw both sides of the question. Gwynne was a Tory of strongly patriotic temperament. Bellasyse was ahead of his time in the even-handed way he sought to represent Reuters. He had cultivated good relations with the Boer leaders, who trusted Reuters not to misrepresent them. As a result, W. H. Mackay, the Reuter agent in Pretoria, was even allowed to stay and to report from the Boer side, under censorship, throughout the war.

Canada was the one major part of the British Empire where Reuters stood back for long periods. The wisdom of directing incoming and outgoing Canadian news via AP in New York was questioned at intervals. Under the 1903 agreement with AP its Canadian news for Reuters was no longer edited by AP, but by Reuter staff in New York. Collins told Baron Herbert on 19 November 1906 that Reuters now provided from Canada 'an excellent general service to the British press'. Unfortunately, the British public was little interested in Canadian news; and the Canadians were primarily interested in United States news. 'In Canada, as in Australia,' admitted Collins to Baron Herbert on 18 November 1906, 'there is a danger of drifting from the old country.'

VIII

In sending news round the British Empire and the world Reuters gave much prominence to official and semi-official news issued by British ministers and officials. It also published important pronouncements from foreign Governments. So long as such matter was plainly seen for what it was, there was no danger of compromising the reputation of Reuters for independence. But should Reuters go further, and make itself available to circulate news and opinions covertly fed to it by the British Government?

Towards the end of the century Arnold Gawthrop, the Reuter diplomatic correspondent, kept in regular private contact with the Foreign Office, in particular with Sir Thomas Sanderson, the permanent under-secretary from 1894 to 1906. For some years these contacts were on a formal basis. In July 1894 Engländer had proposed comprehensively to Sanderson:

> That the Company will forward all political telegrams to the person designated by the Secretary of State as soon as they are received.
>
> That in regard to any telegrams of which the correctness may seem doubtful, or the publication inexpedient, time will be given for rectification before they are sent to the press.
>
> That confidential reports of information received from your Agents on the Continent will be compiled by Dr Engländer and forwarded for the Secretary of State's information.
>
> That the Company will publish on its own authority through its Agents abroad any statements or announcements which may be requested by the Secretary of State, strict secrecy being observed as to the source from which they are derived.
>
> The sum to be paid to the Company in consideration of the above to be £500 per annum.

Lord Kimberley, the Liberal foreign secretary, agreed to try this arrangement for six months, 'with a further prolongation if it should be found to work well'.

The only known doubts about the arrangement were to come, not from Reuters, but from the British Government. Three years later Lord Salisbury—the prime minister as well as foreign secretary—minuted on a Foreign Office internal memorandum, dated 10 August 1897: 'I am sceptical of the advantages of our connexion with Reuter—so is Lord

Kimberley to whom I spoke about it.' Francis Bertie, the assistant under-secretary, shared these doubts. Salisbury's private secretary recorded that 'Bertie when in charge is always very much exercised by the frequent visits of Reuter's agent'.

On at least one important occasion Gawthrop provided a link between a foreign Government and British ministers. In September 1899, as the threat of war with the Boers grew daily, Gawthrop had been in contact with Montagu White, the Transvaal representative in London. Gawthrop reported to the Foreign Office that White was complaining bitterly about the way Joseph Chamberlain, the colonial secretary, was conducting negotiations with the Boers. White would not go to the Colonial Office, reported one Foreign Office official to Lord Salisbury on 23 September, because he believed that he would not be listened to. 'But he is anxious that Your Lordship should be aware of his views on the conduct of the negotiations, which are those of the Boer Government, and he authorized Reuter's man to let this wish to be known at the F.O.' Three days later White met Salisbury's private secretary. In a personal letter, dated 30 September, Baron Herbert praised Gawthrop's peace-seeking initiative, only regretting that 'the case is past praying for'.

Four years earlier Baron Herbert had arranged with White for Reuters to handle at press rates all Transvaal Government telegrams between Pretoria and London. South African telegrams could be politically very sensitive at this period. A Reuter telegram, sent by Bellasyse from Johannesburg on 28 December 1895, was used by Dr L. S. Jameson as the pretext for launching his disastrous raid into the Transvaal intended to support an uprising against the Boers by the British in Johannesburg. 'Position becoming acute and persistent rumours afloat secret arming mines and warlike preparations women children leaving Rand . . . no business everything politics.'

While Bellasyse was unfairly criticized as pro-Boer, some of his staff were certainly anti-Boer. They supported Jameson and his master, Cecil Rhodes. H. J. Wasserfall of the Cape Town office destroyed all record of compromising telegrams exchanged between Cape Town and Johannesburg before the raid. He did this, he explained to Jones thirty years later, at the instance of Rhodes. Wasserfall was surprised not to be called to London to give evidence at Jameson's trial.

The Rhodes group does not seem to have felt any lasting gratitude for this assistance in their cover-up. Like the *Daily Mail*, Rhodes became convinced in the years between the raid and the war that Reuters in South Africa was pro-Boer. Rutherford Harris, Rhodes's right-hand man, wrote to Gawthrop on 21 April 1899 that Rhodes wanted to meet Baron Herbert: 'all of our group are painfully conscious that, in so far as your admirable Services are concerned, you have had no sympathy with us for the last two or three years.' There is no evidence that Rhodes and Baron Herbert did meet.

Reuters never seems to have realized that the Colonial Office privately shared the doubts of Rhodes and the *Daily Mail* about the agency's patriotism. In May 1897 Reuters even offered to improve its service throughout the Empire in return for £500 per annum from the Colonial Office. Chamberlain, the colonial secretary, eventually ruled against a deal on 16 November:

> I do not like this proposal. The only way in which I think we could enter into special relations with Reuter would be if we wanted fuller Reports of Speeches or Documents sent to the colonies or elsewhere that they would forward in the customary course of their business. But this must be a matter for special arrangement at the time.

In 1911 just such an arrangement was secretly made with the British Government. An imperial news service had been started by Reuters in the previous year. Asquith's Liberal Government wanted full reports, rather than brief summaries, of major speeches made by leading ministers, such as Lloyd George or Winston Churchill, to be circulated regularly throughout the Empire. The Government was prepared secretly to pay the extra cable costs involved. Herbert Jeans, the parliamentary correspondent of Reuters, was approached by the Liberal chief whip, the Master of Elibank. Jeans explained to Roderick Jones eleven years later (19 September 1922) how 'the matter was delicate, for the Opposition might have made trouble, and what Elibank wanted to know was whether I could be trusted to play the game . . . this was the beginning of a long and fruitful association with the Government.' The arrangement became known informally as 'Elibanking'.

Jones in South Africa had been confidentially forewarned in 1911, along with other overseas managers, that reports of ministerial speeches were to be cabled at unusual length. On 4 July Dickinson, the chief editor, tried to be reassuring:

> it is a great advantage to us to act on these occasions as the hand-maid of the Government. Our doing so strengthens our position in this country very considerably, and, at the same time, it shows to those in authority, who have it in their power to be agreeable or disagreeable to ourselves, that our great organization can be of infinite value to them.

Jones, in a letter to Baron Herbert of 3 October 1911, recognized 'the beneficial effect of service so rendered on our relationship in London with the Home Government'. But he obtained permission to trim the reports 'if it seriously threatens to affect our prestige on this side or to interfere with our business arrangements with the newspapers'.

Dickinson had discussed with Elibank's private secretary, R. H. Davies, the problem of how to maintain the reputation of Reuters for independence while taking this money. Davies and Dickinson agreed on 11 August 1911 that the attribution 'at the request of a high quarter' should be used only 'when criticism has been raised or information asked for by a newspaper'.

Davies added that Elibank wished 'that these extended reports should form a natural part of your service, and not be earmarked in any way'. Davies did throw in the qualification that secrecy should be observed 'as far as it is compatible with the interests of your Company'. But such a deal, by its very existence, was incompatible with the claim that Reuters always acted freely in its choice of news. Admittedly, the 1911 arrangement did not go so far as that of 1894. Reuters was not now agreeing to publish covert British Government propaganda. The ministerial speeches were well known to have been delivered. But the agreement to give such speeches full circulation throughout the Empire was to be kept secret as far as possible. And the payments made were to be kept entirely secret. Reuters was compromised.

FOUR

The World's News

1865–1914

I

T HE completion of the world's first transatlantic cable was reported by Reuters on 27 and 28 July 1866. A terse telegram in American English (duly translated) from the managing director of the construction company announced:

> VALENTIA, July 27.
>
> 'O.K.' (All right.)

Then at 12.30 a.m. on 28 July came fuller news:

> VALENTIA, July 27.
>
> Shore end landed and spliced. Completed at 8.43.
> Messages of congratulation passing rapidly between Ireland and Newfoundland. Insulation and continuity perfect. Speed much increased since surplus cable has been cut off.

Equipment failure prevented any news being carried immediately. But repairs were soon made, and on 31 July a new era began when Reuter subscribers began to receive an unbroken flow of news from across the Atlantic by cable. Admittedly, the first item was hardly momentous:

> NEW YORK, JULY 29 (MORNING).
>
> The representative of Tennessee has been admitted to Congress.
> Congress adjourned yesterday.

The speed of news by cable compared with that sent by steamship was immediately brought home to newspaper readers. Reuters published this first cable telegram at the same time as a dispatch datelined 'New York, July 21', carried by the *America* to Southampton. This message had included New York prices of the morning of 21 July. Eight or more days had been the usual time lag. But from now onwards businessmen were able to receive American price information from Reuters in hours instead of day.

On 1 August the first hard same-day news was telegraphed to London —the resignation of the secretary of the interior. Also on 1 August, Reuters explained to subscribers how transatlantic messages were transmitted:

> The President's reply to the queen's message left Washington at 1.30 a.m. on the 30th July and telegraphed from Newfoundland at 3.51 p.m. yesterday, consisting of 405 letters, making 81 words, at a speed of 7.36 words per minute. Sent by Weedon, Newfoundland. Received by Edgar George, Valentia. Message delivered to Her Majesty at Osborne at 5 p.m.

News of the election of General Grant as president in 1868 was published in London on the day after the announcement. Eight years earlier the report of Lincoln's election had taken eleven days to reach London.

Greater immediacy added to the interest of news and helped to sell more newspapers. So also did a continuing story. Accounts of Dr Livingstone's appearances and disappearances in 'darkest Africa' recurred in the Reuter file throughout the 1860s and into the 1870s. Livingstone fascinated the Victorian reading public, including Julius Reuter himself. On 9 January 1868 a personal letter from Reuter appeared in *The Times*:

> Sir, – I have received the following telegram from Alexandria, dated yesterday—
>
> 'Zanzibar, Dec 1. Intelligence from Keelwa states that Dr. Livingstone, or a person resembling him, was seen travelling towards the West of Lake Tanganyika.'
>
> You will see that although the news is similar to that already published by Her Majesty's Government on Second of November last, the date of the above message is Zanzibar Dec 1.
>
> Supposing the latter date is correct, which I have at present no reason to doubt, Dr. Livingstone must have again been seen West of Lake Tanganyika, which increases the hopes of his safety. It must be remembered that Lake Tanganyika is upwards of 300 miles long.

Julius Reuter was thus circulating this latest news without charge, perhaps out of excitement. But it was good publicity for his news service. Reuters was not ahead with the ultimate Livingstone stories. Stanley's celebrated encounter with him in 1871, and Livingstone's death two years later, were reported only at second hand.

Wars were long-running stories of another kind. Nothing sold newspapers more readily. Reuters profited during these years from reporting a succession of confrontations—the Austro-Prussian War of 1866, the Franco-Prussian War in 1870–1, the Paris Commune of 1871, and the Eastern crisis (1876–8).

As a result, the demand for Reuter news was steady and strong. But the price of news by telegraph was high, especially from beyond Western Europe. Earliest rates between London and India, for example, were as much as £1 per word. Consequently, as each new overseas line was opened, Reuter subscription charges to the British press increased—by as much as £100 per annum when the American cable was opened.

Because of high cable tolls, even a short overseas telegram could cost several pounds. Ingenious coding was therefore necessary to save money. Even so, early Reuter cable telegrams to and from the world outside Europe were usually kept to bare essentials. But official announcements and speeches by leading public figures at home and abroad were always given sufficient notice, even if they were being received from or sent to expensively distant places. As a result, Reuters quickly became known as the news agency of official report. This made the service indispensable to newspapers, but also exposed Reuters to recurring charges of working under official influence.

Protection of copyright in Reuter telegrams soon became necessary to prevent less reputable editors publishing news without payment. In August 1870 Reuter telegrams were formally registered for copyright at Stationers' Hall. But protection was still uncertain. Finally, on 6 February 1890 *Reuter's Journal* was launched. This daily publication contained a selection of telegrams printed as a news-sheet, and offered formally for sale at Old Jewry, price 6d. The last number of *Reuter's Journal* was published in 1979.

II

Between 1866 and 1872 the news operation in India was ably developed by young Henry Collins. News was processed either in Bombay or Calcutta, before being transmitted to London or distributed throughout India. Collins introduced full coverage of the Indian frontier wars, which were to continue throughout the period of British rule.

The first colonial war to be reported by Reuters from the front line was the expedition against the Emperor Theodore of Abyssinia in 1867-8. The punitive force under General Napier assembled at Bombay in

October, its size and timetable duly revealed by Reuters without censorship:

> BOMBAY (via Trieste) Sept. 29.—The advance guard of the Abyssinian field force, consisting of about 1,400 troops and 1,000 horses and mules sails on the 5th October, and will be followed a month later by the rest of the expeditionary force.

Reuters had a reporter with the expedition. He may have been a special correspondent, or more probably he was a serving officer. His dispatches were sent to Suez for telegraphing to London. He rode with the column which made the final dash to the Emperor's capital, and on 8 May the newspapers received a Reuter telegram which crisply told all:

> HEADQUARTERS, BRITISH ARMY, TALANTA, April 21.—Magdala and its fortifications have been entirely destroyed. The British expeditionary force commenced its return march to the coast on the 18th inst. All well.

The Abyssinian story ended with the arrival of Theodore's son at Plymouth three months later. Edward Aitken Davies, the Reuter agent there, added a touch of human interest to his report of the formal reception on 14 July: 'He is an interesting little lad, tall for his age (seven years last April), and much delighted with England, exclaiming, "Oh, this beautiful country! I shall never go back."'

During the Franco-Prussian War Reuters supplied a special service of news to the Government of India. Dispatches from many datelines were sub-edited in London into a brief round-up and sent variously by the four available cable routes. War news naturally predominated, but home news was also carried. The queen's speech at the opening of parliament was given at length; debates were noticed in both Houses of Parliament on matters of concern to India; the honours list was reported; a strike of Welsh miners was covered; and the results were given of the Derby and of other classic horse-races. Some news from China was included, and some from the United States. Not least, the beginnings of a domestic service for India were reflected in reports of ship arrivals and departures, and of military and civil appointments.

Thanks to its links with the French and German agencies, Reuters received news of the fighting during the Franco-Prussian War from both sides. But it used its own agents as much as possible. Emil Wolff, who had recently started working for Reuters in London, recollected how its reputation was boosted by its war coverage. Reuters did not expect to match the detailed accounts of the newspaper special correspondents, but it did aim to be ahead with the basic facts. Thus Wolff remembered how Reuters gave the first news of the surrender of Napoleon III and of the French army at Sedan. This was immediately telegraphed to the Viceroy of India. Despite the dramatic nature of the news, Reuters offered no comment. 'Its brief bulletins,' recollected Wolff with complacency, 'without a tinge of sensational prose, were looked upon by the public with absolute confidence.'

Bismarck was supplied with daily war reports by Reuters. He understood the importance of news management, and was prepared to intervene openly as well as secretly. On 2 October 1870 he sent a message in German direct to Reuter in London, which was immediately published in English translation: 'The report of the conversation between King William and the Emperor Napoleon, given by Dr. Russell, the *Times* correspondent, is founded throughout upon mere invention.' Reuters had not itself reported this conversation, and *The Times* did not carry Bismarck's repudiation of it. But Russell was shown the Reuter report in Paris. He immediately sought an interview with Bismarck, who denied sending the message to Reuters, but refused to say so publicly. Russell was unconvinced. He always believed that Bismarck had been upset because the king had told the crown prince (Russell's unattributed source) more about the conversation than the king had told Bismarck. An alternative explanation—eventually accepted by *The Times* itself—was that the message to Reuters had been sent by a member of Bismarck's staff, who had blunderingly turned an intended correction of some of the content of Russell's report into a denial of the whole.

Whatever the truth, Reuter found himself under attack in private both from Russell and from Mowbray Morris of *The Times*. The latter asked, with justice, why having published Bismarck's message without hesitation, Reuters had not published a telegram of self-defence from Russell. 'My statement', declared Russell firmly, 'was not founded on pure invention.' Reuter was probably at a loss which party to believe. But the right course would have been to publish both sides. Had he been too concerned not to offend Bismarck?

Prussia's wars and scheming were closely covered during these years, thanks to the network of Reuter agents and stringers established by Engländer across Central Europe. At the start of the Austro-Prussian War, for example, a single day's publication on 18 June 1866 contained Reuter dispatches about the crisis from eleven datelines—Berlin, Vienna, Frankfurt, Munich, Stuttgart, Dessau, Cassel, Hamburg, Lernberg, Carlsruhe and Florence.

III

While Reuter coverage of Europe was always comprehensive, news from the British Empire grew steadily in quantity as world cables extended and as transmission rates fell. And if news from India at first took most space in the Reuter imperial file, news from South Africa came to surpass it for excitement—reports of major diamond and gold discoveries, of war against the Zulus, of the Jameson Raid, and of two wars against the Boers. The Zulu War gave Reuters a beat that shocked the British people, even though it took twenty days to arrive. After midnight on 10 February 1879 Dickinson was the editor on duty. He received a telegram from St Vincent, relaying a message from Cape Town in code. This reported a battle at Isandhlwana, near Rorke's Drift, on 21 January. It contained a long list of names, not in code, which Dickinson soon realized was a list of officers killed. Here was a major disaster, and he called for relays of hansom cabs to rush the story to the newspaper offices sheet by sheet as it was decoded:

> CAPE TOWN (via St. Vincent), JAN. 27.
>
> On the 21st inst. a British column, consisting of a portion of the 24th Regiment and six hundred natives, with one battery, was defeated with terrible loss by an overwhelming force of Zulus, who numbered twenty thousand.
>
> A valuable convoy of supplies, consisting of one hundred and two wagons drawn by a thousand oxen, two guns, four hundred shot and shell, one thousand rifles, two hundred and fifty thousand rounds of ammunition, and sixty thousand pounds of commissariat stores and the colours of the 24th Regiment fell into the hands of the enemy.
>
> The engagement took place about ten miles beyond Rorke's Drift.
>
> The number of Zulus killed and wounded is estimated to have been five thousand, while our force was completely annihilated.

The British public was further shocked five months later when the Prince Imperial—the son of Napoleon III, and a popular figure—was killed while serving in South Africa with the British army. On 19 June Reuters reported that, after dismounting on reconnaissance eighteen days earlier, the prince and two troopers had been killed by spears in a sudden Zulu attack.

This message, via Madeira, took sixteen days to come from Cape Town; but two years later, when Reuters reported another disaster from South Africa during the first Boer War, Durban had become linked to London by cable. News of the Boer victory at Majuba Hill consequently reached London in less than a day. The Boers had stormed the hill on the morning of 27 February 1881. The special correspondent sent out by Reuters to cover the war had not been allowed to go to the front, and bad communications delayed the news reaching him at Durban. But the correspondent hurried with the story to the cable office just before it shut down at 7 p.m. After sending his message, he took the entire telegraphic staff out to dinner. This ensured that no one else could lodge a telegram: a rival might have bribed the staff to reopen.

The economy of words in the telling of the story added to its graphic quality:

DURBAN, Feb. 28 12.15 A.M..

An account of the defeat sustained at Spitzkap says:—

So long as our men's ammunition lasted the loss on the side of the British was very slight.

It was when forced to retreat that the slaughter commenced.

The two companies of Highlanders who were on the summit of the hill remained there throwing stones down on the advancing Boers, and afterwards received them at the point of the bayonet.

The guns from Mount Prospect checked the pursuit of our men by the Boers to a very large extent, doing considerable execution.

Up to the present it has been impossible to obtain a list of the missing officers, and the correct loss of men cannot be ascertained, as soldiers are still arriving in camp, and it is thought that many others are hiding amongst the rocks.

No fears are entertained for the safety of the camp, but all preparations for defence are being made.

Another account of the engagement is as follows:—

When the ammunition fell short the slaughter was fearful.

Finally, the British troops made a desperate rush, but too late, the Boers triumphing, and firing with deadly effect.

The 60th fought their way gallantly back to the camp, but were hotly pressed on all sides.

It is stated that only seven men of the 58th Regiment have survived.

The Highlanders were much cut up.

The camp is being fortified at every corner.

Commander Romilly is dangerously wounded.

The following troops were engaged in the action:— Two companies of the 92nd, of the 60th, and of the 58th Regiments, and the Naval Brigade.

The guns have been brought back to the camp.

Australia did not produce as much news of interest to British readers as did South Africa or India. There were no wars. The crimes and eventual capture of the Kelly gang of bush-rangers attracted attention, however, in

1879–80. And tours by English cricketers received increasing coverage. Ernest Collins, brother of Henry, was in charge of news out of Australia. He came to be remembered in Reuters for sending what was for many years the most expensive press message ever transmitted by telegraph. His lengthy report of a New South Wales budget in 1875—delivered in the days before the introduction of a press rate—was said to have cost Reuters £1,200. Collins had clearly taken too far the Reuter commitment to full reporting of important official news.

Protection of the lifeline of Empire through the Suez Canal to India and Australia gave the British a permanent interest in the fate of Constantinople, the capital of the decaying Turkish Empire. Britain was prepared to fight rather than to let the Russians take the city. Engländer went there in 1877 to report the war between Russia and Turkey. British warships appeared off Constantinople, and for a time early in 1878 British intervention seemed to be a serious possibility.

Engländer revelled in the atmosphere of intrigue and corruption which surrounded the sultan. He knew everyone who mattered at Court and among the competing European diplomats. In particular, he established good relations with Henry Layard, the British ambassador. This was entirely appropriate for a Reuter correspondent. But Engländer's dealings with Layard were not just those of a journalist. He seems to have acted as a spy-master. Some of his letters to Layard referred to 'the Reporter of Your Excellency'. This person received £50 per month from the British Embassy: such a high retainer suggests that the spy was supplying valuable military and political intelligence.

Engländer's reports to London—which were almost invariably copied to the ambassador—used this source, and also two others. In sending information from 'one of my reporters employed by our agency' on 29 December 1877, Engländer asked that this should not be revealed to his competitors. Such stringers supplied both general and commercial news. In addition, there was a high Turkish official, code-named 'the Gentleman in Question'. This contact leaked official news and documents. He seems to have been very biddable, for on 9 February 1878 Engländer told Layard: 'I have this morning seen the Gentleman in Question who will draw up a complete account of the negotiations which I shall be able to communicate tomorrow.' The importance of this source was demonstrated on 21 February when Engländer was able to telegraph details of the wide boundaries proposed for the state of Bulgaria demanded by Russia as a condition of peace. These terms were not acceptable to the other Great Powers.

As well as supplying Layard with information, Engländer received information from the ambassador in return. The two men met frequently. As a result, Reuter telegrams gave prominence to the official British line. Engländer liked to hint at his inside knowledge, but he could be very wrong. For example, on 10 December 1877 he asserted: 'There is no truth in the rumour current here today that Mehemet Ali Pacha has been recalled.' Yet two days later he was mentioning, in passing and without explanation, that the recall had taken place.

Engländer used various means to get news out despite the strict censorship. He sometimes telegraphed London indirectly by way of Bombay and Odessa, or he sent messengers over the Bulgarian border. His assistant and eventual successor, W. H. G. Werndel, recollected later (21 February 1919) how Reuters employed transmitting agents over the border 'to whom we would address our dispatches, while special codes, worded in homely language, were prepared for the purpose of dealing with any possible contingency'.

Engländer and Werndel seem to have devised their own codes. But in 1877 G. D. Williams composed a 'Political Code', presumably for general use by Reuter correspondents filing to London. In 1889 a printed code in French was issued for exclusive use between St Petersburg and London. Tsar Alexander II had been assassinated in 1881, and other political assassinations seemed likely. As with the 'homely language' used by Werndel from Constantinople, every possible variation of outrage was covered by innocent-sounding messages. Thus 'Vendez à trente huite' meant that the tsar had been assassinated by a bomb explosion; whereas 'Annulez commande papeterie' meant that a bomb attempt had failed, with the tsar unhurt. Other likely weapons and ascending degrees of injury were each coded in combination (see Fig. 9).

IV

During the Eastern crisis Engländer's transmission costs must have been high. This was acceptable to Old Jewry only because of the great importance of the news in terms of European peace or war. As telegraphic charges gradually fell, however, much fuller reporting of less momentous news became possible. The 1875 International Telegraph Convention at St Petersburg recommended the replacement of twenty-word 'telegraphic units' by the more economical method of charging per word.

In addition, extra-low press rates for news-agency and newspaper correspondents were reluctantly and unevenly conceded by the cable com-

CODE SPECIAL.

MOT OU PHRASE DE CODE.	SIGNIFICATION.
fort peiné....................	Assassiné.
envoi fonds.................	Conspiration pour assassiner.
Louis	Assassin.
Lucas	Assassins.
fort troublé par.............	Assassiné par.
Vous ne perdrez rien par faillite	Le Czar est indisposé.
Nous subirons perte fort considerable par faillite ...	Le Czar est légèrement indisposé.
Votre père m'a chargé vous télégraphier ses félicitations ...	Le Czar est malade.
Votre mère s'inqui- ète à cause de votre silence.........	Le Czar est très malade.
Votre femme est très souffrante de...........	Le Czar souffre d'une attaque de.
Père devient très inquiet; écrivez-lui...	Le Czar est gravement malade.
Mon fils aîné partira pour Berlin après demain	Le Czar perd ses forces.

6

CODE SPECIAL.

MOT OU PHRASE DE CODE.	SIGNIFICATION.
Vous faut il cent ou deux cent livres	L'état du Czar est désespéré.
banquiers opposent difficultés	Le Czar est mort.
associé vous ren- -dra visite lors sa prochaine visite Londres...............	Le Czar a été poignardé par un assassin et légèrement blessé.
impossible gagner adhesion mes asso- ciés	Le Czar a été poignardé par un assassin et dangereusement blessé.
contrat association sera signée demain	Le Czar a été poignardé à mort par un assassin.
associé commandit- aire vient retirer son capital; que faire ...	Un assassin a tiré sur le Czar et l'a légèrement blessé.
associé gérant donne sa demission	Un assassin a tiré sur le Czar et l'a dangereusement blessé.
télégraphiez à mon associé retourner sans attendre ré- -ception ma lettre..	Un assassin a tiré sur le Czar et l'a tué.

7

FIG. 9. Reuter code-book: St Petersburg to London, 1889

panies during the last quarter of the century. From the beginning of 1876, for example, a press rate of 1s. per word for uncoded general news was negotiated by Reuters with the Anglo-American Telegraph Company, plus a 12.5 per cent rebate for 'packed work'. In return, Reuters agreed to give its whole North Atlantic business to the Anglo-American provided that Reuter messages were transmitted 'at least as well as they can be forwarded by any other route'. But there appears to have been no press rate out of Egypt until the late 1880s, and news of British victories and defeats earlier in the decade must have been transmitted at full rates. Even when special rates were available, press messages might have to take second place; and Baron Herbert told the 1898 annual general meeting that in order to keep up with competitors in its reporting of the recent cricket tour of Australia, Reuters had been compelled to send many of its telegrams at the high ordinary tariff of 14s. 6d. per word, compared with the press rate of 1s. 10d. per word.

Baron Herbert spoke of 'active competitors'. The growing Victorian demand for news had encouraged the establishment in London of several news-agency rivals to Reuters. Some were small and specialist. One rival agency had been started in 1868 by James McLean, who had been the New York agent for Reuters during the American Civil War. But the most enduring challenge came from Central News (1863), and from the Exchange Telegraph (Extel, 1872). Both agencies sent out war correspondents, although Extel specialized in Stock Exchange prices and financial news. It secured the exclusive right to be represented on the floor of the London Stock Exchange.

The challenge offered in the early 1890s by Dalziel's News Agency was sharp but fairly short. From its headquarters in New York Dalziel supplied cheap and colourful news, albeit American-centred. The British provincial press was soon using it heavily. But Dalziel's greatest coup was to exploit the long-standing reluctance of *The Times* to depend upon Reuters. In October 1890 Dalziel won a contract from Moberly Bell, the paper's new manager, and for a while Dalziel telegrams began to match Reuter telegrams in *The Times* and other London papers. But in its search for exciting news Dalziel started to overreach itself. Too many of its reports were found to be inaccurate or untrue; *The Times* gradually turned back to Reuters. Bell told Dalziel on 25 October 1893: 'Reuters sends us a great deal that we are unable to use, but nothing that would make us absolutely ridiculous if it slipped in.'

The Dalziel challenge helped to encourage a major expansion of the Reuter news service. Some necessary improvements had already been introduced by Baron Herbert in the 1880s. After taking over as managing director in 1878, he had come to realize that the service out of Europe lacked freshness. It depended too much upon news from the allied agencies. To correct this, Baron Herbert appointed to the European capitals (in the words of Emil Wolff) 'a number of absolutely independent correspondents, preferably of British nationality'. And to speed up receipt of news at Old Jewry, correspondents throughout the world were allowed to telegraph directly instead of through overseas Reuter offices.

In 1883 Reuter agents and correspondents were sent the following explicit circular:

TO AGENTS AND CORRESPONDENTS

In consequence of the increased attention paid by the press to disaster &c., of all kinds, agents and correspondents are requested to be good enough, in future, to notice all occurrences of the sort. The following are among the events which should be comprised on the service:—

fires, explosions, floods, inundations, railway accidents, destructive storms, earthquakes, shipwrecks attended with loss of life, accidents to war vessels and to mail steamers, street riots of a grave character, disturbances arising from strikes, duels between, and suicides of persons of note, social or political, and murders of a sensational or atrocious character.

It is requested that the bare facts be first telegraphed with the utmost promptitude, and as soon as possible afterwards a descriptive account, proportionate to the gravity of the incident. Care should, of course, be taken to follow the matter up.

These instructions became famous within Reuters, and were reissued at intervals over the years. They were perhaps written by Baron Herbert himself. Certainly, his correspondence in the 1880s was full of incisive guidance along similar lines. In a letter to W. H. Smith of AP on 21 July 1888, Baron Herbert outlined the Reuter method for reporting set events, such as the recent funeral of the Emperor Frederick:

> one of two things is necessary, either to be first with the news and to receive accounts of the various ceremonies as they take place, or else to wait till the end of the day and send a good descriptive account at the cost of being forestalled. We have always considered the first alternative the more desirable for an agency, and it has been the task of editors in the evening to work up the whole material as best they can.

Three months later on 17 October, at the time of the United States presidential election, Baron Herbert was asking Smith 'to make us a concise and above all prompt service'. Conflicting returns were to be avoided as far as possible. 'The definitive result should be sent at full rates by both routes in two words thus, "Cleveland elected" or "Harrison elected".'

The assassination of American presidents was even hotter news than their election. A junior sub-editor was said to have spiked a New York message on 14 September 1901, commenting: 'These Yanks. They seem to think we're interested in their blooming President's shooting excursions.' The editor-in-charge heard the words and retrieved the cable, which read, 'McKinley shot Buffalo'. This was the first news of the shooting.

Newspapers still published their news more or less as they received it. Telegrams from Reuters and other agencies and from each paper's own correspondents were grouped by topic in columns. Sometimes parts of telegrams were omitted, but the news was not yet rewritten into story form. Even so, newspapers were keen to receive their telegrams in good time for going to press. In a circular issued on 17 May 1906 Reuter correspondents were told that the London papers were now printing about midnight, instead of an hour or more later. No long telegrams were to be sent to Old Jewry after 10.30 p.m., and between 10.30 and midnight 'everything must be rigorously summarized'.

V

The top news story of the 1880s for the British press was the death of General Gordon at Khartoum in 1885. Here was a story centring upon a national hero which came to a shocking climax with agonizing slowness: in short, an exemplary news story. Gordon had featured at intervals in the Reuter file for over twenty years. He personified the Victorian ideal of a muscular Christian, active against the heathen. In the early 1860s 'Chinese Gordon' had been defeating the Taipings; in the 1870s he had been pacifying equatorial Africa, ruling the Sudan, and quarrelling with the authorities in Cairo. Now during 1884–5 he was besieged for ten months by the Mahdi at Khartoum.

Reuter correspondents in Cairo and with the army sent daily reports as a relief column inched its way up the Nile. Reuter copy, which carried a number of forward datelines, was widely used; but the first news that Khartoum had fallen to the Mahdi came from official sources in London. The story, however, was not yet complete. No one knew what had happened to Gordon. There were even rumours that the Mahdi had arranged a safe passage. Then on 9 February John Pigott, the Reuter correspondent with the relieving column, telegraphed:

> Korti, Feb 9. 11.30.
>
> Sir Charles Wilson and Lieutenant Stuart-Wortley have arrived here from Gubat having made the journey in four days. They bring intelligence of General Gordon's death on Feb 4.

The next day this date was corrected. The date of the arrival of the two officers at Korti was 4 February: Gordon had died on 26 January. Nevertheless, Reuters had obtained the beat of the decade.

The papers printed the news on 11 February. All accepted that Reuters was correct in its bad tidings, even though *The Times* began an accompanying editorial: 'A Reuter telegram, which we sincerely hope will not be confirmed . . .' Queen Victoria had already assumed the worst when news of the fall of Khartoum came through. Not until 14 February was there any confirmation, when another Reuter report quoted a dispatch in Arabic found in the saddle-bag of a captured soldier of the Mahdi's. Finally, on 16 February came official confirmation.

Pigott had a long career with Reuters as a war correspondent. He covered the Zulu, Afghan, Egyptian, and Burmese campaigns as well as that in the Sudan. Several times he undertook long and dangerous journeys to get his news through. Dickinson remarked in the *Reuter Service Bulletin* for January 1918 that, while Pigott had not possessed the literary skills of later war correspondents, he could write 'in the plain and unadorned English which was suitable to the days when telegraphy was difficult and expensive'.

Most generals did not like the new breed of war correspondents. The soldiers suspected the correspondents of posing as 'experts' with little justification. Their status was ambiguous. They usually had to make their own arrangements for food and horses; and they had to obtain a licence from headquarters and sign a declaration drawn up by the War Office. Yet they shared many of the risks of death from enemy action, or (more likely) from disease. In May 1885 Frank Roberts, the Reuter special correspondent with General Graham's forces in the Sudan, died of enteric fever at Suakin.

Reuters provided a service of news not only *from* the British army in Egypt, but also *to* the army. From 1885 a daily telegraphic news summary was sent free of charge by the Cairo office, addressed to the 'Army up the Nile'. This service sustained morale by keeping the soldiers in the desert in touch with the outside world. The same service with the same address continued until after the Second World War.

By the late 1880s competition from rival agencies and from newspaper correspondents was posing a serious challenge to Reuter leadership in reporting. Engländer, with his strong news sense, realized this, and recommended changes. He told Griffiths on 20 June 1889:

> I inaugurated myself, nearly thirty years ago, the present service of sober, naked statements of facts for our services, but at that time the newspapers published only a few sober telegraphic announcements of facts, and telegraphy itself was in its infancy:—but your Editors still shrink from developing any light and colour in the service, and believe the dull skeleton telegrams alone to be acceptable.

Engländer argued that Reuters must match the 'special telegrams' of its competitors: 'the only way is also to inaugurate special services.' These had to be additional to the basic general service.

A joint Reuter–Press Association special service was eventually introduced in December 1890. It was charged to newspapers not as part of their subscriptions to the general service, but at so much per word used. By 1907 these charges were varying from ½*d*. per word for telegrams from Europe to 3*d*. per word for telegrams from the southern hemisphere and most of Asia. The special service was described in a circular for correspondents, dated 13 August 1897, as 'a supplementary service of lengthy telegrams of great importance or exceptional interest'. This meant news of military expeditions, of popular disturbances, of 'sensational trials', and of natural or man-made disasters such as a major railway accident or the sinking of a passenger ship. 'If the vessel be a great ocean liner, with many British or American passengers on board, or a British warship . . . the correspondent need never stop to weigh the expense of cabling.'

Guidelines for correspondents in the Far East issued in 1906 reflected the values of the age in suggesting that only the murder of Europeans should normally be reported to London:

> The murder of even an obscure missionary should always be chronicled . . .
> On the other hand, the murder of one Chinaman by another under the most atrocious circumstances is invested with little or no interest in European eyes and can therefore be ignored. This remark, however, does not hold good in cases where the outrage is of a political character.

The same circular illustrated the distinction between general-service brief telegrams and special-service longer telegrams. If a gunboat were 'destroyed by natives', the fact should be briefly telegraphed as quickly as possible. Then if the correspondent were able to obtain good eyewitness descriptions of the attack, he should telegraph this colour at greater length for the special service.

Another undated circular—in French and apparently for European circulation—drew an interestingly different distinction. The general service, it said, was for educated readers who preferred a sober style: the special service was for the majority with limited education and experience who liked colourful and descriptive news.

Characteristically, *The Times* continued to grumble. Bell complained to Baron Herbert on 8 March 1898 that news from the non-civilized world was being automatically charged to the special service. Reuters ought to have a correspondent as a matter of routine 'in every place from which important news may be expected'. And such news should be treated as routine, and be delivered in the general service. 'If in addition to this you instruct him to wire ornate descriptions of his personal adventures and impressions it is quite right that anyone caring to publish them should pay for the luxury.'

From the 1890s the expense of fully reporting non-colonial wars drove Reuters to levy extra charges from the newspapers. Their subscription agreements came to contain a clause requiring, at one month's notice, an additional £16 13s. 4d. per month in times of war, civil, or otherwise, involving Britain or any European Great Power or the United States, 'or during any prolonged political excitement, seriously affecting the international relations of any such Powers'. This latter stipulation meant that in practice the extra payment was demanded even when only small European States were at war with each other.

The number of Reuter overseas offices or news bureaux was growing. The bureaux were mostly one-man affairs, except for major centres such as Paris and Berlin (see Table 4.1). There was no office or bureau in Latin America. Even major centres elsewhere did not maintain more than two resident correspondents. Stringers, many of them local newspaper reporters, provided a vital part of the coverage.

TABLE 4.1. Number of Reuter overseas offices or news bureaux 1894 and 1906

	1894	1906
W. Europe (incl. UK)	8	10
E. Europe	1	3
Africa	2	4
Australasia	6	10
Middle East	2	3
India	5	6
Far East	5	8
N. America	3	3

These fresh services and this extended coverage brought good results. Whereas in 1891 the chairman was referring at the annual general meeting to complaints that Reuter reports 'too drily chronicle events', six years later he was telling shareholders that, 'judging from letters received', the reports supplied to the newspapers from the recent Ashanti, Sudan, Niger, and Benin expeditions had all given satisfaction.

VI

At the start of every war Reuters nominated one or more correspondents, who were given precise instructions. Those for William Wallace in the Niger–Sudan campaign were printed on 19 November 1896. Wallace was required to file a daily bulletin of fifty words; but if 'any very important fighting' occurred, he was to send an immediate short message. 'Mr. Wallace can draw on us at three days' sight for salary at the rate of 20/- a day and expenses.'

During the Graeco-Turkish War of 1897 Reuters had correspondents on both sides—H. A. Gwynne with the Turks, Kinnaird Rose with the

Greeks. Rose's vivid coverage of the retreat from Larissa was long remembered. In the next year Gwynne was the only civilian correspondent allowed up the Nile with General Kitchener's avenging Sudan expedition, which culminated in the victory of Omdurman. Gwynne was the outstanding Reuter correspondent of the period. Dickinson described him as 'a man of exceptional physical power, capable of any endurance'. He was also said to possess 'moral qualities which gained for him the complete confidence and approbation of the commanding officer wherever he served'. Kitchener, in particular, trusted Gwynne when he was chief Reuter correspondent for the Boer War of 1899–1902. He reported to Baron Herbert on 12 July 1901 that he was allowed to see Kitchener, now the commander-in-chief in South Africa, twice a week. 'One day talking of correspondents, he told me that he would like me as Reuters Correspondent to be the official chronicler in every war so that other correspondents whom he could not trust should not be with the army.'

Gwynne had charge of about a hundred Reuter correspondents and stringers during the Boer War. Twenty-one of them were awarded the Queen's South Africa Medal; none was killed or injured. Henry Mockford kept his war documents to the end of his life. These included a licence permitting him to 'draw Rations for himself and one servant, and Forage for one horse on payment'. Mockford had accepted the printed 'Rules for Newspaper Correspondents Accompanying Troops in the Field'. No ciphers and codes were to be used. 'All communications to the press must be confined to events that have occurred.' Messages must be in English. 'The Press Censor will have full discretionary power.'

Despite the censorship, the Reuter war correspondents delivered a steady stream of reports which won praise for their speed, trustworthiness, and colour. The chairman told the 1900 annual general meeting that Reuters had 'not hesitated to send a large quantity of news at the full rate of 4s a word'. The beat in that year on the relief of Mafeking has remained one of the greatest Reuter news coups. The resistance offered by Colonel Baden-Powell's force under siege in the town, although not of great military importance, had caught the anxious imagination of the British public. Some news did get out during the siege, only to whet the public appetite for more. J. E. Pearson, an American working for Reuters, was sent in. He avoided the Boer patrols, bicycled to the outskirts, and slipped in and out under cover of night. Reuters had its story. Vere Stent, the Reuter correspondent in the town, had kept a diary which provided the basis for a telegraphed account of the town under siege. The message to London was said by Collins to have run to 10,000 words.

Not long afterwards Mafeking was relieved, and Reuters achieved its famous beat. The British relieving column could only report back to headquarters from Mafeking by mounted messenger. The breaking of the news by an official announcement was therefore bound to be delayed for at least two days. But, fortunately for Reuters, the Boers told W. H. Mackay, its Pretoria correspondent, of their setback. They wrongly assumed that he would not be able to get the story out. Enterprisingly, he saw that he might avoid the Boer censorship by going to the frontier with Portuguese Mozambique. There he handed his dispatch to an engine-driver, who delivered it to the Eastern Telegraph Company at Lourenço Marques. Tradition has it that he paid the driver £5 to hide the message in one of his sandwiches.

The relieving column had broken through on 17 May, and on the following evening at 9.17 Reuters told the world. The news was sent to Queen Victoria, who asked to see the original telegram, to the prime minister, and to the Lord Mayor of London, who read it out from the steps of the Mansion House. The country went wild on the strength of the Reuter report, even though it was not to be confirmed from army headquarters in South Africa for two days. Reuters was trusted. Soon after midnight on 18–19 May, in answer to a question in the House of Commons, A. J. Balfour, the first lord of the treasury, accepted that, although there was no official confirmation of the Reuter telegram, there was 'good reason to think it may be true'.

VII

A few copies have survived of Reuter bulletins supplied to subscribers by the *Bangkok Times* in 1894. These contained a mixture of British, world, and local news. News in March, for example, of the final resignation of Gladstone as prime minister appeared alongside news of the sinking of a Thai rice-boat. A telegram telling of the assassination of President Carnot of France in June 1894 rated a bulletin to itself.

Copies have also survived of Reuter telegrams sold in January 1901 in the form of handwritten news-sheets to passing liners at Port Said. The Boer War was still being reported in detail; but the main news was of the final illness of Queen Victoria at Osborne House on the Isle of Wight (see Plate 15). Arnold Gawthrop had been sent to the island to cover the awesome story for Reuters. He worked closely with the PA correspondent, who had contacts within the royal household. Gawthrop organized a prearranged signal to pass between the house and the telegraph office as soon as Victoria was known to have died. When this happened on 22 January, Gawthrop's reports—sent as priority messages throughout the world—included officially sourced deathbed scenes and last words.

The volume of news and the demand for it were still growing, as was the cost of reporting. Shareholders were told in 1903 that in covering the Somaliland expedition 'the expense in camels, servants, runners, and supplies of all sorts, has . . . been out of all proportion to the amount of intelligence received'. But most newspapers were depending entirely upon Reuters for news of the expedition. A year later the chairman remarked that the Somaliland costs had continued for much longer than expected. 'This is one of the risks which we are compelled to run in our business if we are to maintain our position in the news world.'

The war in Tibet in 1904 was another expensive far-away story which Reuters was expected to cover for the newspapers. Henry Newman accompanied Sir Francis Younghusband's expedition to Lhasa. Like Pigott and Gwynne before him, Newman contrived to establish close relations with the man at the top. Correspondents were not normally allowed to report until two hours after the official communiqué had been transmitted on the one telegraph line. But after the battle of Guru Younghusband allowed Newman to file ahead of the official message, thereby giving Reuters a two-hour beat.

The chairman told the 1904 annual general meeting that the Russo-Japanese War was making heavy demands, financial and otherwise:

> as Europeans are not able to subsist on the fare provided for Japanese troops, the different correspondents have been obliged to make arrangements with a contractor to 'furnish cooks and to provide and prepare each day three good plain meals of European food'. Interpreters are also indispensable, because messages sent over the Japanese field wires must be written in Japanese.

The reputation of Reuters in Japan was much enhanced by its coverage of the war. The Japanese public first heard through Reuters of the breakdown in diplomatic relations with Russia, and throughout the war the Japanese press was full of Reuter reports about European attitudes.

The long voyage of the Russian Baltic fleet to defeat in the Far East led to a most serious case of misreporting by Reuters. In October 1904 the Russian ships had fired on British fishing vessels off the Dogger Bank in the North Sea, believing that they were Japanese torpedo-boats. One trawler was sunk; two fishermen were killed and many injured. British public opinion was outraged. Early in 1905 an international inquiry was convened in Paris. At its conclusion a Russian diplomat revealed to a

Reuter reporter what he said was a summary of the forthcoming judgment; this exonerated the Russians. Reuters published the news without a source on 22 February. In fact the judgment, when announced a few days later, said exactly the opposite: the Russians were censured. Reuters had unwittingly helped them to put up a smokescreen. A letter to *The Times* on 28 February from Bradshaw, the company secretary, accepted that Reuters had been deceived by 'a manœuvre designed to mislead the public'. Years later Dickinson, the chief editor, admitted that his staff ought not to have been so gullible.

In 1912 came the almost unbelievable news of the sinking of the 'unsinkable' *Titanic* on her maiden transatlantic voyage. Reuters was two hours ahead in London with the report of the liner hitting an iceberg at 10.35 on the night of 14 April. When the flash came through one of the night-duty telegraph operators at Old Jewry was asleep, and the other was otherwise occupied. A young messenger boy, Leslie Smith, tapped out the startling report to the newspapers. Reuters had a beat, but thereafter came doubt. This reflected the confusion in New York, where news about the fate of the vessel was being collected. For example, *The Times* of 16 April contained one Reuter telegram which reported dramatically but reassuringly: 'The Titanic sank at 2.20 this morning. No lives were lost.' But the same number also included another Reuter telegram, which was nearer the truth: 'The White Star officials now admit that many lives have been lost.'

Reuters was contradictory, but the Central News was worse. It published a colourful description of the supposed rescue of passengers from the sinking liner by other ships. In reality no vessels reached the scene before the *Titanic* sank.

VIII

Public interest in sport had become intense throughout the British Empire by the turn of the century. The cost of sports detail was high. Reuters devised codes especially for each cricket tour by the English, Australian, or South African teams. Thus one cabled word such as 'GUUKKAFY' would reach Old Jewry from Cape Town. The sport sub-editor would then refer to the codebook, and find 'GU' to mean 'Rain stopped play', 'UK' to mean 76, 'KA' to mean 2, 'FY' to mean 'lunch'. So the message would go out: 'Rain stopped play. Lunch being taken with South Africa 76 for 2.'

Cricket was important in cementing imperial unity, but for many sub-scribers boxing mattered even more. From the earliest days Reuters had reported boxing in the United States, and by 1899 the special service was carrying a 1,400-word round-by-round account of 'The Great Glove Fight in America. Tom Sharkey v. Kid McCoy'. Association football, Rugby Union football, and horse-racing featured prominently in the Reuter sports file, with results being sent regularly to colonial subscribers in Africa, Asia, and Australasia. A system was devised to communicate the weekly British soccer results overseas. Only the numbers of goals scored were telegraphed. These were compared at the receiving end against the known fixture list.

When the first modern Olympic Games were held in Athens in 1896, results and descriptions came through only irregularly, apparently at the whim of a local stringer. By 1912, when the games were held in London, Reuters was offering complete coverage. The Reuter commitment to accuracy was both a recommendation and an imperative for the reporting of sports results.

FIVE

Wartime Reconstruction

1914–1918

I

SIX months after the outbreak of the First World War Baron Herbert wrote on 22 January 1915 about the character of the conflict to Roderick Jones in South Africa. Despite the German origins of his family, Baron Herbert wanted a total British victory:

> We here who have professionally to watch and follow, and, for the proper conduct of the Reuter organisation, interpret the meaning of all that unfolds itself to the eye of the observer, are staggered by the energy, resources, organisation, and skill with which the Germans entered into, and have conducted this stupendous conflict. Every day I realise more deeply the colossal task before us, and the necessity of sparing no sacrifice to succeed where failure spells ruin to three Empires, and will involve the unspeakable blight of German military tyranny over the whole Continent.

Baron Herbert, who had spent his whole life in England, regarded himself as a patriotic Briton. But he bore a German name. And the question was publicly asked in the early months of the war whether he could be trusted, even whether Reuters itself was safely 'British'. Had it been subverted by German influences?

These questions were given focus by the publication in September 1914—a month after the start of the war—of pre-war dispatches from the British ambassador in Berlin 'respecting an Official German Organization for Influencing the Press of Other Countries'. The formation of this semi-official body had been inspired early in 1914 by the head of the German Press Bureau, who had rallied the support of Krupp and other industrialists. They wanted to colour the supply of news about Germany sent to foreign agencies and newspapers. They planned to advertise only in foreign papers which received their German news via approved channels. The British ambassador reported on 27 February 1914 that Havas had agreed to take its news about Germany only through the Wolff bureau, which was to be fed propaganda by the new body. 'The company intends to make a similar arrangement with Reuter's Telegraphic Bureau.'

When this report was made public in September it was naturally asked in the British press whether Reuters had made any such deal. In fact no approach had been made to Reuters up to the outbreak of war; and Havas had rejected the German pressure. But four letters from Baron Herbert to *The Times* were needed to establish the innocence of Reuters. At first he had tried to be dismissive. A *Times* leader of 26 September thought his lack of clarity suspicious. On 27 September a fourth letter from Baron Herbert—composed by Dickinson—finally succeeded in removing 'the singular suggestion that our news service is used for the purpose of misleading British opinion in favour of Germany'. On the contrary, the letter continued, German newspapers were full of rancour at the patriotic handling of war news by Reuters.

The fiftieth anniversary of Reuter's Telegram Company in February 1915 provided a good chance to proclaim the Britishness of the agency. A jubilee leaflet, anonymous but written by Dickinson, declared firmly: 'Reuter's Agency has always been recognised as a British institution representing the English point of view.' Baron Herbert was described as 'in all respects an Englishman. The Directors, the Editorial Staff, and the correspondents are British pure and simple, and so, with the exception of a score, are the 1,200 shareholders.'

An article in the *National Review* for October 1914 had listed 146 holders of 100 or more Reuter shares. Unlike Dickinson, the review found the ownership 'curiously cosmopolitan'. There were only about ten German surnames, addresses, or institutions in the list, but the article still asked of Reuters: 'Are its numerous German shareholders participating in the distribution of its ample dividends?' The question implied that Reuters was flourishing. It was not. Throughout 1914 its reputation and its finances were under increasing pressure. Reuter shares, which had stood at £12 in 1912, were down to £5 by March 1915. The advertising fiasco and the launching of Reuter's Bank were continuing problems. The war immediately added another. For reasons of security, Reuters was told to stop using its codes. This seriously damaged both the private-telegram and remittance traffic: uncoded messages were expensive. Reuter staff in London and throughout the Empire had to be given notice.

Before the war highly cost-effective new codes—abbreviating over a million phrases or word combinations—had been compiled by S. C.

Clements, the assistant secretary. Although the private-telegram business was already declining, the remittance 'traffic' had been doing well. A thousand messages per day were being encoded. The British Government was told that whereas the private-telegram and remittance services had made an estimated profit of £6,542 for the last seventeen months before the war (March 1913 to July 1914), they had lost £17,346 during its first seventeen months (August 1914 to December 1915) because of the coding ban. Early in 1916 Reuters asked the Government to advance £50,000 on easy terms in part compensation. In the event this request became forgotten when Reuters was reconstructed with Government financial backing later in the year. Not until after the return of peace in 1918 was Reuters again allowed to use its codes.

Worry about 'traffic' losses was adding to the pressures upon Baron Herbert during the first months of the war. These pressures included family problems. He was estranged from his only son, Hubert, who had disappointed him by working only briefly for Reuters. Hubert was of an artistic temperament, and wrote poetry. His idealism led him to volunteer for the British army early in the war, and to die a gallant death in Flanders in 1916.

Baron Herbert had reproached Hubert for enlisting against his mother's wishes when she was fatally ill. She died on 15 April 1915. Three days later, a Sunday, Baron Herbert shot himself at his country house near Reigate. He left a letter addressed 'To the spirit of my dear wife Edith': 'Death shall not separate us for we will repose in the same grave.' So ended, suddenly and sadly, the family involvement in the management of Reuters.

Senior staff at Old Jewry mourned their chief sincerely; but for several years the opinion had been growing that Baron Herbert was losing his grip. At the next annual general meeting on 3 June 1915 discussion of the severe difficulties now facing the company led to revelations about Baron Herbert's recent mishandling of Reuter affairs. Mark Napier (1852–1919) was in the chair at this tense meeting. He had become chairman in 1911, in succession to his uncle by marriage, Sir John Hay. Napier had sat on the board since 1888 without making much obvious impact. But he was destined to play a crucial part in the reconstruction of Reuters during the next few years. He was a lawyer by training, and had shared chambers in the 1870s with H. H. Asquith, who was now the Liberal prime minister. Asquith was later to describe Napier as 'one of the most lovable men I have known', with 'a shrewd native intelligence, infinite courage, fine old-fashioned manners'. This combination of attractive qualities predisposed Asquith to respond favourably when in 1916 Napier made representations to him on behalf of Reuters.

With the death of Baron Herbert, Napier was left as the most senior of the four surviving Reuter directors. Two others had joined the board in 1912. They were George Grinnell Milne, and the Hon. Edmund W. Parker, a businessman with New Zealand connections. The third member was Gerald W. Williams, a leading stockbroker, who had joined in February 1915 to become chairman of Reuter's Bank. He was the most weighty businessman on the board, well respected in the City of London. His stockbroking firm had raised large subscriptions when new capital was being sought for Reuter's Bank in 1912, and he had expressed concern about its management at the 1914 annual general meeting. He aspired to displace Napier as chairman of Reuters.

Williams seconded the adoption of the report and accounts at the 1915 annual general meeting, but he did not pretend that all was well, either with the news agency or the bank. Napier had already admitted as much in moving the adoption. He spoke of the interruption to the flow of news and trade caused by the war, and the associated breaking of contracts. He mentioned the losses caused by the ban upon the use of codes. He regretted that a major fraud upon the Sydney branch had cost the company at least £29,000. He reported that Hajduska, the Hungarian manager of the bank, had been on leave in Austria when the war broke out, and had been called up to fight on the enemy side. This was not in fact true: Hajduska was left stranded throughout the war in Holland. An Englishman, G. H. Butterfield, had been appointed in his place. Napier reported that Baron Herbert had allowed Hajduska 'a too wide discretion' to invest in schemes 'which involved the locking up of part of our capital which would have been better left liquid'. Although profits for 1914 totalled £35,725, Napier admitted that they would all be needed to meet current difficulties. No dividend was to be paid.

Williams, in his seconding speech, was more directly critical of Baron Herbert, even while describing him as a man of 'singular charm':

> He had a grave defect as a Managing Director of a Bank, and that was that he knew very little about banking. His brilliant idea of adding a banking branch to his business was remarkably sound, but he put the wrong man in command of that branch, and when he had put him there he backed him up through thick and thin.

Worse still, concluded Williams, Baron Herbert had left his fellow directors in ignorance about what he was doing. Williams did not reveal

that he had threatened—only a few days before Baron Herbert's suicide—to resign from the bank chairmanship and from the Reuter board if
the managing director made any more bank loans upon his own initiative. From the floor, one businessman shareholder, Brodie James, delivered a strong attack upon the board for trying to shift all the blame upon
Baron Herbert and Hajduska. James quoted some of the large promises
about the bank's future made by Napier at the 1912 and 1913 general
meetings. The directors had admitted the slackness of their supervision:
'you have forfeited the confidence of the shareholders and must go.'
James demanded a poll for the re-election of Napier as chairman. There
was never any danger to Napier, for the directors had some 1,500 proxies
in their pockets. He was re-elected by 1,762 votes to 626. Nevertheless,
this significant minority vote constituted a warning that the Reuter board
must quickly put its affairs in order. The death of Baron Herbert had
removed one obstacle; but even if he had lived, Reuters would have been
bound to be reconstructed. Could he therefore have continued as managing director for much longer?

II

Who would now succeed Baron Herbert? Dickinson, the chief editor,
was sure that it ought to be Jones, the general manager in South Africa.
For several years Dickinson had been encouraging Jones's ambitions for
the succession. He had written to him on 5 December 1913 about
prospects for 1914: 'One wonders each time that the year goes up a tick
what is in store . . . all sorts of things may happen in a very short time.
We sadly need some young blood.' Jones—still aged only thirty-six—did
not disagree. After the war had started and with problems for Reuters
becoming threatening, Jones wrote to Dickinson on 4 January 1915
about the crisis. 'There are not so many gentlemen in the Service
[Reuters] . . . and there is a danger of a brood filling the bill who in the
end will not exalt the Agency's name.' Interestingly, Jones himself had
been born scarcely a 'gentleman'. And his struggle throughout life to
improve his social standing shaped his character, which in turn shaped his
impact upon Reuters.

Roderick Jones (1877–1962) had been born near Manchester. His
father—about whom he never spoke—was a hat salesman there. His
mother, by contrast, had a family link both with A. C. Tait, Archbishop
of Canterbury, and with the Scottish Earls of Cassillis. Unfortunately, his
mother had lost all her money in the Bank of Glasgow crash in 1878, a

family disaster never forgotten by Jones. It meant that he could not attend a leading school or go to university. This deficiency was partly remedied by instruction at home from his maternal grandfather, William Tait— instruction described by Jones in his reminiscences as following 'a strong literary and biblical direction'. He continued his education as a young man through wide reading. Jones never mentioned, but almost certainly knew, that his parents had been married only five weeks before his birth. In 'respectable' Victorian England this was socially damaging.

These insecure origins marked Jones for life. He overcompensated by acting too emphatically as if he came from a 'good' family and had received a 'good' education. He dressed with excessive correctness. He never missed a chance to make money, much of which he spent while head of Reuters upon living in conspicuous style, both in a London mansion at Hyde Park Gate and in a country house at Rottingdean in Sussex. Perhaps Jones's assertiveness and display also owed something to the fact that he was a little man, only five feet five inches tall. For years, his passport claimed his height as three and a half inches more, thanks to built-up shoes. His marriage in 1920 at the age of forty-two was a society event. His bride, Enid Bagnold, later the celebrated author of *National Velvet*, alone knew of the vulnerability beneath Jones's grand manner. She passed him a revealing note when he was presiding over a dinner at the Savoy in 1933: '*Darling*. You sit there looking so real, so humorously critical, so (fallaciously) good tempered—so clean cut, such an intelligent gentleman, that you *can't* be so dissatisfied with yourself as you sometimes seem. You are an ass, Darling, about yourself . . .'

Though pretentious, Jones could also be engaging. His appealing eyes were often remarked upon, while his voice has been remembered as unusually compelling. His intelligence and his strength of purpose were both apparent. Subordinates in Reuters were shown this strength without hesitation. Among social equals or superiors, Jones was gentler, but always purposeful. He impressed by the fund of knowledge and experience, tempered by good judgement and good humour, which he displayed in conversation. He was under thirty when he became general manager in South Africa, and looked even younger than he was. Yet leaders of local politics and business were soon asking for his views, and giving their own in return. This trust was the more remarkable since Jones was well known to be the representative of a world news agency.

Jones explained in his reminiscences, *A Life in Reuters* (1951), how he had entered journalism as a step towards becoming prime minister of a united South Africa. He was soon to give up these adolescent political ambitions under the spell of journalism for its own sake. He had been sent out in 1895 to live with a married aunt in Pretoria, the capital of the Boer republic of the Transvaal. He started work on the only daily paper in the town, the *Press*. From that time Jones was to make steady progress as a journalist. He could write equally well in a factual or a colourfully descriptive style. He added greatly to his usefulness by learning to speak and write Afrikaans. By 1896 he was known to Louis Botha, the future Boer leader, and two years later he first met Jan Smuts. The Boer War was soon to break out, and the tension between Britons and Boers meant that news from South Africa was in steady demand. On 2 January 1896 Jones was allowed by the Boers an exclusive first interview with Dr Jameson upon his arrival under arrest at Pretoria after the failure of his raid into the Transvaal. This was Jones's first scoop for Reuters.

Following the outbreak of the Boer War in October 1899, Jones had to withdraw to Cape Town. He became chief sub-editor on the *Cape Times*, and then chief cable correspondent for Reuters. This gave him a key role. Finally, in the spring of 1902, with the war at last ending, he sailed back for England. He had been recommended by the general manager, J. A. Barraclough, to take charge of the new South African section in London. Jones rightly saw this as a good career opportunity, despite a drop in earnings. His salary was £400 a year, increased to £500 in 1904.

Jones successfully developed the Reuter service to meet the growing expectations of the South African press. He was soon a favourite with Dickinson, the chief editor, and eventually became on good terms with Baron Herbert himself. In May 1904 an article by Jones, entitled 'The Black Peril in South Africa', appeared in *The Nineteenth Century*, a leading monthly. Baron Herbert read the article, and summoned Jones to discuss it. Jones had urged Britons and Boers to unite against 'the oncoming hordes of superficially civilised blacks'. Thereafter Jones was invited for frequent talks by his chief.

This intimacy bore fruit when in the autumn of 1905 Jones was appointed general manager in South Africa. His salary was to be £600 per year, plus 10 per cent commission with a £400 minimum. He eventually became sufficiently affluent to invest profitably in the Johannesburg market, with its gold and diamond shares. That market expected speedy news from London, while London was equally eager for economic news from South Africa. Reuters dominated this news exchange. Some newspaper proprietors were jealous, however, of its predominance, especially as it was also gaining control of internal news supply. About a hundred newspapers subscribed to South African news from Reuters. It employed about 250 correspondents and stringers throughout Africa south of the Zambesi.

During 1908 the anti-Reuter newspapers (the *Cape Times*, *Cape Argus*, and *Rand Daily Mail*) set out to establish their own organization, the South African Amalgamated Press Agency, for the collection of both world and internal news. Here was a great challenge, which lasted for nearly eighteen months. Jones succeeded in keeping the provincial press loyal, while he slowly wore down SAAPA. 'Had we refused to fight,' he later told Napier (19 September 1915), 'or had we failed in the fight or in the subsequent negotiations, we should have been forced to abandon our South African press business.'

South African profits were important to Reuters, and Jones was congratulated by the board for his skilful negotiation of a settlement. This contrived to save the faces of the SAAPA newspapermen while ensuring Reuter predominance. A new South African Press Agency was formed early in 1910, within which Reuters kept a seven-twelfths holding; the three principal newspaper groups shared the rest of the ownership equally. The Boer press remained outside the arrangement, but was given equal access to Reuter news. On 22 September 1913 Baron Herbert praised Jones for the 'Pax Romana that your skilful diplomacy has established throughout journalistic South Africa'. South African profit for 1914 was £9,381.

Baron Herbert was also much impressed by Jones's success in raising the prestige of Reuters through personal contacts in the highest social and political circles. Although Reuter general managers could expect some recognition within colonial society, Jones won remarkable acceptance for himself. He became, for example, secretary and later master of the Cape Town hunt. He was well aware that most leading figures were hunt members. Lord Gladstone, appointed in 1910 as the first governor-general of united South Africa, became a member, and Jones soon made a personal friend of him. Jones had lost no time in renewing friendly contact with Botha and Smuts, the Boer leaders. As prime minister first of the Transvaal and then of the newly united dominion, Botha always favoured Reuters. This meant that it got first news of official announcements. Occasionally, Jones was deliberately allowed to leak inside information—as when he publicized Botha's intention to deport the syndicalist leaders of the great 1914 Rand strike. Jones claimed that during his ten years as manager in South Africa Reuters was never once beaten on an important story.

By the immediate pre-war years Jones was looking to his future. He had received tempting job offers in South Africa, but he had remained loyal because he was proud to serve Reuters. Pride in his work was now leading him, however, to aspire to succeed Baron Herbert as head of the whole organization. After the victory over SAAPA, Jones revealed his hopes to Dickinson, who promised to listen for hints of Baron Herbert's intentions about retirement. In 1912, while on a visit to London, Jones himself spoke out boldly to Baron Herbert. The managing director was apparently well disposed towards the idea of eventually handing over to Jones; but he did not commit himself about timing.

III

Baron Herbert's suicide came at a bad moment for Jones. The dead man had done nothing to prepare the ground for a successor. The four Reuter directors, who had the power of choice, knew Jones only by name. The candidate they knew best was Bradshaw, the veteran company secretary. Jones did not dare to challenge Bradshaw outright. Instead, on 20 April 1915—only two days after Baron Herbert's suicide—he sent Bradshaw a carefully worded cable, and also a letter: 'failing yourself I should wish to press my own claims strongly upon directors in view my admitted services and assurances Baron gave when last in London.' Next day Jones wrote directly to Napier, the chairman. Jones asked, although he was 'totally unknown' to the directors, for his letter to be read to the board and for his claims to be considered. He was prepared, he told Napier, to sail home at short notice.

On the same day Jones confessed confidentially to Dickinson that he was prepared to serve as deputy to Bradshaw, with the right of succession. Jones now sent Napier copies of letters of commendation he had received from Baron Herbert. These included a copy of a 1908 letter to Rudyard Kipling in which Baron Herbert wrote that Jones combined 'to an eminent degree the almost mutually exclusive capacities of journalist and businessman'. As further evidence of his suitability Jones told Napier that he had been 'repeatedly' entertained and consulted by successive governors-general and also by Botha and Smuts.

All this was to no avail in the short term. The board appointed Bradshaw as general manager, although not as managing director. Given the bad state of the company's affairs, the directors announced their intention of taking a more active part than in Baron Herbert's day. His commendation of Jones had counted for little.

Bradshaw quickly proved unable to cope. He was a natural lieutenant, not a leader. The board was soon thinking again, and Jones's hopes revived. Lord Gladstone, who had returned in the previous year from South Africa, had already been prompted by Dickinson to write to Napier on behalf of Jones. Although his intervention had come too late to prevent the appointment of Bradshaw, Gladstone's support was to be important. Napier and Gladstone were old political friends, members of a network of leading Liberal families connected by marriage and friendship—Napiers, Gladstones, Asquiths, Tennants. This network was to play a key part in the restructuring of Reuters. Jones took care to commend himself, directly or indirectly, to these great people.

The agency's losses were continuing. The board was told on 28 July that these were estimated at £6,652 for the first half of 1915. The Newspaper Proprietors Association (NPA), representing the London papers, was also alleging a decline in the quality of the news service. At last Jones was recalled for consultations. Within days of landing on 31 July he was meeting Napier. The chairman was soon convinced that Jones, although young for the job, was the man to lead Reuters.

Napier was not all-powerful, however. An outside candidate might be preferred by the other directors. The only other internal candidate was Samuel Carey Clements (1866–1947), the assistant manager. He had been close to the centre of affairs for many years, having joined Reuters in May 1884 upon the recommendation of Gawthrop, and became assistant secretary in 1890. Clements was competent, thorough, and ambitious. The attention he had given to devising his ingenious codes for Reuters reflected all three attributes. He was not modest. 'On two or three occasions I have succeeded in turning the fortunes of the Company when it reached periods of crisis,' he later told Jones (3 July 1925). 'That was true of the time I produced the Code.' Clements had certainly made his codes pay well for himself in paying well for Reuters: his commission totalled £40,000 by 1925. In the same letter to Jones Clements claimed that 'the principal sources of revenue of the Company' were all 'based on the outcome of my ideas'. 'What extravagant talk', scribbled Jones in the margin. Clements served as general manager and secretary until his retirement in 1931.

Like Clements, Jones was ambitious and self-promoting. But he possessed one quality which Clements lacked. This was not so much warmth as magnetism; Jones could win over people. He had won over Napier. And Napier now gave him a clear chance to reveal his quality to the board. Jones was asked to write a report about Reuter problems and prospects. He was good at written analysis and exposition. His six-page document, dated 20 September 1915, was a model of clarity and conciseness. It recommended, firstly, that the bank should be entirely separated from the news agency, and if possible sold off. He had found that the commercial and advertising departments were still showing a profit, but that the private-telegram and remittance services were losing heavily. Jones recommended their immediate closure, if the Reuter codes could not be used. The editorial department, 'in spite of the war, with its impoverishment of newspapers on the one hand, and our special expenses on the other', was still making money, although not enough to balance the losses on 'traffic'. The PA subscription of £8,000 per year, unchanged for over forty years, was far too low, and ought to be increased. The London newspapers were paying nearly three times as much; but, noticed Jones, they were grumbling and needed careful handling. Covenants with overseas agencies produced a fair return, while some subscriptions from Empire countries were lucrative. South Africa alone, he noted with tacit self-congratulation, contributed as much in annual profit as the PA paid in subscription. India was profitable, but Australia yielded only £2,500, even though it possessed four times as many newspapers as South Africa. Canada contributed nothing in press revenue, 'a truly astonishing state of affairs'. Further economies in staffing at head office were possible, Jones concluded, but the editorial department should be protected. 'It is here that the future of the Agency lies. Go where you will, at Home or abroad, the name of Reuter continually confronts you.'

Jones accompanied his submission of this report with a formal application for appointment as general manager. He listed his achievements in South Africa, but he made a virtue of not promising instant success. In his own support he named 'four of my friends, all public men', who would be willing to act as referees: Lord Gladstone; Sir Matthew Nathan, a former governor of Natal; Sir Starr Jameson, of 'raid' notoriety, but more recently prime minister of Cape Colony; and Sir Lionel Phillips, head of Wernher Beit and Company.

On 6 October 1915 Jones was offered and accepted the post of general manager, at an annual salary of £1,400 plus £400 representation allowance. Almost immediately the agency's fortunes began to improve. Economies, suggested by Clements even before Jones returned from South Africa, were beginning to bring benefits. Undoubtedly, however, Jones's very active presence in charge soon made an immediate psychological difference. By November 1915 operations had moved out of loss overall, and the year eventually showed a modest net profit of £3,942. No dividend was paid.

Jones wrote in his reminiscences that he entered office with four objectives: Firstly, to overhaul the internal running of Reuters; secondly, to rescue it from 'incipient insolvency'; thirdly, to reconstruct the limited company; and fourthly, to deliver Reuters 'into the permanent keeping of the newspapers of the United Kingdom'. Jones claimed that he found the first two objectives comparatively easy to attain. The staff were 'strong in the Reuter tradition', and eager for a lead. Economies were made, and new sources of revenue were discovered. But he found that the reconstruction of the company was a much more difficult challenge.

Jones hoped to ensure the survival of Reuters in the long term through its transfer into the control of the British press, London and provincial. But what about the short term? As a private limited company, with some 1,200 shareholders whose first thought was dividend, Jones believed that Reuters was wrongly structured, especially for operation in wartime. Such an imperial institution ought not to be exposed to the whims of a large body of shareholders.

The British Government shared Jones's concern. It was worried about the functioning of Reuters in the middle of a war in which news management had become important as never before. Ministers feared that a majority of shares in the company might fall into the wrong hands, perhaps foreign. Even before his appointment as general manager, Jones was outlining ways in which Government help might be used to prevent this. He wrote a memorandum, dated 14 September 1915, which defined 'the object to be achieved' as 'to prevent the control of the company from passing into undesirable hands'. Jones suggested two possible ways of doing this: either by appointing a managing director with full powers for the duration of the war, 'with a guarantee of dividends'; or by creating a new company, 'whose shares should be in safe hands: the shares to be non-transferable for a period long enough to secure the object above stated'. The first scheme, he noted, would not guarantee the safety of Reuters after the war, nor would it prevent unsuitable people from gaining control. Jones therefore strongly recommended the second proposal. As soon as he became general manager, he set out to find ways of implementing it.

Twice he was to be frustrated. His first suggestion was for the existing company to go into voluntary liquidation and for a new company to be formed. Reuters was to be lent a maximum of £100,000 by the Bank of England to buy out shareholders. The bank was also to provide a maximum of £50,000 as working capital for the new Reuters. The British Government was to guarantee these advances; repayment was to be made over an agreed period, some shares in the new company were to be held by Government nominees with powers of veto; and directors were 'to be appointed and the management to be effected by agreement with the Government'. Nothing came of this scheme because, according to Jones's reminiscences, Williams mishandled negotiations with potential investors. Further mishandling aborted a second scheme early in 1916.

A third initiative, started in the autumn of 1916, with Jones and Napier now taking the lead to the exclusion of Williams, was finally successful in reconstructing the company. Jones himself was now one of the largest shareholders, having invested all his South African savings and having borrowed to the limit. In September 1916 Godfrey Isaacs, managing director of the Marconi Wireless Telegraph Company, had begun to reveal an interest in Reuters. Isaacs was regarded in the City of London as a sharp character. He had been involved in the 'Marconi scandal' of 1912–13, when insider dealing nearly destroyed the political careers of Lloyd George, the chancellor of the exchequer, and of Rufus Isaacs, the attorney-general, brother of Godfrey. The official report on the Marconi affair largely exonerated the two Liberal ministers; but an unofficial report, drafted by Lord Robert Cecil, a Conservative, was less indulgent. It also spoke severely of evidence given by Godfrey Isaacs as 'not satisfactory'. By 1916 Cecil was serving as foreign under-secretary in the wartime coalition. One of his responsibilities was to promote good publicity for the British cause overseas.

Cecil was determined to prevent the untrustworthy Isaacs from gaining control of Reuters. Rather than allow this, the Government would have intervened openly. It was glad, however, to consider proposals from Jones and Napier which would make that unnecessary. Luckily for Jones, his contact in the Foreign Office was John Buchan, an influential imperial politician and writer, already famous as the author of *The Thirty-nine Steps*. Buchan and Jones had first met at the beginning of the century in South Africa. Jones supplied arguments for a memorandum which Buchan sent to the foreign secretary, Sir Edward Grey. This 'provisional plan' still envisaged a continuation of the existing company; but Jones and Napier gradually realized (in the plain words of Jones's reminiscences) 'that the only way to make certain of Reuters' safety, and of our own personal security in Reuters, was to get rid of the shareholders altogether'.

How such a numerous ownership could become an embarrassment was now alarmingly apparent. The Reuter directors might well feel bound to put to their shareholders some tempting bid from Isaacs. He was ready to offer £10 per share. Jones and Napier therefore moved in quickly with a higher bid of £11 per share. Isaacs was finally given the hint that any still higher offer from him would be blocked by the Government, using its powers under the Defence of the Realm Act. Jones and Napier set out to raise the necessary £550,000. Napier was a friend and fellow countryman of the chairman of the Union Bank of Scotland, Lord Glenconner, who was the brother-in-law of Asquith. On 3 October Napier wrote to ask Asquith for an interview. Old friendship and perception of the national interest pointed in the same direction. The outcome was that the Union Bank offered the required money on the security of Reuters as a going concern. So much became public knowledge, because it had to be put to the shareholders. For them, the prospect of a windfall was irresistible. It was gratefully accepted at an extraordinary general meeting on 30 November 1916. The shareholders were not told that the British Government had guaranteed repayment of the loan within three years.

It was also not revealed that Jones and Napier were set to emerge as equal sole owners of the new Reuters. This might well have provoked jealous resistance. 'It was essential', wrote Jones in his reminiscences, 'that I keep myself out of the picture.' So the formal purchase of the old company was made in the names of Napier and of three public figures above suspicion, who were willing to lend themselves as Foreign Office nominees. The three were Glenconner, Jameson, and Viscount Peel, a sometime war correspondent and a grandson of the great Conservative prime minister.

The new private company, Reuters (1916) Limited, started with an authorized capital of £200,000 and a share issue of 999 £1 shares. Napier and Jones divided 498 shares between themselves. The Foreign Office nominees held 500 until such time as the bank guarantee was no longer needed. One public-policy share remained. This allowed the Foreign Office secretly to nominate one director with powers to veto the appointment of any other director; to veto any share transfer; and to exercise a veto on questions of public policy. In a letter to Napier dated 8 December 1916, Cecil defined public policy in both specific and general terms:

> the Foreign Office should be able both to prevent the Company from taking any action which might be contrary to public policy (such as the dissemination of reports prejudicial to the national interest, the employment of undesirable correspondents or other employees, the undertaking

or continuation of undesirable contracts with other news agencies, or the admission of undesirable persons as shareholders or directors) and also to secure that the Company's operations and actions are in conformity with public policy or the national interest, and that information of national importance is properly collected and circulated.

Buchan became the first Foreign Office director. The powers of veto were never used, and were given up in 1919.

Jones did well financially out of these manœuvres. He had bought Reuter shares at £6 or less and sold them at £11. After Napier's death in 1919 he held 60 per cent of the new Reuter shares, leaving the Napier family with only a minority interest. In addition, he was paid £5,000 a year as managing director of the new company.

It was only appropriate, Jones argued, that his personal interest in Reuters and the national interest in Reuters should be made to coincide. In 1918 his solicitor, who also became the new company's solicitor, circulated a retrospective memorandum about Foreign Office relations with Reuters since 1915. Cecil then minuted, on a copy returned to Jones, that it was 'right to record' how this 'extremely successful transaction' had depended upon 'the loyal and patriotic cooperation of Reuters and particularly of Sir Roderick Jones'. 'I quite agree,' added A. J. Balfour, the foreign secretary.

Reuter's Bank had been renamed soon after Jones took over. It was now known as the British Commercial Bank, to separate it as far as possible from the news agency. But the reconstruction process had still left Napier and Jones as proprietors of the bank as well as of the agency. Jones was sure that the bank should be sold, although only at a fair price. How much was it worth? An auditor's report of 9 November 1916 had summed up its career as 'unfortunate'. No dividend had been paid after its first year. Profits of £35,721 for 1914 and of £12,100 for 1915 were not distributed. Some of the bank's difficulties could fairly be blamed upon the war: it had conducted considerable business inside Germany and Austria. But it had also advanced £50,630 against Mexican Government bonds of doubtful marketability.

The bank was clearly in difficulties, but it was not bound to fail. The auditors valued the surplus assets at over £450,000. But they reported that £50,000 more capital would be needed to put the business upon a sound basis. In the end, Jones was able to exploit an effect of the war. Clarence Hatry, a financier who later went to prison for fraud, wanted to control a bank. Yet in wartime it was not possible to start a new one. Here was an existing foundation, which had tempting unissued capital in the form of 50,000 £10 shares. In his reminiscences Jones told a tale flattering to himself of his long negotiations with Hatry during 1917. These concluded in October with the sale of the bank on good terms for Reuters. Hatry paid the substantial price of £477,500, partly in cash and partly in guaranteed paper. All but £50,000 of the loan from the Union Bank was now cleared off. Jones and Napier bought back the frozen foreign investments of the bank for a sum higher than Hatry believed them to be worth. After the war, claimed Jones, he was able to sell them at considerable profit.

So Jones, in removing an encumbrance from Reuters, had made good money for Reuters. And since he and Napier were now the only shareholders, this meant that he had also made good money for himself.

IV

Jones conducted these bank negotiations while heavily engaged upon war work.

In both world wars he believed that patriotism required close contact between Reuters and the British Government. The question was: How close could such contact be without undermining the independence of the agency? Such independence was essential for the good worldwide reputation of Reuters in peacetime. Even in wartime, Jones argued in public and in private, the national interest would be best served by maintaining the independent reputation of Reuter news. In September 1918 he told the *Reuter Service Bulletin*: 'Our relations with our own and with other Governments have been intimate and friendly but never subservient. Such as they have been they remain.'

In reality, had the relationship ever been so clear and so clean? Reuters always wanted to follow the patriotic course. Yet it wanted also to claim that its news reporting was objective. Jones contrived to reconcile in his own mind these two apparently conflicting requirements. He had given his definition of objectivity in an interview for the *Observer* on 24 October 1915 at the time of his appointment as general manager: 'We should preserve a cold and judicial impartiality.' This sounded clear enough. But Jones then added what for him—as for his colleagues in the higher management of Reuters—was a natural gloss. 'At the same time, as a British agency, when we are dealing with international affairs we naturally see them through British eyes.' Objectivity, therefore, did not exclude writing from the British point of view: it only excluded taking sides *within* the British point of view. And since almost all shades of

British opinion supported involvement in the two world wars, Reuters was left free—indeed, was expected—to support the war effort. Thus were 'patriotism' and 'objectivity' reconciled.

A wartime Agence-Reuter service had been started at the end of 1914 by arrangement with the Foreign Office. This service was for the circulation of news and comment to which the British Government wished to give publicity. Agence-Reuter was kept separate from the normal Reuter news services, but it was entirely produced at Old Jewry. Its output went to Allied and neutral countries in Europe and the Middle and Far East, and to every part of the British Empire. By November 1917 about a million words per month were being circulated under the Agence-Reuter credit. The cost to the British Government in that year was £119,835. Yet Reuters made a profit of only £8,231 on the service, without allowing for overheads—a patriotically small return.

Jones described the Agence-Reuter service in a memorandum for the Department of Information, dated 10 November 1917. The department had been formed early in the year, with Buchan at its head. Jones was given charge of its cable and wireless propaganda, working part time and unpaid. This enabled him to supervise the content of the Agence-Reuter service when acting as a departmental official, while at the same time overseeing its distribution when acting as managing director of Reuters:

> Its object is to secure that a certain class of news, of propaganda value, is cabled at greater length than would be possible in the normal Reuter service. . . . The principle observed in shaping this service is a simple one. While bearing in mind that the proper presentation of the Allies' point of view is the main object of the service, the fact is not forgotten that this object can best be attained by a candid and exact description of events as they occur. A military operation, for instance, in which the Allies have not been successful, is not ignored, but is set out soberly in its proper perspective. Nor are Allied successes made the subject of paeans of enthusiasm. They are recorded in measured language . . . Many years' experience in the handling of news has shewn that these methods provide the best means of creating that intangible atmosphere of confidence which is indispensable if the service is to be trusted.

Reuters was placing its reputation as well as its network at the service of the British Government. 'At Reuters', wrote one Department of Information (DOI) official revealingly on 11 July 1917, 'the work done is that of an independent news agency of an objective character, with propaganda secretly infused . . . it is essential that independence should be preserved.' He knew that so long as Reuters continued to be trusted, even avowedly official news or comment circulated through the Reuter network would be more likely to be believed. On 29 November 1917 the *Daily Telegraph* published a letter in favour of a negotiated peace from Lord Lansdowne, a former foreign secretary. The obvious question among neutrals was 'Are the British cracking?' The 'Weekly Agence Report' of 3 December explained that the Agence-Reuter service had 'made it abundantly clear to the Continent and South America that the country does not subscribe Lord Lansdowne's views'.

From early in the war Amsterdam, Copenhagen, and Berne became centres for collecting news out of Germany and for feeding propaganda in. The Foreign Office paid for the removal of Reuter news handling in Amsterdam from the control of Abraham Delamar, the Dutch manager, whose family had served Reuters for fifty years. Delamar had been continuing the pre-war practice of issuing Reuter, Havas, and Wolff material together, all under one umbrella Reuter credit. The primary concern of the British authorities was the heavy output of propaganda through Wolff, with which Reuters could not compete. Finally, complaints from *De Telegraaf* in June 1915 revealed that Delamar had been passing on the New York Stock Exchange prices to Wolff ahead of Reuters. A separate Reuter Amsterdam office was opened under W. J. Moloney. The original office under Delamar was renamed the Nederlandsch Telegraaf Agentschap, and left to publish Wolff news.

Jones claimed in his memorandum of 10 November 1917 that his cable and wireless section was clearly winning the propaganda war with Germany. He quoted an article by Dr Paul Roche in the Berlin *Vossische Zeitung* of 15 August 1917: 'We might march into Petrograd or Paris tomorrow . . . if Reuter, the day after, assured the honest neutral that it was of no importance, he would be believed. Reuter rules the market, not Wolff; London makes foreign opinion, not Berlin.' German material, complained Roche, was too wordy. Neutral papers understandably preferred fifty lines from Reuters to a long-winded German article.

Alongside the Agence-Reuter service Jones ran an Official Service for the Department of Information. The Foreign Office had started this service early in the war. By November 1917 it was publishing about 150,000 words per month. It was less effective than the Agence-Reuter service because it was more obviously dealing in propaganda. Over half of its material was delivered by cable, but the rest was transmitted by wireless—an indicator for the future.

The overlap between Jones's position at Reuters and his work for the Department of Information eventually provoked questioning from the Press Advisory Committee. Could he serve two masters? Jones did not doubt that he could and should, in the national interest. 'The major portion of the telegraphic propaganda is conducted through Reuters,' he wrote to Buchan on 21 January 1918. 'As long as I remain managing director I can control this side of the propaganda.' When the Ministry of Information (MOI) was formed early in 1918, with Lord Beaverbrook as minister, Jones became its full-time director of propaganda. He still refused a salary. His functions as managing director of Reuters were now put into commission, but he did not resign. In July 1918 this drew criticism from the Select Committee on National Expenditure as 'on principle open to objection', because the ministry was making large payments to Reuters. Jones's position was defended in the House of Commons by Stanley Baldwin, the financial secretary to the Treasury, and in a letter to *The Times* from Napier. Both men emphasized that Jones had nothing to do with payments to Reuters.

It was certainly the case that Clements, the Reuter manager and secretary, Dickinson, the chief editor, and Murray, the assistant secretary, together conducted negotiations in the summer of 1918 for a formal contract governing payments from the MOI to Reuters. Hitherto, there had been only a verbal agreement for the sake of secrecy. Yet Jones watched over every move from the Reuter side. He minuted to Napier on a copy of a letter from Clements to Beaverbrook on 17 June: 'Of course this is my letter. I simply got Clements to sign it.'

Jones refused to admit any possibility of conflict of interest between his official position and his position at Reuters. Under continuing pressure to make a choice, he was bound to choose Reuters, where his heart and future lay. In September 1918 he therefore resigned from the Ministry of Information, ostensibly on grounds of ill health. Beaverbrook thanked him warmly on 30 September for his services to the nation, which were 'not perhaps the kind of work which most readily attracts public attention'. Jones made sure, however, that they did attract attention after the war by publishing Beaverbrook's letter in the *Reuter Service Bulletin* for April 1919.

Without doubt Jones had been an effective conductor of British wartime propaganda. In the process, he had exploited the good name of Reuters; but at least he had conducted the Agence-Reuter service separately from the other Reuter services. He believed that he had kept the promise made when he became general manager—to reconcile patriotism with objectivity. But he had done so only within his own definition of terms.

Once again he found his reward, this time not in money. On 8 January 1918 Jones was gazetted one of the first knights of the new Order of the British Empire. He revelled in his fresh style. Henceforward he was 'Sir Roderick'.

V

The demands of war brought changes to Old Jewry. The pressure of editorial work was now always heavy and continuous; there were no longer any intervals without news coming in. The stress was aggravated because the flow of news, inwards or outwards, was often impeded by censorship, or by breaks or difficulties in communication.

The names of 115 men who had joined the Allied forces were listed in the *Reuter Service Bulletin* for September 1918. Eighteen men killed in action were eventually named on the Reuter war memorial. All who served were generously granted half pay, and they were promised jobs on return.

Women were recruited for editorial work for the first time; the experiment was apparently successful. But by the last year of the war serious complaints were being voiced about the heavy workload, shortage of staff, and the reduction in the real value of pay owing to inflation. Reuter wage rates for boy and girl messengers, for girl telephone operators, and for manifolders had all become uncompetitive. The manifolders also pointed out that they were working seven days a week because of lack of numbers. And the traffic superintendent, F. J. Griffiths, reported on 4 June 1918 that the only boys now offering as messengers were 'not of the best'. In September the messengers even threatened to strike unless they were granted a basic wage of 15s. per week. 'I am afraid we shall have to give in,' Griffiths lamented to Jones, '. . . now that the police have set so bad an example we must not be astonished at anything.'

Some senior staff were likewise inclined to complain about erosion of the real value of their salaries. In his 1917 end-of-year message Jones fairly reminded them that Reuters still paid income tax on salaries, despite the very great increase in tax rates. The same message also reminded staff that they and their families were now insured by the company, free of charge, against death or injury caused by air raids. Raids sometimes interrupted work at Old Jewry, although never for long. As a precaution against being bombed out, plans were made in September 1917 to continue editorial work from the basement of the British Commercial Bank in Coleman Street: 'it is well to complete all preparations in order that the work of the Agency should not be interrupted for want of foresight on our part, and in order not to give cause for rejoicing to our enemies, who have a particular dislike of Reuter and all it stands for.'

War News

1914–1918

I

THE outbreak of the First World War was not foreseen by Reuters, even though it had been busy reporting the tensions of the immediate pre-war years. Instructions in French to European agencies, issued from Old Jewry on 1 January 1914, were still emphasizing that the British public was little interested in the internal affairs of European States, or even in their attitudes towards international relations. The European agencies were told to send no more than brief summaries of the proceedings of foreign parliaments, unless the debates directly affected British interests.

These same instructions had stressed, however, that the British public expected full and fast reporting of assassinations of leading figures. Archduke Franz Ferdinand, heir to the Austro-Hungarian throne, was assassinated at Sarajevo on 28 June. The first Havas message communicated to Old Jewry by telephone from the Paris office of Reuters reported tersely: 'Sarajevo Ferdinand Deste assassiné.' That was all. The sub-editor who took down the message was awaiting the result of the Paris Grand Prix horse-race. He took this to be it, and prepared story on the lines of: 'The result of the Grand Prix at Paris this afternoon was 1. Sarajevo. 2. Ferdinand. 3. Assassiné.' Fortunately, before this ludicrously mistaken story was circulated a more senior editor intervened and realized that in fact the report told of the assassination of the archduke, whose full territorial title in French was 'd'Autriche-Este'. Within a month Europe was slipping into general war.

The British found themselves becoming enmeshed in the crisis despite their lack of interest in European affairs. The announcement of the British entry into the war caused unexpected difficulties for Reuters. During the last hours of peace on 4 August 1914 the British Admiralty was intercepting wireless messages to German shipping warning that war with Britain was imminent. So it was. But the Admiralty wrongly interpreted these signals as meaning that the Germans had anticipated the expiry of the British ultimatum by themselves declaring war. The British Foreign Office therefore issued a statement, which Reuters published in two versions:

August 4th 1914 (11.16 p.m.).

Reuter's Agency learns that a state of war exists between Great Britain and Germany.—Reuter.

August 4th (11.45 p.m.).

Reuter's Agency learns that Germany declared war at 7 o'clock to-night.—Reuter.

The Foreign Office soon found that it had blundered. The British ambassador in Berlin telegraphed to say that the German chancellor had told him by telephone that Germany would not be replying to the British ultimatum, timed to expire at 11 p.m. There was to be no declaration of war from the German side. Britain was being left to declare war on Germany.

Soon after midnight Reuters corrected itself, again in two stages and at first still giving 7 o'clock as the starting-time for hostilities:

August 5th (12.13 a.m.).

Reuter's Agency is informed that it is now stated officially at the Foreign Office that it was Great Britain who declared war against Germany at 7 o'clock yesterday evening.

The original statement was issued by the Admiralty, and it was to the effect that Germany had declared war.—Reuter.

August 5th, 1914 (12.24 a.m.).

Reuter's Agency is informed that the following statement was issued from the Foreign Office at 12.15 a.m.:—

'Owing to the summary rejection by the German Government of the request made by His Majesty's Government for assurances that the neutrality of Belgium would be respected, His Majesty's Ambassador in Berlin has received his passports, and His Majesty's Government has declared to the German Government that a state of war exists between Great Britain and Germany as from 11 p.m. on August 4th.

— Reuter.

Reuters was subsequently attacked by the *Daily Mail* for putting out false news. In reply the agency was persuaded not to expose the Admiralty and the Foreign Office to embarrassment in wartime.

Newspaper editors were simply sent a printed explanation from Bradshaw, not for publication. This spelt out in detail why Reuters was not to be blamed for misleading the public about one of the most important moves in modern diplomatic history. 'The "mistake"', wrote Bradshaw fairly, 'was an official mistake and not that of Reuter's Agency.'

II

An anonymous typescript account of 'Reuters and the War', written in March 1919, recollected that the speech of Sir Edward Grey, the foreign secretary, on 4 August 1914 explained the reasons for the British declaration of war. This had been cabled in full to the Empire, where it had 'kindled at once a glowing fire of indignation against the aggressor'. Throughout the war Germany was to be regarded by Reuters as an aggressor.

Did such an attitude constitute unsuitable bias? The management of Reuters did not believe so. The revealing interview, reconciling 'patriotism' with objectivity, given by Jones on his appointment as general manager in 1915 has already been noticed. Objectivity with regard to British policy was appropriate, Jones argued, only when British opinion was divided, not when it was nearly unanimous. And especially not during such a tremendous war. 'Discussion and controversy which might be tolerated in peacetime', exclaimed Jones on 4 March 1918 in a private letter to General H. T. Lukin of the South African Brigade, 'are not to be suffered in war, certainly not in a war like this one.' Dickinson, in a letter of 26 June 1917 to A. H. Kingston, the Reuter manager in India, admitted frankly that 'the man who at the present time and in existing circumstances can give a plain and impartial record of the world's events must possess exceptional qualities . . . Here in London the presentation of events is almost necessarily one-sided.'

This did not mean that Reuters regularly expressed its own opinions in its telegrams; but it did decide what news to circulate, and it did select purposefully among the opinions of others. Marriott disingenuously explained this away in his unpublished history of Reuters, written in 1919: 'If to the transmission of facts was sometimes added the transmission of opinions they were not Reuters opinions; they were the opinions of the accepted leaders of thought in this and Allied countries, as stated on public platforms, or the opinions of writers in the public press of every political shade.'

One early wartime report showed Reuters giving acceptability to an anti-German story without quite going so far as to confirm its truth:

BRITISH RED CROSS NURSES KILLED BY GERMANS. HOSPITALS FIRED UPON.

Paris. Oct 14.

The latest example of the contempt of the Germans for the laws of war is contained in intelligence from Braisne (Aisne) which states that the Germans systematically shelled a Red-Cross hospital, killing two British nurses.

In the last year of the war the Reuter report on 21 April of the funeral of Baron von Richthofen—the German air ace at last shot down—did not allow British chivalry simply to speak for itself:

Baron von Richthofen's funeral this afternoon was a very impressive spectacle. The fallen airman was buried in a pretty little cemetery not far from the spot where he was shot down. A contingent of the Royal Air Force attended. We may not feel that it is our national role to try and impose Kultur upon the rest of the world, but we certainly do continue to practice chivalry towards our enemies.

Marriott noticed with satisfaction that wartime news from Reuters had both rallied opinion throughout the Empire and greatly influenced the attitudes of neutral countries. The Germans themselves admitted this. The *Berliner Tageblatt* explained the same point in grander language: 'Mightier and more dangerous than the Fleet and Army is Reuter.' The German humorous magazine, *Kladderadatsch*, devoted its whole issue of 31 March 1917 to Reuters, entitled the 'Reuter (Lies) Number'. The front and back pages each carried full-page cartoons. The front one (see Plate 22) showed a man in hunting-gear striding along the top of telegraph wires. He exhibited the protruding teeth which every good German knew to be the peculiar mark of the Englishman, and from his mouth issued forked tongues which turned into telegraph wires. From a huge cornucopia he was scattering a shower of unpleasant creatures, representing Reuter news. A duck (German *Ente* also means 'a false rumour') followed the striding figure, while a smug-looking Jew lurked below. The caption beneath—*Es ist fabelhaft, wie schnell der Kerl vorwärts schreitet trotz seiner kurzen Beine* ('It is amazing how quickly the fellow strides on despite his short legs')—referred to the German saying 'Lies have short legs.' The cartoon on the back page showed a globe grasped by an imp-like figure. From his large claws sprang lines of cable encircling the world. Underneath came the rhyming legend *Die Lüge ist der Welt*

Gesetz—dies lehrt das Reuter-Kabelnetz ('The lie is the law of the world—
so teaches the Reuter cable network').

III

On 29 July 1914, with fighting already breaking out in the Balkans,
Bradshaw, the Reuter secretary, sent a circular to all the London newspapers. It announced that Reuters was 'making arrangements to cover fully
in our Special Service all developments connected with the War'. The
charge for war news was set at a uniform rate of 1*d*. per word used.

Joint Reuter/PA correspondents were eventually sent to all the battle
fronts in which British or imperial forces were engaged. Lester Lawrence,
the Reuter correspondent in Berlin, had got out of Germany on the
British ambassador's train to Holland. He was to become the most mobile
Reuter correspondent in the early days of the conflict: first in Flanders
during 1914; then with the fleet off the Dardanelles in February and
March 1915; then at Gallipoli until the evacuation at the end of the year;
then in Egypt. Always eager for action, he pressed to be posted back to
Europe, where from 1916 he served as chief Reuter correspondent with
the French army on the western front.

Lawrence was often in danger. Dickinson wrote to him admiringly on
27 April 1918 that he was 'right in deciding to remain in reach of the bat-
tlefield', even though rival correspondents might occasionally pick up
some fresh news by staying at French headquarters. A good example of
Lawrence's style, which contrived to be reasoned yet optimistic, was a
dispatch of 26 March 1918 about the new French line on the Oise:

> I spent this afternoon on the new French front on the Oise among the
> troops who with such admirable courage and method are retarding the
> German advance down the river valley, making the enemy pay dearly for
> every fresh yard of ground and keeping him in play until the moment
> comes for the counter-offensive.
>   The belief of the men that this is inevitably the last great effort of the
> Boche is sustained by the recklessness with which the enemy hurls his bat-
> talions to certain destruction.

In this way the opening sentences set the tone of the whole dispatch,
which explained away any loss of ground in confident terms and demonstrated Lawrence's involvement. In more recent times no Reuter correspondent would have dreamt of using such an emotive word as 'Boche'.
Lawrence's last paragraph wound up neatly, in the same optimistic spirit
as the first:

I have met no one who has seen a German tank, although it is said that small ones may have been employed. The gas the enemy used was neither particularly new nor particularly deadly. He is staking all upon his numbers, and these are being wasted at a rate that cannot be maintained for many days more.

The first war correspondents with the British troops in Flanders were based at headquarters and were allowed to make only occasional forays to the front line. Representing Reuters in this group was Douglas Williams, a son of the former chief editor. In May 1915, after persistent pressure from the news agencies and newspapers, five correspondents were assigned to the British front in France. They included Herbert Russell for Reuters and the PA. Russell had previously covered the Gallipoli landings. His daily reports from the British front in France soon made him the best-known of all Reuter war correspondents (see Plate 21).

The newspapers had begun to credit the correspondents by name; and the provincial dailies, lacking men of their own at the front, used Reuters heavily. Russell later described himself and his fellows as being 'independent eye-witnesses on behalf of the nation'. They were not part of the army and they paid for their accommodation, food, and transport. When they were invited to accept honorary military rank, they refused lest this might seem to compromise their independence. They simply wore officers' uniform, without badges except for a distinguishing green brassard.

Reuter war correspondents, especially in France, had to see quickly and to write often. They were expected to file separate reports each day for both the morning and evening papers, and also for the Sundays, which were without separate representation. These were heavy demands, quite apart from the danger of death, injury, or illness. Russell's reward came after the war when he was knighted.

Russell reported the first day of the battle of the Somme for Reuters: 1 July 1916. On this single day some 60,000 men from Britain's fine new volunteer army were killed or wounded, many of them in the first morning hour. In retrospect the five-month battle was to be recognized as a huge failure, even as a turning-point in the history of the British Empire. Russell's first telegrams did not have the benefit of such hindsight. Initially he does not seem to have known the truth about the number of first-day casualties. He therefore started by reporting optimistically:

The British Offensive
From Reuter's Special Correspondent

British Headquarters, France
July 1. 9.30 a.m.

At about half past seven this morning a vigorous attack was launched by
the British Army. The front extends over about 20 miles North of the
Somme. The assault was preceded by a terrific bombardment lasting about
an hour and a half.

It is too early as yet to give anything but the barest particulars as the
fighting is developing in intensity but British troops have already occupied
the German front line. Many prisoners have already fallen into our hands
and as far as can be ascertained our casualties have not been heavy.

This first report was sent out to the newspapers from Old Jewry at 12.22
p.m. Another Reuter telegram, timed at 1.15 p.m., talked about 'good
progress into enemy territory'. British troops were said to have fought
'most gallantly', and to have taken many prisoners. 'So far the day is
going well for Great Britain and France.'

At 8.50 a.m. on 2 July came a summary of the first day, with more
emphasis now upon the severity of the fighting. 'The progress of the battle has been marked by steadily increasing intensity throughout the day.'
Here was the first hint of heavy casualties. A telegram at noon on the
second day was noteworthy for what it did not say. The hoped-for great
breakthrough had not taken place. Readers were left to work this out for
themselves, but the telegram gave the hint in its first sentence: 'The situation on the British front appears not to have changed since yesterday
evening. I hear that a strong counter-attack on Montauban during the
night was repulsed and heavy loss inflicted on the enemy. The troops are
in excellent spirits.' So the Germans were still well enough placed to
launch a counter-attack. And what was the implication of being told
about the spirit of the troops? If things had gone well such a statement
would have been superfluous. Yet there was nothing here to activate the
censors.

IV

Throughout the First World War Reuters complained frequently to the
Press Bureau about inefficiencies and inequalities of the censorship system. At the start of the war the censorship had been ham-fisted and damaging. Cable lines to Europe and the Empire were cut at a moment's
notice, or were interrupted. This impeded the collection of news by
Reuters, just when it was most in demand. At the end of August 1914
Reuters lost a major beat on the battle of Tannenberg because of the cen-

sorship. The Russians, who had advanced recklessly into East Prussia, were routed by the Germans. Deliberately or otherwise, the vital telegram to Reuters from the Russian agency was mislaid in the censorship bureaucracy. Soon afterwards Reuters suffered again when the news of the fall of Maubeuge was withheld. The chief of the Press Bureau admitted that the telegram to Reuters had been kept back by a censor 'because if Reuter published the news, it would be believed, and the public is already discouraged enough'. He promised that such a perverse compliment would not be paid again.

Reuters remained liable to be blamed for deficiencies in news coverage which were in fact the result of censorship. When German communiqués began to have some of their content silently removed before being passed for publication, Reuters circularized the London newspaper editors on 7 October 1915 to explain that it was not responsible for the mutilation, as the Germans were claiming. In the summer of 1915 the South African newspapers had become so dissatisfied with the Reuter news service that one of them, the *Rand Daily Mail*, even threatened to give up taking Reuters. Rival agencies were said to be sending a 'brighter' service. The Reuter board cabled an explanation to Jones, the general manager in Cape Town, for communication to the South African papers:

> think your papers cannot appreciate situation London. We can only cable what available. Veil overhangs all war centres. We send everything interesting that penetrates and cable systematically every graphic descriptive any value. News Dardanelles most intermittent always belated. London newspapers always publish what you getting thereanent nothing else. We must maintain general sequence events which naturally come scrappily sometimes dull. Opposition would promptly seize anything omitted. We reject what believe untrue including various bright items. Communiques form sole source daily official information. Always leading feature every paper closely studied elaborated brightened by newspapers themselves.

Although Lawrence was with the warships which bombarded the Turkish forts in the Dardanelles, the first Reuter reports of the Gallipoli landings on 25 April were datelined Malta, and were based only upon interviews with the wounded. Lawrence was eventually allowed to file from Gallipoli, but other correspondents had done so sooner—hence the South African complaints.

The Turkish Empire began to disintegrate during the last two years of the war. Fergus Ferguson followed General Allenby's advance through Palestine. In the words of the *Reuter Service Bulletin* for January 1918, newspaper readers wearied by news of static trench warfare were exhilarated by Ferguson's accounts of 'long night marches, wide turning movements, assaults in front and flank, and above all brilliant cavalry charges, knee to knee, sabres flashing'.

The close relationship between Reuters and the Indian authorities encouraged Buck, the correspondent with the Government of India, to organize a service of stories about loyal Indian support for the war effort. This propaganda service using the Reuter name started at the end of 1914, and was paid for by the Indian Government. 'Buck will from time to time cook up suitable telegrams for transmission, through Reuter, to all parts of the British Empire.' So explained one Indian Government official. Buck did not hesitate to insert comments. For example, on 10 November 1914 he sent the following to London for publication:

> War has united Hindus and Muhammadans in one great body determined to lay down their lives for Empire and to sacrifice everything for ultimate victory of England . . . The small section of seditionists about whose activities much was heard prior to the war has receded into the background. Meanwhile Moslem messages of disgust at manner in which Germany has duped and misled Turkey into disastrous war.

In 1917 a supplementary Imperial Service was launched from Old Jewry, subsidized by the British Government through the Department of Information. An editorial order of 19 March explained that the intention was to stimulate the interest of different parts of the Empire in each other, and 'in the continued vigorous prosecution of the war'. At intervals the chief editor received summaries of telegrams circulated:

INTER-EMPIRE ITEMS

SYDNEY SCOTSMEN URGE FORMATION OF KILTED BRIGADE
(Sent to Canada)
23/6/18

LLOYD GEORGE, SPEAKING AT WELSH BAPTIST TABERNACLE, SAYS THE WORLD MUST BE MADE FIT FOR EVERYBODY—THERE MUST BE NO ROOM FOR MILITARISM, MAMMONISM OR ANARCHY.
(Sent to America, Canada, India, Far East, South Africa and Australasia)
23/6/18

A Reuter ticker was installed for the British prime minister, Lloyd George, at 10 Downing Street in September 1917. Previously he had found himself waiting for the newspapers to tell him what Reuters was reporting from overseas.

V

News about the attitudes and actions of the United States assumed increasing importance as the war progressed. The Allies needed American munitions, and preferably American entry into the war. The Reuter manager in New York, Lawson, worked closely with E. M. Hood of AP. Hood, who had good contacts with Woodrow Wilson's administration, supplied Reuters with early news of official American policy initiatives. Reuters was 'miles in front', Jones reminded J. L. Garvin of the *Observer* on 19 February 1917, when the United States broke off diplomatic relations with Germany. Wilson's speech of 2 April 1917, asking Congress to declare war, was cabled as it was being delivered via a prearranged 'clear wire' to London. An opening message from Reuters was accepted worldwide as sufficient evidence that America would join the Allies: 'President Wilson tonight asked Congress to declare that a state of war existed between Germany and the United States.' Wilson's famous '14 Points' speech to Congress in January 1918, laying down his programme for future world peace, was initially reported by Reuters as containing only thirteen points. Point one, calling for 'open covenants openly arrived at', was reported rather laboriously: 'Open Covenants of Peace only arrived at, after which there shall be no private international understandings of any kind, but diplomacy shall proceed always frankly and in the public view.'

From America as from other countries, Reuters was usually efficient in handling official matter. It was also good at reporting speeches by leading figures, and at covering anticipated big events. United States presidential elections fell into this last category. Unfortunately, in 1916 Reuters published the result too soon, and got it wrong. A flash at midnight on 8 November announced:

MR HUGHES ELECTED.

This was confirmed at 12.15 a.m.:

MR HUGHES HAS BEEN ELECTED.

This sounded conclusive. But at 6.20 a.m. on 10 November came:

WILSON REELECTED.

An explanatory telegram followed (time not given):

MR WILSON HAS CARRIED CALIFORNIA.

Then 'later' came the final confirmation:

MR WILSON HAS BEEN REELECTED FOR THE PRESIDENCY.

H. F. Prevost-Battersby, a trained soldier as well as a poet, playwright, and author, was appointed Reuter correspondent with the American troops in France. He had previously served as a *Morning Post* correspondent and had been wounded. In the last days of the war he was severely gassed. Battersby's telegrams were cabled day by day to the United States, where they were available to the AP. The Americans also assigned their own correspondents to France. Because of heavy official traffic and inadequate cable maintenance, press messages were now taking up to forty-eight hours to cross the Atlantic.

Battersby's full description of the capture by the Americans of the St Mihiel salient on 12 September 1918 was clear and good on topography, although characteristically 'literary':

> This is open rolling grassland country very much resembling Salisbury Plain, broken here by small and there by larger woods, chiefly of fir and pine, the scrub being framed on either side by the two nearly parallel scarps of hills deep into which both the Meuse and the Moselle have cut their way. Hence one has this open green plain before one, stained in places with heliotrope by the autumn crocus, with the purple ridges of hills on either hand.
>
> Simpler fighting ground it would be difficult to find, and the Americans found it to present but few difficulties after the four hours of bombardment. The Germans were undoubtedly getting their guns away, and the support thus offered to their sacrificed infantry was weak in the extreme, while of the counter-battery work there seemed to be none at all. Though the day was most unpropitious for aircraft, our planes did splendid work, swooping down on the retiring infantry and driving them clear off the roads besides pushing every German plane out of the sky, and bringing down several balloons in flames.

VI

While the Americans were entering the war, the Russians were withdrawing from it. The Tsarist Empire collapsed and two revolutions in 1917 were followed by a civil war.

The Reuter correspondent at Petrograd since 1904 was Guy Beringer. His greatest pre-war coup had been to obtain the text of the 1907 Anglo-Russian agreement several hours before it was officially released. During 1917–18 Beringer was not put off by personal danger or by food shortages. He was eventually arrested by the Bolsheviks, and spent six months under threat of execution in an overcrowded prison.

In covering the first revolution in March 1917 Beringer had enjoyed a virtual monopoly of cover, to the great advantage of Reuters:

> March 16, 10.14 a.m.
>
> Three days' silence from Russia has been broken by a despatch from Petrograd dated 13th instant describing a revolution which resulted in the Duma, aided by the Army, assuming the Government and the arrest of reactionary Ministers and ex-Ministers whom the people have long suspected of pro-German sympathies which are responsible for the lack of food and lack of enthusiasm in conducting the war. Popular discontent smouldering on the 10th, flamed up on the 11th, and became a conflagration on the 12th, when there was fighting in the streets in which soldiers fought soldiers and people. The fighting ended in the troops, including the Guards and the Navy, joining the Revolutionists.
>
> March 17, 3 p.m.
>
> (Petrograd).—The Tsar abdicated at midnight on Thursday on behalf of himself and the Tsarevitch in favour of the Grand Duke Michael. The latter abdicated on Friday afternoon and the Government is now vested in the Executive of the Duma and a National Cabinet.

The British Government opened a propaganda bureau in Petrograd, but Jones assured Beringer that Reuters would continue to be recognized as 'paramount'. In the summer of 1917 Clements was sent to Russia and China on a visit of inspection. He seems to have established good relations with the new Russian Government, but the position of Reuters again became uncertain after the Bolshevik take-over in November. The Bolsheviks now controlled Vestnik, the Petrograd news agency with which Reuters dealt. Jones told the Reuter board on 12 December 1917 that the relationship was delicate, 'but our policy was to maintain it, at least for the present, and avoid a rupture, in the national interest'. Vestnik gave Reuters a beat in London with the terms of the armistice agreed by the Bolsheviks and the Germans on 16 December 1917. Jones told Beringer on 21 January 1918:

> The official service from Petrograd has continued unimpaired, and it has been well supplemented by your own telegrams. On this side we were told more than once that your telegrams were thought to be reflecting overmuch the Bolshevik view, but our opinion is that this notion arose mainly out of a natural misconception in London as to what the actual situation in Petrograd was.

Jones congratulated Beringer on 'the adroitness with which, while avoiding anything calculated to affront the ruling party, you act as a commentative chorus upon events in Russia':

Nov. 8, 8.30 a.m.

(Petrograd).—Armed naval forces under Maximalist orders have seized the offices of the Russian Official News-agency, also the Central Telegraph Office, the State Bank and the Marie Palace where the Preliminary Parliament which was suspended had been sitting. No disorders are reported.

At this period, the Bolsheviks were usually referred to by Reuters as 'Maximalists', meaning supporters of the maximum socialist programme.

9.25 p.m.

Reuter has received telegrams from the official Petrograd Telegraph Agency, which is now in the hands of the Maximalists, stating that they hold the City and have arrested the Ministers. Lenin, who is the leader of the movement, has demanded an immediate armistice and peace.

Nov. 13, 9.34 p.m.

. . . Trotsky has issued a proclamation as follows:—
History will record the night of November 12th . . . The sailors, soldiers and workmen of Petrograd know how to impose, and will impose with arms, the will and power of democracy. The Bourgeoisie endeavoured to separate the army from the revolution, and Kerensky attempted to break it by violence and Cossackism; both efforts have failed.

Vestnik outlined its news needs in a service message to Old Jewry on 17 December:

Please greatly reduce reports speeches newspaper articles stop Substitute short news of more general character for long accounts speeches stop We particularly interested know how various classes receiving successive stages events and peace steps also facts about labour movement.

A Reuter editorial order in response, dated 19 December, warned that, although Vestnik had asked for the views of the Labour papers, 'we must not on any account be led into playing into the hands of the peace party'. Articles and speeches in favour of peace 'must be carefully eschewed'.

Early in 1918 internal chaos caused a breakdown in communications; and this resulted in Beringer's withdrawal to Finland. Soon, however, he returned to Russia to report from Moscow, now the capital, even though communications were still bad. Personally, Beringer was decidedly anti-Bolshevik, and he was at great risk. In a private letter to Jones on 22 June 1918, almost certainly read by a Bolshevik censor, he claimed that the Red Army was a 'rabble' and that 'the Bolshevik bubble' was on the point of bursting.

1. *top of page* Founder and son: Julius and Herbert, *c.*1870

2. *above* Charles Havas

3. *right* Bernhard Wolff

4. Pigeon messages: Aachen, 1850

5. Sigismund Engländer, revolutionary and reporter, 1845

6. The new hub of the world: The offices of the British and Irish Magnetic Telegraph Co., 1859

7. Meeting the mail-boat: Cape Race, Newfoundland, 1861

8. Henry Collins, the first Reuter 'proconsul', sent east in 1866

9. Storming of Magdala, Abyssinia: The first colonial war for Reuters, 1868

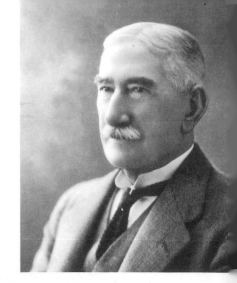

10. Siege of Paris, 1870: Balloon message from Havas to Reuters and the world

11. The telegraph pioneers: Julius
Reuter and James McLean (*top right*)
represent the news agencies, 1883

12. Reuter messengers, 1896

13. Pretoria office, 1900

14. The stars: Boer War correspondents Perceval Landon (*The Times*), H. A. Gwynne (Reuters), Rudyard Kipling, Julian Ralph (*Daily Mail*)

REUTER'S TELEGRAM COMPANY, Ltd.

Port Said Branch

TELEGRAMS: *(All Rights Reserved)*

London 19th Janry:
Bulletin noon: The Queen is suffering
from great physical prostration accompanied
by symptoms, that cause anxiety. The Prince
of Wales who intended proceeding to Sandringham
today has left for Osborne. ——

15. The end of an age: Port Said telegram, 1900

16. Reuter bulletin-seller, Port Said, 1938

17. Outpost of the Reuter empire: Kalgoorlie, Australia, c.1900

18. Meeting the tourists, 1905: Reuters in Invercargill, New Zealand

19. 'Reuter's Advertising Agency', 1910

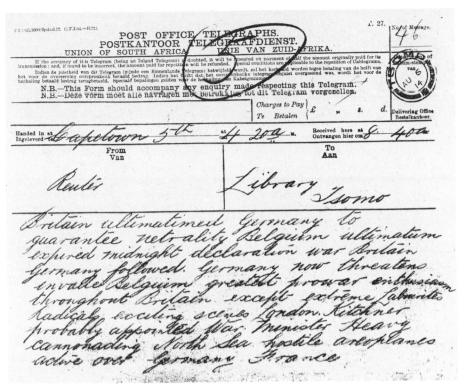

POST OFFICE TELEGRAPHS.
POSTKANTOOR TELEGRAAFDIENST.
UNION OF SOUTH AFRICA. UNIE VAN ZUID-AFRIKA.

If the accuracy of this Telegram (being an Inland Telegram) is doubted, it will be repeated on payment of half the amount originally paid for its transmission : and, if found to be incorrect, the amount paid for repetition will be refunded. Special conditions are applicable to the repetition of Cablegrams.

Indien de juistheid van dit Telegram (zijnde een Binnenlands Telegram) betwijfeld wordt, zal het herhaald worden tegen betaling van de helft van het voor de overseining oorspronkelijk betaald bedrag. Indien het blijkt dat het oorspronkelijke telegram onjuist overgeseind was, wordt het voor de herhaling betaald bedrag terugbetaald. Speciale bepalingen gelden voor de herhalingen van Kabelgrammen.

N.B.—This Form should accompany any enquiry made respecting this Telegram.
N.B.—Deze vorm moet alle navragen met betrekking tot dit Telegram vergezellen.

| | Charges to Pay | £ | s. | d. | Delivering Office |
| Te Betalen | | | | | Bestelkantoor. |

Handed in at Ingeleverd — Capetown 5th at 4 20a M.   Received here at Ontvangen hier om 8 40a

From / Van — Reuter

To / Aan — Library Isomo

Britain ultimatimed Germany to guarantee neutrality Belgium ultimatum expired midnight declaration war Britain Germany followed. Germany now threatens invade Belgium greatest prowar enthusiasm throughout Britain except extreme Labourites Radicals exciting scenes London. Kitchner probably appointed War Minister Heavy cannonading North Sea hostile aeroplanes active over Germany France

20. 'Hostile aeroplanes active': Reuters tells the Empire
of the outbreak of war, 1914

21 Herbert Russell presented to King George V: France, 1917

22. German wartime propaganda: 'Reuter Lies Number', 1917

23. Mark Napier, chairman 1910–19

24. John Buchan, board member 1916–17 and 1919–35

25. Servants of the Raj: William Moloney, Roderick Jones, and Edward Buck, 1924

26. Commercial services pioneer: Dorothy Nicholson with manager James Lelas and Karachi staff, *c.*1925

27. Delhi office, *c.*1920

28. Messenger girls, *c.*1920

29. The code-books in use: London private-telegram department, 1923

30. Frederic Dickinson, chief editor 1902–22

31. The new editor-in-chief: Bernard Rickatson-Hatt with assistants, 1932

Letters were taking as long as two months to reach Old Jewry, and Beringer realized that many of his telegrams were not getting through at all. He was reduced to sending batches of telegrams with his letters, for use by the newspapers in retrospective accounts of the civil war. The last of these telegrams mailed to London was dated 8 July 1918. Beringer was presumably arrested on that day or soon afterwards.

Several of his telegrams in June 1918 gave an indication of the fate of Nicholas II:

> [18 June] bolshevik official germans landed 3000 infantry cavalry artillery poti blacksea stop reported petrograd extsar murdered stop soviet circles state received no such news

> [22 June] murder extsar still officially undenied although report repeated various sources one version killed red guards railway train wherin taking unknown destination after czechslovaks began threaten ekaterinburg stop

VII

The beginning of the end of the war came in the Balkans, where the conflict had started. Werndel, the old Middle East hand, secured a three-hour beat from Salonika with news of the Bulgarian surrender on 29 September 1918. The surrender of the Germans on 11 November was preceded by several days of tantalizing uncertainty while negotiations continued. As at the outbreak of the war in 1914, Reuters was misled. On 7 November it circulated the following wrong report to the London evening papers: 'Reuter's agency is informed that, according to official American information, the armistice with Germany was signed at 2.30.' In reality an armistice was not to be concluded for another four days.

Reuters organized an immediate inquiry into this very visible and damaging error. It discovered that on the morning of 7 November someone in the French War Ministry had telephoned the American embassy in Paris to say that an armistice had been signed, and that hostilities would cease at 2 p.m. This story was then telegraphed to the American admiral at Brest, who released it to the press for transmission across the Atlantic. Simultaneously, the news was issued by the American naval authorities in London. The Reuter report was taken from this source. Fortunately, on this occasion—unlike 1914—Reuters had covered itself by giving a source. As had happened four years earlier, the report was 'killed' within a few minutes.

When on 11 November Reuters at last received the official announcement in London that all fighting was to stop at 11 a.m., it responded

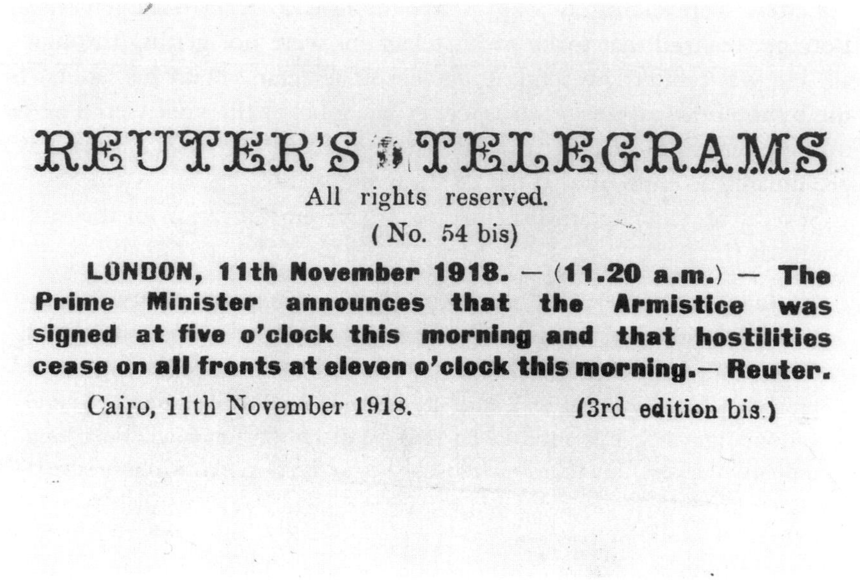

REUTER'S TELEGRAMS

(No. 54 bis)

LONDON, 11th November 1918. — (11.20 a.m.) — The Prime Minister announces that the Armistice was signed at five o'clock this morning and that hostilities cease on all fronts at eleven o'clock this morning.— Reuter.

Cairo, 11th November 1918.   (3rd edition bis.)

FIG. 10. Reuter reports the armistice, 11 November 1918

impressively. The good news from Old Jewry reached many parts of the British Empire well ahead of any Government communication.

For four years one topic had dominated the Reuter file. Even so, Reuters still aimed at comprehensive coverage, and much other news had continued to be reported, not least because non-war stories provided contrast. World commercial news remained important, sport was still covered, and to the end quite trivial social news was being noticed.

The volume of words handled by Old Jewry reached unprecedented levels during the war. The Agence-Reuter and other services for the British Government alone added ten million words to the file. Reuters had entered the war in serious difficulties, financial and otherwise. By the end of the war these had been overcome, and the reputation of Reuters as the news agency of the British Empire had been restored.

SEVEN

The Autocracy of Roderick Jones
1919–1934

I

SIR RODERICK JONES ran Reuters as an autocracy. This had been his style in South Africa, and it was even more his style as head of Reuters between the wars. At first Dickinson, his early mentor, was still present to influence Jones, who genuinely respected his judgement. Jones made him a director in 1918. But in 1922 Dickinson died suddenly. Napier, the chairman, had already died in 1919. Jones, now the majority shareholder with a 60 per cent holding, became chairman as well as managing director, the unquestioned boss of Reuters. Even after the reconstitution of the ownership in 1926, although the new board contained a majority of PA nominees, Jones was left with a free hand. Into the 1930s he continued as before, unchallenged, always smoothly courteous to his provincial newspaper colleagues, but keeping control of policy and management in his own hands.

Jones liked to present himself as successfully continuing in the dynamic spirit of Julius Reuter. He certainly tried to conduct Reuters as the news agency of the British Empire; and he also tried to maintain the ring combination of news agencies which Reuter had helped to form. But in both connections the policy of Reuters was no longer dynamic: it was defensive. Between the wars Reuters faced increasing difficulty in protecting its position throughout the world. In particular, it found the challenge of the thrusting American news agencies hard to meet.

The weakening position of Reuters in the world mirrored the weakening position of the British Empire itself. Jones was well aware that he was living in a period of imperial difficulty and prospective change. He wrote to his wife on 19 February 1924 from Government House, Madras, of the pomp and circumstance 'of a system which soon may pass away, or at least be modified, under the democratic influences of the time'. Yet Jones showed no desire to separate the fortunes of Reuters from those of the formal and informal British Empire.

How far, then, should Reuters be associated with the British Government in protecting or promoting British interests worldwide? In peacetime should there be any such association at all? Here was the question which had posed itself before 1914, and which had troubled Engländer and Dickinson surprisingly little. Jones was more careful. He repeatedly declared that Reuters was, and must remain, independent. 'We are not suppliants in any sense,' he told the Foreign Office on 2 April 1925. Nevertheless, Jones always emphasized that Reuters could choose to make contracts with the British Government so long as the terms of such contracts did not concede any control overall. In other words, Reuters was willing to work closely *with* the British Government, but was not willing to work meekly *for* the British Government. This distinction was sufficient, in Jones's view, to leave Reuters independent.

Jones regarded such an attitude as both justifiable and patriotic. It was also convenient, for throughout the period Reuters wanted Government money to help balance its books. The Government, for its part, was inclined to accept Jones's logic, since it realized that a Reuters proclaiming itself independent was much more likely to be useful than an obviously subsidized mouthpiece.

At the end of March 1919 the wartime Agence-Reuter service was shut down. Jones had argued strongly against closure, because of the need to compete with French- and American-angled news, especially in Europe, the Far East, and South America. Instead, an agreement was made with the Foreign Office for Reuters to circulate specific messages overseas upon instruction. The Foreign Office agreed to pay the cost of extra wordage. This contract, renewed in 1921, declared that Reuters would distribute only news 'consistent with their independence and their obligations to the newspapers'. This agreement, and a similar one with the India Office, remained in force throughout the interwar years.

The British Government did not depend solely upon Reuters for circulating favourable news and views. The Foreign Office decided in 1919 to continue with the British Official News Service started during the war. This now became known as the British Official Wireless. In the opinion of Jones this service constituted unfair and unnecessary competition for Reuters because overseas newspapers could use it without payment. Jones was the more irritated because he had himself built up the service during the war. There was always the danger that the Foreign Office would prefer to use the facilities of another British news agency, probably Extel.

One ground for Government doubts about Reuters was its closeness with Havas and other foreign agencies. The pre-war ring combination between Reuters, Havas, Wolff, and AP had been renewed in 1919—with the sphere of Wolff now confined to Germany. In quick succession, the news agencies of all the smaller States of Europe, old and new, became allied with Reuters and Havas. Rosta (later Tass), the news agency of Bolshevik Russia, also became associated with the alliance through a contract made with Reuters in 1924. The relationship remained uneasy, however. Reuters kept a correspondent in Riga, the capital of independent Latvia, but did not send one to Moscow because of the censorship. First news of the banishment of Trotsky in 1928 came via Riga.

The old misunderstanding persisted that involvement with Havas and other agencies meant that all news received by Reuters out of Europe was coloured at source. In reality, Reuters was not bound to use the output of the allied agencies; and it remained free to collect news from its own correspondents or stringers in any country. The fact remained, however, that in the immediate postwar years Havas held the central position in the supply of news to and from Europe, and this worried the Foreign Office. Germany was almost entirely dependent upon Havas for its foreign news. A plan to make Berlin a centre for circulating British news supplied by Reuters was discussed with the Foreign Office in 1922, but came to nothing.

II

Buchan was available during these years to make representations on behalf of Reuters in official circles. His involvement with Reuters during the war has already been noticed. In June 1917 he resigned as the Government-nominated director on the new Reuter board upon becoming head of the Department of Information, which had financial dealings with Reuters. Buchan returned as a Reuter director in 1919, and served as deputy chairman while Jones was away on a world tour in 1923–4. At a Reuter dinner before Jones left Buchan praised him as 'one of the whitest men God ever created'. Buchan was elected a Conservative Member of Parliament in 1927. He finally left the board upon becoming governor-general of Canada in 1935.

In September 1922 the sudden death of Dickinson, the chief editor, necessarily brought changes in the editorial department. Herbert Jeans, a Reuter veteran, was finally made chief editor. He had joined in 1898, eventually becoming the highly respected chief of the Reuter parliamentary staff at Westminster. Reuter news under Jeans remained heavily political and official. He died in post in 1931.

The successor whom Jones installed to modernize the editorial side was Bernard Rickatson-Hatt (1898–1966). On the recommendation of Buchan, Hatt had joined the editorial staff straight from the army in 1923. He had served in the Coldstream Guards during the war, and retained a military appearance at Reuters. He was always immaculately dressed, invariably wore a guards' tie and sported a monocle, and outdoors always wore a bowler hat and carried a rolled umbrella. There were oddities; Hatt's complexion was abnormally pink and white, 'no stranger to cosmetics', according to some observers; and he was suspected of wearing a corset. He often came to the office carrying a small poodle. All this suggested a need to put up a façade, conventional and idiosyncratic at the same time. Hatt's nerves had been shaken by his wartime experiences. He found relaxation in reading the Greek and Roman classics, and at his death left a collection of pornography said to be one of the best in the world.

Hatt served as personal assistant to Jones on his world tour of 1926, when despite Hatt's officer-class appearance he got on well with the Australians and Americans. At the end of the tour Jones left him in New York, and in 1930 made him chief correspondent there. Hatt was particularly interested in sports reporting, and one anecdote said that a fight at Madison Square Garden was once delayed to await his late arrival at the ringside. He learnt fast about American news methods, and Jones brought him back in 1931 to apply some of them in London. One early symptom of a less formal atmosphere was Hatt's use in conversation of first names rather than surnames.

Another influential figure between the wars was W. L. Murray (1877–1947). Murray had joined Reuters in 1899. He had served as a correspondent in Europe during the pre-war years, notably as the discreet Reuter royal-watcher who accompanied Edward VII on his annual trips to take the cure at Marienbad. At the outbreak of the First World War Murray became liaison officer for Reuters with the official Press Bureau. By 1923 he was company secretary, and in 1932 he was made European manager. He had a sharp mind for economy, but there is no evidence that he possessed vision. He retired in 1937.

H. B. Carter (1897–1964), a cousin of Dickinson's, started with Reuters in 1919 as private secretary to Jones. He came to combine this nerve-testing job with that of assistant company secretary under Murray.

Jones treated him as an elevated office boy. From 1932 he was himself secretary. He retired in 1959.

Jones justified his insistence upon the highest standards of performance within Reuters by emphasizing how the organization depended especially heavily upon its staff. 'We have no tangible machinery, no equipment,' he wrote in his 1938 new year message: 'just men and brains.' Reuters at that time employed over 1,000 people worldwide, about 370 of them in London. The London editorial department consisted of 12 senior staff and 120 others, the commercial department employed 4 seniors and 86 others.

Jones once described to a would-be recruit his selection policy for those who wanted to become overseas correspondents and who might later become managers. The qualities needed, he wrote, were a mixture of those expected by the Civil Service and those necessary for a business enterprise. Recruits must show themselves to be hard-working and healthy, good at languages, good with people, ready to travel, and ready to commit themselves wholeheartedly to Reuters. Remembering his own early progress, Jones liked to encourage young men. Older men were rarely brought into Reuters.

Jones was often accused of having a snobbish preference for public-school recruits (especially Old Etonians), with Oxbridge degrees and with private means. Yet snobbery may not have been the whole reason for the noticeable influx of public-school trainees during these years. They were thought most likely to possess that social polish which Jones and Hatt felt to be essential. Reuter correspondents and managers were expected to mix easily with top people in every country.

Women had been taken into the editorial department during the First World War, but few were recruited after the war. Muriel Penn, who joined in 1931, was the exception—a formidable personality who flourished upon her own terms. She was engaged as a sub-editor, and became at various periods a foreign correspondent, a fashion reporter, and a copytaster. Women staff at all levels were expected to retire upon marriage. Ellen Bayliss, who began as a messenger girl during the First World War, and became a parliamentary correspondent during the second, was the first woman to be allowed to stay on after her marriage in 1932. The terms of employment for Reuter male staff still required them to ask permission to marry.

Jones liked to think of the Reuter staff as a worldwide 'family' of which he was the head. In the 1920s the Joneses attended Reuter garden parties hosted by the Napier family at Puttenden Manor, a visible expression of a tacit feudal relationship. Jones also gave his support to a staff social club, to a literary and debating society, and to the Reuter cricket club. He was said always to partner the prettiest girls at Reuter dances. Yet junior staff who encountered him at work were usually terrified of him, fearful of instant dismissal. Only a few knew that if cases of sickness or misfortune came to his notice he could be constructively kind.

At a time when a single week's paid holiday was regarded as generous, Reuters allowed even juniors a fortnight. On the other hand, trade unions were not permitted to make demands about holidays or wages. In 1934 Jones did enter into what he called a 'gentleman's agreement' with the National Union of Journalists (NUJ) to pay at least the union minimum rates; but he refused to sign a formal agreement. He told the union secretary on 14 June that 'nobody at home or abroad could ever say that they had turned to me in vain.' For that reason, he 'was not prepared to allow any outside organisation, whether the NUJ or another, to come between me and my people'.

But holding out against the unions was becoming increasingly difficult by the late 1930s. In 1939 Reuters reluctantly joined with the other agencies in recognizing the National Society of Operative Printers and Assistants (NATSOPA). The Reuter board was told on 6 June that the extra cost in wages would be about £1,000. In September 1940 Reuters signed an agreement with the National Union of Press Telegraphists (NUPT). Job descriptions, wages, hours, overtime rates, and holiday entitlements were now all spelt out in agreements. The 'family' atmosphere was going out: labour relations were coming in.

III

Economy drives at intervals during the 1920s and 1930s produced redundancies, which conflicted with the 'family' image. Strict economy was necessary at all times because Reuters was never comfortable financially. Payment of income tax upon the salaries of management was finally abandoned in 1920. In 1921 there were actual salary cuts—10 per cent in the case of top salaries; proportionately less for lower salaries; the cuts were gradually restored in the mid-1920s. Revenue and profits were never sufficient to pay for all the development needed to meet growing competition (see Table 7.1).

Jones's speeches at annual general meetings between the wars voiced a recurring theme—that the subscriptions from the British newspapers,

TABLE 7.1 Revenue and profit figures between the two world wars (£)

	Total revenue all sources	Revenue from largest territories					Net profit after tax
		UK	Europe	India	Far East	N. America	
1918	266,300	49,400	31,600	35,200	16,200	800	4,600
1928	382,500	62,400	32,800	81,500	66,400	2,400	27,000
1938	517,800	145,000	42,400	126,300	73,200	1,700	117,100

London and provincial, were much too low in relation to the costs of the extensive services provided. London morning-newspaper subscriptions remained unchanged at £2,400 per annum throughout the 1920s and 1930s. Any attempt to increase these charges might have caused the London papers to desert Reuters for other agencies. The PA differential during the 1930s—the difference between what the provincial papers paid Reuters for world news (£36,000) and what Reuters paid them for British news (£22,000)—was only £14,000. As owners of Reuters, PA members could not be persuaded to subscribe more. They insisted upon being served at below cost price.

At the time of the negotiations for the purchase of Reuters by the British press in 1925, Price Waterhouse produced revenue and expense figures for the previous five years. The fortunes of the various departments within Reuters were compared. The news side had failed to improve its margins; the advertisement business was still profitable; but private-telegram and remittance traffic, once the financial mainstays, had fallen into decline. The contribution of the new commercial service was becoming important (see Table 7.2).

Reductions in charges by the cable companies meant that it was no longer worth while for private customers to code their telegrams through

TABLE 7.2 Comparison of departmental revenue and expense figures for 1919 and 1924 (£)

	1919	1924
News subscriptions at home and abroad		
Revenue	199,000	208,000
Expenses	131,000	134,000
Commercial and trade service		
Revenue	15,000	72,000
Expenses	8,000	55,000
Private-telegram and remittance traffic		
Revenue	35,000	35,000
Expenses	29,000	37,000
Advertisements		
Revenue	13,000	18,000
Expenses	8,000	10,000

Reuters. The service was stopped in 1926. The remittance service lingered on in parts of the Empire, the end not coming until the closure of the Bombay remittance office in 1954. The London advertisement department was shut down in 1942, and the Australian advertisement service was sold off in 1945.

IV

Old Jewry had been overcrowded for many years. At last in November 1923 the top management (now known as 'the administration') and the news staff were transferred to 9 Carmelite Street, off the Embankment. This was a long narrow building with some pretensions to Queen Anne style.

The move to Carmelite Street cost the considerable sum of £4,195, and required careful planning to ensure that services were not interrupted. Douglas Williams described the move to Jones, who was on his world tour:

> Mr Jeans brought the Baron's bust down in his car. . . . then they found that all the men had gone to lunch. . . . So for ten minutes the poor Baron sat forlornly on the pavement with Mr Carter's bowler on his head, much to the joy of passers by . . . The Editorial looks most impressive and they have six lovely big new oak tables and a new bookcase with a table under it, and the gallery looks much better than was expected but the staircase up to it is so steep that it is easier to fall down than walk down. I don't think Mr Kemp is very happy—he likes a mess, you know, and he can't throw his tea leaves on the floor. . . . The Editor-in-Charge sits with his back to the fireplace with the Dominions on his left and the messengers on his right, and on the other side is the French staff and all the rest.

There were just over 12,000 square feet at Carmelite Street, still not enough to take all the Reuter departments, some of which remained at Old Jewry.

All floors were linked by a small lift. The arrival and departure of 'Sir Roderick' each day by this method were occasions of some tension, for Jones did not expect to wait. Bells rang to announce his coming and going. His personal messenger boy was in attendance to operate the lift. And to speed the evening departure, another boy was sent to press the pneumatic pad which controlled the nearby traffic-lights.

The first story on the wire from the new headquarters was about the appointment of a new German chancellor. This news was telephoned from Berlin. By the 1930s important news from most parts of Europe was being telephoned. A special continental bell rang with the noise of a fire alarm so that correspondents were not kept waiting. Stenographers wrote down the messages, which were also recorded on dictaphones.

Reuters prided itself in the 1930s upon receiving or sending news by teleprinter across the world in a matter of minutes. Four machines were involved in each news chain—one at Reuter headquarters, one at the cable office in London, one at the receiving cable office, and one at the overseas Reuter office. When Amelia Earhart flew from Honolulu to California in 1935, Reuters had the news distributed in London within nine minutes of her landing. The message had crossed America, been edited by Reuters in New York, relayed to London, and put out to the newspapers.

Such news for the London papers, and for the provincial papers via the PA, was delivered on Creed machines. These typed capital letters on foolscap paper at sixty-six words per minute, or faster at risk of break-down. As each letter was typed in Carmelite Street it appeared simultaneously on machines at the newspaper offices. These Creed machines, successors to the old column-printers, had first been installed in 1928. Important news could be dictated directly to the Creed operator. A light or buzzer then gave warning in the newspaper offices.

Baron Herbert had been very interested in wireless developments. As early as 1903 he told the annual general meeting that some transatlantic steamers were being supplied with the latest Reuter intelligence by Morse code. During the First World War wireless made great progress. With all their cables cut, the Germans could only send news overseas by this means. The British Official News Service was transmitted from Hornsea Island and Caernarvon, and after the war from Rugby. Jones was well aware of wireless developments, British and foreign, through his work for the Ministry of Information. In his news-agency role he was particularly concerned that the Marconi Company, which had tried to buy Reuters in 1916, would be able to offer strong competition in peacetime. Under the protection of the Admiralty, Marconi had been allowed a monopoly of news received by wireless. This gave Marconi's Wireless Press news an advantage, since Marconi could pick up enemy news direct from the Continent, while Reuter agents had to send the same news by cable.

After the end of the war Jones campaigned hard to prevent Marconi being allowed to continue combining the functions of a news agency with those of a major wireless carrier. He argued that the free flow of news might be endangered by such a combination. The days when Julius Reuter had aspired to be a cable owner as well as a cable user were long past. Reuters did not now seek to control either the old cable network or the new wireless stations.

But Jones did want Reuters to make full use of wireless for news transmission. In this purpose he was fortunate to find a young man already on the Reuter staff who combined enthusiasm for wireless with business sense. This was Cecil Fleetwood-May (1893–1971). The money made and saved by Fleetwood-May's development of wireless services and of commercial services for Reuters between the wars was to prove vital to the finances of the company.

Fleetwood-May had joined as a sub-editor in 1917. In 1919 he submitted proposals to Jones which were to lead to a transformation of the commercial services. In his prime Fleetwood-May was a likeable and yet purposeful personality—genial, boisterous, hard-working, a little man with large but practical ideas. In 1930 he was given the title of wireless manager in addition to that of chief of commercial services. He revelled in both responsibilities. Sadly, as European manager after the Second World War—in which his only son was killed—he was no longer so happy. His younger colleagues found him old-fashioned. It became hard to credit the story that his fluency in French and German had been acquired in his youth while playing the piano in the taverns and bawdy-houses of the Continent.

The success of the new commercial services depended heavily upon speedy delivery of price and other statistical information. This led Fleetwood-May in the 1920s to look into the possibilities of broadcast wireless telegraphy. A large number of receiving points throughout the world might be able to receive messages in Morse code simultaneously, whatever the distance, instead of by the usual series of cable relays. Such relays inevitably meant that some places got information ahead of others; and Julius Reuter had long ago understood the advantage of providing simultaneous price information to commercial clients, even if it meant locking them in one room at Aachen. Could the whole world now begin to take the place of that single room?

Fleetwood-May applied to the British Post Office for a licence 'to study the application of wireless to news dissemination'. This professional application was turned down. Fortunately, he was able to make some progress early in 1922 through listening as an amateur to the various experimental wireless emissions being broadcast at that time. But he was soon short of money to buy equipment. He plucked up courage to ask Reuters for £30 to buy more. He was called to a meeting of senior executives, who were unenthusiastic. Fortunately for Reuters, Jones overruled them. Fleetwood-May got the money to set up a more sophisticated listening-post. His suburban London home was connected to Reuters by a telephone line which, through a transformer, could be connected directly to the wireless sets.

Fleetwood-May described years later how difficult it was at first to persuade the editorial department that any news 'picked up' by wireless could be authentic. The news room would not accept the result of a football match in Paris until it had been confirmed by cable. However, experiments by German and Swiss agencies in using wireless for commercial news broadcasting soon changed attitudes. To meet this competition, Reuters negotiated with the Post Office for a service of long-wave transmissions—'circular toll broadcasts'—in Morse from Northolt, addressed to news agencies on the Continent. The new service went out under the address 'Reuterian'. So began an association between Reuters and the Post Office which gave a lead to the world in the use of wireless for news distribution between the wars.

In 1923 the Reuter Continental Broadcasting Service began sending out price quotations and exchange rates at set hours seven times a day. Frequently expanded, it remained the leading commercial service for Europe throughout the 1920s and 1930s.

In November 1929 the Post Office offered the use of a powerful short-wave transmitter at Leafield. As the charges were reasonable, Reuters started to employ this outlet for sending general as well as commercial news to Europe. The Post Office was soon persuaded to allow keying direct from Carmelite Street, but only on condition that the keying was done there by Post Office employees.

A novel form of news transmission by wireless was introduced in 1935 and it soon took over much of the service to Europe. This employed a type of wireless tape-machine, developed in Germany by Dr Wolff Hell and known as the Hellschreiber. Fleetwood-May had seen Hell give a demonstration in Athens and had been much impressed. The Hell system became widely adopted by the European agencies. Electrical impulses, transmitted via Leafield, sent words and numerals from Reuters to Hell receiving machines anywhere in Europe. The incoming news was printed on narrow paper tape at the rate of sixty-six words per minute. In bad transmitting conditions Hell messages could become garbled. But they were less vulnerable than messages sent by radio teleprinter, the rival technology prematurely favoured by the American agencies.

Reuters wanted to reach subscribers quickly throughout the world, not just on the Continent. At Rugby the powerful long-wave transmitter built by the Post Office for the Admiralty during the war lay idle for much of the time. Its facilities were offered to Reuters. The minimum charge for starting up was £5, even for a message of a few words. But Morse signals from Rugby could be picked up in Reuter offices all over the world, and also by overseas newspaper subscribers. The Reuterian world service began in March 1931. A coding system made key words unintelligible to eavesdroppers. By 1938 this service was being directed to twenty-six destinations—along the fringes of Europe, over the Middle and Far East including India, to Africa, and to South America.

By the late 1930s about 90 per cent of Reuter news was going out by wireless. Fleetwood-May, steadily supported by Jones, had brought about a transformation in world news supply. Cable transmission remained useful for communication with fixed points; but outward cable messages were now confined mainly to news of special interest to particular countries and therefore unsuitable for broadcast distribution by wireless. To the benefit of Reuters, the formation of Cable and Wireless Limited from 1929 brought the British Empire's communications network under one control.

Fleetwood-May became a key participant in annual conferences of the European agencies, held in different capitals every year between 1924 and 1939. Much time was spent considering how Reuter services to Europe might be improved. At the first conference in 1924 Fleetwood-May found that many of the national agencies, especially the Scandinavians and the Hungarians, wanted news direct from London.

With the introduction of wireless transmissions in Morse, many Europeans also came to prefer news from Reuters in English rather than in French, thus avoiding the delays and pitfalls of double translation. Wireless was obviously working to the advantage of Reuters. But subsidized foreign competitors—French, German, Italian, Japanese—were setting up world or regional wireless news services. Although Reuters kept ahead, its rivals had much less need to count the cost.

V

Under the skilful direction of Fleetwood-May, the commercial services offered by Reuters expanded impressively between the wars. These became very important to the economic life of the formal and informal British Empire, and also of Europe.

A prices service had continued from Victorian times, run by a handful of staff. But Fleetwood-May, who had acquired experience on trade journals before joining Reuters, realized that a fuller service could be offered. Commercial information could be collected through the existing network at only a small extra cost. Much was already reaching the newsroom only to be 'spiked'. Junior though he was, Fleetwood-May began to press during 1919 to be allowed to explore the possibilities, starting with the trade journals. On 4 October Jones granted him an interview; after hearing Fleetwood-May's ideas, he authorized the making of preliminary enquiries.

Within two months a circular was announcing 'a special service of industrial, commercial, and financial messages', to be known as 'Reuter's Trade Service', and starting on 1 January 1920. The service was available on free trial for four weeks; subscriptions varied from £15 to £200 per annum. Information was circulated through printed weekly and monthly bulletins. Within a few years, greatly helped by the use of wireless, this trade service had expanded into a full commercial service.

Fleetwood-May eventually recruited a London staff of about ninety clerks and financial writers, special market reporters, engineers, and telegraph operators. Jones told the 1928 annual general meeting that 'our telegraphic service of Financial and Commercial quotations and Markets intelligence generally is now, after several years of assiduous labour, easily the largest, the most widely distributed, and the most trusted in the world'. A favourite story of Jones's told how business on the Shanghai Stock Exchange was once completely suspended for thirty-six hours because a communications break had stopped the inflow of Reuter prices. The new service had added a fresh dimension to the prestige of the old name.

By the end of 1930 a total of 737 commercial messages each week, 6,100 words in all, was being transmitted to the Continent; and 459 messages totalling 10,620 words were reaching India, the Far East, Australasia, Egypt, and the West Indies. Fleetwood-May told Jones in July 1934 that a one-minute cotton service was now operating from New York, via Liverpool, London, and Rugby, to Bombay, at the rate of twenty-two messages per day. In Bombay, when the Washington cotton-crop reports were due Reuter subscribers were locked in a room to receive the information on equal terms—just as subscribers had been locked in by Julius Reuter at Aachen.

At successive annual general meetings Jones was able to describe how the commercial service was cushioning losses on the editorial side. By 1933 annual profits of the commercial service were £23,600. In that year commercial subscriptions from the Far East alone were bringing in

£59,900. This was £11,000 more than total United Kingdom newspaper subscriptions.

The introduction in 1928 of the City ticker service to private firms in London constituted a breakthrough. It was the first printer service for the delivery of Reuter statistics. Jones told the 1934 annual general meeting that tickers were now placed in seventy-five banks and business-houses in the City, including the Bank of England, 'at first a rather shy recruit'. Between 1928 and 1939 over £90,000 was spent upon 'telegraphic instruments'. Shanghai had followed London with a ticker service in 1930, and then India, South Africa, and Egypt.

In 1933 Sydney Gampell started the Reuter commodity index. Two years later he began to write the weekly *Economic X-Ray*, which was subtitled *World Business Analysis*. By 1938 the *X-Ray* reached about 350 subscribers, chiefly within the British Empire. It did not hesitate to discuss political as well as economic matters. Jones's fair comment upon one number was: 'racy and amusing but risky for Reuters.' It was nevertheless highly esteemed, and continued to be published until Gampell's retirement in 1974.

Jones described the commercial services to the 1934 annual general meeting as 'a particular hobby of mine ever since the War'. He also called them 'half-brother to the News Services'. Despite this support from the top, the editorial staff always looked down upon Fleetwood-May's department.

VI

When under pressure to resign in 1940, Jones marshalled his defence in an *aide-mémoire* to himself entitled 'What I have done for Reuters'. The second item read: 'Preserved it for the newspapers of this country, in particular for the Press Association, when I could have cashed out on far better terms'. Jones always asserted that he could have floated Reuters as a public company, and thereby made much more money than he did by selling out in two stages to the PA in 1926 and 1930.

A public flotation would have exposed Reuters to the danger of control by undesirable shareholders, the danger which had threatened in 1916. Jones was undoubtedly sincere in his wish to protect Reuters by selling it to the British newspapers. There is more of a question about the financial terms which he exacted. His critics were later to contend that he obtained a very generous price in return for following the public-spirited course.

The idea of a co-operative news service for Britain, run by the newspapers themselves, can be traced back at least to an article in the *Nation* of 24 April 1915, published after the death of Baron Herbert. Jones later claimed that he was himself already looking forward at the time of the 1916 reconstruction to transferring the ownership to the British press, but that such a big change was not practicable in wartime. He was probably right, for when negotiations did begin in 1925 they turned out to be long and difficult. Nevertheless, the nine-year delay proved very profitable for Jones. A deal with the newspapers made in 1916 would have simply meant selling his holding in the old company, at a time when he was no more than one large shareholder among others. From 1919 he owned 60 per cent of the shares in the new company. He was now in a commanding position.

In March 1922, during the course of a long conversation with Jones, Lord Northcliffe, founder of the *Daily Mail* and the 'Napoleon of Fleet Street', offered his support for the idea of newspaper ownership of Reuters; but he died four months later. Jones, however, had other influential contacts, notably Lord Riddell, chairman of the *News of the World* and vice-president of the Newspaper Proprietors Association, and J. J. Astor of *The Times*. After Jones's return from his world tour of 1923–4, he began informal soundings both with members of the NPA, representing the London papers, and with the PA, representing the provincial papers. An element of urgency had been added by the formation of the first Labour Government in January 1924. Jones and others in Reuters feared that Labour wanted to interfere with the press. They believed that there would be greater safety under co-operative ownership.

Discussions began in earnest in May 1925. Jones prepared documents for the NPA and PA which presented the affairs of Reuters in a surprisingly favourable light in view of the difficulties which he had been emphasizing earlier. Jones had told Northcliffe in 1922 that the profits were 'poor, if not non-existent.' The annual report for 1923 had declared a loss of £3,927. Yet in 1925 Jones was able to convince two firms of auditors—first Deloittes, called in by himself, and then Price Waterhouse, called in by the NPA—that Reuters had been continuously profitable since the war. Jones's final 'proposal for sale' to the British press, dated 2 November 1925, based upon the auditors' reports, showed an average net profit of between £25,000 and £26,000 per annum. In what seems to have been a private *aide-mémoire* of 13 October Jones had argued: 'I cannot allow years 1921, 22 and 23 to be counted against us. They were fortifying and entrenching years.'

In his reminiscences Jones portrayed Sir Andrew Caird, the representative of the Northcliffe–Rothermere newspaper interests, as his chief adversary. Caird seems to have been unimpressed by Jones's optimistic presentation of the financial position of Reuters. In an effort to satisfy Caird and other critics within the NPA, Jones modified his original proposals considerably. He offered the newspapers 40,000 'A' preference shares in Reuters at £4 per share, the NPA and the PA to have 20,000 each. These 'A' shares were to enjoy the same voting-rights as the remaining 35,000 'B' ordinary shares, held by Jones and by Napier's two sons.

Ownership of the 'A' shares would therefore have given control of Reuters to the newspapers. The 'A' shares were also to possess special dividend rights, ensuring a minimum return of 7.5 per cent. Finally, the newspapers were to be allowed a three-year option to buy the 'B' shares at £4. 10s. each, thereby becoming sole proprietors.

Although, according to Jones, the attractions of the scheme were recognized by all parties, a majority within the NPA refused to accept equality with the PA in the ownership of Reuters. Jones, for his part, insisted that the PA must not be left in a minority position or excluded. In the event it was the NPA which came to be left out: Jones's scheme was taken as the basis for an agreement with the PA alone. He was apparently encouraged in this by Riddell, who had despaired of the NPA. Jones convinced himself that ownership by the provincial press would provide sufficient protection for Reuters. But he retained the hope that all the London newspaper groups would one day come in. Until they did, there was always the risk that one or more of them might ally with one of the American news agencies to the detriment of Reuters.

The PA paid Jones and the Napiers, as owners of Reuters, the £160,000 which Jones had previously asked from the PA and NPA together. By an agreement dated 23 March 1926, issued capital of 75,007 shares in Reuters was divided into 50,000 'A' shares, 25,000 'B' shares, and 7 'C' (directors') shares, all of £1. Jones and the Napiers contracted to sell to the PA 31 250 'A' shares and 8,750 'B' shares, all at £4 per share. The agreement gave the PA the option to buy the remaining Jones–Napier shareholding by 31 December 1930 at £4. 10s. per share—18,750 'A' shares and 16,250 'B' shares. This was duly done at the end of 1930, for a price of £157,500. So in total the PA paid £317,500 for Reuters. Assuming that Jones received 60 per cent of this sum, he got £190,500.

Jones was allowed a nominal holding of 1000 shares until his retirement. He had made his continuance as managing director a condition of the negotiations, and the 1926 agreement confirmed his position. From

1926 until 1930 the Reuter board consisted of the four senior members of the PA board, plus Jones, Buchan, and Claude Napier. After the second purchase all six PA directors served on the Reuter board, along with Jones and Buchan.

Given that the directors believed Jones to be indispensable, he was able to secure generous terms as chairman and managing director. In 1926 he signed a ten-year contract at a salary of £300 as chairman, £4,200 as managing director, plus £2,000 representation allowance, and commission of 10 per cent on profits over £13,000. In 1931 his salary was increased by £1,500 and the representation allowance by £500. During the 1930s his commission varied from a high of £3,592 in 1932 to a low of £623 in 1938.

So, notwithstanding the financial tightness of Reuters, Jones prospered during these years. At the time of his marriage in 1920 he had told his prospective father-in-law that his income was between £5,000 and £6,000 a year, with the bulk of his capital tied up in Reuters. Within ten years all that capital was released, and in addition he was being paid more than ever before.

But his skill in drawing money to himself was not what Jones wanted to be noticed. What he wanted to be recognized was his achievement in at least partially realizing his 'vision' for Reuters—putting it safely into the co-operative ownership of the British press.

VII

As head of Reuters, Jones regarded himself as one of the great servants of the imperial idea. In this role he undertook between the wars five visits of inspection or negotiation to main overseas centres of the Reuter empire within the British Empire.

As in Baron Herbert's day, Reuter general managers acted as proconsuls, with considerable independence in the management and development of their areas but regularly in touch with Jones in handling major problems and in applying overall Reuter policy. Seven general managers were in post in the 1920s—at Shanghai, Bombay, Cairo, Melbourne, Cape Town, New York, and Ottawa. Europe was managed from London, as was South America and much of Africa.

In a letter to his wife of 21 February 1924 while on his world tour, Jones listed the contents of one morning's post:

> one of our remittance clerks in Australia caught stealing cash; an action against us in Calcutta for £2,000 damages brought by blackguard who

owes us an immense sum, won't pay, and is countering with this action; men in India getting allowances to which they have no right (thank goodness I shall be there tomorrow); Douglas Williams wasting money in New York; Barraclough (our G. M. in Australia) quarrelling with our biggest newspaper clients simply because he is a tactless, rude, and bad tempered old devil (I am going to rap him over the knuckles); damages we have had to pay in Johannesburg because a clerk made a word wrong in a coded telegram to London with the result that the wrong goods were shipped (I am vexed about that because we ought not to have paid: our contracts protect us); a new nationalist internal news agency being started by influential Indians (natives) against the Eastern News Agency (owned by Reuters) which hitherto has had the field to itself; and a whole heap of minor vexations.

The fatigues of travel were eased by the fact that, as head of Reuters, Jones could expect to stay at Government House in each territory. Here was recognition of the important function of Reuters within the British Empire. But Jones liked to take it also as a personal compliment, and he revelled in the privileged surroundings. 'I love the pomp and circumstance,' he told his wife on 17 February 1924 from Government House, Madras, 'and wish I were staying here longer.'

Relationships between Reuters and the Dominions—South Africa, Australia, New Zealand, and Canada—had been established well before 1914. The strongest link was with South Africa. By far the weakest was with Canada, where Jones had only limited success in his attempts to strengthen it. This was mainly because of Canadian satisfaction with the service received from AP, but partly because of the Canadian newspaper proprietors' deep suspicions about the attitude of Reuters towards Canadian Government subsidies. A visit to Toronto in 1920 for the Imperial Press Conference gave Jones the opportunity to meet proprietors and executives of the Canadian Press news agency (CP). It received its foreign news from AP, including some originating from Reuters. This arrangement was continued; but from 1921 Reuters added a 600-word special daily service containing British and imperial news of interest to Canada through AP's New York office. In 1923 CP opened a bureau within the Carmelite Street headquarters of Reuters.

In 1926 Jones visited Australia, where the position of Reuters as the supplier of world news to the Australian press had long been difficult. As early as the 1870s Reuters had given up hopes of securing a dominating position within the local newspaper scene. By the twentieth century two cable news organizations were in competition—the Australian Press

Association, and the United Cable Services. The APA was backed by the *Herald* and *Telegraph* in Sydney, and by the *Argus* and *Age* in Melbourne; the UCS was controlled by the *Sydney Sun* and the *Melbourne Herald*. The two organizations were rivals. Yet they had now formed what Jones described to Clements on 31 July 1926 as an 'offensive and defensive alliance'. The only newspapers outside this combination were small and weak. Once again, the Australians were able to squeeze Reuters: 'at almost all costs,' admitted Jones to Clements, 'we must come to terms with the Combine'.

Jones therefore made a virtue of negotiating with the two organizations as one, blandly claiming at the time and in his reminiscences that this was his own particular wish. The Australians and New Zealanders had been paying £6,000 for Reuter news, and wanted (according to Jones) to pay even less. Under the new deal on 31 July 1926 they agreed to pay £11,000 for five years, and £12,000 for ten years thereafter, less £4,000 paid by Reuters for Australian and New Zealand news and office accommodation. Jones was well pleased with these terms. In reality the deal did not earn as much as he had expected, because he had concluded the contract in pounds Australian instead of pounds sterling. By 1941 this oversight had lost Reuters more than £14,000.

After 1926 the Australians acted no less independently than earlier. They were the more able to do so because Jones had been forced to allow them to edit their news for themselves in London: they had complained loudly about British bias in the file. Like the Canadians, they now set up a bureau at Carmelite Street.

Complaints were also coming from South Africa, where feeling was growing among both the English-speaking and Dutch South Africans that the internal news service should be in their own hands, not controlled by an outside organization. By 1938 the pressure had become irresistible, and Jones made his last overseas journey to negotiate a new contract.

He decided that the prudent course would be to assist himself in setting up a co-operative, non-profit-making organization, a South African Press Association. Reuters relinquished to SAPA the handling of internal general news, while retaining the exclusive right to supply world news. In 'What I have done for Reuters' Jones drew attention to the payment of £21,000 by the South Africans for goodwill, 'which nobody else possibly could have obtained'. The fact remained that this payment was simply a sweetener.

At the other end of Africa, Reuters had been established in Egypt since the 1860s. During the interwar years the large Egyptian Government payment of £2,300 per annum continued to be vital. On 30 June 1930 the Egyptian Ministry of Communications described the money plainly as a 'subsidy'. In a letter of 6 July Gerald Delany, the Reuter general manager, wrote of the Government 'contribution'. The Egyptian newspapers were still too weak to support a Reuter news service by their subscriptions alone.

Dorothy Nicholson was sent out in 1931 to expand the commercial service to Egypt. She was doing well until the finance minister suddenly told Delany that the service must be stopped because it encouraged gambling, which was against the teaching of the Koran. Miss Nicholson remembered sixty years later how she persuaded the minister at an interview 'that we were doing exactly the opposite, as now everyone received the prices at the same time—all private cables had stopped and no one did any business until they had received the authentic Reuter Prices'.

VIII

Miss Nicholson had earlier helped to develop the commercial services in India. She went on to set up similar services in Australia and South Africa. These were much boosted by the introduction of the Reuterian wireless service of prices, notably of New York cotton prices for Bombay. During the 1930s India was the leading overseas profit centre: profit on Indian-press business reached over £17,500 in 1935, which more than counterbalanced the loss on home-press business. Indian commercial-service profit was then about £7,500 annually.

A new generation had come to the fore in India, led by William J. Moloney, the general manager from 1923 to 1937. His predecessor in India, A. H. Kingston, had been killed by a fall from a railway train. J. S. Dunn, the general manager in South Africa, was sent to assess the situation. He reported to Jones on 27 April 1923 that Kingston had neglected his work and had become 'sexually unhinged . . . He mixed with the wrong people and could perhaps be described as haunting the underworld thus becoming somewhat notorious . . . none of the people who should have been Reuters' friends in Bombay would know Mr Kingston socially.' Dunn welcomed the appointment of 'a man of the charm and social status of Mr Moloney'. Moloney, an Irishman—as was Delany in Egypt—contrived to gain acceptance by the white community and in official circles, while maintaining a sympathetic attitude towards Indians and good contacts with the nationalists. He returned to London in 1937 to serve as joint general manager, and retired in 1944.

In a retrospective note dated 11 July 1944 Moloney listed the most important features of his work in India:

(1) 'The closer association of Indians with the management of the branches (there were no Indian managers in Reuters on my arrival in India).'
(2) The merging of the staffs of the Eastern News Agency and of Reuters, which led to great economies.
(3) The supplying of Reuter news to vernacular newspapers.
(4) 'Successful resistance to the tendency to sell out in India as we had done in Australia, Japan and South Africa.'

This last achievement was indeed noteworthy. In India between the wars the Reuter rearguard action was entirely successful, although it was still a rearguard action. Reuters restructured its organization but held its ground. It continued to supply India with most of its world news, and it continued to dominate the supply of internal news.

The Eastern News Agency, started by Reuters in 1910, had absorbed the Associated Press of India. API had been launched by Indians as a domestic news agency to collect news about India for the Indian press, but it was never financially viable. Its moving spirit, K. C. Roy, was an able journalist, and a nationalist who advanced his cause through charm and moderation. Roy joined Reuters at the take-over, and served loyally, becoming head of the news department until his early death in 1931.

In the meantime API kept its own name within the Reuter organization. It gave full coverage to the nationalist movement while at the same time reporting all official news. A conflict of loyalties was avoided because API did not add comment. None the less, through the circulation of so much nationalist material the cause of self-government was well publicized. Neither Jones nor Moloney was expecting a self-governing India to be an India without Reuters. Their aim was to secure the agency's long-term position by making it indispensable to the Indian press.

Moloney was succeeded as general manager by John Turner, who had gone out to India in 1930 as chief accountant. He was widely liked by the Indians, and it was at Turner's prompting that Gandhi gave API exclusive rights to his personal news. Turner returned to England in 1951 and was appointed chief accountant in 1954. He retired in 1960.

The close Reuter relationship with the Indian Government and with the India Office continued throughout the interwar years. The India Office paid 7*d.* a word for news transmitted at its request, reduced to 6*d.*

when cable tariffs were lowered in 1927. Ministers and officials in London and New Delhi frequently complained about what they considered to be inaccuracies in the Reuter file to India, about an excess of trivia, and about alleged pro-nationalist bias.

For example, Sir Samuel Hoare, secretary of state for India, complained on 5 December 1932 because Reuters had reported an India League meeting in London which had attacked the Government's policy towards India. Hoare dismissed the occasion as 'scurrilous', and claimed that only the *Daily Herald* among the London papers had thought it worth noticing. 'This is not the sort of thing for which publicity in India seems to us desirable.' Hoare also suggested that Reuter news sometimes showed a pro-Hindu bias. Jones answered on 8 December in characteristic terms, seeking to claim both objectivity and patriotic intention for Reuters 'whose sole aim and purpose are faithfully and dispassionately to represent to the people of India facts as they are and not as Congress propagandists strive to make them out to be. Without for one moment taking sides in any controversy, Reuters are *in effect* fighting your fight.'

The Government of India's payments to Reuters were admitted by Dunn to Jones on 27 April 1923 to be 'handsome'. The three main Government news subscriptions were worth R2,600 (about £200) monthly. The Indian News Agency (an offshoot of API) was also paid for news supplied to the Indian provincial governments. Nationalists in the Legislative Assembly were told that these were not subsidies but payments for services rendered. A similar answer was given to a question in the House of Commons on 12 December 1938.

Significantly, however, Turner was already thinking about a future without British rule. He warned Jones on 6 December 1937 that 'British control in India is being relaxed . . . We are not in favour of unduly emphasizing British or Empire news at a time when Indian Nationalists are taking an ever increasing share in the Government of this country.'

IX

China was the part of the world outside the British Empire where Reuters was most prominent during the interwar years. Reuters supplied not only world news to the Far Eastern press, but also a regional service from local correspondents, Reuters' Pacific Service. Chinese-language papers such as the *China Times* paid Reuters monthly for news; only British-owned titles, such as the *North China Daily News*, were allowed more generous credit.

The high status enjoyed by the agency in China impressed Jones on his world tour of 1923–4. 'A Note on Reuters', which he seems to have written for internal circulation after returning to London, rejoiced that Reuter price quotations and Reuter political and commercial news were 'paramount' on every stock exchange throughout the Far East.

William Turner was appointed general manager in the Far East in 1920. Jones had known Turner as a journalist in South Africa, and in 1915 had put him in charge of the South African service from London. In a memorandum of 25 June 1921 Turner warned Jones that the main challenge to the British position in China was coming from American, French, and Japanese competition in trade and in supplying news: 'the quiet British atmosphere of the treaty ports is being rapidly effaced by a restless internationalism, in which commercial jealousy, and jealousy of the British especially, plays a leading role.' Despite this, the Reuter commercial service expanded rapidly under Turner's direction during the 1920s. As a result, Far Eastern revenue more than quadrupled, growing from £16,200 in 1918 to £66,400 in 1928. In 1932 Turner became overseas general manager in London, retiring in 1941.

During the 1920s the main challenge to Reuters in the Far East was coming from UP. The other American agency, AP, was still a member of the ring combination. Nevertheless, it complained increasingly about the quality of Reuter news from the Far East. This was said not to match UP's in suitability for the American market or in colour. Equally, AP complained that news about the United States circulated in the Far East by Reuters for the ring combination dwelt too much upon the seamy side of American life, highlighting the activities of gangsters and film stars.

These complaints reflected an underlying desire within AP—strongly promoted by Kent Cooper, its general manager from 1925—to quit the ring combination, and preferably to break it up. Cooper wanted free competition in news worldwide. What did Reuters want? When Jones spoke at the Royal Institute of International Affairs in 1929 about 'The Control of Press News in the Pacific' his discomfiture was apparent. He knew in his heart that the old ring combination—and the leading position of Reuters within it—could not last much longer. AP would not allow it:

> Americans and other people talk a great deal about the 'Reuter monopoly' . . . The Americans realize that the presentation of news from an American angle, not only American news but news of the world generally, is calculated to create a state of mind more favourable to American trade in the Far East than the state of mind created or maintained if the people of the

Far East are dependent in the main upon a service which either is British in its substance, or, in so far as the substance is foreign, British in direction.

In response to AP pressure, a Reuter American Service had been started in 1924. But Jones admitted in his lecture that this service out of London had still not satisfied the Americans: 'even if Reuters were as fair as the Recording Angel, they still do not want the Far East to get its American news from Reuters, because it is handled by Englishmen. I do not blame them. If the position were reversed I should say the same thing.'

Jones explained that Reuters had added a service of news direct to the Far East from San Francisco. Although AP-originated, Reuters would have been entitled under the ring-combination agreements to label this news as its own. Jones had decided, however, to call it 'the Associated Press Service'. In other words Reuters had not dared to assert its rights. Even so, why should AP not circulate this news for itself? The ring-combination barriers were looking increasingly artificial.

If China was unsettled during the 1920s, it became even more so during the 1930s, when Japanese aggression was added to internal conflict. Reuters had prospered during the troubles of the earlier decade, because its good name made it acceptable to all parties. But in the 1930s it became more vulnerable, although still profitable. Far Eastern revenue rose from £66,400 in 1928 to £73,200 ten years later.

The young man chosen as Turner's successor to handle this increasingly difficult situation was Christopher Chancellor (1904–89). He came from a Lowland Scots landowning family and was educated at Eton and at Cambridge University, where he took a first-class degree in history. He went into business, but in 1929 found himself suddenly without a job. His wife Sylvia wrote in desperation to Jones, whom she had known since girlhood. She was by birth a Paget, one of the influential families cultivated by Jones. He interviewed Chancellor and made him a trainee in the editorial department. Jones claimed in his reminiscences to have immediately spotted that the young man possessed an 'executive outlook'—quick intelligence, plus energy, toughness, and patience.

After mastering the editorial work in London, Chancellor was sent to report the League of Nations at Geneva. Then in January 1931 he took over as general manager for the Far East at Shanghai. Jones had boldly decided that his protégé was already qualified for top management. Although not himself a journalist, Chancellor soon showed that he could control journalists. He ran the organization efficiently, while at the same time representing Reuters to the outside world with polish and tact. His diplomatic skills were more than ever needed after the Japanese invasion of China in 1937. The Japanese respected him not the less because they were certain that he was working for British intelligence as well as for Reuters. The Chancellors became leading figures within the Shanghai social élite. Yet at all times Chancellor kept a cool head for business, disconcertingly cool for some. In 1939 he returned to London as an assistant general manager. He was being groomed by Jones for the succession.

By the late 1930s business in China was declining fast, and (in Jones's words to the 1936 annual general meeting) 'drastic economies vigorously carried out' proved necessary to maintain margins. Far Eastern commercial subscriptions had dropped from £70,198 in 1935 to £49,140 in the following year. At the 1938 annual general meeting Jones summed up the position of Reuters in the Far East as 'no longer undisputed' but 'still supreme'.

X

Chancellor admitted in a lecture of 1939 that the British were trying to maintain their large commercial presence in China by a mixture of bluff and compromise, 'without power to make our will felt'. In Japan the Reuter bluff had already been called. Here was another country where Jones found himself forced to sell out, boasting in consolation that the terms were good. He wrote in 'What I have done for Reuters': 'I got £20,000 out of the Japanese merely for the *right* to exclude Reuters name from Japan. It is secured to us by a Debenture on the whole undertaking of the Japanese Agency, on which Debenture we draw 5 per cent—a steady £1,000 per annum.'

But the withdrawal of its name amounted to a major climb-down for Reuters. This was the more serious in a country where 'face' mattered greatly. Japan had been Reuter territory since the early days of the ring combination in the 1870s, and Reuters had largely controlled the supply of news into and out of the country. The first significant change had occurred at the end of 1913, when a Japanese agency, Kokusai, had been started. From 1 January 1914 Reuters was associated with this national agency, whose first managing director, John Russell Kennedy, became the Reuter agent. All Kokusai's world news came from Reuters, which retained exclusive rights to Kokusai's Japanese news.

After the war Japanese national feeling was intensifying while British influence was declining. The name of Reuters was less of a recommendation, and Kokusai wanted to remove the attribution even while continuing to take Reuter news. At the end of 1923 Kennedy was succeeded by a

Japanese, Yukichi Iwanaga. At this point Jones arrived in Japan on his world tour. He landed just after the disastrous Yokohama earthquake, which dealt a severe blow to the business of Kokusai. According to Jones, Iwanaga had not expected to pay Reuters any compensation for the withdrawal of the Reuter credit; but Jones insisted upon a high payment of £20,000. 'Of the two alternatives before you I suggest you would be wise if you chose that of keeping the Reuter name and saving your twenty thousand pounds.' But the Japanese were adamant, even though financially hard pressed. Jones then suggested the debenture scheme as a means of easing payment. The Japanese agreed, and from 1 February 1924 the Reuter credit disappeared from general news distributed in Japan, although it was retained for commercial news.

In May 1926 Kokusai was absorbed into a co-operative of national newspapers, known as Rengo. In the same year Kokusai had opened a London bureau, housed in Reuters. The bureau chief began to advise on the Reuter service to the Far East; this meant that Reuters was no longer the unquestioned master. Reuters next allowed Rengo to send news direct to Shanghai for circulation to client Chinese papers. This concession, though small in itself, meant penetration by the Japanese of previously exclusive Reuter territory in China.

From 1926 Reuters also allowed AP to supply news directly to Rengo, even though the terms still recognized the primacy of Reuters. In his reminiscences Jones explained away this shift as 'no more than consistent with conditions in the Far East'. But consistency with the new realities was becoming uncomfortable. Jones kept the concession secret from Havas and Wolff. In the following year Reuters, Havas, and Wolff agreed to give up the differential which AP had always paid them within the ring combination. AP news out of America was now accepted as worth just as much as news for America from Europe and elsewhere.

Even so, AP remained restless within the ring combination. In 1930 Iwanaga of Rengo and Kent Cooper of AP agreed in principle that they would enter into a full exchange of AP news for Rengo news once Rengo's current contract with Reuters had expired in the middle of 1933. Rengo's rival, Dentsu, was doing well because of its links with UP, AP's main rival in the United States. AP and Rengo needed to mount a counter-attack.

AP was feeling less and less obliged to humour Reuters. It was now strong enough to stand alone anywhere in the world, and it intended to become a truly international news agency. As a co-operative, serving a population of 100 million, it possessed a powerful home subscriber base which could not be threatened by any rival. Cooper was particularly keen to sell AP news directly to the Far East. Conveniently, he was able to promote these materialistic purposes by talking not of influence and profit but of freedom in news. His reminiscences, *Barriers Down*, published in 1942, claimed that he was pursuing 'practical idealism in international news relationships'. The idealism was the more sincere because it paid off.

Cooper had written to Jones on 15 February 1930 telling him plainly that AP 'must have a free hand in the Far East'. At the end of the year AP gave a year's notice of withdrawal from the ring combination. Frank Noyes, the AP president, wrote to Jones on 26 December 1930 to explain the American agency's position. Noyes said that AP did not want a complete break with Reuters and the combination, only a less restrictive relationship: 'Conditions have changed materially in forty years.' AP wanted free entry into China; Noyes suggested that his agency would be competing with UP to supply American news to the Chinese rather than with Reuters to supply non-American news. Jones had already half conceded free entry on 17 November: 'Come in by all means.' But he still wanted 'a working agreement of some kind on the spot. After all we are allies, not rivals.'

With regard to Japan, Noyes argued that Rengo ought not to be denied the natural right of choosing AP rather than Reuters as its main partner, if it so wished. Jones countered that Reuters had 'carefully nursed the Japanese field' in the expectation of 'a legitimate reward' once the Japanese press had become stronger.

UP was well aware of these growing strains, and in April 1931 Edward L. Keen, its European general manager, asked Jones whether Reuters would be free to deal with UP in the event of a a split with AP. Jones said yes. He wanted to keep the UP alternative open as a bargaining ploy, even though he regarded its news handling as too sensational. The difficulty was that Cooper was willing to risk Reuters doing just such a deal.

On 30 June 1931 the Reuter board discussed the coming crisis. Jones asked whether, 'if the Associated Press took up too strong a line', Reuters should stay with AP and break with the continental agencies, or stay with the Europeans and break with AP. He inclined towards the latter course. In the short term, a breach was avoided. In April 1932 a new agreement was signed between Reuters, AP, Havas, and Wolff. Cooper now assumed that his proposed news-exchange deal with the Japanese would not be open to question. Jones, on the other hand, still thought that—

since the 1932 agreement was supposedly a continuation of the old friendly relationship—AP would never push to the point of directly threatening an established Reuter interest. In a long letter to Jones, quoted in *Barriers Down*, Cooper gave his own version of news-agency history in Japan:

> for twenty years the Associated Press has deferred to Reuters as respects Japan. But the Associated Press has denied itself meeting its own necessities as long as it dares . . . I was astonished to learn that you are opposed to the Associated Press sharing equal responsibilities and financial returns with Reuters as respects relations with Rengo. It is due you, therefore, as an ally and friend that you know how fairly we feel we are dealing.

Cooper was here being disingenuous, for he had just signed a contract with the Japanese without involving Reuters in the negotiations and without telling Jones of his intentions. This contract, concluded in May 1933, did permit the Japanese to make a subsequent deal with Reuters, but it did not require them to do so.

Jones was furious, not only because the AP–Rengo deal removed Reuters from its position of primacy, but also because of the way Cooper had acted. Guided by Jones, the Reuter board gave AP formal notice to terminate the 1932 four-party agreement, with the object of renegotiating the whole relationship. He now demanded payment of a £10,000 differential for the Reuter service: this would have been a step back for AP. Jones claimed in his reminiscences that this demand was not made without consideration. Havas and Wolff had expressed support, as had Turner and Chancellor, the past and present Far Eastern managers.

The decision to break with AP was made at a special meeting of the Reuter board on 30 June 1933. Jones spelt out the situation as he saw it: 'Mr Kent Cooper is deliberately intriguing against us in the Far East, if not elsewhere.' The Americans were trying to undermine the British business position in the Far East, and AP was joining in the attempt. As for the AP–Rengo contract:

> it places Rengo in the position of being able to put a revolver at our head if we are weak or foolish enough not to call their bluff . . . I would like to have authority to give notice to the Associated Press to terminate our Treaty with them. I am of opinion that the best defensive is the offensive.

In answer to a question, Jones expressed confidence that the serving of notice would bring the Americans and Japanese to heel: 'Both the Japanese Agency and the Associated Press will take our action as a sign of strength.' Jones was sure that the outcome would be an offer of favourable terms for Reuters in Japan. He admitted, though, that Cooper's attitude posed a problem. 'I have never liked the man,' commented Buchan. 'He is a low stamp of American, of a different class altogether from the old Associated Press men.' The discussion then concluded with a formal resolution, carried unanimously, 'that the matter be left entirely in the Chairman's hands'.

The outcome was not as Jones had forecast. Cooper made it clear that AP could do without Reuters anywhere in the world. Could Reuters, with no service of American news of its own, really do without AP? Could Reuters hope to compete successfully with a hostile AP, which would be able to spend heavily to promote its services? Would not a new relationship—partly of association under contract and partly of friendly rivalry—be more comfortable for Reuters than total war? In the end, such a new relationship was negotiated. But to achieve it, Jones had to climb down a long way.

The PA directors on the Reuter board had not fully realized the implications of what they were doing. AP news suited the provincial press; UP news would not do as a substitute. Cooper wrote to the general manager of the PA, H. C. Robbins, telling him what was happening. 'I would be glad indeed', he remarked cunningly, 'if a way could be found to have a direct relationship with the Press Association, although I fear that Reuters would not permit that.'

Robbins was horrified at the prospect of losing AP news. He convinced the PA board that negotiations must be started to prevent this happening. Jones's 'offensive' had obviously failed, and the PA representatives on the Reuter board now wanted peace. This was the first time that they had ever asserted themselves against Jones on a matter of importance. Ever adroit in adversity, Jones seems himself to have drafted a conciliatory cable for Robbins to send to Cooper: 'Wishful as we are that the two American British cooperative enterprises Associated and Press Association should continue together instead of being in opposition camps we prepared use our influence with Reuters.' The cable concluded by offering a meeting in New York 'to clear up all causes of misunderstanding'. Jones, in other words, was now prepared to cross the Atlantic on a journey of appeasement.

He never admitted that he had been forced to climb down. He liked to claim that he had simply responded to pleas from Iwanaga. And he blandly gave the impression in his reminiscences that the initiative for talks came almost as much from Noyes of AP as from himself. Jones sailed for New York in February 1934. Cooper later admitted that he forced unequal terms upon Reuters. He began the negotiations by saying that he was interested only in a contract with the PA. Eventually, Jones had to take whatever else AP would offer. In exchange for the Reuter world news service, plus the PA service of British news, Reuters had to accept not the equivalent AP service but only its home service. This was designed for the American newspapers, and was little suited to Reuters.

AP was now left free to compete with Reuters anywhere in the world, including the British Isles. A direct contract was signed between AP and the PA. The division of the globe into exclusive news-agency territories had gone for ever. Cooper was well satisfied. This, he explained in *Barriers Down*, was the climax of his career. 'Reuters had slipped from the throne that had given it hegemony over the news of the world.'

Jones summed up very differently. 'We had given new life to an international league', he claimed in his reminiscences, 'which, if not radically reformed, very soon would have broken down.' Yet in truth what was completed in 1934 was much more than a radical reform of the old news order: it was the ending of the old order. Jones's talent for self-deception, here exemplified, was to contribute to his eventual undoing.

EIGHT

The Decline and Fall of Roderick Jones

1934–1941

I

RODERICK JONES spent his last eighteen months as head of Reuters in a brand-new headquarters building at 85 Fleet Street. It was opened in July 1939, only weeks before the outbreak of the Second World War. The new building was the physical expression of Jones's vision of Reuters as the news centre of the world. For years he had talked about the need for such a building. But the long process of construction during the late 1930s was to produce noticeable friction between Jones and some of his PA colleagues. And this friction contributed to a growing atmosphere of criticism of Jones by members of the Reuter board, criticism which eventually brought about his downfall in 1941.

The new building was intended for joint use by Reuter and the PA, with Reuters requiring by far the greater space. Jones had hoped to keep the land and building under Reuter control; but instead it emerged in PA ownership, with Reuters simply as tenants. The Reuter board had agreed on 11 December 1934 that Jones should submit a plan in writing to the PA. But the PA board meeting on 11 January 1935 did not accept the idea of a long lease for Reuters, and eventually decided to go ahead with the scheme as a purely PA-financed venture. This PA board meeting was attended by the same five men as had attended the Reuter board meeting on 11 December. They had listened to Jones at the one meeting and turned him down at the other.

Jones was thus rebuffed early. Nevertheless, his enthusiasm for the project never diminished. He was appointed chairman of a joint PA–Reuter building committee. This involved him in much extra work during the next four years. He visited the site at weekends, climbing ladders energetically to check progress. The final total cost of about £500,000 was far in excess of original estimates. Some hint of the accompanying boardroom tension was given by Jones in a letter to Buchan, dated 27 November 1937:

> There is an underground tendency in certain quarters to treat the structure as a Press Association Building, quite as much as a Reuter Building, if indeed not more so.
>
> This is due partly to a complex of senior PA executives, and partly to the fact that new PA directors, who do not know the early history of this enterprise, year by year come on to the Reuter Board to take the place of older Directors well acquainted with its origins.

This comment by Jones was revealing. He was still trying to pretend that the venture was chiefly a Reuter concern. Here was another instance of his capacity for self-deception. The new directors were doing no more than taking the fact of PA ownership as they found it.

Even over the choice of architect Jones ran into difficulties. His nominee was his friend Sir Edwin Lutyens, the architect who had designed New Delhi and who had also lavishly reconstructed the interior of Jones's London house at Hyde Park Gate. The Reuter directors were not so sure about Lutyens. They were concerned about the day-to-day interior functioning of the building at least as much as about its exterior grandeur. In the event, a compromise was reached. Lutyens was made responsible for the structure, including the outside appearance and the decorations: Smee and Houchin, who had recently designed the inside of Bush House, prepared the working interior.

Lutyens's first sketch was too elaborately expensive even for Jones. A second sketch, which became the basis for the completed building, was rather more restrained. It sought both to overcome the constriction of the site area and to blend with Wren's adjacent church of St Bride's. At a late stage the upper levels of the building were cut back to meet a complaint from the Dean and Chapter of St Paul's that it would obstruct the view of the cathedral from Fleet Street. The outline gently converged from pavement to cornice, the facing blocks of Portland stone being cut at a slight angle. This, in Jones's view, achieved distinction without ostentation.

There were eight floors to be shared with the PA inside the new building, linked by four 'fast' lifts of which Jones was very proud. Reuters rented almost 40,000 square feet out of the 72,000 available. Jones professed disappointment when the PA insisted upon a full economic charge;

eventually £20,200 was agreed, plus half-rents of £600 for the basement and £500 for the restaurant. Departments were transferred from Carmelite Street in stages during the first half of July 1939, the editorial staff moving into the fifth floor on Sunday, 9 July.

The layout of the editorial resembled that at Carmelite Street, but was more spacious. For incoming news, a pneumatic tube ran from the Post Office headquarters at St Martin's-le-Grand; five teleprinters were linked to receive news from the cable companies; and there were seven sound-proofed telephone cabinets. Outgoing messages prepared by the General News Desk were typed in sextuplet on flimsies and each sheet from these 'sandwiches' went to a separate destination. The top copy was slipped by the chief sub-editor through a slot in the partition immediately behind him, and was taken by the operator on duty to the dispatch room, where it was typed out and transmitted by teleprinter to the London newspaper offices.

II

By the late 1930s Jones was losing the confidence of his fellow directors, and also of the British Government. In the early days of PA ownership the provincial newspapermen on the Reuter board seem to have been mesmerized by him. Then during 1933–4 came his mishandling of relations with AP, and his authority was never quite the same again.

Jones's sixtieth birthday fell in October 1937. He had negotiated a new five-year contract in 1936, still more favourable to himself. For the present, there was no suitable successor available within Reuters. But his performance and future were now under increasing private discussion by the directors. These included several PA newspapermen of markedly higher calibre than most of those who had served on the board previously. Among the new men was Alexander McLean Ewing (1870–1960) of the *Glasgow Herald*. He had first joined the Reuter board in 1932 and continued until 1945. He was a good conciliator, and his talents in this regard were to prove invaluable. Jones regarded him as a friend; yet Ewing always remained determined to put the interests of Reuters before those of friendship, a priority which Jones never quite grasped.

Another newcomer was Samuel Storey (1896–1978) of Portsmouth and Sunderland Newspapers Limited. He had joined the Reuter board in 1935, and quickly became the most unqualified critic of Jones. As well as being chairman of his family newspaper group, he was a Conservative Member of Parliament for over thirty years, becoming a prominent

back-bencher and ending up as deputy speaker. For his political services
he was made a life peer in 1966, taking the title of Lord Buckton. On the
board of Reuters he quickly decided that Jones must be removed so that
changes could be introduced; he hoped himself to become chairman.
Jones soon saw the danger and began to speak strongly in private against
his enemy. James Henderson of the *Belfast News-Letter*, a board member
from 1936, emerged as Storey's closest supporter.

William John Haley (1901–87) joined the Reuter board in 1939. He
was to become the most formidable of Jones's critics. Like Storey, Haley
was ambitious for Reuters and for himself. He was a self-made newspaperman, who had started in 1919 as a copy-taker on *The Times*. By 1930
he was managing editor of the *Manchester Evening News*. This was owned
by the *Manchester Guardian*, and so gave Haley a prestigious background.

At meetings of the Reuter board Haley began to ask searching questions and to expect full answers. He was particularly sensitive about the
good name of Reuters, and told Jones with conviction on 11 November
1939:

> From my earliest days as a journalist, I was imbued with the tradition of
> Reuter's accuracy. So are most other journalists—to such a point that in
> the more responsible papers a sensational flash will often be held up a
> moment or two 'to see if we get confirmation from Reuters'. Such a repu-
> tation is the most valuable asset Reuters has.

Throughout his career Haley was to be high-principled, perceptive,
and determined. This combination of strong qualities sometimes caused
friction, the more so as he possessed no talent for small talk. But Haley's
strength was much used during his comparatively short period on the
board of Reuters, even though formally he was never more than a part-
time director. He resigned in 1943 upon becoming editor-in-chief of the
BBC, being promoted to director-general in the next year. In 1952 he
returned to newspaper work as editor of *The Times*. Haley thus served
three great media organizations in succession. He implemented great
reforms in each one.

III

During the late 1930s Reuters was under a variety of pressures. Financial
crises recurred. In 1936 Hatt instructed correspondents to cut wordage by
a quarter, 'not by ignoring stories but by covering them more briefly'.
There was never any margin to meet emergencies. This was demonstrated at the time of the Munich crisis in September 1938, when a great

extra effort had to be made. The estimated loss for the month reached £3,861.

Long before the Munich crisis, Jones wanted to circulate more Reuter news to compete with the propaganda coming from the German and other foreign agencies. He told the 1938 annual general meeting plainly: 'We must have more money if we are to extend our organisation.' Informed opinion recognized that Reuters needed help. For example, Sir Arthur Willert, a former head of the Press Department at the Foreign Office, explained the difficulties in a collection of essays entitled *The Empire and the World*, published in 1937. Willert rejected all forms of subsidy for Reuters, but he accepted that Reuters and the other British news agencies were justified in asking for cheap rates for their wireless transmissions, when even the Americans enjoyed cheap transmission rates across the Pacific and to South America. In 1939 the subsidized French, German, Italian, Japanese, and Russian agencies were each carrying between 5,000 and 6,000 words per day, compared with 3,000 from Reuters.

Jones and his colleagues liked to claim that Reuters offered a superior service, and would do even better with help. The British Government was not so sure. In March 1937 Anthony Eden, the foreign secretary, told one Reuter director, Arthur Mann of the *Yorkshire Post*, that 'Reuter is not always dependable'; Mann passed the comment to Jones. In October 1935 Sir Samuel Hoare, the previous foreign secretary, had complained about Major Jim Barnes, who had been chosen as a Reuter correspondent to cover the war between Italy and Abyssinia. Barnes, wrote Hoare concernedly, was 'generally regarded as an ardent Italian propagandist'. Hoare was right: Barnes's book on *The Universal Aspects of Fascism*, published in 1928, had contained a foreword by Mussolini. Jones explained to Hoare on 19 October that Barnes's 'valuable connections' were one reason why he was being sent to report from the Italian side. 'Barnes is now sufficiently trained in Reuter ways to know that his first duty is to be accurate, objective, and dispassionate.' Barnes left Reuters when his contract expired in 1937. Jones told him on 27 April that, although there was no complaint about his work, he was 'unfitted by personality' for a Reuter career in which he would be expected always to show objectivity. Barnes subsequently adopted Italian nationality and broadcast from Italy in support of the Fascist cause during the Second World War.

Also in 1935 came a blunder from the Paris office. Gordon Waterfield, the number two correspondent, telegraphed that the French prime minister had handed to the British ambassador proposals from Mussolini for a settlement of the Italo-Abyssinian dispute. Waterfield's only authority was a report in the *Paris-Soir*: this was a doubtful source. But the damage was made worse because Reuters issued the story without naming any source at all, which gave an impression of authority. On 25 October Jones wrote in agitation to Randal Neale, the chief Paris correspondent, exclaiming that surely Waterfield must have known that any statement coming from Reuters with the introduction 'It is understood', was always taken as officially inspired. Jones condemned this as 'one of the most criminal blunders ever committed in the history of the Agency . . . I cannot recall its equal.' Sir John Simon, the home secretary, assured the House of Commons on 24 October 1935 that there was 'no truth in this wild exaggeration at all'. The sorry episode of the Hoare–Laval Pact, concluded and repudiated a few weeks later, suggests that the story was not so 'wild'.

The Foreign Office did not forget mistakes by Reuters, real or alleged. Ministers came and went, but the permanent officials stayed, and their opinions mattered. For example, Rex Leeper, head of the Press Department, was a persistent and influential critic of Reuters. He favoured the British Official Wireless and also Extel.

On 28 November 1936 Eden invited Jones for a talk at the Foreign Office. Jones wrote up a full account. The foreign secretary began by saying that two Reuter stories had recently been discussed in Cabinet— one alleging that the Government was contemplating a naval agreement with Italy, the other about naval movements in the Mediterranean. Both reports were wrong, and both had been embarrassing because on the Continent (as Eden reminded Jones) what Reuters published about the British Government was taken as officially inspired. Jones admitted the mistakes.

He then widened the discussion. He told Eden that the maintenance of Reuter standards was becoming ever more difficult. Reuters was fighting for survival overseas; it needed to do well there since little more than 10 per cent of its revenue came from the United Kingdom newspapers. Jones emphasized that Reuters did not want a subsidy, but it did want a 'revised and strengthened' relationship with the British Government. The Germans had feared Reuters in the last war, recollected Jones, and the agency hoped to be no less effective 'next time'. He concluded by claiming that Reuters was getting the worst of all worlds. It was a target for complaints from the Foreign Office, and yet it was not helped to compete effectively upon the international news scene.

Despite Jones's representations there was no response from the Foreign Office during the first ten months of 1937. In April the indiscriminate

German bombing of Guernica during the Spanish Civil War produced another widely publicized blunder from Reuters. Its first report gave the type numbers of the planes involved (Heinkel 51 and 111, Junkers 52) as the numbers engaged. The Germans were able to hide behind derision at this foolish mistake.

Finally, in November 1937 Jones took what he described in his reminiscences as the 'extreme step' of appealing directly to the prime minister, Neville Chamberlain. After an interview with Chamberlain on 17 November Jones sent him a short *aide-mémoire*. This emphasized the threat to British news throughout the world from subsidized foreign competition. Havas was getting £250,000 a year in subsidy; Deutsches Nachrichtenbüro (DNB), the Nazi agency which had replaced the Wolff bureau, probably received even more. Although foreign newspapers still wanted to take Reuter news 'because of its reputation for accuracy and independence', they were being tempted to prefer news from Paris or Berlin 'for which they paid nothing'. Such news was often anti-British. Jones ended by repeating the now familiar request, asking not for a subsidy but for special transmission rates from the British Post Office.

Eden prepared a memorandum entitled 'British News Abroad', dated 8 December 1937, for a Cabinet meeting on 15 December. This paper reiterated the old Foreign Office concern that Reuters served as a vehicle for propaganda from its associated agencies. A close check would be necessary, Eden argued, to stifle such propaganda. He believed that Reuters would be willing to enter into 'an informal agreement to this effect'. Looking more widely, Eden suggested that a Cabinet committee under Sir Kingsley Wood should consider whether it was desirable 'to assist Reuters to enlarge their service of news to foreign countries'. In particular, the committee should recommend whether Reuters ought to be granted reduced rates for use of the Rugby transmitter. Eden commented that this 'would be practically equivalent to the grant of a subsidy'. The outcome was that Jones met the Kingsley Wood committee, and asked for Government help for Reuters to send 6,000 words per day to the Continent and 6,000 words to the rest of the world—a sixfold increase.

Jones thought that he had impressed the committee concerning the urgent needs of Reuters. So he had. But he had not yet realized the lack of confidence in official circles over his own leadership. In the eyes of the Government, and particularly of the Foreign Office, his replacement had become imperative. There had been too many blunders, and he had made powerful enemies.

This was revealed to him at an interview on 30 March 1938 with Sir Horace Wilson, the senior civil servant who was Chamberlain's confidant. Wilson noted that the revelation shocked Jones. 'He was not conscious of any need for any change.' Whereas in 1916 the British Government had worked to keep Jones at Reuters, now it wanted him to go. Jones was alerted. Henceforward, in his negotiations with the Government on behalf of Reuters he was also negotiating to save himself. On both counts he conducted himself with characteristic tenacity and adroitness.

Jones was prepared to negotiate, but not to abdicate. A peerage was hinted at, if he would accept some titular role within Reuters— 'President', 'Governor'. Jones turned this round by hinting at the appropriateness of the award of a peerage in return for implementing his own ideas. In a memorandum sent to the Foreign Office, dated 12 June 1938, 'Upon a Possible Financial Relationship between the Government and Reuters in the National Interest', he argued that although Reuters could not take subsidies, it could accept more subscriptions from embassies and colonial governments. The long-standing relationship with the Government of India, claimed Jones, had demonstrated that this could be done 'without derogation from Reuters' unofficial status'. With the increased revenue thus made available, Reuters could extend its services and reinforce its representation overseas.

All Jones's thinking assumed that he would continue in office as chairman—even if not as managing director—for up to ten more years. This was not what the Foreign Office wanted. In consequence, the arguments about the future of Reuters continued inconclusively throughout the spring and summer of 1938. Meanwhile the Foreign Office looked about for possible outside successors to Jones, either as chairman or as managing director. Moloney and Turner, the only obvious internal candidates, were ruled out as inadequate. Among possible outsiders, Leeper suggested Douglas Crawford, who had once been a protégé of Lord Northcliffe's. But Wilson dismissed Crawford on 11 July 1938 as 'quite one of N's worst!'

Both Jones and the Foreign Office agreed that British news services to key areas, such as eastern Europe and South America, needed improvement. Both sides also agreed that the independence of Reuters must not seem to be compromised in the eyes of the world. Jones, for his part, insisted that a real distinction might be drawn between unspecific subsidies, on the one hand, and specific payments for additional services or extra transmissions, on the other. He contended in a memorandum for

the Reuter board of 27 July 1938 that this was 'not hair-splitting . . . let
the Government straightforwardly pay Reuters for news services rendered
as they would pay a shipyard for building a cruiser'. Jones claimed that
until recently he would have resisted even payments of this kind. But
now the democracies had been made to understand that 'a great international news agency is an important instrument of policy'.

So far Jones had shown a willingness to discuss every proposal—except
his own total retirement—that came from the Government. But his
stance at any one moment must not be taken as necessarily representing
his real mind. He was a supple negotiator, always probing. When the
Munich crisis erupted in September 1938, he tried a change of tack.
Instead of talk he offered action: he pressed to be allowed to distribute an
enlarged wireless service of news overseas. Sir Horace Wilson agreed at
once ('World opinion is uncertain, and we must not run any risks'), and
the service began on the very next day, 22 September. Reuter wordage
was trebled, from 1,000 to 3,000 words per day. The extra wordage was
given the address 'Globereut'.

After the crisis had passed, Jones tried to exploit this breakthrough by
urging ministers to make the arrangement permanent, at an annual cost
of £25,000 plus Post Office charges. Ministers and civil servants disagreed
among themselves. Kingsley Wood was in favour, whereas Lord Halifax,
the foreign secretary, was reported by Leeper on 2 February 1939 as saying that the sum was too small to compete with DNB, 'too large to
escape criticism and to avoid the discrediting of Reuters as an independent service'.

At the end of 1938, and again in March 1939, questions were asked in
the House of Commons about the enlarged service which Reuters had
provided at the time of the Munich crisis. In general, the House was in
favour of some permanent arrangement with Reuters. Storey, speaking as
a Reuter director as well as a Member of Parliament, presented the case
well. Nevertheless, even as late as the summer of 1939, with war only
weeks away, nothing had been agreed.

Ministers and civil servants now decided that they must negotiate
urgently for a simple settlement. They had reluctantly accepted that Jones
could not be displaced for the present. Instead, he was to be encouraged
to appoint a younger additional general manager as a prospective successor, a man acceptable to the Government. Chancellor was emerging as
this mutually acceptable figure. On 2 August 1939 Jones sent a 'Note on
Mr Christopher Chancellor' to the Foreign Office. Jones praised his
'most efficient administration' in the Far East, and added that Chancellor

was personally known to R. A. Butler, the foreign under-secretary, and to Lord Perth, the director-general designate of the revived Ministry of Information. Jones assumed that these connections would assist the defence of his own position. In the event, Chancellor was to use his influence in high places not to protect Jones, but to undermine him.

IV

The Reuter board met on 12 September 1939, nine days after the British declaration of war on Germany. How could the agency support the war effort without compromising its independence? This question was now being asked by the directors with an insistence not found during the First World War. Increasingly irritated by Jones's autocratic style, they suspected that he might already have committed them too far. In advance of the meeting, Ewing, the deputy chairman, circulated a memorandum to the other directors, but not to Jones. This surveyed the one-sided relationship between the PA and Jones since the 1925 purchase. It concluded that he had then sold out at a very favourable valuation, and had since been remunerated over-generously. 'I doubt if any Director has ever had the temerity to ask what his "commission" amounted to.'

On 12 September Jones put to the board, for retroactive approval, a 'Memorandum of Arrangements relating to the provision of additional services by Reuters at the request of His Majesty's Government'. This had been finalized between Jones and the Foreign Office days before the outbreak of war; it dealt with news supply and payments. But accompanying the memorandum was a 'private and confidential' letter which Jones did not circulate to the board, dated 24 August, from Lord Perth 'setting out certain understandings which, although unnecessary in the formal document, are an integral part of the arrangements'. This, the 'Perth letter', was to have momentous repercussions for Jones and Reuters eighteen months later.

A copy of the letter has survived in Jones's papers, annotated by him at the time. These annotations show, what he was always to insist, that he did not accept all of Perth's conditions. Furthermore, as he was also to insist, Jones never acknowledged the letter. In the hectic circumstances of the outbreak of war, the ministry seems simply to have assumed that Reuters had taken the letter as binding, even though Perth had ended in terms which required confirmation from Jones and a further letter from himself: 'On hearing from you that you concur in the above I will give instructions for the issue of an official letter inviting

Reuters to enter into arrangements on the lines embodied in the enclosed Memorandum.'

The Reuter board meeting of 12 September accepted these memorandum proposals. Jones emphasized that this would be a sound business deal, bringing in over £18,000 each year. He had earlier spoken to the board of getting much more, even £100,000; but any larger sum, he now explained virtuously, could only have been obtained by the sacrifice of independence. Jones did not reveal the existence of the Perth letter. Why not? Because, as he later explained in self-defence, it was a draft, not a finalized proposal. According to the board minutes, he mentioned only 'verbal discussions' extending over two years, which 'might well' come to be confirmed 'in private correspondence between the Secretary of State and himself'.

Jones did read out in full the key clause B of the Perth letter, but without revealing its context: he explained only that this undertaking had been accepted by him as 'verbally understood'. The clause declared that Reuters 'will at all times bear in mind any suggestions made to them on behalf of His Majesty's Government as to the development or orientation of their news service or as to the topics or events which from time to time may require particular attention'. Jones marked this passage 'Yes' in his own copy; and after prolonged discussion on 12 September he persuaded the Reuter board that he would never accept official direction on the strength of the words 'bear in mind'. He reminded the board that 'Reuters has always taken into account the official point of view, but never to the surrender of their own final judgment and independence'.

There were four other clauses in the Perth letter, none of which Jones revealed on 12 September. Clause C simply covered effective use of transmission time (annotated 'Yes'); clause D ('Yes') left the Government free to employ other agencies as well as Reuters. Clause A proposed that an additional general manager be appointed, who would be superior to the two existing managers, Turner and Moloney. The new man was to be 'in immediate charge' of the new arrangements, and was to be designated chief general manager within eighteen months. Jones marked this proposal 'No'. And he put double question marks after a sentence urging separation within five years of the offices of chairman and managing director. Jones added at the foot of the page: 'If HMG terminate the contract in a year or at any time we are saddled with the consequences of A. This is not sensible.'

So Jones had important reservations about clause A—no doubt for the sake of Reuters, but also for reasons of self-preservation. None the less, in the national interest, he was prepared to respond as far as he thought prudent. A postscript to the letter said that Perth had now heard of Jones's intention to appoint Chancellor to the clause A post. This would be 'acceptable to His Majesty's Government'. Jones seems to have told Chancellor about his intention on 28 August.

When knowledge of the Perth letter leaked out to the board in 1941, Jones was condemned for being willing to tolerate such secret Government interference in the making of senior appointments. Did Chancellor, the chief beneficiary of Jones's fall, himself know about the Perth letter at this time? Probably not. Did he at least know—if not from Jones, then from his friends in high places—that he was officially endorsed as well as being Jones's personal choice? Probably.

Jones announced the appointment of Chancellor as a third (but not senior) general manager to the board on 3 October 1939. The members acquiesced; but the way Jones had simply invited Chancellor to attend recent board meetings, and had now 'decided' to make this appointment, angered the directors. Dissatisfaction with Jones's high-handedness became open. Ewing, as deputy chairman, was sent to tell Jones that the right to make such appointments lay with the board, and that he must never again take such unilateral action. Jones was genuinely surprised, having down the years (as he wrote in an *aide-mémoire*) effected 'about a dozen' such senior appointments in this way. He made no mention of the reference to Chancellor in the Perth letter, which he was now treating as inoperative. Perth himself had survived as director-general for only a few days after the outbreak of war.

Losses were again mounting, and at an informal meeting between Jones and the directors on 6 November 1939 they demanded to be given more information about Reuter business. From January 1940 Jones provided monthly reports. Two accounts of the 6 November meeting have survived, one by Haley, the other by Jones. Haley's version reveals Jones to have been pressed hard, with the directors leaving him on probation: 'they proposed to leave everything over for the time being.' His own account was more self-indulgent: 'as I have always assumed, I am there for life if I choose'.

Jones obviously thought that he could still dominate the Reuter board. His error suddenly became clear to him on 10 April 1940. On that day he was told by Ewing and Henderson at a hurriedly called private meeting that he had lost the confidence of the directors, and should resign. He described himself in a letter to Ewing on 12 April as '*thunderstruck . . . a very dark hour for me, the darkest in my life!*' When pressed for reasons,

Ewing and Henderson blamed Jones's autocratic personality for stifling initiatives put forward by the general managers. Jones's arrogance, added Ewing and Henderson, had aggravated the crisis with AP in 1933–4. Jones denied the charges, and demanded to meet the full Reuter board next day at the Victoria Hotel.

His is the only record of this confrontation. Jones had now realized that the three general managers had been complaining to the directors over his head. 'Chancellor and Turner, I am told, have chimed in with all this, and Moloney made an impression upon the 3 directors by his intensity on the subject.' Jones found Chancellor's action 'the most hurting . . . I have cherished him'. Jones wondered about going to law, but reluctantly decided to accept retirement if unavoidable—so long as it was hon-ourable, and the financial terms were good. It was on 24 April that he drew up, for his own eyes alone, his memorandum on 'What I have done for Reuters'. The fact that Jones was now thinking in terms of gratitude in business showed how much he had been shaken.

At the Victoria Hotel meeting Jones defended himself at length against the charges of being a dictator; the directors declined to argue. Jones was told that his resignation was expected: 'The sooner the better,' said Herbert Staines, the current PA chairman. This gave Jones a chance to divide his critics. It was not fair to rush him: 'The whole of my career was at stake.' Ewing was sympathetic. Eventually it was agreed that no announcement would be made until the annual meeting on 2 July. Jones was now manœuvring—at best to save his job, at worst to get good retirement terms (£5,000 a year: half his present remuneration). He floated the idea of at least retaining the chairmanship. Storey was identified as 'the Arch-Enemy'. Haley, noted Jones, needed careful han-dling.

Jones poured out his sense of shock at a private meeting with Ewing. Jones mentioned the names of several respected national newspapermen whom he regarded as friends, and to whom he might turn—notably Astor of *The Times* and Lord Camrose of the *Daily Telegraph*. On hearing this, Ewing became worried, although he did not reveal this to Jones. Afterwards, Ewing told Staines that mention of these friends had made him wonder whether the directors were being prudent in seeking to remove Jones so brusquely. Astor and Camrose might well persuade the Newspaper Proprietors Association that the Reuter board had acted unwisely. The NPA might then 'become much more unfriendly than it already is'. The national newspaper owners were well known to have a low opinion of the judgement of the provincial newspapermen. Ewing began to recommend delay. The board, he now argued, should use the excuse of the disastrous course of the war during the spring and summer of 1940 to retain Jones in office for the time being. Very reluctantly, the other directors agreed to this reversal of attitude, but only under threat of resignation from Ewing.

Jones was reprieved. The date of his departure was postponed—probably until the end of 1941, when his contract expired and when he could retire without loss of face. His hopes revived: perhaps he could contrive to stay on longer still, at least as chairman. On 31 July 1940, according to Jones's account, Ewing even assured him privately that he had regained the confidence of all the directors, excepting Storey: 'he believed they were thankful that they had been saved from making a bad blunder.' Had Ewing really gone so far? This may have been another instance of Jones hearing what he wanted to hear.

The day before, Jones had boldly read the board a lecture, deploring the way he had been treated and insisting upon a *modus vivendi* for the future. This, he announced blandly, involved him in taking steps to pave the way for his retirement as managing director. He proposed that in future the general managers should report directly to the board. One of them might eventually be designated chief general manager, and thereafter Jones might hand over to him as managing director, while remaining as chairman. This was an adroit scheme. It seemed to meet many of the board's wishes; yet it sought endorsement for Jones to remain at the centre for a further long period. The directors were adroit in turn. They welcomed the proposal for more delegation, but contended in an immediate written answer of 30 July that because of the uncertain national situation 'it would not be in the best interests of Reuters for there to be at this stage any precise scheme regarding the future'.

In the autumn of 1940 the directors resumed their pressure. They decided to insist that Jones's contract should not be renewed. He would therefore retire at the end of 1941. This was the inoffensive yet decisive course. The necessary formal notice was given to Jones in November 1940. Even after this, he still retained hopes of surviving as chairman. In the event, he was not destined to survive in any post for more than a further three months.

The Ministry of Information was now aiming to play a more positive part in promoting publicity for Britain overseas. A new director-general, Frank Pick, had been briefed about the Jones problem. Nevertheless, the two men seem to have got on well during detailed discussions about a new Reuter contract. On 5 December 1940 Jones put to the board proposed 'Heads of agreement', to which he added a clause-by-clause commentary. Reuters was to be split into two halves. All Government-supported services were to be conducted separately, but still under the umbrella of one overall Reuter management. Jones expressed satisfaction with this separation plan. Any problems in working were to be submitted to a joint standing committee, which was to hold frequent regular meetings. Nevertheless, the committee was not, as Pick had originally intended, to be given any power to interfere. Jones assured the board on 5 November, and repeated to Ewing on 28 November, that he had made 'short work' of a proposal to appoint a Government director. He did not reveal that this had been the 1916 arrangement.

No member of the board liked the Pick draft as it stood, despite Jones's insistence that the independence of Reuters was not threatened. Without telling Jones, the directors had met privately in Leeds on 4 December. Also without telling him, they sent Storey to talk to Pick and Wilson. Jones heard about the visit, but thought that Storey was acting on his own initiative. Eventually Storey, Haley, and Jones were appointed to a subcommittee which met Sir Walter Monckton, Pick's successor, on 14 January 1941. The three men had been given authority to continue the talks about an agreement with the Government.

On the previous day Jones ventured upon an off-the-record meeting with Monckton. According to his own account, Jones told Monckton that he had always insisted upon complete independence for Reuters, but that Storey 'for his own ends had worked up the feelings of the rest of the Board in order to undermine my position, and he had made them fearful of the Government's intentions where there was no ground for fear'. Jones was obviously trying to ingratiate himself with Monckton; yet he was probably unwise to reveal the extent of his own insecurity within Reuters. Monckton was among those who wanted him to retire, and he knew more than Jones realized. Chancellor had been so revealingly hostile about Jones in official quarters that Sir Alan Barlow of the Treasury had even warned him on 12 October 1940 to 'refrain from any further overt action'. Not surprisingly, Monckton seems to have decided to exploit the disarray on the Reuter side—perhaps to get favourable terms, at least to get rid of Jones.

So Monckton opened a second meeting with the subcommittee on 20 January 1941 by casually referring to the Perth letter of 24 August 1939 as part of the existing arrangements now under revision. Storey was absent; Haley and Jones exclaimed that they knew of no such letter. Haley may have meant 'no letter at all': Jones meant 'no *binding* letter'. The revelation of its existence was made to seem innocent on Monckton's part, but probably was not. Haley's 1981 *Dictionary of National Biography* article on Jones summed up tersely: 'The Ministry deliberately betrayed him.'

Four days later the subcommittee met Monckton again, this time with Storey present. The status of the Perth letter quickly came under discussion. Jones recorded the exchanges. 'Monckton was under the impression that I had accepted that letter.' Jones insisted that he had not even replied to it; he urged that they should now start afresh: to no avail. 'Storey and Haley clearly wanted to delve into the past, so I said I certainly would see what my file produced.'

On 29 January Jones visited Monckton to explain what the file had revealed: 'There were points in the draft which I wished to alter . . . Meanwhile a week later war was declared, and everybody's idea, both Government and ours, was to get on with the work. The Perth letter was never mentioned again—we all forgot about it. In any case I never answered it.'

This explanation was not good enough for Storey and Haley. They persuaded the other directors—Ewing, Staines, Henderson, W. R. Derwent, and F. C. Whittaker—that Jones, in his arrogance, had deliberately deceived them: he had not revealed the full extent of his concessions to the Government in 1939. An overview written by Ewing after Jones's resignation took it for a fact that Jones had accepted the Perth letter 'over the telephone', and had later confirmed his acceptance in writing. No such confirmatory letter has been found and none was sent. Jones was telling the truth. He was not believed.

On the morning of 3 February 1941 Storey and Haley asked to see Jones to discuss the minutes of the meeting of 24 January. This proved to be the decisive encounter, which ended Jones's resistance. He has left the only account; folk memory within Reuters has wrongly placed these exchanges at the board meeting next day. Storey began by asking about 'these letters covering the Government contract'. Jones answered that there were 'no letters . . . only a draft letter'. He showed a carbon copy of the Perth letter, which Storey and Haley read carefully and which Storey kept. 'They maintained that I should have disclosed paragraph A (CJC etc.) to the Board as well as paragraph B.' Jones argued that he had still been in negotiation. He had not wanted to place Chancellor over Turner or Moloney. 'Also I did not feel we should be left saddled with this and its consequences while the Government had the power to terminate the contract any year.'

These were indeed points which Jones had scribbled on his own copy of the letter at the time. 'I reported to the Board the essential clause B, which was to my mind the essence of the "Gentlemen's agreement", and I also at the following meeting reported my appointment of CJC':

> At one stage after repeated reassertion of complaint by Storey and Haley, I said to Haley, in reply to an invidious remark he made: 'Do you suggest that I deliberately concealed this from the Board?'
>
>   Haley: 'Yes, I do.'
>
>   Jones: 'Then I can only say that I am sorry for you. I did no such thing.'

This time the loss of confidence was clearly final.

Had Jones really sacrificed the independence of Reuters, and then deceived the board about it? His many *aides-mémoires* from the period— written for himself alone—show clearly that he sincerely believed in his own success in preserving the independence of Reuters. If he was deceiving the board, he was also deceiving himself.

At the board meeting next day, 4 February 1941, Jones quietly submitted his resignation. Three years later (3 March 1944) he explained to Ewing that he was 'too tired and disheartened after the harassing events of the previous year, too exhausted and utterly disgusted to do anything but resign'. Staines had remarked to Ewing on 10 December 1940 that Jones was in poor health, and 'could not combat the present position as he would have done in ordinary times'. Jones made only one stipulation—that he should be paid his full salary until the end of the year, followed by the agreed good pension thereafter. Both sides agreed not to issue any public explanations.

It was ironic that a revelation about how Jones had allegedly compromised the independence of Reuters in relation to the British Government should have come from the Government itself. It was ironic, too, that Jones should have been blamed for supposedly promoting Chancellor under Government pressure, when he did so not because he had to, but because he wanted to. It was further ironic that Chancellor then actively conspired with the Government against him.

Jones himself saw another irony. He argued in his reminiscences that it was his very success in resisting the Government which 'increased the doggedness of elements in Whitehall bent upon bringing Reuters under subjection'. This intention, he believed, had required his own removal. In reality the Government wanted him removed, as did his critics within Reuters, so that its services could be improved.

V

If only Jones had retired on his sixtieth birthday in 1937, his period of personal rule over Reuters would have ended in harmony. His style could even have been defended as unsurprising in his day. Sir John Reith's autocratic management at the BBC in the same period has been accepted as much more beneficial than damaging. Jones, for his part, believed that Reith was far more autocratic than himself. The two men were, of course, pursuing quite different objectives. Reith was creating a new inheritance: Jones was defending an old one.

Jones was never given the peerage which he long expected would be his reward for serving the British Empire through Reuters. His claims were put forward more than once by political friends—Amery, Buchan, and others. In 1936 his name seems to have figured in a draft new year's honours list, only to be taken out at the last moment. Jones's name was withdrawn perhaps because the Government wished to retain the prospect of a peerage as bait while pressing him to retire. He had apparently decided to take the title of 'Lord Rottingdean', from the Sussex seaside village where he owned a house. His family jested that he would become 'Lord Rotters of Reuters'.

After his enforced retirement in 1941 Jones's friends tried again. Chancellor—a protégé, but not a friend—was asked for his opinion. Chancellor described his reaction in an interview in 1976. 'I told them what an awful man he was. How he'd been destroying Reuters, and couldn't possibly get one. He didn't.'

NINE

News between the Wars

1919–1939

I

SHORTAGE of money had limited the range and quality of Reuter reporting before the First World War. Reporting was even more affected by financial constraints between the wars—at a time when competition was strengthening from the American agencies, and from subsidized agencies in Europe and elsewhere. Roderick Jones reminded Douglas Williams on 1 March 1924 that Reuters was restricted by 'the unwillingness of the newspapers to pay more. In the last analysis the papers get what they pay for.'

Reuters could never afford to maintain as many news bureaux or to appoint as many full-time correspondents as it needed. In 1920 there were forty-three offices and bureaux throughout the world: by 1932 there were only twenty-seven. Reuters had to depend increasingly upon stringers, who were either foreign newspaper reporters, freelances, or even local businessmen. Between 1920 and 1932 their numbers more than trebled—from 70 to 234. By 1938 the number of 'resident correspondents' worldwide was 676, 282 of them in Europe. But only 19 of the latter were full-time staffers. There were staffers in twelve Indian and eight Chinese cities; but elsewhere in Asia only in Tokyo, Singapore, and Manila. A single full-time Johannesburg correspondent was expected to cover most of Africa. And there were only two staff correspondents in the United States, based in New York and Washington. Remarkably, the Washington appointment had not been made until 1937, and then with much hesitation because of the cost.

Reuters always tried to suggest that it was adequately represented throughout the world. But on 8 December 1923 a well-informed exposure appeared in the *Nation & Athenaeum*, entitled 'Reuter's Monopoly in Foreign News'. The article was widely noticed overseas as well as in the United Kingdom. Its author was Herbert Bailey, London correspondent of the *Melbourne Sun*. Bailey pointed out that most foreign news in the British papers came from Reuters. Yet, claimed Bailey, its wartime links with the British Government had been maintained. And because it had too few correspondents of its own to collect news overseas, it was forced to recycle propaganda from the foreign agencies with which it was allied by contract. These agencies were under official influence: 'we are constantly flooded with the views of foreign Governments disguised as pure news.'

There was sufficient truth in the article to make it damaging. Jones was on tour, so Buchan sent an answering letter as deputy chairman, published on 22 December. He insisted that the wartime connection with the British Government had ended. All news from foreign agencies, claimed Buchan, was 'checked and supplemented by the correspondents of Reuters'. A week later Bailey came back strongly. He contended that Reuters simply did not maintain sufficient numbers of British-born staff overseas to check the news as Buchan contended. Bailey asked Reuters to reveal how many 'Englishmen' were employed in each European country; Buchan did not respond. In 1924 Bailey became managing editor of the British United Press. He appointed correspondents worldwide, lightened the presentation of foreign news, and won for BUP a prominent place in the columns of the British press, much to the discomfort of Reuters.

Not all Reuter correspondents were good journalists. Jeans, chief editor during most of the 1920s, admitted in October 1922 that few Reuter men in Europe or elsewhere 'have had actual experience of newspaper work or have been trained to look at matters from the sub-editor's desk in a newspaper office'. They reported the facts, noted Jeans, but were often weak on background. Although Reuter correspondents were not expected to comment as freely as newspaper correspondents, 'we can be clearer and more explanatory'. When a big story broke, complained Jeans, many Reuter correspondents still waited for some related newspaper reaction, and simply reported that response. D. C. Pendrigh, the Dominions editor, demanded an end to all telegrams beginning with the tired formula from Julius Reuter's day, '*Le Matin* says'.

In a lecture to the Press Congress of the World at Geneva in 1926 Jeans claimed that improvements in cable communications and reductions in rates meant that correspondents need no longer write so tersely. A correspondent could now 'telegraph his story in his own words with all its lights and shades'. Jeans's use here of the word 'story' was significant. Correspondents were now being asked to send not 'telegrams' or 'messages': they were expected to send 'stories'—or rather, the raw material for stories. These could then be written up by the sub-editors at Carmelite Street, or in the newspaper offices.

How far could Reuters go in 'brightness'? Apparently, not very far. Roderick Jones disliked a Reuter story in the *Observer* of 4 September 1932, which told how the secretary of state for war, Lord Hailsham, had taken third place in a wild-cow milking contest at a Canadian rodeo. The dignity of Cabinet ministers, thought Jones, should be protected even against themselves.

The Reuter ideal with regard to news handling was well expressed in the contract made with SAPA in 1938. All news supplied to South Africa was to be 'independent, unbiased and impartial'. It was to be supplied in a form suitable for publication in any newspaper, 'irrespective of the political view of the paper, without modification other than curtailment'. And all Reuter services were to be free from propaganda content, 'except such as is inseparable from the fair reporting of public utterances by men of public importance or events of general news interest'.

In 1918 Reuters appointed a labour correspondent. This was Vernon Bartlett, who was to become a distinguished newspaper columnist and also a Member of Parliament. Jones had been persuaded by Bartlett that it was desirable to take an interest in left-wing politics. But, according to Bartlett's reminiscences, this was not done in order to counter the impression that Reuters was merely an official mouthpiece. On the contrary, it was done because the agency hoped to continue in that role 'after the revolution'.

II

The greatest story of 1919 had unquestionably been the peace conference at Versailles. William Turner led a strong team of correspondents. The wartime British Press Bureau had been closed down, and Reuters was selected to provide the British official summary of the peace terms, for circulation to the Empire and the world except North America. The NPA and PA relied on Reuters to cover the conference. Early on 7 May 1919 Old Jewry issued the 12,750-word official summary of the treaty. This unprecedentedly long message, split into sixty-six sections, was cabled to South Africa in four hours, and to India in eleven. Here was a great success for Reuters.

A bound volume has survived of all telegrams transmitted in 1923 to the Seychelles, a remote British colony in the Indian Ocean. A daily bulletin was compiled by the local Seychelles authorities out of the service delivered to East Africa. These telegrams provide an example of the sort of news thought appropriate for imperial outposts. The file contained a mixture of important world stories, news about the Empire, and 'home' news from the United Kingdom. Familiar names from the war years—Lloyd George, Lenin, Allenby—continued to feature regularly. But new names were appearing—Hitler, Mussolini, Mustapha Kemal, Gandhi. Reuter correspondents in Germany had already appreciated the potential importance of Hitler. They gave detailed coverage of his abortive Munich beer-hall *putsch* on 9 November:

> After the dictator Von Kahr had spoken at a large Nationalist demonstration at the Burgenbrauen Beer Cellars denouncing the Marxist principles, the Fascist leader Von Hitler entered with 600 men and announced that the Bavarian Government had been overthrown; he added that the new Government was in the hands of Ludendorff who is commander-in-chief, while Von Hitler will be his political adviser; further the chief of the Munich police, Von Poehner, has been appointed administrator, and General Von Lossow Minister of Defence. Von Hitler's troops then surrounded the cellars; later the troops of the Oberland organisation with the Reich colours occupied a number of places, particularly open spaces; there is no further news from the cellars where it is believed Von Kahr and Von Hitler are negotiating; the attitude of the Reichswehr is unknown; Bavarian police have occupied the telegraph office.

The status of Indians within the Empire was of obvious interest to the Seychelles. Reuters reported policy statements and noticed relevant letters and editorials in leading newspapers. Both the Kenya Constitutional Conference and the Imperial Conference on tariffs were handled in great detail.

British politics received full coverage in the Seychelles service—results of by-elections, House of Commons debates (especially on imperial topics), news of Bonar Law's health and of his resignation as prime minister, and of Baldwin's appointment as his successor rather than Lord Curzon. The inconclusive general election and subsequent negotiations between the political parties were treated in depth. Running stories—such as the results of the general election—were covered minute by minute. The wedding of the Duke of York (the future George VI) and Lady Elizabeth Bowes-Lyon presented an opportunity for descriptive writing; but the Seychelles file did not contain much colour or lightness. An exception was a 200-word story about Christmas Day in England, obviously aimed at expatriate colonial readers.

Most stories were straight reports, clearly sourced; but in some cases the sourcing was vague, hinting at official contacts—'Reuter learns', 'a Reuter lobbyist learns'. Occasionally, unsourced interpretative articles appeared. An example, timed 'London 31st August 6.55 a.m.', began: 'The danger of flinging lighted torches in the Balkans was not more dangerous in the days of the Sarajevo incident than today when the Lausanne Treaty has left neither Turks nor Greeks completely satisfied.' The article noted that the London newspapers deplored 'Mussolini's precipitancy' in threatening intervention against the Greeks. 'Soberer commentators believe that Mussolini will not proceed the length of his words.'

The Seychelles file contained reports of horse-racing in England throughout the season, and frequent accounts of boxing matches. The main British sporting-cum-social occasions were covered—the Derby, Wimbledon tennis, Henley rowing. The Oxford and Cambridge University boat race on 24 March was given priority, though an error crept in greatly flattering to the victors, Oxford:

6 p.m.   Boat Race: Oxford won by nearly a length.

6.20 p.m.   Boat Race: Official: Distance three quarters of a mile [sic!];
            Time: 20 min. 50 sec.

A 200-word description of the race followed at 7.20 p.m., nearly two hours after it had ended. In 1923 the Football Association cup final was played at Wembley Stadium for the first time. Seychelles readers were told how 'pressure on the terraces was so terrific that the authorities had to allow late comers to take positions on the running track whence finally they were swept over the pitch'.

In the same year the massive Tokyo earthquake destroyed three Reuter offices in Japan, but the agency still got the news out. The commercial manager in Osaka, which was not affected by the quake, managed to get in touch with Japan and Yokohama. His usual task was to supervise the transmission of London prices to Japan; but on this occasion, like many other Reuter commercial managers before and after him, he acted as a journalist in an emergency. Reuters also quoted Radio Corporation of America bulletins from San Francisco, as well as other wireless messages monitored in Peking and New York. It used news reaching Shanghai, reported a cable received by the Japanese consul-general in Liverpool, and gave earthquake measurements from a Belgian observatory. Eventually there were brief reports from the stricken cities of Yokohama and Nagasaki themselves.

The discovery in 1923 of the intact sarcophagus of the ancient Egyptian King Tutankhamun led to a great Reuter beat. Valentine

Williams had been sent to Egypt as a special correspondent, even though *The Times* had negotiated exclusive rights to the whole story. He contrived not only to obtain the news of the discovery within minutes, but also to get a 'flash' out first and quickly to the world. The climax came on 16 February, when Williams rightly guessed that the final breakthrough into the chamber would be made. Reuters had bought him a new car to speed the news from the Valley of the Kings to the western bank of the Nile. He had also hired a boat for the day to take the news across the river, and six fast donkeys as back-up. He had arranged for a local car to carry the news from the eastern bank to the cable office at Luxor. As he waited near the tomb entrance, Williams kept in his pocket two prepared cables, each marked URGENT (triple rates). One read 'Tomb empty', the other 'King's sarcophagus discovered'. Williams told in his reminiscences how he had seized his chance when he saw an Egyptian official leaving the tomb:

> I summoned to my aid one of the oldest devices of the reporter for getting at facts, the pretence of knowledge. I addressed the Egyptian in French, because French is the language of polite society in Egypt and I knew it would flatter him, and I called him 'Excellency' because thereby I implied that he was a Pasha.
>
> 'Excellency,' I said, removing my sun helmet with a bow, 'is it true that they have found two sarcophagi?'
>
> 'No, no,' replied the fat man importantly in French. 'Only one.'
>
> 'Quite plain, they tell me?'
>
> 'No, no,' he said again. 'It is magnificently decorated, all blue and gold.'

Williams dared not risk another question. He had his flash. Within thirty seconds his Egyptian assistant was on his way in the car. The London evening papers put the stop-press news on the streets even before the archaeologists had left the tomb. *The Times* retained its monopoly of subsequent descriptive stories, but Reuters had alerted the world.

There was intense competition from both Extel and the International News Service (INS) over the progress of the 1929 Wall Street crash. The New York office of Reuters provided fast and colourful coverage, while other bureaux weighed in with reaction:

> New York Tuesday [29 October]: Wall Street has never witnessed such a wild opening as this morning. Practically all the leading stocks opened with initial sales of from 10 000–15 000 shares, with average decline of up to 10 points . . . the closing gong at three o'clock ended a day of greater pandemonium, apprehension and general uncertainty than any broker has previously experienced.

Two years later Hatt was among editors summoned to 10 Downing Street on Sunday, 20 September 1931, to be told that Britain had gone off the gold standard. Reuters flashed the news round the world, well ahead of its official transmission to British representatives overseas. In India the viceroy took the necessary action on the strength of the Reuter report alone.

III

On the first day of 1931 Jones nominated for the *World's Press News* 'the ten greatest news stories of 1930'. He explained that his choice was made with the preferences of the British public exclusively in mind. His list reflected Reuter news priorities in a year which had not seen any dominating political story. Consequently, the traditional Reuter interest in disasters featured strongly: six of Jones's ten stories fell into this category. They were headed by the R101 airship crash, which Jones named as the top story of the year. Amy Johnson's flight to Australia came second, and Kingsford-Smith's victory in the race there by air was placed ninth. King Carol's dash by aeroplane to seize the Romanian throne came fourth. Only one other political story was selected by Jones—Gandhi's civil-disobedience march in India.

The rapid development of broadcasting in the United Kingdom during the 1920s and 1930s presented a challenge to the British newspapers. To what extent should the British Broadcasting Company—given semi-official status from 1927 as the British Broadcasting Corporation—be allowed to carry news bulletins? The newspaper proprietors feared that such bulletins, especially if broadcast at times when the morning and evening papers were appearing, would seriously reduce sales. Therefore should the news agencies, which supplied the newspapers, be left equally free to supply the BBC? And if they did supply news, should there not be restrictions upon BBC usage? A news-agency alliance, consisting of Reuters, PA, Extel, and Central News, was formed to find answers to these questions.

Reuters dominated this alliance. Jones had much in common with Sir John Reith, the autocratic director-general of the BBC. In their recurring negotiations the two men treated each other with warm but wary respect. Jones wrote in a memorandum on 'Sir John Reith and Broadcasting Questions' of 21 October 1927 that Reith had given the BBC 'a holy mission' to raise standards in society. Reith, noted Jones, was an admirer of Reuters; but he had his own ideas about 'what the BBC should do in news'. Increasingly the initiative was with Reith. The news agencies found themselves conducting a long rearguard action.

The first agreement to supply news to the BBC was made on 11 November 1922. The service was to consist of 1,200–2,000 words per day, supplied by the four agencies through Reuters. Payment was to be made on a sliding scale related to the number of wireless receivers licensed, with a minimum payment of £4,000. There was a verbal understanding that no news was to be broadcast before 7 p.m., and each bulletin was to include the acknowledgement 'Copyright News from Reuters, Press Association, Exchange Telegraph and Central News'.

This formula was eventually reduced to 'copyright reserved'. Jones told the 1935 Ullswater Committee on Broadcasting that the purpose was to prevent listeners from taking down and publishing any broadcast news. He explained that the agencies were really trying to stand on property right rather than on copyright, since copyright related only to the form of words, not to content. The agencies claimed property right so long as an item had news value. That right, they argued, was not automatically abandoned on first publication, either in print or over the air. Such a right of property had been established in United States law by a Supreme Court decision obtained by AP in 1918. Between the wars Jones campaigned for the acceptance of this right in English law.

In the early years the newspapers and news agencies were very reluctant to allow the BBC to report events as they happened by means of outside broadcasts. Meetings of newspaper and news agency representatives with Reith (4 November 1924 and 20 February 1925) insisted that this was 'their province'. Some curious compromises were negotiated:

> Regarding the Derby, the Company could microphone what might be termed natural sounds—the noise of the horses' hoofs, the shouts of the crowd, and so forth—and the Agencies would not object to the microphoning also of manufactured sounds, consisting of burlesques by John Henry and other comedians, very much as was done with the Lord Mayor's show.

Such extreme restrictions could not last for long. The first running commentary was broadcast in January 1927.

The general strike of 1926 had given a great boost to the aspirations of the BBC. Few newspapers had appeared during the strike, and the first news both of its starting and of its ending came from the BBC. All restrictions upon the times of news bulletins were temporarily relaxed. The BBC organized an emergency news room, and gathered its own material for the first time. Afterwards it pressed for the right to edit the news supplied by the agencies. It began to complain about both content and presentation. 'In the BBC mind,' wrote Valentine Harvey, the broadcasting editor of Reuters, on 30 January 1929, 'the Agencies are no longer "the news" but are merely contributors to a BBC news service.' The agencies formally accepted this new reality at the end of 1929. The BBC agreed to add an extra £2,000 to the £14,000 annual subscription which it had paid since 1927. In place of a 5,000-word news selection, the BBC was to be supplied with the full agency services.

From 1927 the BBC was broadcasting to the British Empire. At first the agencies refused to allow news bulletins to be included in the service. Here was another extreme restriction that could not be maintained: the agencies gave way in 1930.

In March 1929 atmospherics prevented the BBC from broadcasting live President Hoover's inaugural address. The BBC was forced to fall back upon the news-agency summary, which was available only a few minutes after Hoover had finished. Four years later, however, the direct broadcast of Roosevelt's inaugural speech was successful. This new development was described by the Reuter board on 7 March 1933 as 'a considerable threat to newspapers and news agency interests'.

The four agencies successfully resisted pressure from the BBC during the 1930s to be allowed to take news from the British United Press. Jones made it plain that Reuters would not supply the BBC if it took BUP news. The four agencies were facing strong competition from the BUP's 'bright' news service, which they claimed was placing speed and sensation before accuracy. BUP, despite its name, was indirectly American-owned. Jones argued vigorously against such an unscrupulous and foreign agency being allowed to provide news for the British national broadcasting network.

In 1932 Reith tried to detach Reuters, which supplied most of the BBC's foreign news, from the other news agencies. He offered a direct news contract. If this had been accepted, he would have then been free to deal directly with BUP. The four agencies had always shared the BBC subscription equally, even though Reuters provided much more than a quarter of the volume. Nevertheless, Jones declined to break with his allies. He told Reith on 16 November 1932: 'Human reasons sometimes weighed in business affairs.'

It was only a matter of time before the BBC began to appoint its own correspondents. Reith wanted to send a man to report the war between Italy and Abyssinia in 1935. Jones told him on 18 September that it would be a waste of money, since the BBC would be getting 'a splendid service' from Reuters. Reith pointed out that the BBC had for some time been getting its own reports from the main European capitals.

In the following year the BBC appointed Richard Dimbleby and Charles Gardner to cover home news stories. With the outbreak of the Second World War in 1939, Dimbleby was sent to France as the first BBC war correspondent. By the time of the preparations for D-Day in 1944 the Reuter board was noticing with concern that whereas BBC reporters were sure of places to report all military operations, Reuters could not be equally certain of recognition.

Such was now the power of the microphone. Live news by radio had an immediacy which newspaper reports could not match. And yet, fortunately for Reuters, the fear that the broadcasting of news would reduce the sale of newspapers—and therefore the demand for agency news—had not materialized. Reuters remained a national institution, even though the BBC had also become one.

IV

In the early 1930s Reuters attempted to reform its methods of news collection, editing, and distribution. Hatt's new title of 'editor-in-chief' was deliberately chosen. It was a forceful-sounding Americanism, thought to be more up to date than the old title of 'chief editor'.

Hatt quickly produced a report, dated 11 April 1931, on the reorganization of the London editorial department and of the news services. He began by complaining about the lack of drive within Reuters. 'Editors have come to regard themselves not as newspapermen or journalists, but as conscientious cable transcribers.' Stories, he noted, were often too long, sometimes issued piecemeal, and diminished their impact by putting the main point at the end instead of at the beginning. Hatt described the Dominions department, which sent news to the self-governing Empire, as 'perhaps the premier standard-bearer' for Reuters. F. W. Emett's intelligence department (diplomatic department) was dismissed as 'an almost contemptible farce', and he was retired. Hatt appointed three new diplomatic correspondents, emphasizing that Reuters must cease to be 'a mere purveyor of Foreign Office and Embassy statements'. He also confirmed what Bailey had asserted eight years earlier, that there were 'some terribly weak spots' in the coverage by Reuter correspondents overseas, especially in Europe. Correspondents and stringers needed instruction in the kinds of stories now required.

Hatt's report had hoped that by 1935 there would be enough suitably trained Reuter correspondents in post. This hope was not to be realized: coverage and performance remained uneven. For example, on 30 January 1933 BUP beat Reuters by ten minutes with the momentous news of the appointment of Hitler as German chancellor. Extel and Central News were also behind, indicating that BUP had become the main competitor. On 1 February Reuters was reporting from Berlin: 'There appears every prospect that Hitler will remain Chancellor for a considerable time and that his regime will not bring the disasters which many expect.' The first speculation was perhaps permissible, but the second comment committed Reuters to a compromising value-judgement. This was bad practice— quite apart from the fact that the forecast was spectacularly wrong.

Victor Bodker was soon afterwards replaced as chief correspondent in Berlin by Gordon Young. Young brought about an improvement in performance, even though he was at first working with only one full-time assistant, compared with the four or five staffers employed by the other agencies. By 1938 Reuters itself had four full-time correspondents in Berlin. It also ran a network of fifty-nine stringers across Germany. Hatt told Jones on 6 December 1934 that they did good work, despite the Nazi censorship. 'Harmless stories are telephoned and dangerous copy is mailed.'

William Turner, the overseas general manager, believed that Hatt was more successful in reforming the inward news service for the London and British provincial newspapers than in improving the outward service. Turner argued that overseas newspaper-readers were of 'considerably higher' intelligence than British readers. He gave examples of what he regarded as good and bad handling of stories for the outward service. He described the following interview by Bodker with von Papen, the German chancellor, sent in cablese to the world on 17 August 1932, as 'a good summing up of the German situation':

> we remain office longtime declared chancellor exclusively Reutered von-papen confident his appeal commonsense political parties would successful but should vote noconfidence be adopted government would take action accordance situation cumevery intention respecting constitution . . . declared germanys claim equality with other nations regards disarmament was vital progermany who would unlonger submit discrimination be treated as secondclass power germany still aspires return some her colonies retention whereof was unjustifiable discrimination antigermany which must remedied sooner later hoped nazis unwould resort illegal measures but anycase government unhesitate suppress revolt promptly force arms.

The Reuter editorial log for the day noted that most British newspapers gave the interview prominence. '*The Times*, piqued perhaps by our coup, did not publish a word.'

The *Reuter Review* for January 1938 boasted that Reuters had secured more than eighty major beats during 1937. It did not say whether this was more than BUP or AP had achieved. Was Hatt too ready to settle for trying to be first? He was known in his own department as 'a man of glass'—with a quick news sense, but not much depth of interest. By the late 1930s the British press was becoming critical of Reuters. And during the first year of the Second World War the Reuter board itself began to question Hatt's effectiveness.

If he had not achieved all that he had hoped for when he took over full of energy and American ideas in 1931, Hatt had achieved something. The Reuter file was livelier and better presented than before. It stood comparison with the output of its rivals, even though they had greater resources. To achieve more, Reuters needed to invest more. The extra money could only come from the British newspapers or from the British Government or from both. Yet the newspapers and the Government were reluctant to provide further money, at least while Jones and Hatt remained in charge.

V

The Reuter file was to be dominated during the 1930s by the activities of the totalitarian regimes in Germany, Italy, Russia, Spain, and Japan. In 1933 Reuters won praise for its coverage of the show trial in Moscow of a group of British engineers. These men, who had gone to Soviet Russia to work on various construction projects, were used as scapegoats for short-comings in Stalin's programme of rapid industrialization. They were charged with sabotage and espionage. The Reuter reporter at the trial was Ian Fleming, who had joined Reuters in 1931, well connected and well recommended. Hatt told Jones on 1 October 1931 that Fleming had made a good start. 'His languages are sound. His appearance is good, and his manners are agreeable.' Also, unlike some other Old Etonian recruits, Fleming was hard-working and could write effectively. His 'curtain-raiser' to the trial on 12 April 1933, with its attention to descriptive detail, gave a hint of the writer who twenty years later was to create the fictional James Bond:

> (Moscow, Wednesday)—As the famous clock in the Kremlin Tower strikes twelve the six Metropolitan-Vickers English employees will enter a

room which has been daubed with blue in the Trades Union Hall and thronged with silent multitudes in order to hear an impassive Russian voice read for 4 or 5 hours the massive indictment which may mean death or exile. Within the packed room there will be a feeling of the implacable working of the soulless machinery of Soviet justice calling to account six Englishmen to decide whether the Metropolitan-Vickers raid was a vast bungle or a Machiavellian coup.

Fleming liked Reuters but chafed at his low salary of £300 per annum. Jones was keen to keep him, and on Fleming's return from Moscow offered him the post of assistant general manager in the Far East. Jones mentioned £800 per annum 'in the tone of one offering sacks of gold'. Fleming still left to become a stockbroker. Jones knew that Fleming's Moscow reporting had brought credit but not profit to Reuters. He had been filing up to 2,000 words a day on the trial. Total expenses had been £634, whereas extra payments from the London papers and the PA had amounted to only £511.

All British subjects working in the totalitarian states ran the risk of being treated as British intelligence agents. This was especially the case with Reuter correspondents who, like other good reporters, were bound to keep themselves informed by trading information with diplomats. Ivone Kirkpatrick of the British Embassy in Berlin remarked in 1939 that the Reuter and *Times* correspondents were 'often useful scouts and touts for the Embassy'.

As early as 6 December 1931 Hatt was writing to Bodker, who had received complaints from the Nazis about inadequate coverage, that Reuters had given the rise of Hitler 'as fair and impartial a show as we could . . . more space has been devoted to the Hitlerites by Reuter than to any other political party in Germany'. There was severe internal censorship in Germany and Italy, but no restriction upon outgoing news. On the other hand, if foreign correspondents filed stories to which the authorities took strong exception, they were likely to be expelled. Reuters had to walk a tightrope, trying to avoid giving offence without suppressing important but sensitive news. From many countries in Europe and elsewhere there was direct censorship of messages to London.

Reuter dealings with foreign diplomats in London required care. Jones claimed in his reminiscences that he had avoided social contact with von Ribbentrop when he was German ambassador in London. But the avoidance had not been total. When the Czechoslovak crisis was building up, Jones sent Ribbentrop a 'personal and confidential' letter on 9 June 1938 which expressed 'very kind regards', and offered to send a senior Reuter representative to interview Hitler.

Jones's wife, Enid Bagnold, visited Germany in 1933, and revealed herself in a *Times* article on 2 June as half-impressed and half-repelled by what she saw of Nazism. Hitler's friend Ernst Hanfstaengl, who had met the Joneses in London, invited them to attend the 1933 Nuremberg Nazi rally. Jones claimed in his reminiscences that he declined 'without hesitation', because to have attended would have compromised his position as head of Reuters.

News out of Italy was more than usually important during the 1930s because of the ambitions of Mussolini. The Italo-Abyssinian War of 1935 received much attention from the press of the democracies. Indeed, Jones complained to Kent Cooper on 11 November 1935 that the news agencies and newspapers were spending far too much money on the war. Reuters, he wrote, had sent eight full-time correspondents to the various fronts, plus assistants: large numbers of stringers were also engaged. Reuters was represented on both sides. The Cairo bureau was reinforced, and correspondents sent to Eritrea, Italian Somaliland, and French Somaliland.

Dick Sheepshanks, an engaging Old Etonian and a particular favourite of Jones, had been briefly engaged in Abyssinia. Sheepshanks was one of the Reuter team of four sent to cover the Spanish Civil War; he reported from Franco's side. On the last day of 1937 he was killed when a shell landed close to a car in which he was sitting with three other correspondents. The only one to survive was the *Times* correspondent, Harold Philby—already a Soviet agent. In the *Reuter Review* for May 1938 Jones described the Reuter ideal in war reporting as a 'combination of dispassionate reliability and vividness'. This quality came through strongly in a report from Joseph Swire, datelined Valencia, 13 June 1938:

IN A PATHETIC PROCESSION REFUGEES FROM THE VILLAGES WHICH HAVE FALLEN TO THE NATIONALISTS IN THEIR ADVANCE ON CASTELLON ARE ARRIVING IN VALENCIA.

MULECARTS CARRYING AGED WOMEN AND BABIES AND LADEN WITH HOUSEHOLD EFFECTS, FLOCKS OF SHEEP AND GOATS, AND ARMY TRUCKS, PACKED WITH WOMEN AND CHILDREN MINGLE WITH TROOPS ON THE ROAD FROM CASTELLON.

THE CIVILIAN RETREAT IS VERY ORDERLY AND THERE ARE ABSOLUTELY NO SIGNS OF PANIC.

VALENCIA'S YELLOW TRAMS, WHICH STILL RUN HALF WAY TO THE ANCIENT ROMAN TOWN OF SAGUNTO, MIDWAY BETWEEN VALENCIA AND CASTELLON, ARE PACKED LIKE SARDINES WITH REFUGEES.

SAGUNTO IS RUINED AND DESERTED IN CONTRAST TO CASTELLON, WHERE MANY OF THE INHABITANTS STILL REMAIN. WITH INTER-CONNECTED AIR-RAID SHELTERS DUG OUT BENEATH EVERY HOUSE CASTELLON RESEMBLES A RABBIT WARREN.

THE NATIONALIST OFFENSIVE IS BEING SUPPORTED BY HEAVY AIRCRAFT BOMBARDMENTS.

I TRAVELLED ALONG THE ROAD TO CASTELLON YESTERDAY AFTERNOON AND ON FOUR OCCASIONS I HAD TO TAKE REFUGE AMONG THE ORANGE TREES, LYING FLAT ON MY STOMACH, WHILE A FLEET OF PLANES DROPPED OVER A HUNDRED BOMBS ON THE ROAD.

SOME 25 BOMBS, WHISTLING DOWN, EXPLODED ABOUT TWO HUNDRED YARDS OF WHERE I LAY, RAISING CLOUDS OF SMOKE.

SOME OF THEM LANDED EVEN NEARER AND I COULD FEEL THE BEAT OF THEM AS THEY EXPLODED.

VI

Reuter coverage of the Munich crisis in September 1938 was ambitious and expensive. Jones took over as in effect editor-in-chief throughout. Early in the crisis Guy Bettany attended the Nuremberg rally to cover Hitler's speech of 12 September. A direct telephone line to London was held open for four-and-a-half hours, and the Reuter report started running only five minutes after Hitler had started speaking. Chamberlain, the British prime minister, had asked for copies of the Reuter tape to be sent to him immediately at 10 Downing Street. A motor-cycle messenger did the round trip from Carmelite Street in twelve minutes, so enabling batches of copy to be delivered at fifteen-minute intervals. Downing Street was delighted with the service.

Young led teams of correspondents to cover the visits of Neville Chamberlain to meet Hitler at Berchtesgarden, Bad Godesberg, and finally at Munich. Chamberlain's decision to return to London from Bad Godesberg on 24 September gave Reuters a forty-one-minute beat and an exclusive statement from the prime minister. This received great play in the evening papers.

Regardless of expense, Reuter correspondents made much use of air travel to and within Germany. During the first three weeks of September this helped them to match the strong competition from other agencies. However, as the probability of a breakdown into war came closer, Jones and Hatt wondered how many reporters to leave in Germany, or even in Czechoslovakia. If war came, they feared that all Reuter correspondents would be interned, including many of their best men. Nearly all of them were therefore told to withdraw from Prague and Berlin to Zurich, Amsterdam, and Budapest. The Berlin office was briefly left in the charge of just one correspondent. But when news of the intended Munich meeting came through unexpectedly on the afternoon of 28 September, the withdrawal policy was suddenly abandoned. Here was a dramatic moment in history. Reuters simply had to report from Germany and Czechoslovakia with as many men as it could muster.

Unfortunately, these comings and goings affected the quality of the Reuter report during the later stages of the crisis. This showed in comparison with the performance of the American agencies, whose correspondents were not at risk. Even the *Reuter Review* for November 1938 admitted shortcomings. 'At Munich we were compelled to register certain opposition beats, but our sober, full, and accurate report, made in difficult circumstances was eloquent of the work done.'

William Turner, the joint general manager, referred plainly to 'our failure at Munich' in a report for Jones on 11 October 1938. He blamed this partly upon the failure of DNB, the German agency allied with Reuters, to provide 'influential assistance', especially with communications out of Germany. The *Reuter Review* complained that telephone calls had taken up to eight hours to be connected. On 30 September Reuters had secured one late beat, but it came out of London not Germany. Martin Chisholm of the diplomatic staff obtained from the Czechoslovak legation the first news that Czechoslovakia had reluctantly accepted the Munich terms.

The cost of all this Munich activity was over £3,000, and unbudgeted. Afterwards economics had to be enforced. The result was a poor showing during the early months of 1939. Remarkably, Prague news was left to a single local stringer. This was done despite the continuing tension which led eventually to the German take-over of Czechoslovakia.

VII

An angry exchange between head office and Cornelius Murphy, the Rome correspondent, demonstrated the problems faced by hard-pressed bureaux. Jones had cabled testily on 12 April 1939: 'Disgracefully forestalled Mussolini Greek communique imperative you take measures to tighten up service.' Murphy replied equally testily on 17 April that tightening up would require manning the office round the clock 'as the opposition does'. Yet Reuter staff were too few to do so. 'We are doing our best in the worst equipped office in Rome, consistently working longer

hours than anyone.' The delay complained of, Murphy added conclu-
sively, was a consequence of a recent instruction that cable tolls were
never to exceed £3 per day.

Although BUP and other agencies often had the advantage over
Reuters on spot news, Reuters led on interviews. Its reputation gave its
correspondents access to key figures in most countries, for talks both on
and off the record. Thus, during the Munich crisis Young told Jones
about interviews with the British ambassador in Berlin, Sir Nevile
Henderson. Henderson was strong for appeasement: 'Why should a little
shyster lawyer (Sir Nevile used these words) like Dr Benes be allowed to
drag Britain into war? . . . I think we shall be all right if only the British
Government sticks fast and doesn't get misled by any false prophets like
Winston Churchill.' None of this was for publication.

Reuters had interviewed many of the leading Nazis down the years. A
revealing hour-and-a-half interview was given by Dr Joseph Goebbels,
the propaganda minister, to Young on 12 November 1938—apparently at
the request of Jones. Goebbels told Young: 'We desire that England shall
take no interest in the way we solve the Jewish question.' A room was set
aside in the Propaganda Ministry with two secretaries and a stenographer
from DNB, so that Young could afterwards compile his report in time
for use by the British Sunday newspapers. Such was Goebbels's desire to
publicize his views through Reuters.

Reporting of Nazi anti-Jewish policy was vetted by Jones himself.
Young had assured Goebbels during his interview that Reuters would
always be 'objective'. What did this mean when dealing with anti-
Semitism? Jones explained in a letter of 10 February 1939 to Sir Neil
Malcolm, high commissioner for German refugees, that Reuters was trying to strike a balance. 'Horror stories are dangerous, the newspapers
rightly are chary of them, and the public do not particularly want to read
them. Decrees are in a different category. These and other measures will
continue to take their place in the Reuter report.' Jones appended a list of
twenty-seven Reuter reports of anti-Jewish decrees issued since October
1938.

VIII

Sport and politics mixed at the 1936 Berlin Olympic Games, opened by
Hitler. The Germans recognized the importance of Reuters and gave its
sports editor, Vernon Morgan, a privileged viewing-box. Except for the
Olympic Games held every four years, Jones had ruled in 1931 that for

reasons of economy Reuters should concentrate upon the sports of the widest popular interest—cricket, football, and boxing. Gilbert Mant, an Australian member of staff, was sent to cover the 1932–3 England cricket tour of Australia. The tour was nearly abandoned because of England's 'bodyline' bowling. Mant disliked 'bodyline', but he respected the Reuter tradition by supplying the scores and a factual account of the play without partisan comment. On his way back by sea, however, he began to write a personal account of the tour, condemning 'bodyline' as unsporting. Jones refused him permission to publish, on the ground that Mant's controversial opinions might be taken as those of Reuters. For the same reason, Jones refused to allow Young to publish a book about Hermann Goering, Hitler's deputy.

Withholding opinions could be defended. But what about withholding news? Reuters assisted the British press during 1936 in its voluntary blackout over the relationship between King Edward VIII and Mrs Wallis Simpson, an American. Hatt had served in the First World War with Mrs Simpson's current husband, Ernest, and their friendship led to Hatt's inclusion within the social circle round Edward. Hatt was present at York House in February 1936 when the king told Simpson that he wanted Wallis to become his wife and to be crowned queen.

Far from publishing such inside information, Hatt and Jones played their part in the cover-up of the relationship by the British press. They knew of the stories which were circulating in the American press, many of them sent from London by AP and UP; but Reuters said nothing. When the British papers at last began to write about the affair early in December 1936, Jones personally supervised the Reuter handling of the story night by night. Valentine Harvey, the chief parliamentary correspondent, was informed of the king's decision to abdicate on 11 December shortly before the official announcement. Hatt was rumoured to have known sooner still, and to have offended Jones by not telling him.

Jones told Samuel Storey, a Reuter director, on 10 May 1937 that Reuters had been 'soft-pedalling' on the latest twists in the story of the ex-king (now Duke of Windsor) and Mrs Simpson. They married in June. Newspaper interest in their doings continued, not necessarily sympathetically. On 18 May 1938 the Duke requested Hatt's assistance. A dinner-party was being given for the couple by the British ambassador in Paris, and the Duke asked Hatt to ensure that the event received 'good publicity'. Hatt obliged, and subsequently sent the Duke newspaper clippings to illustrate the restrained reporting of the occasion in the British press. The Duke was well satisfied, but not the Buckingham Palace authorities. The Reuter correspondent in Paris was summoned to the British Embassy to explain how Reuters had found out the names of the guests. They had been supplied by the Duke himself through his equerry. Matter of such triviality would soon cease to be important. War was again approaching.

TEN

War News

1939–1945

I shall never forget the extraordinary sensation of looking down—I repeat 'down'—on the Heinkels and Junkers as they roared past the ships and turned sideways to launch their loads.

(Arthur Oakeshott, Arctic convoy to Russia, 1941)

During the night brave Cossack cavalrymen watered their horses in the Dniestr. *(Harold King reporting from Moscow, 1944)*

When I left the fighting area I left something behind me—my face print in the mud of Normandy's beaches.

(Marshall Yarrow, D-Day, 1944)

The Atomic Bomb wiped out over four square miles.

(Jack Smyth covering Hiroshima from Guam, 1945)

I

REUTERS had a good war—in the end. It sent correspondents to all the main battlefronts. The extracts quoted above were just a few of their more striking or momentous turns of phrase.

The London editorial floor quickly developed a new spirit of professionalism after Walton Cole and Sidney Mason took over in 1942. The result of their work as news manager and chief news editor respectively soon began to be noticed outside Reuters. The *Newspaper World* of 9 January 1943 remarked that the outstanding feature in the journalistic world during the previous year had been 'the remarkable transformation of Reuters'. Earlier in the war its performance had been generally unimpressive. Answering complaints about BUP and AP 'space superiority' during August 1940, Hatt had feebly admitted in a report on 1 October that 'some of our centres have been weak lately. We have been unlucky, too, in suffering from temporary disadvantages in one or two places. Remedial action has been taken wherever possible.'

Remarkably, the cost of war coverage was unbudgeted. Early in the war, correspondents often filed even big stories at cheaper (because slower) rates, leaving Reuters behind with the news. Fresh instructions were not issued until March 1941. The American agencies had more men in the field; and for over two years, until the entry of the United States into the war in December 1941, the Americans were able to file directly out of Germany, Italy, and occupied Europe, while Reuters had to rely mainly upon radio monitoring. Jones was justified, however, in praising to the board on 9 November 1939 the 'excellent listening-in system' organized by Reuters. Throughout the war Gothic House (renamed Radio House) at Barnet secured some notable beats on news out of enemy countries.

These were, of course, not beats gained by Reuter correspondents. Their calibre at the outbreak of war was mixed—a few good, some adequate, many neither. From February 1941—after the departure of Jones and Hatt, and probably at the insistence of Storey and Haley—deficiencies in both men and methods were admitted by the deputy editor-in-chief, Neale, in his reports to the board. Some of Neale's comments were devastating: 'his news judgement is not remarkable'; 'his is a long record of inexcusable failures and irrefutable excuses'; 'unreliable and unequal, nor is he responsive to service suggestions and instructions'; 'an old Levantine who serves other masters'.

Everything had to be passed by British Government censors in the newsroom before transmission. Delay on big stories was minimized by devising a new drill for super flashes, which warned the outward wireless services when an important message had been handed to the censor. In 1941 a flash of twenty words was taking three minutes fifty seconds from writing through censorship to transmission. Later in the war this was reduced considerably.

Censorship of news for the United Kingdom was always tight, but Reuters was left with more freedom over what it delivered abroad. Even so, censorship caused frequent irritation, both in the field and in London. Rear-Admiral George Thomson, the chief press censor, sent out a stream of 'D notices' (Defence notices) giving sometimes oracular guidance on what could not be published or what should be submitted. The censor enjoyed power without responsibility: 'the fact that matter is passed for publication by the censorship does not mean that it is guaranteed as accurate or that its publication is desired.'

Censorship in the Middle East was particularly bureaucratic. Messages from the desert war were delayed, not just because they had to be sent back by lorry over bad roads, but also by double censorship. Reports had to be passed by a censor with the 8th Army at the front, and again in Cairo. Inward and outward messages had all to be submitted to the Cairo censorship office, which closed for siesta between 13.00 and 16.00 hours, and again from 02.00 to 08.00. If there was any doubt, messages were referred to one of seven different authorities.

In 1942 Cooper of AP and Haley of Reuters defined their agreed attitude towards the censorship of news in wartime. 'There is acceptance of the right of government to have us withhold news for the common good, but no acceptance of any right of government to say how we shall word what we do transmit.' The latter insistence meant that, even with news passed by the censor, there could be clashes with the authorities. For example, the British Foreign Office took exception to reports from Martin Herlihy during a trip to neutral Turkey in July 1942. Herlihy explained: 'while taking the general British line of policy, I endeavoured not to be a mere mouthpiece and to introduce more information and criticism than would have been welcome some years ago.'

II

Germany invaded Poland on 1 September 1939, and Britain declared war two days later. During the very last days of peace the British Government was anxious that the United Kingdom press and news agencies should not publish anything which, by upsetting a temperamental Hitler, might make him decide for war rather than for peace. On 30 August Sir Samuel Hoare, the home secretary, called in five representatives of the British news agencies to offer them 'guidance', which was readily accepted by Hatt and Neale representing Reuters. 'It was advisable to avoid any personal references whatever to Hitler at the present time.' On the positive side, suggested Hoare, it would be helpful if the news agencies reported that the British people were perfectly calm; 'and, above all that we were resolutely determined to honour our obligations towards Poland.'

As in the First World War, Reuter correspondents were posted with both the French army and the British Expeditionary Force. On 9 November 1939, however, Jones cryptically reminded the board of another source of news. 'Reuters have the important direct channel known to the Directors and accessible to nobody else in the British Isles.' Was this a reference to information gathered by the British intelligence services? To boost morale at home or to gain propaganda advantage abroad, some of this information may have been fed to Reuters for circulation as its own news. Certainly, evidence has survived of the War Office trying this method on at least one occasion. On 18 October 1939 Major Blumenfeld of the War Office sent a story to Hatt, 'concocted (for your private ear) in collaboration with Foreign Office': 'we shall be greatly obliged if you can arrange for this to be put out, under a Shanghai dateline as from your own correspondent, for tomorrow's morning papers. Naturally you will not disclose its real source of origin—and we are not giving the cable to any other agency.' The story was issued as requested. Hatt asked editorial how much it had been used by the newspapers. He was told that it had not been used at all, either in the London or provincial press. The piece—headed 'Tommies Defy China Floods', and telling of the resilience of the British army garrison at Tientsin—was obviously judged by the papers to be of little interest. Even so, the fact remained that Reuters had allowed itself to be exploited. Other plants may have been arranged over the telephone, as this one initially was.

At a meeting with editorial staff on 27 July 1939, Jones had discussed how 'news which impinges on what you might call the official area' should be handled in wartime:

> Reuter must never lose sight of the national interest. Reuter is authoritative, more so than any other British press organ, even including *The Times*, and Reuter is so regarded abroad. This places Reuter under the obligation to observe great prudence in handling any news which may possibly involve the national interest, and to act in close collaboration and accord with Whitehall in this connection. . . .
>
> On a lower plane, Whitehall is a most important source of news to Reuter, and any failure on Reuters' part to conform to the principle and practice of close collaboration with Whitehall would ipso facto *close that source of news to us.*

Such an attitude, Jones decided, was 'perfectly compatible' with independence. 'It is not submission to dictation, but consultation of expert advice.'

Support for the national interest could involve suppression of news, even without reference to Whitehall. In the first week of the war Reuters did not issue a report from its chief correspondent in Copenhagen that propaganda leaflets intended to be dropped from the air over Germany had fallen upon Denmark. The Danes had realized that the leaflets might have been bombs: 'better send your pilots school learn some geography.'

A curious episode—barely reconcilable with the Reuter tradition—was a letter published in *The Times* of 18 June 1940. This was the month of the fall of France to the Germans. The letter was signed by Gordon Young, who described himself as 'Reuter's Chief Berlin Correspondent for three years under the Nazi regime' and now 'Reuters Special Correspondent in Turkey'; Jones had approved the letter. Young warned against 'over-estimating the power and resources of our enemy'. The policy of Goebbels and the Nazis, he wrote with unbelievable optimism, had always been to exaggerate their strength: 'our victory may be much less remote than it appears to be.' Here was the good name of Reuters being used for morale-boosting. Even at a time of greatest national crisis, ought such a letter to have been sent? The answer presumably was that Reuters was British; and therefore the letter—which was obviously expressing an opinion, and was not trying to present opinion as fact—justified itself under the circumstances.

Reuters had insisted upon its right to publish enemy communiqués. Yet in doing so it took every chance to play them down, as the following example showed:

> The Nazis this morning are reticent about last night's RAF raid on naval bases in north-western Germany but as usual give extravagant accounts of their raids on Britain, says Reuter.
> All they say about the RAF raid is that 'Weak forces flew into the North German coastal area'.
> They do not say that any bombs were dropped.
> Here is the official German news agency's report.
> 'Last night weak forces of the enemy flew into the north German coastal area.
> 'The German airforce last night successfully attacked a town on the English south coast.
> 'Heavy explosions and large fires which quickly spread and were visible from a great distance as well as numerous smaller fires in the harbour installations were observed.
> 'There was an enormous cloud of smoke over the target area.
> 'One fire was visible 50 miles away.
> 'Further objectives were attacked in eastern England'.

In January 1943 Stewart Sale filed a graphic 1,500-word report after flying in a bomber on a raid over the German capital:

> I saw Berlin burn from the nose of a Lancaster, one of the many scores converging on the city. I looked down on hundreds of points of fire—incendiaries which had just struck and looked like strings of gems, others were already an angry red. There were also dark crimson puff-balls thrown up by the big bombs. . . .
> . . . Most of the pilots, it seemed, thought the flak over Berlin was light. My own captain thought it rather bad. I know it was bad enough for me. We made another run to release our other bombs, among them hundreds

of incendiaries. I tensed myself again for the sickening sensation as the nose went down. For a wild moment the redness that masked Berlin seemed to rise until it was in line with my shoulder.

I expected banks of searchlights. I saw not more than half a dozen tapering down to pinpoints. The fires behind spread and brightened. Incendiaries streamed across the city in glittering laces. Looking down on the furnace, I remembered nights on Fleet Street roofs when the bombers were over. By the time the bombers following us were through with it, Berlin too would know what bombing means.

Eight months later Sale was killed while reporting from Italy. In all, five war correspondents on the Reuter staff were killed during the Second World War. A further eight members of staff died in action as members of the armed forces.

The German press, itself controlled by Goebbels, had no doubts that Reuters was a British propaganda outlet. The Germans sometimes referred back to what they ruefully regarded as the successful propaganda role of Reuters in the previous war. *Der Neue Tag* of 3 October 1939 recollected how 'the poison cooks of Reuters' had functioned then. They had turned the 'fabrications' of Lloyd George and Churchill 'into the easily understood "objective" language which, by its pretended nobleness, attained the desired impression'. When Jones resigned in 1941, Barnes, the Fascist one-time Reuter correspondent, exclaimed on Rome radio that the departure of this 'very astute man' was a sign that Britain was cracking up. 'We shall not be surprised if the next we hear of him is in Portugal and then in South America.'

The Germans monitored all news put out by Reuters, ever ready to take advantage. Reuter mishandling of the news of the assassination of Admiral Darlan in Algiers in December 1942 gave them such an opportunity. Reuters published the story in a version which carried overtones of satisfaction at the removal of Darlan; these overtones had been added by the Reuter diplomatic staff. This version was soon 'killed', but not before damage had been done. The British Government had distrusted Darlan, whereas the Americans had been favouring him. The German propaganda machine was able to play up this difference with help from the Reuter report. The gift to the enemy was admitted in a warning instruction to Reuter staff on 31 December 1942: 'Our message was of such a nature that the Germans were able to make insinuations which did not easily permit of a ready rebuttal, and it caused considerable concern in high places in this country. . . . in political matters we must never express a view of our own.'

III

A Reuter correspondent who achieved notice early in the war was Desmond Tighe. He had started in 1930 as a Morse operator in London. From 1935 he worked for the commercial service in Egypt; but he was in London on leave at the outbreak of war, and he stayed on to become a war correspondent. He arrived in Oslo in April 1940 at the same time as the invading Germans, only getting away to Sweden by the last train after walking past German army pickets at the railway station. He then travelled to Namsos by sledge to interview the British army commander. He had to make a 7,000-mile trip via Moscow, Odessa, and Bucharest to reach Paris. At the fall of France he again got out just in time, on the last plane to London.

Tighe eventually succeeded Massey Anderson as Reuter correspondent with the British Mediterranean fleet. Like Tighe, 'Jock' Anderson had served with the commercial service in Egypt. He lost his life in December 1941 when his ship was torpedoed off Alexandria. Tighe covered the Allied invasion of Italy in 1943 from on board ship, and his report of the Salerno landings in September was widely used.

Reuters did well with its coverage of the European war at sea. Arthur Oakeshott sailed bravely on ten Arctic convoys to Russia. John Nixon covered the successful pursuit of the German battleship, *Bismarck*, across the Atlantic in 1941, including the early sinking of the British battle cruiser, *Hood*. The *Evening Standard* in June noted that 'wearing a raincoat over a lounge suit and a soft hat, Mr J. R. Nixon, a fair-haired, lean-jawed Englishman stood on the bridge of a destroyer dodging shell fragments as the *Hood* went down'. Was Nixon's determination to wear his own unsuitable clothes a sign of arrogance? War correspondents were under considerable temptation to become prima donnas. They knew that they were writing about tremendous events. They were exposed to great strain and sometimes to great danger, and yet they carried no weapons for self-defence.

Well aware of these pressures, Cole and Mason used service messages and personal letters to guide and control their correspondents. Quite often this meant praise and encouragement through 'herograms'. Sometimes it meant criticism, either gentle or sharp, as when Cole sent a service message to Denis Martin in Algiers (18 June 1943) which contained a classic of cablese:

WHEN OFFBROWNED OFFLET STEAM ME ETBE UNPRIMADONNAISH

Correspondents were regularly reminded that the British newspapers wanted small personalized stories as much as great descriptive pieces. The names and home towns of individuals mentioned in reports were of particular interest to the provincial press.

While Cole and Mason kept up a barrage of instructions to correspondents, the accounts department was not far behind, questioning expenses and explaining allowances. Correspondents have traditionally taken a generous view of their entitlement to expenses. The precarious state of Reuter finances meant that only half-salaries were paid to staff interned or captured.

AP and UP, usually with more correspondents in the field, provided very strong competition throughout the war. For example, when in 1943 Reuters was being regularly beaten out of Algiers with news of the Anglo-American campaign in North Africa, troubled service messages flowed from London to the Reuter correspondents. These referred on 23 April 1943 to 'upward' (codeword for UP) and 'apathy' (codeword for AP):

> what route used upward yesternight eightharmy attack on which we disastrously beaten fullstop fyi lloyd williams sixhours after opposition self and martin about twohours.

> Grateful reply speediest how many correspondents apathy upward have northafrica etof total how many algiers.

IV

Reuter reporting during the Second World War first achieved consistent success with its coverage of the eastern front between Germany and Soviet Russia.

Reuters began with a notable beat from London giving the first news of the German invasion of Russia on 22 June 1941. The German Foreign Office had put out a statement saying 'We are expecting a quiet weekend.' This struck Geoffrey Imeson, the editor-in-charge, as disingenuous, and put him on his guard. Normally both Reuters and DNB shut down their monitoring about midnight and resumed at 6 a.m. This unofficial truce was intended to give translators a rest. On this occasion Imeson asked Nina Gee to stay listening all night—just in case. In the small hours she told Imeson excitedly over the telephone that 'Germany has invaded Russia'. Imeson immediately sent out a worldwide flash. Only after this had been transmitted did Nina Gee explain that all she had heard was an announcement about a proclamation from Hitler denouncing Soviet policy. This was shortly to be broadcast by Goebbels. Did it really mean war? In fact it did. The reputation of Reuters was enhanced; but it would have been seriously damaged if the dramatic flash had turned out to be wrong. In later years Imeson was to describe his ten-minute beat as 'ill-deserved'.

In the summer of 1942 Harold King, who had been a part-time reporter for Reuters in Paris before the fall of France, was sent to the Soviet Union to cover what proved to be the turning-point of the war on the eastern front. King taught himself Russian, rejected an approach to supply material secretly to the British Embassy, and sent back a steady stream of stories. The *Newspaper World* article of 9 January 1943 was full of praise: 'greatly impressed with the way in which Harold King, with no "dead" periods to ease his task, has supplied graphic news commentaries and spot news. Tribute to his work is reflected in the number of times he has ousted the newspapers' correspondents from their own front pages.'

King was not a particularly good writer, but he supplied the essence to London and his stories were written up there. In his unpublished reminiscences he claimed that he was read worldwide in over 4,000 newspapers, 'just because of that tense suspense all over the globe about which side was going to win'. In May 1943 King obtained from Stalin a personally signed statement announcing the dissolution of the Comintern:

> I feel that the dissolution of the Communist International is perfectly timely because it is exactly now, when the Fascist beast is exerting its last strength,—that it is necessary to organise the common onslaught of freedom-loving countries to finish off this beast and to deliver the peoples from Fascist oppression.
>
> With respect,
J. Stalin

This was taken as evidence that Stalin had given up the dream of 'Bolshevizing' the world.

Stalin began to say that the Red Army's objective was to clear the Germans out of the Soviet Union, but not to go beyond. He said this not because he meant it, but to lull the Russian people into thinking that their sufferings would end the sooner. The Russian censors began to be coy about just how far their armies had advanced. King cleverly got round this by saying: 'During the night brave Cossack cavalrymen watered their horses in the Dniestr.' They were into Romania.

V

Cole and Mason made careful plans for covering the Anglo-American landings in Normandy, which started on D-Day, 6 June 1944. Mason himself and two others were assigned to Supreme Headquarters in London to handle incoming material. Four extra staff reinforced the Reuter contingent at the Ministry of Information, which became the channel for all copy. Their task was to co-ordinate the flow of all material—Reuter stories, pooled dispatches, official hand-outs and communiqués, and backgrounders. Each agency had been allocated a room at the MOI, with a direct printer back to head office. Reuters, however, developed its room so that it became a small copy of the Fleet Street newsroom, with lines connecting directly to the British national newspaper offices. When important news broke, a switch enabled the Reuter room to cut out head office.

Recruitment of extra journalists for D-Day had started in 1943. Doon Campbell, destined for a long career in Reuters, was spotted by Cole on a visit to the *Evening Dispatch* in Edinburgh. Campbell had been rejected for military service because from birth he had lacked a left forearm and wore an artificial limb. At twenty-four he was to be the youngest war correspondent reporting the action in Normandy. There were few other competent British journalists available. Most young men were in the forces, and at that time no editor would have dreamt of sending a woman to cover the landings. Cole, a good spotter of talent, had therefore interviewed over forty candidates while on a visit to North America. With some difficulty, he had found enough experienced American and Canadian newspapermen willing to accept Reuter salaries, which were substantially below North American rates. The difference would be offset, promised Cole blandly, by the lower cost of living in Britain. 'The recruits are joining Reuters', he assured the board in February 1944, 'because of their belief in our future and the important role we are destined to play in post-war Europe.' Notable newcomers were Charlie Lynch and Marshall Yarrow from Canada and Bob Reuben, Bill Stringer, and John Wilhelm from the United States. Stringer was killed near Chartres in August 1944.

Recruits were also found in neutral southern Ireland. Moloney, the joint general manager until 1944, had been alarmed at what he regarded as the lowering of tone within Reuters after the arrival of Cole and Mason. He felt that they were introducing too many journalists of their own unpolished kind. He had therefore gone to his native Ireland to collect men of a better sort. They were known in the office as 'Moloney's revenge'.

At the very start Reuters had a beat from the Allied side with its report of the first Normandy landings. The news broke at 6.33 a.m. on 6 June: 'Allied forces began invasion of Europe landing on Normandy beaches today.' Transocean, the German overseas news agency, had made the first announcement, and this was heard by Radio House. Comparative times on the printer in London were: Reuter, 06.33 a.m.; BUP, 06.35; AP, 06.38.

What the Reuter editorial log for 6-7 June claimed as 'the best published descriptive dispatch of the invasion' was by Tighe. It was used by every London paper:

> From Desmond Tighe, Reuters Special Correspondent for the Combined Press aboard British Destroyer off Bernière-Sur-Mer, Tuesday—Dawn.
>
> Guns are belching flame from more than 600 allied warships. Thousands of bombers are roaring overhead, fighters are weaving in and out of the clouds as the invasion of Western Europe begins.
>
> Rolling clouds of dense black and grey smoke cover the beaches south east to Le Havre as the full fury of the allied invasion force is unleashed on the German defence. It is the most incredible sight I have ever seen.
>
> We are standing some eight thousand yards off the beaches of Bernière-Sur-Mer and from the bridge of this little destroyer I can see vast numbers of the naval craft of all types.
>
> The air is filled with the continuous thunder of broadsides and the crash of bombs. Great spurts of flame come up from the beaches in long snake like ripples as shells ranging from 16 inches to 4 inches find their mark. In the last ten minutes alone more than 2,000 tons of high explosive shells have gone down on the beach head.

Monty Taylor, correspondent with the RAF sub-beachhead forces, sent back a message by carrier pigeon in the best Reuter tradition: 'We are just 20 miles or so off the beaches. First assault troops landed 0750. Signal says no interference from enemy gunfire on beach. Passage uneventful. Steaming steadily on. Formations Lightnings, Typhoons, Fortresses crossing since 0545. No enemy aircraft seen!'

The editorial log for 9–10 June noted with satisfaction that invasion stories from Reuter correspondents were featuring prominently in the pool dispatches used by the British national newspapers, especially stories from Lynch and Campbell. Campbell, the first British seaborne correspondent to land, went in shortly after 9 a.m. with the marine commandos on Sword Beach. His opening report from 'a ditch 200 yards inside

Normandy', handed to a naval officer to take back across the English Channel, never reached Reuters. But subsequent graphic stories—the more believable because they described the dangers and difficulties—did reach 85 Fleet Street:

> It is a miracle that I'm alive to write this despatch—that I've survived 24 hours on this beachhead bag of tricks . . . Much of my 24 hours have been spent flat on my face burrowing into sand or earth—the good earth . . . the front is fluid, so fluid that I crouched for two hours in a ditch before realising I was a good 100 yards ahead of the forward troops.

Yarrow served with the Americans. He wrote with stark economy:

> I landed in Normandy with the first glider forces of the invasion. It was dark, it was deadly, and we landed in a country of stinking swamps and hidden snipers . . . I crawled as I have never crawled before.
>
>   When I left the fighting area I left something behind me—my face-print in the mud of Normandy's beaches.

The enterprise shown by Reuter correspondents could sometimes lead to their undoing. John Wilhelm and Seaghan Maynes each temporarily lost their accreditation for technical breaches of regulations. In the absence of his conducting officer, Wilhelm had driven his jeep through the German lines and had a narrow escape from capture or death. Maynes had slipped into Paris ahead of the troops—with help from the novelist Ernest Hemingway, who had contacts with the Maquis. The Resistance possessed an underground radio transmitter, and Maynes broadcast a dispatch 'onpass Reuter' which got through. This was technically in breach of censorship, and Maynes was suspended for three months. During that time he flew in a Canadian aircraft over Nijmegen, and filed a report. As he was still under suspension, his action caused some concern at 85 Fleet Street. Fortunately, no one seemed to notice, and both Maynes and Wilhelm were soon back in Europe.

On D-Day plus six (12 June) General Montgomery gave a briefing at his headquarters to nearly fifty correspondents, including Doon Campbell (see Plate 37). 'Monty' was full of confidence. To report such briefings, Campbell developed what he found to be an unbeatable technique. First, he delivered a series of two- or three-line 'snaps' on the highlights— 'won the battle of the beaches', '7,000 prisoners taken to Sunday night', 'German women snipers killed'. These snaps, being short, were likely to be quickly cleared by the censors. Next he sent a full account. And finally he offered an overall 'lead' or 'intro', ready made for the tabloid papers.

The abortive Arnhem landings in September 1944—intended to force a crossing of the Rhine—were covered for Reuters by Jack Smyth. He landed by parachute. But he was injured during the fierce fighting, and was captured. For seventeen days he was roughly interrogated by the Gestapo, and was even threatened with death. While a prisoner of war, he sent Cole a card of apology, dated 11 October. 'A fine correspondent I turned out to be! Four days in the field, a solitary despatch and then captured.' Smyth's dispatch, the only press report from the landing zone, had been published in the London papers on 22 September:

> With Airborne Force, Arnhem Area, Sept 21
>
> On this fifth day our force is still being heavily mortared, sniped, machine-gunned, and shelled by self-propelled guns. But, as their commander says, they are in good heart.
>
> The medium guns of the Second Army have just come into communication, and have begun shelling enemy targets that we have signalled. Maybe the tanks will arrive today. Anyway we are holding on until they do.
>
> These airborne men are magnificent. They fight individually as well as in platoons and companies. When the Second Army arrives and relieves this crowd, then may be told one of the epics of the war. In the meantime they just go on fighting their hearts out.

Reuters had successfully covered the Allied advance from Normandy to the Rhine. But the old cry for economy was being heard again before the end of the year. Campbell and Lynch were asked by Mason on 13 December 1944 to cut down their filing 'while the front is quiet'. In the event, the quiet was not to last much longer, for three days later the Germans launched their Ardennes counter-offensive.

The Rhine was finally crossed in March 1945. For the crossing, Reuters had Campbell with the 17th American Airborne Division, and Maynes with the British 6th Airborne Division. Campbell landed by glider and Maynes dropped by parachute. He described the drop as 'one of the fastest and most effective operations in military history', adding that 'the full story of this great airborne battle is one of heroism and men who fought grimly'. In a vivid dispatch, which was used throughout the world, Maynes accurately reflected the dangers faced by war correspondents and described how he had actually helped capture some Germans:

> It was a slight consolation to know that the Germans on the ground were probably more scared than I as the paratroops came into Germany and leaped into action with machine-guns firing against them.

The hunting horns of the paratroop commanders sounded the tally-ho to rally the units. There was too much happening to think clearly.

With Captain Gus Moore, the steeplechase jockey, I dashed into the woods at a crouching run past the crumpled bodies of paratroopers to find ourselves, suddenly, within a few yards of a German machine-gun nest.

Captain Moore, who was slightly hurt in the leg, covered me with his Sten gun while I yelled 'hands up' and then I dodged behind a tree . (War correspondents are not permitted to carry arms.)

The trick worked. Five Germans with a machine-gun marched out, their hands in the air, while we shouted orders to imaginary paratroopers in case the Germans should change their minds and fire on us. They had with them one of our paratroopers as prisoner. Another hung dead on his parachute near the machine-gun.

One of the Germans, also a paratrooper, offered us cigarettes. We were glad to smoke as our kit had been scattered everywhere.

Reuters enjoyed a notable world beat on 28 April with news of an offer of surrender to the Western Allies from Himmler, the Gestapo chief. Another beat which told about the disintegrating Nazi leadership was secured by Duncan Hooper, King's successor as chief correspondent in Moscow. Hooper got news of the suicide on 1 May of Goebbels. A Soviet official had approached Hooper at a party and said: 'It is very sad about Dr Goebbels.' Knowing nothing, Hooper had responded carefully: 'Very sad.' The official then revealed all. 'You know they killed all the family. They killed the children in the bunker and then killed themselves.'

Hitler had shot himself in the same Berlin bunker on the previous day. He did so after hearing, courtesy of Reuters, that Himmler was treating with the Allies. This news had been a last blow. Hitler had access to a Reuter Hellschreiber, perhaps in his bunker but more probably in the nearby Propaganda Ministry. He had always trusted the accuracy of Reuter news.

News of the discovery of what was thought to be Hitler's body a fortnight later provided Hooper with another beat. He had reached Berlin from the east four or five days after the German surrender on 9 May. American correspondents with AP and UP had also arrived in Berlin. They were ahead of Hooper in hearing that the Russians had found a body in the bunker, which had been identified as Hitler's from dental records. As there were no direct communications out of Berlin, the Americans had decided to fly all the way back to Paris to transmit the news from there.

This gave Hooper his chance to finish ahead after all. He found a British dispatch rider who was on his way to the airport to take a flight to Lübeck, the nearest communications head, a distance of 150 miles. After hastily scribbling a message, Hooper handed it to the dispatch rider, and told him that if he delivered it to Lübeck he would be rewarded with a bottle of Scotch. About four hours later the Reuter story was being broadcast by the BBC. The Americans were still in the air, keeping their news to themselves.

VI

The war in Europe took priority for Reuters—as for the United Kingdom—over the war with Japan, which had started with the attack upon Pearl Harbor on 7 December 1941. Relations between Reuters and the Japanese authorities had been growing increasingly strained during the years before the war, even though links with the Domei news agency remained cordial. On 29 July 1940 Jimmy Cox, chief Reuter correspondent in Tokyo and a Far East veteran, died in mysterious circumstances while in police custody. He fell to his death from a third-floor window at the secret police headquarters after being arrested upon suspicion of spying. Ten other British subjects were detained at the same time.

Cox had been questioned for fifty-five hours. Did he jump? Was he thrown? Kenneth Selby-Walker, Chancellor's successor as general manager in the Far East, had visited Tokyo during the previous May and had found Cox 'in somewhat of a nervous state'. Cox felt that he was being watched. Selby-Walker reported to Jones on 14 August, after a visit of enquiry to Tokyo, that Cox 'did take his own life'. 'I feel that, in his nervous state, he decided it was more than he could bear to go on indefinitely suffering the acute physical discomfort of his surroundings, the indignities of the situation and the mental bullying.' An American doctor's report, communicated to the British Foreign Office, said that foul play was not suspected. Cox's injuries were consistent with a fall of about forty feet. The body was some way forward from the wall, as would be likely if Cox had jumped from a window. An alternative suggested by an American journalist, who had himself suffered arrest, was that Cox became disorientated from ceaseless questioning, and thought that he was escaping by a ground-floor window.

Either way, Cox cannot be said to have been murdered. Postwar evidence from a Japanese secret-police commander, who was in charge of the section dealing with Cox, suggested that the police had no wish to murder him, but that they did believe him to be an intelligence gatherer. Cox's files were found to contain information about the Japanese army and navy, but these may have been no more than cuttings and other material such as any Western journalist would have expected to collect. Even such a collection was suspect in a totalitarian country where, as Selby-Walker explained, 'technically the mere possession of such information is a crime'.

Was Cox therefore totally innocent of spying? He left a note for his wife which could be read as meaning that he was about to crack and reveal something, or simply (as Selby-Walker argued) that he was choosing suicide because he could take no more: 'See Reuters re rents. See Cowley re deeds and insurance. See H.K. Bank re balance and shares in London. I know what is best. Always, my only love. I have been quite well treated but there is no doubt about how matters are going.'

The Japanese police commander claimed that Cox was known to be passing material to the British Embassy in Tokyo. In a public statement Reuters issued 'a flat denial' of the charge that Cox and other Reuter correspondents had official connections. Reuters did not reveal that at this very period the salaries of several of its correspondents in the Far East were being supplemented by payments from the Foreign Office. Nearly fifty years later C. R. Graham-Barrow admitted in an interview that he had been sent to Manchukuo in 1939 'officially to sell the Reuter service, but (I don't think Reuters would like this) I was loaned to HMG for the period to keep an ear to the ground'. The British Government paid Reuters £926 per annum for Graham-Barrow. When he was repatriated after the outbreak of war, he sailed on a ship with British diplomats and officials, much to the surprise of other journalists.

The Japanese were embarrassed by the Cox tragedy. Through the Japanese ambassador in London, Matsuoka of Domei, the Japanese news agency gave 100,000 yen (over £5,800) to Cox's widow as a personal and private gesture of sympathy.

Selby-Walker was himself to meet a violent end. His Cambridge tutor had written of him on 14 June 1934, when he was applying for a job at Reuters, that he was 'far better able to think for himself than the average Etonian . . . he is a sticker at a job'. Alas, these commendable qualities seem to have contributed to Selby-Walker's death. He had withdrawn through South-East Asia before the Japanese advance at the turn of 1941–2, and had reached Java. Reuters in London told him on 5 March 1942 to report until the last moment, 'but remember we do not want you be caught'. The warning was already superfluous. Selby-Walker's last message by cable next day said bravely:

> eyem afraid its too late stop eyve only myself to blame goodluck hope see you all sooner than you expect.

He tried to escape that night with three other journalists, but all were supposed drowned when their boat was torpedoed off Sumatra on 7 March.

Reuters took a long time to recover from these Far Eastern shocks, and coverage remained uneven throughout 1942. As late as 9 December a service message to Bombay from London was full of complaints. The Bombay office was in charge of South-East Asian reporting:

> we lacking news exburma frontier fullstop extel have number small stories emphasising imminence action this theatre fullstop others have stories such as experiences small force british australian commandos who treked four-thousand miles when returning exbritish mission china fullstop we want this type story.

The momentous news of the dropping of the first atomic bomb on Hiroshima on 6 August 1945 came from Washington at 16.23 local time:

> PRESIDENT TRUMAN ANNOUNCED HERE THAT THE FIRST ATOMIC BOMB, MOST POWERFUL BOMB IN THE WORLD, HAD BEEN DROPPED 16 HOURS AGO ON HIROSHIMA (WEST OF KOBE) JAPANESE ARMY BASE, BY A US PLANE.
>
> IT IS MORE POWERFUL THAN 20,000 TONS OF TNT AND HAS MORE THAN 2,000 TIMES THE BLAST POWER OF THE BRITISH 'GRAND SLAM' HITHERTO THE LARGEST BOMB USED IN WARFARE.

News from Guam on 8 August was sent by Smyth, now serving in the Pacific after recovering from his experiences as a prisoner of war in Germany. He followed up by filing an eyewitness account from the pilot of the plane:

> 'IT WAS HARD TO BELIEVE WHAT WE SAW' IN THESE WORDS COL PAUL W TIBBETS, PILOT OF THE SUPERFORT WHICH ON MONDAY DROPPED THE FIRST ATOM BOMB ON JAPAN DESCRIBED THE RESULT OF THE EXPLOSION . . .
>
> ASKED IF IT WAS DANGEROUS FOR THE PLANE TO CARRY THE ATOMIC BOMB GENERAL LEMAY REPLIED 'WHAT DO YOU THINK!' CAPT WILLIAM PAR-SONS OF THE US NAVY WHO WORKED ON THE DEVELOPMENT OF THE BOMB RODE IN THE SUPERFRONT TO OBSERVE THE EFFECTS. HE SAID 'THE WHOLE THING WAS TREMENDOUS AND AWE INSPIRING. AFTER THE MISSILE HAD BEEN RELEASED I SIGHED, AND STOOD BACK FOR THE SHOCK. WHEN IT CAME THE MEN ABOARD WITH ME GASPED "MY GOD" AND WHAT HAD BEEN HIROSHIMA WAS A MOUNTAIN OF SMOKE LIKE A GIANT MUSHROOM.'

O 8.8.45..

ATOM

SNAPFULL

Japan
AIR OPS: *8 AUG* *atomic bomb*

GUAM, WEDNESDAY — T ATOMIC BOMB
WIPED OUT OVER FOUR SQUARE MILES OR
60 PER CENT OF HIROSHIMA, IT WS ANNOUNCED FROM GENRL
SPAATZ'S H Q TODAY. REUTER MF 0500 '''''

ATOM

SNAPFULL 2

T COMM BASED ON RECONNAISSANCE PHOTOS SD "ADDITIONAL
DAMAGE WS SHOWN OUTSIDE T COMPLETELY DESTROYED AREA.
REUTER MF 0501 '''

XXX ATOM

SNAPFULL 3

FIVE MAJOR INDUSTRIAL TARGETS WR WIPED OUT IN T CITY
T AREA O WH WS SIX AND NINE TENTHS SQUARE MILES. REUTER
0508 ''''''

VIII

Even in wartime, many days were not days of excitement. For example, the day-duty log for 15–16 February 1941 began simply: 'There was no big foreign news.' On such days Reuters had to make the most of what news there was. Reuters had also to remember that newspapers in Britain and elsewhere had sports columns to fill even in wartime. Although Malta was under fierce siege by air, Mabel Strickland, the doughty proprietor of *The Times of Malta*, once cabled: 'would appreciate full list of Derby runners as soon as possible.'

In November 1942 Cole used his contacts to obtain a copy of the famous Beveridge report on social welfare a week before publication. This enabled Reuters to publish a detailed summary as soon as the document was released. Here was a blueprint for postwar Britain. What about postwar Germany? Mason was very interested in the state of German public opinion during the war. At the time of the final push into Germany in 1945, he asked for full coverage of more than the fighting:

> The story has still to be told in connected fashion of the life of the Germans under Hitler since 1939, and the angles to this are so many that any correspondent could think up enough to fill a couple of books . . . Are the Germans going to be any better in the future than they have been in the past? Are they really beaten? Are we going to have to feed and clothe them, or are they sufficiently well off?

So Reuters prepared to report the painful return of peace to the world, just as it had reported the destructive course of war. It had done well. Its reputation as a news agency stood much higher in 1945 than in 1939. In wartime people everywhere read newspapers with extra attention, and the name 'Reuter' was often attached to the war news. And yet what perhaps fixed the Reuter name in the subconscious memory of the world in these years, as much as any war reporting, was a Hollywood film. In the United States it was called *A Dispatch from Reuters*; elsewhere it was entitled *This Man Reuter*.

The film was released in London in September 1941, when the United States had not yet entered the war but was sympathetic towards the British cause. The film was a good piece of pro-British propaganda. Through the example of the career of Julius Reuter, it illustrated the commitment of both Britain and America to freedom and honesty in news; and it showed how, in order to create a news agency which successfully promoted such freedom, Reuter had chosen to leave Germany and to set up in London. The geographical moral was tacit but obvious.

The decision to make a film about Reuter had been taken before the war. Even in peacetime the need to stand up for freedom in news was apparent in the face of the manipulation of the media by Goebbels and others. But at that time Hollywood was probably more interested in Reuter as a good subject on biographical grounds. Films about two other European celebrities of the nineteenth century, Zola and Pasteur, had been well received. Several approaches from film-makers had been made to Reuters in London during the 1930s. These had come to nothing. But on 6 December 1938 Jones reported to the board that he had settled with Warner Brothers. Jones had required that the script should be approved by Reuters.

As finally made, the film was misleading in many details. For example, the Crimean War of 1854–6 was substituted for the 1859 War of Italian Liberation as the occasion for Julius Reuter's earliest news scoops. Nevertheless, the film succeeded in conveying the atmosphere of the early days. Reuter was played by Edward G. Robinson, best known for sour gangster parts. He rightly portrayed Reuter as cheerfully purposeful.

Jones wanted an epilogue to be added to the film, sketching the later history of Reuters. It was to include shots of himself as a young man in South Africa and as chairman in London; the implication would be that he was a second Julius Reuter. An outline script was sent to Hollywood, where a Warner Brothers executive dismissed the idea sharply: 'it STINKS.' By the time of the film's release Jones was no longer in charge of Reuters.

ELEVEN

The Last Days of the Old Reuters
1941–1963

'In the nature of a trust' 1941–1951

I

CHRISTOPHER CHANCELLOR led Reuters through the difficult period after the Second World War. He served as joint general manager from February 1941, and as sole general manager following the retirement of Moloney in 1944.

Chancellor told a meeting of journalists in Washington on 28 January 1946 about the changes in the company since the resignation of Sir Roderick Jones in 1941: 'I think it is right and necessary for me to explain that the Reuters of today is a *new* Reuters, and that the Reuters of the past has on occasion stepped perilously near the abyss. In 1941 Reuters was reconstituted as a cooperative press association.' In that year, continued Chancellor, the Reuter board 'had the courage to say to the British Government that it would be better for Reuters to disappear from the face of the earth than for Reuters to receive any form of favoured treatment or subsidy. All such arrangements were cancelled. It was then that the new Reuters came into being.'

How valid were these claims? The present chapter will demonstrate that in reality the freedom achieved for Reuters after 1941 was not so complete as Chancellor suggested. The changes in the attitude of the Reuter management may have been total, but the changes in practice were incomplete. Reuters after the war simply did not possess the resources to operate independently in as many countries as it would have wished. Even the Reuter Trust deed was eventually found to be no more than a shareholders' agreement, which could be—and ultimately was—altered.

The old Reuters was reformed, but not transformed. This can best be understood by comparing what happened to Reuters under Chancellor with what happened after 1963 under a later general manager, Gerald Long. Then there was indeed a transformation.

II

Long once likened Chancellor to Horatius at the bridge—successful in holding his chosen ground, but limited in what he could attempt. The shortage of money which had driven Jones to seek Government help in the 1930s was still restricting improvement in the 1950s. Chancellor's style in facing these old problems was calm and polished, but also alertly intelligent. He was good at analysing problems and imaginative in proposing solutions. He could communicate clearly both in speech and writing, and he was very hard-working. Was there a flaw? Years after his retirement Chancellor was still remembered by some former colleagues and board members as 'devious'. He did not look you in the eye. Some Australians called him 'crafty Chris'—in contrast to Tony Cole, his right-hand man, who was 'phoney Tony'. Many who dealt with Chancellor in important negotiations—Kent Cooper of AP, for example—never felt quite at ease with him.

Nevertheless, Chancellor remained in successful charge of Reuters through most of two decades. His talent for manœuvre was what the agency needed in his time as general manager. He was trying to rebuild Reuters with limited resources against the odds. He had to conceal weakness while trying to find strength. A more straightforward personality might have done less well.

Chancellor's burden was the greater because the Reuter board possessed no regular chairman. Its membership fluctuated in quality. In 1945 Chancellor persuaded three major national newspapermen to become directors—Lord Rothermere, Sir Walter Layton, and H. G. Bartholomew. They joined three provincial newspapermen of stature—J. R. Scott of the *Manchester Guardian*, Malcolm Graham of the *Wolverhampton Express and Star*, and Harold Grime of the *Lancashire Evening Gazette*. With such a strong board behind him, Chancellor was later to remark that the next few years of postwar reconstruction constituted the high period of his time as general manager.

Chancellor was fortunate to find a deputy upon whose lively ability and commitment he could depend. This was Walton (Tony) Cole (1912–63). Cole had begun as a reporter in his native Scotland at the age of fifteen. In 1935 he moved to London as a reporter for the PA, and by 1939 was its night editor. Cole and Chancellor came to know one

another when both were serving as privates in the joint Reuter–PA company of the Home Guard. This had been formed in 1940 when a German
invasion of England seemed imminent. In March 1942 Chancellor
invited Cole to become news manager of Reuters. He had rightly realized that here was the man to modernize the news service and to sell it
worldwide.

Cole possessed both the right practical experience and the right hust-
ling personality for the job. During his time with Reuters he became a
massive figure, physically and psychologically. He was huge, weighing
eighteen stones or more: this gave him presence. Indeed, he so much
resembled King Farouk of Egypt that on one occasion, when he and
Chancellor arrived together at Cairo airport, the guard turned out. Not
that Cole possessed all the social graces. At table he devoured food and
drink—soda water after he gave up alcohol—in astonishing quantities,
which he seemed able to convert into instant energy. He needed little
sleep. He worked early and late at his desk, and was ever ready to travel
far and often. He lived for Reuters.

Cole was very much a working rather than an intellectual newsman,
but he subscribed to an overall ideal—truth in news. He believed that
Reuters had a mission to spread the truth worldwide through speedy,
accurate, and objective reporting. When he spoke about this in his own
Scots/mid-Atlantic drawl, there was no doubting his missionary sincerity.
His arguments and example readily persuaded most Reuter correspondents that they were privileged to work for an organization with such a
great purpose.

Cole was not himself a good writer. He had no foreign languages, and
his written English could become wordy and involved. But he was an
intuitive journalist. He had a nose for news, and was able to inspire much
better reporters than himself. He was also an eager salesman, revelling in
the negotiation of contracts with foreign agencies and newspapers. After
each negotiating trip, he returned to London full of excitement. He often
did well, but sometimes less well than he imagined. In some instances he
had seriously underestimated overheads, or forgotten about taxation or
inflation.

Cole was at his best with colleagues who were obviously junior to
himself. With possible rivals for the succession to Chancellor he pursued
a policy of divide and rule, encouraging and discouraging by turn, but
building up no one too high. His many tours to overseas offices were
occasions for developing local contacts and signing contracts with
Government and media figures; but while passing through he would

watch the progress of Reuter people. His visits were therefore occasions of considerable tension. In January 1955 David Chipp—then a South-East Asia correspondent, and later (1958–60) personal assistant to Cole—described in his private diary a visit by the editor to Rangoon and Bangkok:

> Wed. Jan. 19. After days of anxious waiting the great man arrived . . . In great good form and luckily impressed with my airport contacts. Carrying a huge briefcase called 85 Fleet Street . . .
>
> Sat. Jan. 22. Vital day. Clinched deal with The Nation, and laid foundation for economic one with the government. First Prof. Tun Thin who had schedule for Comtel all prepared. Obviously very keen.
>
> Thought Information Minister, Tun Win, was going to run out on us, but he saw WAC in end. Latter was very tough and impressive . . .
>
> Sun. Jan. 23. Arrived at WAC's room at 0645 and we got straight down to report. With only short break for breakfast we went on right to lunch.
>
> Tues. Jan. 25. Impressions of Cole—obviously NOT a gent and likes to hear good opinions of himself. Wears made-up bow ties. But he certainly gets things done and is a real worker; a good companion. Completely ruthless, and I found myself going under his spell.

The partnership between Chancellor and Cole was effective but curious. Chancellor treated Cole with a mixture of liking and disdain. Apart from both being Scots, the two men were very different in their social origins and in their personalities. But they shared a commitment to Reuters, and that was what mattered.

Two very different men worked closely with Cole in implementing editorial reforms. These were Geoffrey Imeson and Sid Mason. Imeson had joined Reuters in 1931. He served under Chancellor as chief editor in the Far East, and from 1942 to 1944 he was in New York. He was then brought back to London as deputy news manager. Imeson was an English gentleman. Mason was a Cockney orphan—pugnacious and foul-mouthed, known for ostentatiously wearing both a thick leather belt and braces. His early job as a newspaper copy-taker had taught him how to become a reporter. Spotted by Cole as a key man at BUP, Mason was persuaded to become night editor at Reuters in December 1942. He soon changed the news-room atmosphere by establishing his authority both as an editorial craftsman and as a personality. In 1944 he was made chief news editor, organizing the incoming file. Most Reuter correspondents in the field idolized him. They knew him to be a hard taskmaster, but they also knew him to be their protector at 85 Fleet Street.

III

The Chancellor and Cole era can be divided into four periods:

1. The wartime years after the resignation of Sir Roderick Jones (1941–5);
2. The period of busy post-war reconstruction, which lasted approximately until the Reuter centenary year (1945–51);
3. The later Chancellor period, ending with his resignation (1951–9);
4. The brief rule of Cole as general manager (1959–63).

After Jones's resignation in February 1941, the rest of the year was dominated by negotiations to bring the London national newspaper groups into the Reuter partnership, on terms acceptable both to them and to the provincial newspapermen who were the existing owners. The provincials were represented by the PA, the national newspapers by the NPA.

Jones's successor as chairman was Storey, who had been his most persistent critic. At the request of Storey and Haley, Sir Walter Monckton, the director-general of the Ministry of Information, agreed to withdraw clause A of Perth's letter of 1939 and the related postscript. This clause had requested the appointment of a deputy to Jones, while the postscript had indicated the Government's willingness to endorse Chancellor as such a deputy. The two passages were no longer specifically applicable, since the Jones problem had been solved. The requirement in Perth's letter 'that Reuters will at all times bear in mind any suggestions made to them on behalf of His Majesty's Government' was not withdrawn. 'The rest of the letter will stand,' wrote Monckton to Wilson of the Treasury on 27 February 1941. Monckton was exploiting the acceptance on the part of Storey and Haley that the letter had been in full force since 1939. In order to bring Jones down, the two directors had insisted upon adhering to this belief, despite Jones's claim to the contrary. So, paradoxically, Reuters was more certainly bound by the Perth letter after Jones's resignation than before it. Before challenging the letter's main provision, Reuters needed to find strength by extending its ownership and by improving its services.

Storey's ambition to become chairman of Reuters was suddenly achieved at the board meeting of 4 February 1941, which received Jones's resignation. Henderson, Storey's chief ally, proposed him. He immediately began to play an active part, more like that of a managing director. Indeed, Ewing and some other directors were soon complaining that Storey had assumed an almost full-time executive role not voted to him by the board.

Following Hatt's departure in the wake of Jones, Neale was appointed deputy editor-in-chief, the editorship being held open. Overseas staffing was reorganized, and the wireless service was aligned to directional beams. But Storey's main attention came to be concentrated upon the possibility of the NPA joining in the ownership of Reuters. He regarded this prospect with caution, whereas Haley believed that Reuters would be greatly strengthened if its ownership could at last be widened to represent the whole British press.

During February and March 1941 Haley, Chancellor, and others made informal contacts with members of the NPA. Among those sounded was its chairman, Lord Rothermere, chairman since 1932 of Associated Newspapers, the *Daily Mail* group. On 21 March the NPA formally requested a meeting with the PA to talk about the future of Reuters.

How should the PA respond? It soon became clear that the NPA would never accept less than equality. The meeting took place on 8 April, when Rothermere tabled a long memorandum. This recognized the need to strengthen the independence and efficiency of Reuters, noticed the increasing American competition, and proposed joint working between the provincial and national newspapers. The PA was asked to sell half its holding to the NPA. These were constructive proposals; but the memorandum was also threatening:

> If common agreement cannot be found we would have to ask Reuters to disclose to us what steps are being taken to organise the collection of news in the present German-controlled countries and elsewhere. Agencies that are now mere puppets of their governments must be suspect for many years, and we would have to know the sources of foreign news so that we could determine whether we should remain as subscribers or organise our own news collecting agency, or make other arrangements. We doubt if the provincial newspapers have the experience to satisfy us who have our own representatives in all parts of the world.

The possibility of the national newspapers setting up their own rival agency had been feared by Reuters ever since 1926.

The PA was seriously divided over its response to this NPA approach. A large and active minority, including Storey, concluded in the light of past experience that the PA would be unwise to allow the national-newspaper bosses an equal position within Reuters. During the interwar years they had shown how unscrupulous they could be. They had fought bitter newspaper wars with each other, both at the national and local levels, bankrupting independent papers in the process.

These proprietors were as distrustful of Storey as he was of them.

Some NPA members, influenced by Jones, doubted his integrity. Others simply did not believe that any provincial newspaperman could be sufficiently competent to preside over a major business such as Reuters. Quite quickly, and to his great frustration, Storey found himself being pushed aside—both by the NPA leadership and by a majority of the PA directors. The process was helped by the accident that his tenure of a seat on the PA board expired on 6 May 1941. Storey's version of events during 1941 is unfortunately much less well documented than that of his opponents.

Ewing of the *Glasgow Herald* now became chairman of the PA for a second time. He was widely respected as a firm yet conciliatory figure. Despite the opposition of the Storey minority within the PA, he was keen to bring the NPA into the Reuter partnership, and was made chairman of a PA negotiating subcommittee. Informal exchanges of view took place after meetings of the Newsprint Supply Company, which contained both PA and NPA representatives.

Haley's diary sketched the slow progress of the negotiations between the PA and the NPA:

22 June
During the last three months [there] have been the long negotiations with the NPA . . .

13 July
The Reuter deal still hangs fire . . .

21 July
Ewing rang from Glasgow this morning. The NPA are biting again . . .

3 August
Spent four days in London this last week trying to settle the Reuter business. At last we have got the NPA into line but Storey threatens trouble. I am more than sure the deal should go through and the Trust [be] set up.

14 September
I have had four days in London on the run, Sunday to Wednesday, trying to finish up the Reuter's Trust. At last we have it all straightened out with the NPA, and it is only a case of waiting to see if Storey will summon a meeting of the members. Even so the thing should go through, and I can take a fair share of the credit . . .

The terms finally agreed were skilfully designed by Haley and Ewing to protect the PA partners in Reuters from selfish scheming by the NPA partners, while none the less giving the NPA an equal share in the ownership. Only Lord Beaverbrook's *Daily Express* group, which disliked the asking price, refused to participate. The other NPA members agreed to buy half the issued capital of Reuters at £4. 10s. per share, the price paid by the PA in 1930. The NPA paid paid £168,768 for 37,504 shares. This holding was designated 'B' stock, the remaining PA holding 'A' stock.

No executives were made Reuter directors, although the general manager always attended the board. Its composition was carefully balanced. It was to consist of three directors from the PA and three from the NPA; even if one or two directors were absent, each party was to retain its power of casting three votes. No permanent chairman was to be appointed. The directors were to take the chair in turn at each board meeting, and there was to be no casting vote. All this was intended to prevent the acquisition of too much power by any one person—by another Jones from within the Reuter management, or by another Storey from the PA side, or by some press baron from the NPA side. 'How Storey will like the idea', wrote Haley in his diary on 21 July, 'I do not know, but I am convinced it is all wrong and too dangerous for Reuters to be under his or any other person's single control.' Storey apparently thought otherwise, as Haley noted on 12 October:

> Storey is spreading it abroad that I am ditching him so that I can get his chairmanship. The complete answer to that is that it is I who have destroyed the Chairmanship. As I said to Bracken [*minister of information*], 'Reuters has been run by a Baron, it has been run by a Knight, it is now being run by an MP. It was time it was run by some honest to goodness newspaper men.' Bracken agreed.

IV

Haley was the man most responsible for the terms of the Agreement of Trust made on 28 October 1941 between the PA and NPA. This agreement immediately became one of the most important documents in the history of Reuters.

The 'trust' idea had come into the world of journalism in various forms between the wars, for the defence of quality newspapers against predators. Haley had himself been appointed one of the first *Manchester Guardian* trustees in 1936. *The Times*, likewise, was protected by restrictions which made any transfer of shares subject to the approval of a committee consisting of the lord chief justice and other worthies.

The idea of a Reuter Trust began to circulate in the summer of 1941. It aimed to protect the agency from outside influence and interference, notably by the British Government. But equally it aimed to protect

Reuters from inside corruption, from any abandonment of standards by the directors or management. Even after his enforced resignation, Jones was being kept surprisingly up to date with developments by Ewing and others. On 9 June 1941 Ewing gave Jones a copy of a typed draft headed 'The Reuter Trust'. Ewing remarked that 'the original notes were Haley's some time ago', but that the draft was a combined effort drawn up 'one night recently at the Savoy'. This draft already included most of the provisions and much of the wording of the October final version, including the key phrase 'a trust rather than as an investment'.

It is not clear whether Storey was shown this draft. He had refused to surrender the chairmanship of Reuters, even when asked to do so in June by a deputation consisting of a majority of the PA board, led by Ewing. Haley and Ewing concluded that Storey was totally opposed to an equal partnership with the NPA. They seem to have decided to keep him in as much ignorance as possible.

Because of this, at the Reuter board meeting on 29 July 1941 a confrontation occurred. Storey asked for an account of the state of the PA negotiations with the NPA. Ewing answered that it was a matter for the PA board, not for the Reuter board. The subsequent exchanges with Storey—and with Henderson, his chief supporter on both boards—were described by Ewing to Jones, who next day wrote up an account:

> Storey said emphatically he was of opinion that he, as Chairman of Reuters, ought to have been consulted, and Henderson supported him in this . . .
>
> Needless to say, Derwent and Haley (and I daresay Staines) fully backed up Ewing, and the proceedings became so hot that Ewing said there was nothing to do but to adjourn the meeting.
>
> 'Until when?,' said Henderson.
>
> 'Well—until some time tomorrow, or even maybe Thursday if we don't get the NPA response in time for further consideration by the PA Board.'
>
> Henderson: 'In that case I shall not be able to be present.'
>
> Ewing: 'That I fear will be no loss. So far you have not assisted the proceedings. Quite the reverse.' (Henderson silent, pale and furious!)
>
> Storey got up and stalked out of the room. The other directors then got up from the table, and Henderson said: 'Well this is a pretty mess we've got ourselves into.'
>
> Ewing: 'For which you are mainly responsible. It was you who moved Storey Chairman, the moment Sir R. J. left the room upon his resignation.'
>
> Henderson: 'I fear I must admit that. It was an unwise step.'

Although Storey was no longer on the PA board, he was qualified to speak at a PA emergency general meeting on 17 October. It lasted all day, and revealed the depth of division within the PA. The Storey party accused the NPA of being 'unfriendly' or worse. There was much discussion of the content and spirit of the March memorandum from the NPA. Storey's supporters dwelt upon its threatening tone, whereas Ewing called it a 'remarkably reasonable statement', and Haley thought that it merely contained 'statements of fact'. The proposed trust agreement was dismissed by the Storey party as unworkable, and therefore meaningless; the main complaint was that the trustees had no power. Haley answered that 'they have the power to decide any matter the Board cannot decide. They cannot be removed, but they can remove directors.' A hostile resolution was eventually defeated by forty-three votes to seventeen on a show of hands. Henderson thereupon demanded a full poll. The resolution was then defeated by 5,024 to 2,288.

Storey's dogged opposition led him to make one last effort in 1941. He was now even prepared to welcome Government intervention to settle terms for reconstructing the Reuter ownership. He engineered a debate about the new partnership in the House of Commons on 22 October, three days after the decisive PA meeting. Attendance in the Commons was small, but a useful discussion took place. Behind the scenes, Storey had tried to arouse the concern of the Labour Party and of the backbench Conservative 1922 committee. He wanted, he said, all-party backing for Government intervention. All the speakers expressed concern about the independence of Reuters being left at risk. Most wanted some sort of trust. No one explained the case for what was already being done. But Brendan Bracken—the minister of information, and himself a newspaperman—knew more than most members about the new arrangements, and was not disposed to be as alarmed as Storey. The Government, he said, had been 'keeping a fatherly eye' on developments.

Next day (23 October) Bracken and Sir Kingsley Wood, the chancellor of the exchequer, met a deputation consisting of Ewing, Haley, and Derwent from the PA, and Rothermere, Kemsley, and Astor from the NPA. Kingsley Wood emphasized that the Government did not want to run Reuters itself; but it did want an independent outside chairman of the Reuter board, or at least of the new trustees—to be appointed not by a minister but by the lord chief justice. This approach meant that the Government was not seeking to challenge the new joint-ownership and trust arrangements. It was merely proposing additional safeguards in response to the thrust of the Commons debate. Both sides finally agreed that the chairman of trustees should be an outsider. The official report of the meeting noted that Haley accepted this only 'after some hesitation'. A Government request that the trust should function for a minimum of ten years was readily accepted. At the end of the meeting Haley pressed for speedy Government endorsement of the new arrangements, subject to the agreed changes. If not, he alleged, Storey 'might cause serious harm to the organisation'.

V

The preamble to the 1941 agreement of trust referred to the 'national interest' in wartime:

> The Press Association and the Newspaper Proprietors Association, recognising that the present national emergency and the uncertainties of the future render necessary special precautions to ensure in the national interest that Reuters be so established and consolidated that in every event it shall preserve its position as the leading world news agency, have mutually agreed to enter into this Agreement.

Here was shrewd manipulation of the idea of 'national interest'. Far from denying its relevance, the preamble simply assumed that the intention to secure the independence of Reuters must obviously be in the national interest. The preamble was omitted in the postwar version. The main part of the agreement of trust was clear in purpose:

> The Press Association and the Newspaper Proprietors Association hereby record their mutual agreement that they will regard their respective holdings of shares in Reuters as in the nature of a trust rather than as an investment and hereby undertake to use their best endeavours to ensure:
>
> (a) That Reuters shall at no time pass into the hands of any one interest group or faction.
>
> (b) That its integrity independence and freedom from bias shall at all times be fully preserved.
>
> (c) That its business shall be so administered that it shall supply an unbiased and reliable news service to British Dominion Colonial Foreign and other overseas newspapers and agencies with which it has or may hereafter have contracts.
>
> (d) That it shall pay due regard to the many interests which it serves in addition to those of the Press, and
>
> (e) That no effort shall be spared to expand develop and adapt the business of Reuters in order to maintain in every event its position as the leading world news agency.

The PA and NPA were each to appoint four trustees, under a chairman to be nominated by the lord chief justice. The trustees were given a five-year term. Their function was 'to act in a consultative capacity with the Board' and 'in accordance with the principles enunciated in this Agreement'. They were also to appoint 'A' directors from the PA and 'B' directors from the NPA in accordance with the articles of association. But, as Storey and others complained, the articles restricted the trustees' choice to nominees of the PA or NPA. The trustees therefore had power of rejection or dismissal, but not of free choice. The trust was to last for a minimum of twenty-one years, rather than the ten-year minimum agreed at the meeting with ministers on 23 October.

At the Reuter board meeting on the morning of 28 October Storey, who still refused to resign, was formally removed. The PA board had met under Ewing to authorize the transfer back to the PA of Storey's single share as a Reuter director. This was done—with Storey still in the Reuter chair. The minutes recorded: 'Mr. Storey having thus ceased to be a Director he then withdrew.' That same evening, Ewing described the occasion to Jones. 'Storey as Chairman said the transfer was in order. He signed it and then said: "Gentlemen, that naturally severs my connexion with Reuters and the Reuter Board. Good day."' So, for the second time within the year, the chairman of Reuters—first Jones, and now Storey—had left office in dramatic fashion.

The man selected as chairman of the Reuter trustees was Sir Lynden Macassey, a leading arbitration lawyer. He was eased out of office at the end of 1950. In that year a legal opinion had revealed that the agreement had no special status: it was merely a shareholders' agreement, which the shareholders could alter or even scrap. The requirement for an independent outside chairman of the trustees was now removed. But no publicity was given to the discovery that the much-publicized 1941 arrangements for the protection of Reuters were so fragile.

The declaration that the PA and NPA would treat their ownership of Reuters as a trust rather than as an investment brought its reward in the form of low assessments for the supply of Reuters news. The owners preferred to benefit in this way rather than to declare dividends, upon which they would have had to pay tax. Asked during the 1941 negotiations what return the national-newspaper proprietors could expect, Haley had replied: 'the establishment of Reuters as incontestably the greatest news agency in the world; and the use of its steadily improving services at gradually lower prices.' Haley remarked forty years later that this assurance had closed the discussion.

VI

As soon as the new ownership had been established in October 1941 Reuters began to seek a fresh relationship with the British Government— a relationship no longer conditioned by the Perth letter. At the beginning of that year the Ministry of Information had tried to prohibit the publication of enemy communiqués in the overseas services of Reuters, but the idea of such prohibition had been firmly resisted. Reuters insisted that it must publish all the news, even bad news for the British cause. Monckton, the director-general, had eventually agreed with Storey on 21 February 1941 that 'Reuters are still to be at liberty to include the substance of enemy communiques in their service in a form which would exclude propaganda'.

The joint committee of Reuters and the MOI continued to meet. Reuters produced a paper for the committee on 11 February entitled 'Some proposed methods of combating the effect of enemy communiques other than by suppression'. It recommended 'a persistent spoken, written, broadcast and whispering campaign' to undermine confidence in enemy communiqués. Reuters would continue to publish the communiqués, but counter-propaganda from the MOI could be included in the same overseas wireless transmissions.

The difficulty was that this combination required the submission of every enemy communiqué to the ministry, in case it wanted to comment. Reuters began to find such delay damaging. On 10 December 1941 publication of the Japanese communiqué announcing the sinking of the British warships *Prince of Wales* and *Repulse*—a major disaster in the new war in the Far East—was delayed for an hour. Meanwhile, AP had sent the news from London to New York. The New York office of Reuters complained that the delay had given the impression to American subscribers that Reuters was trying to suppress unpleasant news. An explanation on 23 December from Cyril Radcliffe, Monckton's successor, was more alarming than soothing: 'Any other arrangement would leave Reuters in effect in the same position in its relations with the Ministry as any other news agency with which we maintained no special connection. But, of course, we have special connections with Reuters.' This answer, if accepted, would have left Reuters tightly bound.

With this in mind, on 27 January 1942 the Reuter directors, plus Chancellor and Moloney, met Radcliffe; Haley presided. The discussion proved to be fruitful. The Perth letter had declared 'that Reuters will at all times bear in mind any suggestions made to them on behalf of His Majesty's Government'. Radcliffe now accepted that Reuters 'would not be expected to include anything in its service as a result of Government directives'. He did ask, however, for more effort by Reuters to understand 'how news which it sends abroad can affect Government policy throughout the world'. On the question of enemy communiqués, the meeting agreed that there must be consultation 'where a major British disaster is in question'. Otherwise, if no speedy comment came from the MOI, Reuters was to be free to transmit a communiqué abroad. In this way Reuters clarified its relationship with the British Government over the handling of news. In the following year it secured a complementary clarification of its financial relationship.

By 1941 British Government payments for extra wordage in Reuter wireless transmissions overseas were running at almost three times the payment to the British Post Office from Reuters itself—£15,000 per annum from Reuters and £44,000 from the Government. Did these large Government payments constitute a subsidy? The Reuter board decided that, at least in their existing form, they did. On 1 June 1943 the board therefore resolved 'to complete the liquidation of the emergency arrangements with the Ministry of Information'. In a letter to Radcliffe of 22 September 1943 Chancellor included a transcript of this resolution. He explained that it covered all arrangements between the Government and Reuters 'dating from 1939, details of which will be available to you at the Ministry'. Thus, in this decisive but unexcited fashion, were the provisions of the Perth letter finally repudiated by Reuters.

Yet the same board resolution promised that there would be no contraction of Reuter activities. How then were Government payments to the Post Office in aid of Reuter transmissions to be reconciled with the new spirit? At a meeting on 7 September the Reuter board decided that the continuing need for cheap transmission rates could be satisfied, without hint of subsidy, if cheap rates were made available to all. A low tariff for every user, Chancellor told Radcliffe, 'could in no way be called a subsidy to Reuters and it would be analogous to the Empire press rate'.

So a low tariff was introduced, in theory open to all but not publicized. Reuters agreed to pay £20,000 for the year from 1 July 1943, subsequently increased to £30,000 for the year from 1 July 1944. Actual transmission costs for the latter year were £90,000. Reuters persuaded itself that this did not amount to a £60,000 Government subsidy because the same low tariff was nominally available to others.

The new emphasis upon independence in relation to the British

Government at home did not mean that Reuters felt that it could now do without support from the British Government overseas. At the very same board meeting on 1 June 1943 which had repudiated all existing contracts, Haley raised 'the question of what was to be the future attitude of the Government towards Reuters as a great independent British agency'. Haley's combination of adjectives was revealing. Reuters now regarded itself as independent, but it still saw itself also as British—with a right to expect help from British diplomats overseas.

On 24 June 1942 Chancellor had visited Eden, the foreign secretary, to ask for such support. On 11 August Eden lunched at 85 Fleet Street with the Reuter board, and toured the editorial department. Upon his own initiative, he promised to circulate a note about Reuters to British missions abroad. In a draft for Eden's guidance Chancellor emphasized the Britishness of Reuters as well as its independence. 'It is of great importance for the maintenance of British prestige', he told the foreign secretary, 'that news from Great Britain and other parts of the world should be provided so far as possible through a British channel.'

Eden's circular of 20 July 1942 was less supportive than Chancellor had probably expected:

> The present management admit that Reuters' standard of efficiency in recent years has left much to be desired and declare their anxiety to improve matters . . . Reuters naturally desire that their representatives abroad should receive all possible help from His Majesty's Missions. . . . While helping Reuters in every way, it would of course be unwise to discriminate against competent and well-disposed correspondents of other British or American agencies or newspapers.

Here was more qualification than commendation.

VII

The Foreign Office remained keen for Reuters to establish itself in Latin America. The 1927 renewal of the ring combination had finally allowed Reuters the right of entry, in return for allowing Havas into the Far East. In 1931 Jones decided upon a big effort. After a sales-promotion visit to South America, the Prince of Wales had spoken publicly of the need 'to improve the present very inadequate British news service in South America'. Here was a challenge to Jones's patriotism. Reuters started to distribute its news in South America through a service centred upon Argentina. But this comprised only 1,000 words per day, compared with between 10,000 and 15,000 daily from the American agencies. After three years the losses had become insupportable, and Reuters withdrew.

The fall of France in 1940 brought a new opportunity. The Foreign Office asked Reuters to take over from Havas. Chancellor went out in the summer of 1940 (and again in 1943) to organize the service. Initially this largely meant re-engaging the Havas staff, although most were later replaced. Reuters started with what Jones described to the board on 1 November 1940 as a 'blanket grant' from the British Government of about £30,000 to cover expenditure not met by revenue. Transmission to South America of the Globereuter and other wireless services was subsidized to the extent of 11,000 words daily.

Gross revenue from South America built up well: 1941, £72,914; 1945, £88,357; 1950, £107,997. These totals exceeded the current revenue from North America, and made South America in 1950 the third overseas revenue-earner after Europe (£235,122) and the Far East (£126,658). Yet once again Reuters failed to establish itself upon a profitable basis. With the coming of peace, concentration upon Argentina, Chile, and Brazil was tried. But this did not solve the underlying problem. Reuters could not afford to mount a service of Latin American news, preferably in Spanish, for local sale alongside its world news. The 1951 centenary history of Reuters recorded the amazement among its competitors 'that Reuters stayed in Latin America at all'.

VIII

A relationship of friendly rivalry was cultivated with the Associated Press from 1942. This was established thanks to the negotiating skill of Haley, who spent from April to June 1942 in the United States and Canada drawing up a new contract. For three weeks Cooper of AP would not meet Haley at all, but Haley waited patiently. He eventually persuaded the distrustful American that the principles which now guided Reuters were the same as those which guided AP—commitment to truth in news, news collected in free competition without official interference or subsidy.

The end was harmonious, but the Reuter board had been prepared for failure. On 10 March 1942 it denounced the 1934 contract as 'intolerable'. The board was prepared for a complete break if better terms could not be obtained. Haley told Cooper plainly that in calling Jones's bluff in 1934 AP had forced 'a vindictive contract' upon Reuters. Cooper did not deny this.

In a long report on the negotiations, dated 1 July 1942, Haley described Cooper's remembrance of Jones as amounting to 'almost a phobia'. Jones's cold and patronizing manner had made Cooper suspicious of everything to do with Reuters. On five separate occasions Cooper told Haley how twenty years earlier he had approached Reuters with an offer of friendship, and how Jones had rebuked him for his presumption. This personal dislike was joined to the belief that Reuters was subsidized by the British Government. In reply, Haley gave Cooper a copy of the new trust agreement, and was able slowly to convince him that Reuters was now eager and fit to join in the campaign for truth and freedom in news. 'We agreed that the basis covering our relationship should be "Compete and co-operate".'

In this spirit, Reuters and AP became (in Cooper's phrase) 'blood brothers'. New and equal terms were agreed. AP was to have full access to the Reuter and PA news service, as delivered to London newspapers for use anywhere in the western hemisphere. In return, Reuters was to have full access to the AP news service, as delivered to New York newspapers for use in the eastern hemisphere. This represented a great improvement upon the 1934 agreement, which had delivered to Reuters only AP's North American news. As before, this news exchange was to involve no money payment.

Reuters had found it hard to sell news to American newspapers, especially outside New York, where the *New York Times* was an old and valued customer. One of Cole's greatest coups came in 1944 when he signed a contract with the *Chicago Tribune* for delivery of the Reuter service in London and New York. This contract represented a triumph of personality. Cole had to win over Colonel Robert McCormick, the owner of the *Tribune*, who was well known for his anti-British views. Cole volunteered to visit Chicago to demonstrate to McCormick that Reuters was an efficient and reputable partner, no longer under the influence of the British Government. Before signing, McCormick sent his managing editor, J. L. Maloney, to sit in the newsroom at 85 Fleet Street. Maloney liked what he saw, and the Reuter service to the most influential newspaper in the Middle West started on 1 December 1944. The *Tribune* paid $200 per month for the Globereuter service, and £2,400 for the Reuter and PA service to newspapers in London, as also supplied to the *New York Times*.

In February 1945 a second contract was signed. This arranged for the *Chicago Tribune/New York Times* News Syndicate to market Reuter news in the Middle West and South on a profit-sharing basis. In return, Reuters was to market news from the syndicate throughout the United Kingdom, Europe, India, and South Africa.

IX

At the end of 1942 Haley went to Australia to negotiate a new contract with the Australian Associated Press (AAP), successor to the Australian Press Association, which had negotiated the expiring 1926 contract. Before setting out, Haley wrote a comprehensive report on 'Reuters in Australia', dated 25 October 1942. He concluded that the history of Reuters in Australia was 'the record of an attempt by powerful newspapers acting in combination to keep Reuters from establishing itself there'.

As expected, the negotiations were tough. But Haley was able to establish good personal relations with two of the Australians—Rupert Henderson of the *Sydney Morning Herald*, and Sir Keith Murdoch of the *Melbourne Herald and Sun*. Henderson, who was to be closely associated with Reuters for over forty years, was described by Haley as 'one hundred percent a newspaperman': 'He has, far more than Sir Keith Murdoch, a genuine apprehension of American influence in Australia after the war. He is determined to combat it, and he feels a Reuter service, providing it is as good as that of its American rivals, is essential to the Australian press.'

The fixing of the amount payable by the AAP was explicitly treated by Haley as a test of whether or not a new spirit had been created. He told Henderson that he was going to name straight away what he thought to be a fair figure, without starting from a higher figure simply for the sake of bargaining:

> Mr Henderson asked 'And the figure is?'
> I said 'Ten thousand pounds a year'.
> Mr Henderson pursed his lips, looked at me and said 'You want this to be more than a mere business deal?'
> 'Yes'
> 'And you want it to be in a spirit above a bargain?'
> 'Yes'
> 'And you want ten thousand pounds a year?'
> 'Yes'
> A pause. Then
> 'All right. It's done.'

Unlike Jones in 1926, Haley took care to negotiate for pounds sterling, not Australian pounds.

The agreement was for fifteen years from 1 May 1943, but with either party free to give a year's notice on 30 April 1950. For the future, Haley was hopeful but not unrealistic. 'Experience indicates that the AAP's feelings towards Reuters will always be subject to fluctuations. That is the Australian nature.'

During 1941–2 Reuters had been swept out of a vast area north of Australia right up to Manchuria. Chungking became the only office still functioning in the whole of China, and Reuters was the sole western agency still distributing news there. The manager was Tommy Chao. He was the most senior of the local staff upon whose loyalty and dedication Reuters in Asia and elsewhere had always depended heavily. He died in confinement at a Communist reformatory farm in 1961.

The Japanese had seized the Shanghai office on 8 December 1941. Surprisingly—thanks to the personal intervention of the Domei president and of its general manager, Sabaro Matsukata, an old friend of Reuters—the British staff were well treated. The Japanese had even allowed a limited service of commercial and general news to operate during January–May 1942. This excluded any news which 'might give the Chinese people the idea that, although we are winning some victories now, we will lose the war later on'. Cromarty Bloom, the manager, left Shanghai in August 1942, and nearly all the staff of over a hundred were paid off with dollar IOUs, to be honoured (as they were) after the war.

X

Air raids threatened the work of Reuter headquarters in London much more seriously during the Second World War than during the first. Fortunately, the new building at 85 Fleet Street had been built with basement air-raid shelters, where alternative editorial and wireless-transmitting facilities were organized. Even so, 85 Fleet Street was several times cut off from incoming messages because of damage to cables. The teleprinter system out to the British newspapers was never interrupted.

An alternative news centre was set up at a house near Barnet, on the northern fringe of the London telephone network. The entire overseas staff became based there during the worst of the blitz in 1940–1. Emergency lines to the transmitter kept the overseas wireless service operating without interruption. On 17 April 1941 Reuter headquarters came close to being bombed out. A land-mine dropped by the Luftwaffe became caught in cables strung across Fleet Street about half way between the front door of Reuters and Ludgate Circus. No incoming messages were being received. In order to prevent the Germans from knowing that they had almost put the Reuter headquarters out of action stories from back numbers of *The Times* were rehashed as fresh news.

The news report was supplemented by a service of news features called 'situationers'. These were edited by the formidable Muriel Penn. Most Reuter correspondents liked writing situationers because they were widely published, and unlike hard news copy they usually carried the reporter's byline. From 1944 Reuters and the PA jointly produced a feature service and a British news-picture service. Reuters pulled out in 1958 and 1964 respectively, leaving its representatives to regret that they had no picture service to offer when negotiating contracts.

XI

In 1945 Reuters was employing nearly 2,000 full-time staff worldwide for the first time. About a tenth of this number were full-time correspondents. By 1950 large bureaux were operating in twenty-three countries, and small bureaux with one or two staffers in another nineteen. Reuter news was being distributed directly to subscribers in fourteen countries. But distribution through national agencies remained the method for thirty-one countries. Reuter news via radio was received from London by newspapers and radio stations in thirty-five countries, mostly within the British Empire.

Chancellor told the 1948 Royal Commission on the Press that about half a million words per day were now pouring into the newsroom of 85 Fleet Street. At any one time some thirty journalists plus an equal number of typists and wire operators were working in the editorial, which had moved from the fifth to the fourth floor in June 1947. The Central Desk remained the focal point. All news came to it for processing. Target news also went to a growing number of regional desks—Asian, African, European, North American—each with an editor. The regional desks were Cole's response to the realization that overseas subscribers did not want identical services. When he joined in 1942 he had found that the entire news service was produced in just three parts—a direct teleprinter service to the London papers and the PA; a general overseas service; and a service to Europe. The Nor Desk, set up to serve North America in 1944, was increasingly staffed by young Americans and Canadians, who knew what the American papers wanted. Among the Canadians, Stuart Underhill was to progress through the editorial to become a contender for the post of general manager in 1963.

XII

The Paris office in the Place de la Bourse was the largest overseas centre in the immediate postwar period, with a staff of about fifty. It served as a collecting-point for French news; as a distribution centre for Reuter news and commercial services to French subscribers; and as a retransmission post to London for news collected in many other European centres. During the 1950s the news service for France was redesigned and news distribution reorganized. By 1958 trading profit was £45,922, compared with only £686 for 1949. By the late 1950s Reuters in France felt more confident in competing on the home ground of Agence France Presse (AFP), the French Government-subsidized successor to Havas. On the other hand, AFP was an increasingly strong competitor on the world news scene.

Just before the war the news agencies of Belgium, Switzerland, The Netherlands, Finland, Norway, Denmark, and Sweden had come together in the '1939 Group'. It continued active during postwar years, pressing Reuters for lower subscription rates. At first Chancellor and Fleetwood-May, the European manager, responded over-generously, being more interested in consolidating community of interest than in extracting maximum financial return. Eventually, however, more realism began to be introduced into contract and other negotiations with the Europeans. The man responsible was Alfred Geiringer, an Austrian by birth, who had started with Reuters in Vienna in 1937.

In 1944 he was chosen to re-establish the Reuter organization in central Europe. Geiringer began with Switzerland, where he was sent to help modernize the Agence Télégraphique Suisse. He persuaded the Swiss that they could not afford to buy news from more than one world agency, and that they should choose Reuters. He also negotiated a direct contract with the Agence Cosmographique for Swiss rights to the commercial service.

Geiringer's greatest achievement came in postwar Germany. Gradual relaxation of Allied control of news supply allowed him time to build up a strong organization in West Germany. Offices were opened in Berlin, Hamburg, Bonn, and Frankfurt. Frankfurt became the editorial centre for central, eastern, and northern Europe. From the beginning, Geiringer recognized that the Germans would soon want to establish agencies of their own. Wisely, he did not try to oppose this. Instead, he took care to ensure that the new co-operative agency—formed by a merger on 1 September 1949 of the agencies in the three Western Allied zones—was firmly linked to Reuters by a five-year contract. The new German agency was called Deutsche Presse Agentur (DPA).

As with the 1939 Group, Chancellor offered collaboration rather than competition. He told Fritz Säenger of DPA on 1 January 1951 that, because AFP had lapsed into being a subsidized organ of the French Government, DPA could readily become the leading continental agency. 'Reuters needs a strong ally in Europe, and I feel that if we work together each can help the other.' In 1949 a West German commercial news agency had also been formed with Reuter support—the Vereinigte Wirtschaftsdienste (VWD). A financial reorganization in December 1951 led to Reuters taking a third share.

Within its limits, Chancellor's European policy paid off. From 1949 Europe became the main revenue-producing area for Reuters, following a sharp decline in revenue from India after independence:

TABLE 11.1. *Gross post-war revenue figures (£)*

	Europe	Far East	Indian sub-continent
1945	55,155	10,980	277,090
1950	235,122	126,658	57,635
1960	526,501	368,471	67,088

XIII

The problem of how to pay for Reuter radio transmissions overseas after the war had become urgent by 1944. The American agencies had asked the British Post Office for similar rates to those enjoyed by Reuters. Reuters could not resist, having itself anticipated allegations of subsidy by insisting in the previous year that equal rates were nominally made available to all agencies.

The outcome was a new higher tariff which presented Reuters with additional expenditure of £64,000 per annum. This was a measure of the hidden official subsidy to Reuters even after the 1943 renegotiation. The British Government remained ready to help: it expressed a willingness to pay generous 'subscriptions'. An agreement was made between Chancellor and Radcliffe on 17 February 1945, summarized for the Reuter board on 1 March:

1. Existing British Government 'subscriptions' totalling about £15,000 per annum were to be 'crystallised' as at 25 January, and were to be altered only to meet changes in 'out-of-pocket' expenses of Reuters. To this end, £10,000 had already been added to the £15,000 from 1 January 1945.

2. British Government offices overseas were to be supplied with the Reuter news service 'for internal use'. This news could be used in some weekly British information bulletins issued locally, but only with specific permission from Reuters.

3. Reuter and Press Association services were to be provided for use in the British Official Wireless service at a subscription of £4,000 a year. 'The Reuter name will not be quoted.'

4. Reuters was to be paid £6,000 a year for transmitting the Force-reuter service to British servicemen abroad on the European and Eastern transmitters.

On 11 April Chancellor explained the new position to the chief Reuter correspondents overseas. Total Government payments 'for services rendered', he wrote, were worth 'approximately £35,000 per annum'. Even so, Chancellor claimed that no special relationship existed between Reuters and the British Government because the payments took the form of 'subscriptions'. Subscriptions were received from other Governments and the American agencies also accepted them. The fact remained that the British Government payments to Reuters were deliberately very generous.

XIV

The commercial services, which had been seriously disrupted in Europe and the Far East, slowly revived after the war. In March 1944 Reuters had bought Comtelburo. This was a private company dating from 1869, which was on the verge of collapse but which enjoyed a virtual monopoly of reporting commercial prices between South America and London. This made it attractive to Reuters, which was now trying to break into South America.

On 14 February 1945 Reuters concluded an agreement with PA and Extel to pool their handling of commercial news. Comtelburo contracted to provide a 'home commercial service', and also the 'overseas commercial, financial and trade services'. Extel agreed to supply the home financial and Liverpool services. The London fast-printer services were to be run jointly. In other words, Reuters was seeking to prosper in supplying commercial news, but it was not yet seeking to dominate the field.

The commercial services shared the Reuter communications network with general news, but not on equal terms. Derek Jameson, then a duty editor, recollected how the Comtelburo staff at 85 Fleet Street were forever trying to get use of the news wires. '"Sorry, cock," we would say, "they've just formed their 29th postwar government in Italy. No room for your crap".' These commercial services were still regarded as subsidiary. Chancellor made this brutally clear in a board paper on 10 June 1947: 'The main activity under the second function (profit-making) is the so-called Commercial Service. This is run for the sole purpose of subsidizing the news service. If it ceased to show a profit we should discontinue it.' In the event, Comtelburo profits doubled during the 1950s, from £68,956 in 1950 to £143,197 in 1959. They were becoming increasingly necessary to maintain the loss-making general-news side.

Progress in communications technology had brought important developments during and after the Second World War. Most of the news from outside Europe was still carried by the cable companies. After the war, monitoring of broadcasts from Communist countries became vital when reporting from inside the Communist bloc was made increasingly difficult. In 1953 a new station was opened at Green End, 30 miles north of London, with a staff of nineteen listeners. Monitoring at Green End continued until 1980.

For outward services, Chancellor told the 1948 Royal Commission on the Press that there had been a 'complete revolution in communications' in recent years. In the days of telegraphy by commercial cable the emphasis had been on condensation of messages because charges were related to wordage. Now leased channels, either land-line or radio, were used. The radio channels were leased from the Post Office for twenty-two hours per day, resulting in an enormous increase in wordage. One hundred thousand words per day were now sent from London: before the war this had been a whole month's total. 'It has altered the whole style of the work, and the tendency is to write the news in London in a much more presentable form.'

High-frequency radio, which had made possible a switch to directional beams in 1941, allowed the distribution of separate Globereuter services with content varied to suit regional interests. After the war Europe and the Mediterranean, North America, South America, Africa, and the Far East received separate beams. In 1949 a high-frequency radio-teletype service was opened between London and New York. This replaced Morse, and reduced transmission time to seconds. Unfortunately, all high-frequency transmissions were often affected by interference, which could block or garble messages. A blackboard in the editorial department, chalked up by hand, showed from hour to hour the wordage being carried on each beam and the backlog. At the end of 1949 the British Post Office at last allowed Reuters to employ its own operators.

Lines were less liable to interruption than radio, and here also big advances had been made. The Globereuter radio service to Europe was replaced in 1949 by a leased-line teleprinter network which provided a two-way link between London and the European capitals. A first stage had been started to Paris in 1947. This European Printer Network (EPN) was financed and operated in association with the European national agencies. Reuters was following the example of the American agencies and of AFP, which had already set up their own networks. Cole told the board in February 1950 that the benefits for Reuter correspondents were large. They now knew that if they were ahead with a story, Reuters would stay ahead in getting it out.

XV

At the end of 1946 the Australian Associated Press and New Zealand Press Association agreed to join in the ownership of Reuters from 1 March 1947. Chancellor and Cole had visited Australia to settle terms for an expanded partnership. No longer was Reuters to be exclusively British-owned. It wanted to broaden its ownership, and it needed capital for development.

An additional issue of 37,500 'C' shares was made at £1 par value. This 'C'-share issue equalled the number of 'A' and 'B' shares held respectively by the existing owners, the PA and NPA. The AAP took up one-third of the issue at the price paid by the NPA for its shares in 1941—12,500 shares at £4. 10s. per share. The NZPA bought 2,500 'C' shares. The Australians thus paid £56,250 to become part-owners of Reuters, and the New Zealanders £11,250.

In place of the 1943 agreement, under which the AAP was a customer, the Australians were to pay an annual assessment of £36,000. This was in proportion to their shareholding, one-seventh of the total assessment. A rebate of one-third was allowed to cover the expenses of Australian staff in London and New York. The AAP was given the right to appoint one director and one trustee. The NZPA was allowed one trustee, and also secured a link with the AAP board.

The Australians were understandably well pleased by these terms. The AAP secretary noted on 18 December 1946 that the agreement assured the AAP of participation in the Reuter service, 'and a seat at the Reuter Board table at which all the principal international news agreements must from time to time be discussed'. All Pacific correspondents were to be AAP-appointed, but they had to be acceptable to Reuters. Three

Australians and one New Zealander were initially selected. General editorial supervision was expected to be exercised from Melbourne.

In his report to the Reuter board, dated 14 December 1946, Chancellor summed up optimistically from his side of the negotiations:

> We shall employ Australians and New Zealanders in Reuters and they will be a source of strength to us; but the AAP news organisation outside Australia will gradually be absorbed into Reuters and the basic news service to Australia—to be called AAP-Reuter—will be increased from about 5,000 words a day to 15,000 words a day. This will establish the Reuter name in Australia and New Zealand and make the Reuter service the main news source for the Australian and New Zealand newspapers. And it will relegate the American services to a supplementary place. To my mind this is just as important as the financial terms of the agreement.

Chancellor told Murdoch in a letter of 22 July 1946 that 'this would not be an ordinary business deal. . . . To a large degree the motive would have to be idealistic . . . designed to widen the ownership and strengthen the competitive power of the only British-owned *world* news service.'

The new stock, part-issued to the Australians and New Zealanders, was available for sale only to Commonwealth press associations and newspaper organizations. The aim was to enable Reuters to become a great co-operative within what was still called the 'British' Commonwealth—Reuter-led from London, but with partners around the world. Murdoch forecast that such an approach would not be confined to journalism: 'we have started a method which will undoubtedly be applied increasingly and over a wide area to British activities, commercial and others.' Murdoch had been responsible for starting the exchanges which led to the new partnership. But it was Henderson's drive which transformed the idea into reality.

So the Australian and New Zealand connection was established. What about Canada, South Africa, and also India—now on the point of achieving independence? From the first, the board had agreed that the door should be kept open for the Canadians and South Africans to follow the Australians. But the Canadian Press was rightly regarded as unlikely to respond, in view of its close links with the United States. Chancellor and Henderson visited South Africa in 1947 and discussed the matter there. But Afrikaaner opinion was against any partnership with Reuters.

XVI

It was fortunate that the South Africans never joined the partnership, and unfortunate for both sides that the Indians did join. The Associated Press of India, a Reuter subsidiary, had been a successful and profitable organization. It was in a dominant position within India, employing about 500 people and controlling 6,000 miles of leased teleprinter lines. Reuter assets at independence in 1947 (including API) were worth about £100,000. Indian subscriptions were much the highest for any area of the world— £277,090; roughly a third of which was profit. Indian revenue peaked about £330,000 in 1948, but never again reached six figures.

On 7 April 1945 the Indian Newspaper Society had resolved to press for a complete take-over of API, and for 'an interest' in Reuter internal services 'with a view to reorganising them on cooperative lines'. At this stage Reuters was ready to concede no more than an equal share in the ownership of API, and no share at all in the Reuter commercial service. This was earning very good profits of about £30,000 a year.

Cole was sent to India to examine the position. He quickly decided that the Indians could not be offered less than sole ownership of API and its internal news service. Terms were eventually drawn up for transferring the ownership of API to a new Press Trust of India (PTI). But the negotiations were aborted when the new interim Indian Government refused to allow Reuters, as a non-Indian organization, rights over internal teleprinter lines. Many nationalists could not forget that Reuters had been an instrument of the raj.

Early in 1947 a fresh start was made. The new president of the Indian Newspaper Society, Kasturi Srinivasan, who controlled the *Hindu* of Madras, was a moderate nationalist. Chancellor wrote to him on 18 March in conciliatory terms: 'this is not just an ordinary business deal: it is much more important than that.' Similar words had been used by Chancellor in his recent dealings with the Australians, and by Haley in his negotiations with Kent Cooper in 1942.

John Turner, the general manager in India, was now instructed to explore the ground. A Turner–Srinivasan agreement, dated 1 June 1947, included a formula for sharing profits between Reuters and the PTI. In a letter to Chancellor on 2 June, however, Srinivasan looked beyond these 'tentative proposals'. He expressed a desire 'to enter into the same relationship with Reuters organisation as the other countries which sit on the Board'. A Reuter subcommittee was appointed to consider this approach. Among the Indians, financial realism was at least as important as idealism about journalistic standards or Commonwealth co-operation. Reuters too had its financial incentive—fear that AP or UP might sooner or later displace Reuters as the main supplier of world news to India, if the Indians were not tightly bound.

On 19 June 1947 the Reuter board agreed to invite the Indians to discuss entry into the partnership on terms similar to those agreed with the Australians. By a coincidence, this was the very first meeting of the Reuter board attended by Henderson as the AAP/NZPA representative. Layton (now Lord Layton) reminded his fellow directors that they were sitting 'for the first time as a British Commonwealth Board'.

Annoyingly for Reuters, the Indian Newspaper Society now hesitated; not until May 1948 did a delegation arrive in London. Apart from Kasturi Srinivasan, its members were his cousin, C. R. Srinivasan, a governor of the Reserve Bank of India; Devadas Gandhi, son of the Mahatma, managing editor of the *Hindustan Times*; Ramnath Goenka of the Madras *Indian Express*; and Swaminath Sadanand, publisher of the Bombay *Free Press Journal*. In a note for the Reuter board, Chancellor warned that Devadas Gandhi exploited the prestige of his father's name but was 'very much a man of the world and a hard negotiator'.

The objectives of the Reuter negotiators were defined by Chancellor at a board meeting on 11 February 1948. They were firstly, 'to retain as high a proportion as possible of the net revenue from India'; and secondly 'to keep India permanently as a Reuter territory'. The negotiations in London dragged on from 21 May to 18 June 1948. They quickly came down to questions of money—in particular, to the amount of assessment. 'The basic point', summed up by Gandhi, 'was that the Press Trust wanted to pay £35,000 and Reuters wanted it to pay £42,000.' Breakdown seemed likely. But at the last moment heads of agreement, drafted by the Reuter side and approved by the Indian Government, were accepted by the Srinivasans and agreed in principle by Gandhi. At a meeting of the Eastern and Indian Newspaper Society from 22 to 24 July 1948 Gandhi spoke out strongly in favour. Goenka and Sadanand spoke against; but the Society publicly announced its acceptance on 21 September 1948.

The heads of agreement of 18 June proclaimed that the PTI 'will assume the same responsibility as the other owners for the Reuter world service and the maintenance of the principles of the Reuter Trust'. The PTI was to take 12,500 'D' shares at £4. 10s. per share—the same number as the AAP. And like the AAP, the PTI was given the right to appoint one director and one trustee. An Indian Desk was to be set up at 85 Fleet Street to take over the work of the Eastern Desk. This desk was to serve Pakistan, Ceylon, Burma, Malaya, and elsewhere as well as India. The Indian news zone was to stretch from Cairo to Singapore, and primary responsibility for collection of news in the zone was to rest with the

PTI. Four extra correspondents were to be appointed. All zone correspondents were to be known as 'PTI-Reuter' journalists.

On transfer day the entire API organization was handed over intact. The PTI paid Reuters the value of net assets, but without attributing any value to goodwill and with payment spread over five years. The Reuter commercial service was included in the transfer. The PTI assessment was fixed at the same nominal level as that of the AAP—£43,333. 6s. 8d. A 'development rebate' for three years cut this by £13,000. Reuters agreed to meet the costs of the Indian Desk in London up to a maximum of £10,000 per annum.

The Indians formally joined the Reuter partnership for an initial four years from 1 February 1949. Jawaharlal Nehru, the first Indian prime minister, described the move in a letter to Kasturi Srinivasan on 23 September 1948 as 'another step in our liberation, for a free Press and a free news service are the most vital characteristics of a free nation'. Chancellor and the Reuter directors were enthusiastic in public, more guarded in private. Chancellor told King on 24 September 1948 that India was 'suffering from a hysterical form of nationalism . . . if we can make this partnership work we shall have done something worth doing. But it will not be easy.'

XVII

In January 1946 the American State Department issued a booklet on *The Post-war International Information Programme of the United States*. A section devoted to Reuters claimed that it was still subsidized by the British Government. In particular, the booklet noted that the Rugby radio transmitters were used by Reuters round the clock to send British news over the world. 'Ostensibly the same facilities are open to American news agencies. But the facilities are limited and apparently not available in volume.'

Chancellor responded immediately to this attack with a 3,000-word statement on 4 January 1946 which was widely noticed. He denied that Reuters received any special privileges, 'and that Reuters as a result of this connection with the British Government "conditions" its news to favour British interests'. Nevertheless, Chancellor had to admit that in practice the Rugby transmitters had not been equally available to all agencies. They would become so 'as soon as the necessary equipment and staff are available on release from wartime service'. This explanation glossed over the past by pointing reassuringly towards the future.

Three weeks after the State Department attack Chancellor gave the address to journalists in Washington quoted at the beginning of the present chapter. He then flew on to Kent Cooper's home in Florida to settle a new contract with AP. Thanks to Haley's good work in 1942, Cooper now accepted Reuters as a partner in the pursuit of truth and freedom in news. He did so even though Haley and Chancellor still described Reuters as 'British'. Was this now merely a geographical adjective, or did it carry overtones of persisting commitment to a British point of view?

In answer, Chancellor was capable of varying his emphasis to suit his audience. For example, he told the Washington journalists reassuringly: 'We are British because we are cooperatively owned by British newspapers. But we are not doing a British job. We are doing an international job.' These words seemed clear enough. Yet to the British Foreign Office, whose generous subscriptions were needed by Reuters, Chancellor spoke differently. On 8 January 1946 he had privately told Ernest Bevin, the foreign secretary, that 'it was an essential British interest for Reuters to develop as a great independent world service based upon London, sharply distinguished from British publicity services in every form'. Chancellor was still here committing Reuters to the independent pursuit of truth in news. Nevertheless, the pursuit of truth—when described as 'an essential British interest'—amounted to 'doing a British job', even though the job being done was not directly for the British Government.

XVIII

In 1951 Kent Cooper was guest of honour at the Reuter centenary banquet. This formed part of celebrations which lasted for a whole week, 9–16 July 1951, and which cost Reuters £25,000—in a year which saw an overall pre-tax loss of £22,925. This large expenditure was afterwards defended on the ground that the celebrations produced highly favourable worldwide publicity for Reuters.

The banquet for over 1,100 guests at Grosvenor House, Park Lane, on 11 July was the social high point of the celebrations, a glittering event which itself cost nearly £7,000. Guests included Clement Attlee, the prime minister, the Archbishop of Canterbury, press chiefs from over fifty countries, and also Sir Roderick Jones. The menu included delicacies supplied from each of the countries in the Reuter partnership. Kent Cooper, three of whose foxtrots were played as part of the background music, proposed the toast of Reuters. Attlee was characteristically brief, pointing out that his Government would leave Reuters alone, 'except when offered their hospitality'.

Other centenary activities included the symbolic releasing of a hundred pigeons from 85 Fleet Street by Chancellor's daughter (cost of pigeons: £56: 13s. 4d.); and a garden party for Reuter staff at Dane End (cost: over £3,500). This was the Chancellors' country house north of London. To ensure that everyone could attend, before or after duty, the festivities began at noon on Saturday, 14 July, and lasted for over twelve hours. Wine and spirits flowed unceasingly; dancing took place indoors; a fireworks' display illuminated the sober and not so sober. The Chancellors circulated with warm smiles, and conducted countless tours of the old house.

This was the last 'feudal' occasion in the history of Reuters, a final memorable expression of that embracing family emphasis which went back to the days of Julius Reuter. Appropriately, Chancellor was now 'Sir Christopher', knighted to mark the centenary. That such an honour should have been offered and accepted was an indication of how much Reuters was still seen—and at heart saw itself—as 'British': not perhaps an organ of the British Government, but none the less a British institution.

On the Brink 1951–1963

I

Looking back at the time of his resignation in 1959, Christopher Chancellor described the 1951 centenary year as the culmination of his period as general manager. He believed that Reuters lost momentum soon afterwards, and admitted that this slackening may have indicated that the moment had come for his own departure. But he believed that the slackening was due also to a lack of interest in Reuters by the London newspaper proprietors. The leading NPA figures who had become directors in 1945—Rothermere, Layton, Bartholomew—had not been succeeded by men of equal commitment. The Reuter board continued unadventurously content with small annual profits, and in 1951, 1956, and 1960 there were actual losses.

Problems in the 1950s were not only financial. Indian participation in the Reuter partnership never worked smoothly, and in 1953 the Press Trust of India withdrew after only four years. Difficulties had recurred over the handling of news from the Indian zone, which included Pakistan

(East and West). The tense relationship between India and Pakistan after independence had not been foreseen. The Pakistanis objected to Indian-born correspondents representing PTI-Reuter in Karachi or Dacca.

In answer to this difficulty Chancellor insisted upon sending corre-spondents from London. He bluntly told A. S. Bharatan, the general manager of PTI, that outside India PTI news about Pakistan was not accepted as objective. As a result, the reputation of the Reuter world ser-vice was being endangered. Another difficulty for Reuters was that PTI reporting from India tended to dwell upon news, such as Nehru's speeches, which interested the Indians much more than anyone else. This heavy matter became known outside India as 'sacred cow copy'.

In his correspondence with the Indians Chancellor was all patience. In private, he complained sharply about what he regarded as their repeated unreasonableness. The partnership agreement was due to expire on 1 February 1953, and the Indians sought to renew it more or less upon existing terms. The other partners demanded changes which would take account of the recent difficulties: the strength of feeling surprised the Indians. A first round of talks in India was adjourned, and a second round began in London in July 1952.

A draft agreement for three years was finally offered to PTI. This laid down the right of Reuters and all member organizations within the part-nership to send correspondents 'as, when and how they please' to any part of the world 'including the territories of the parties to this agree-ment'. More than equal treatment for any partner was ruled out: 'The whole is greater than the part and any rights or privileges of one part should not directly or indirectly affect the whole.'

On 19 August 1952 Nehru wrote to Kasturi Srinivasan, the chairman of PTI, complaining about Reuter coverage of his non-aligned foreign policy. He hinted at the desirability of a break, though he professed to be surprised when it came. The Indian minister for information, B. V. Keskar, had told Srinivasan on 13 August that if the PTI became 'sub-servient' to any foreign network, the Indian Government would consider withdrawing facilities. In the same spirit, the Indian Government was to insist four years later that all internal news distribution must be made through Indian-owned agencies.

The PTI board met on 20 September 1952 and the now inevitable decision was taken to withdraw from the partnership. An ordinary com-mercial contract was concluded as a substitute, under which Reuters settled for a net £30,000 per annum. Reuters ended up with just two staff correspondents at New Delhi, plus five stringers elsewhere in India. As telephone links between Delhi and the rest of India were uncertain, much had to be left to PTI. Some good reporting was still to come out of India, but the great days for Reuters—great in profit, great in prestige—were over.

II

Like India, China had been a major centre of Reuter enterprise and profit. Now China too lost its prominence within the Reuter world operation. The Communists expelled all Western correspondents and managers in the summer of 1949. The locally born veteran Tommy Aldeguer, the news editor, remained in charge for Reuters in Shanghai until he quit in September 1951 after much harassment.

During the next five years coverage of the Chinese scene was left mainly to radio monitoring from Hong Kong. This remained important even after a Reuter correspondent was at last allowed back to Peking in April 1956. This was David Chipp. He spoke no Chinese, which may have been one reason why he was acceptable to the Communist authorities. A correspondent from Xinhua, the Chinese news agency, was posted to London at the same time. Chipp engaged a translator, and started the Reuter service from his hotel room. He laid the foundations for an exchange news agreement with Xinhua, and for a commercial agreement between Comtelburo and the Chinese Government.

The key Singapore office had been revitalized by Graham Jenkins on his appointment as manager for South-East Asia in 1955. Competition from AP and AFP was intense. Jenkins was an Australian, rugged and smooth by turns. He introduced post-colonial attitudes just in time. On the one hand, he deliberately separated himself from the old colonial ruling circle, now in its last days. On the other, he ended the long-standing arrangement under which much of the running of the Reuter office was left to See Gim Hock, a local Chinese, and his relations. See Gim Hock was replaced as office manager by Jimmy Hahn, a Korean by birth, who had worked for Reuters in Hong Kong. New office machinery was installed to encourage a spirit of enterprise. In 1964 Hahn was to become the first Asian to be appointed an area manager.

Singapore was the hub of the Far Eastern communications network. It used Hellschreiber, radio-teletype, and some Morse. Singapore relayed the Reuter service to Hong Kong and Japan, and radiated tailored services throughout the region. Jenkins ensured that these contained plenty of regional news: he had decided very early that emerging Third World countries wanted to hear about each other.

After the war the Japanese (like the Germans) had been keen to restart their own news agencies. In November 1945 two new agencies were formed in place of Domei. One was Kyodo, owned by the provincial Japanese press, and the other was Jiji Press, owned by its staff. Chancellor explained approvingly to the 1951 Reuter annual general meeting that, being a co-operative run by a diversity of newspapers, Kyodo was committed to objective reporting. He had commended DPA, the new co-operative German news agency, in much the same terms. As in Germany, Reuters decided to collaborate rather than to compete, although in the case of Japan action was delayed for several years.

Chancellor told the board in April 1952 that poor radio communications were making the direct Reuter service to Japan very unreliable. Reuters found itself unable to match the American agencies, and Chancellor had concluded that it would be better therefore to operate indirectly. In 1953 a contract was signed with Kyodo. The Japanese agency took over the Reuter English-language service and published it under a Kyodo-Reuter credit. A regional desk, targeting news for Japan and South-East Asia, was opened in London. On 12 March 1952 Chancellor wrote in characteristic terms to Matsukata of Kyodo, revealing once again his liking for beyond-the-ordinary business relationships with other agencies. 'It will be more than just a buyer-seller relationship. It will be a close editorial relationship in which Kyodo will play a constructive part in shaping a basic world service for the Japanese press.' A complementary contract was concluded in the same year with Jiji. This brought a subscription of £24,000 per annum, about a third more than the previous commercial-service revenue from Japan.

A good service from Japan and Singapore constituted an important part of the benefit which the Australians and New Zealanders had anticipated when they joined the Reuter partnership in 1947. At the 1948 annual general meeting Rothermere claimed that the accession of the Australians had been 'a complete success'. This was true for Reuters only in the short term. Cole emphasized in a note for Chancellor, undated but probably from 1955, that AAP was 'an Alice-in-Wonderland operation' rather than a complete news agency. He pointed out that its teleprinter network supplied only overseas news, for which Reuters was the main source. Yet the promised Reuter credits were not to be found in the Australian papers. More than once Reuters tried to raise the AAP payment of 15 per cent of gross revenue from the commercial service in Australia: the rate elsewhere was 30 per cent. In 1959 the Australians reluctantly conceded 20 per cent. AAP profit had more than quadrupled, whereas the payment to Comtelburo had increased only threefold:

TABLE 11.2. *Gross revenue figures for the commercial service in Australia 1948–1959* (£ Australian)

	Revenue	Expenses	Comtel fee	AAP profit
1948	11,756	7,766	1,763	2,227
1959	55,647	40,940	5,348	9,359

III

Kim Rogers, the manager in North America, was described by Cole in September 1962 as 'cautious' about prospects in the United States. The Reuter operation there was still limited. Rogers managed forty-two staff in New York and Washington from the Reuter headquarters in the *New York Times* building. These included sixteen Comtelburo staff, based in the financial district of New York. About 150 stringers backed up this modest number of staffers.

Reuters depended heavily upon its 1947 news-exchange contract with AP. The handful of Reuter staff correspondents could undertake only a limited amount of reporting outside New York and Washington. Salaries were low, and the office atmosphere was penny-pinching; correspondents had to think twice about taking taxis. But John (Pat) Heffernan, who headed the Washington bureau from 1957, developed a good relationship with the White House; in April 1961 a teleprinter carrying the Reuter report was installed there. Shortage of money meant, however, that Heffernan had to be selective in covering presidential trips, and Reuters was not represented in Dallas when President Kennedy was assassinated in November 1963.

The North American radio-teletype circuit to London carried between 30,000 and 35,000 words transmitted each day by radio-teletype. Comtelburo sent another 12,000 words daily. In the opposite direction, from February 1956 a Comtelburo transmission provided a fast commercial service. Reuters leased a 5,000-mile teleprinter network through North America serving news subscribers. In all, there were 400 North American subscribers to the news and commercial services.

In the mid-1950s Reuters faltered once again in Latin America. News revenue collapsed, partly because of local currency devaluations. By 1958 the Latin American surplus was a mere £1,143—with Comtelburo profit concealing a general-news loss. The drastic decision was taken to withdraw general-news provision from Argentina and Chile, the two remaining markets. Chancellor told the board on 9 July that a deficit of at least £20,000 was likely: 'There was no prospect of running a successful news service in South America unless it was heavily subsidised.' In a letter of the same date to F. R. G. Murray, the permanent under-secretary at the Foreign Office, Chancellor had asked for some form of indirect 'subsidy' (his word) of not less than £100,000 per annum. 'The only practicable answer to South America in my opinion would be some sort of ANA [Arab News Agency] set-up. A Latin American news agency could be formed with the support of British interests.' In other words, Chancellor was prepared for Reuters in Latin America—as in the Middle East—to operate through a news agency known to be subsidized by the British Government.

IV

Yet in a 1958 radio programme Chancellor had contended that the commitment of Reuters to truth in news had 'nothing whatever to do with the British Government'. This was the familiar claim, except that Chancellor was now aiming to take it further. By the late 1950s he was seeking not only to deny any connection with the British Government, but also to repudiate any particular commitment to things British. Earlier in his career he had been ready enough to attach the adjective 'British' to Reuters. By the end of his time as general manager he was eager to draw attention to the international content of Reuter news and to its worldwide market: 'Reuters is not just a British news service; it is not an organ for presenting British news . . . It is an organisation to supply newspapers and radio stations of every country of the world with a truthful and complete service of world news.' This significant shift in emphasis owed much to the way Reuters had handled one of the major news stories of the period, the Suez crisis of 1956.

During the preceding years Chancellor had expressed strong sympathy for colonial nationalism. As early as 24 August 1944 he was warning Herlihy, the manager in Cairo, that in the new 'Egyptian Egypt' Reuters would have to win the genuine respect of the people. Not only was such respect duly earned in Egypt during the postwar years, it proved to be strong enough to survive even the 1956 Anglo-French invasion. On 26 July of that year the Green End monitoring station picked up Colonel Nasser's speech announcing the nationalization of the Suez Canal. Reuters secured a world beat with the news. Slowly thereafter the crisis built up to war; and on 5 November Green End heard on Cyprus radio the news of the start of the Anglo-French landings.

On 1 November Chancellor had issued a circular to Reuter staff throughout the world. He began by quoting from that day's *Manchester Guardian*, which had emphasized how deeply British opinion was divided about the rights and wrongs of military intervention. He continued:

> It is the duty of Reuters, both to itself and to the many newspapers all over the world who rely on the Reuter service, to keep this fact in mind and ensure that it is reflected in the news service—that is, so long as it remains a fact and the nation remains, as it is today, divided on the issue of war with Egypt. Reuters does not represent the British Government.
>
> In the strain of the next few days I know the Editorial staff will always bear in mind the fact that Reuters must strive to give a true reflection of opinion in this country. I know full well how great a strain will fall upon our splendid and capable staff during this critical period. I have the fullest confidence in their part in upholding the standards which have made this country great and Reuters a great news service.

On behalf of the NUJ within Reuters, Jameson wrote immediately to Cole welcoming support from the top for 'an objective file'.

But what did Chancellor, Cole, and Jameson mean by objectivity within the Suez context? Was Reuters now taking the high ground? Was it declaring that in future it would not take any side in any war? Or was it simply saying the Reuters would not take sides against the Egyptians in this particular war, because a large part of British opinion was against doing so? A strict reading of Chancellor's words would suggest that he was advancing only the latter justification for objectivity—that British opinion was divided, and that Reuters must therefore take care in its reporting to reflect that division.

Such an attitude implied that Reuters was still operating within a British perspective. Yet the Egyptian Government began to react as if Reuters was now no longer British—as if Chancellor had advocated objectivity because Reuters had become supranational. The Egyptians treated Reuter staff in Egypt with consideration. Admittedly, Gilbert Sedbon, the Cairo chief correspondent, was at first expelled; but he was later invited back, although he chose not to return. Aleco Joannides, a Greek who had been transferred from Athens, was allowed to report for Reuters from inside Egypt throughout the period of military action. In contrast, AFP reporting was quickly stopped. After covering the Anglo-French landings at Port Said, Joannides moved to Cairo, where he took over as chief correspondent.

Cole personally supervised the handling of Suez news at 85 Fleet Street. He visited Egypt in March 1957, at a time when diplomatic relations between Britain and Egypt were still broken off. He was granted a two-hour meeting with Nasser, who remarked that the Reuter teleprinters at his home and office had been of 'immense value' in enabling him to follow events during the Suez crisis. Perhaps this was one reason why Nasser had allowed Reuters so much freedom. But his respect for the agency seems to have been genuine.

V

Geiringer became chief of the commercial services in May 1952, fresh from his successes in restoring the position of Reuters within postwar Europe. Comtelburo profits were to grow steadily during the 1950s. Comparative figures showed how the loss-making general-news services were being subsidised. By 1959 Comtelburo's revenue was amounting to roughly one third of total company revenue:

TABLE 11.3. *Comtelburo revenue and profits, 1950 and 1959 (£)*

| | Comtelburo | | | Reuter overall |
	Revenue	Costs	Profits	pre-tax profit
1950	336,978	268,031	68,956	17,145
1959	748,201	605,004	143,197	35,871

Geiringer brought drive to the running of the existing commercial services; but he could not be expected to foresee the computerized information revolution which was to transform those services and to offer great new market opportunities from the 1960s. On the contrary, he was convinced that, after two world wars and an intervening depression, public opinion would never again leave capitalists free to play the markets and to influence the livelihoods of the world's millions.

Geiringer also wrongly believed that Reuters might make money by telling businessmen about new developments and opportunities. An International Business Unit (1955–8) failed for lack of subscribers, while a bulletin called *International Business Facts* lasted less than a year (1956–7) because businessmen preferred specialist magazines or financial newspapers. *Business Facts* was quite different from the daily or weekly Reuter bulletins about particular commodities. These were well targeted, and accounted for nearly a third of commercial-service revenue from the United Kingdom. Eighteen were being published by 1961.

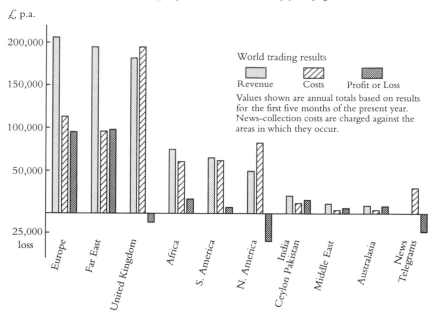

FIG. 12. Comtelburo: World trading results, 1960

    In October 1960 Bloom, who had succeeded Geiringer as manager of Comtelburo, reported that its revenue was being earned chiefly from the sale of fast market information 'covering finance in every aspect, commodities of all sorts and freights and shipping'. In that year Comtelburo employed 186 staff in London and 282 abroad. World trading results by region showed large Comtelburo profits from Europe and the Far East, but losses from the United Kingdom and North America caused by large production overheads (see Fig. 12). Experience had shown, continued Bloom, that Comtelburo did best when it conducted its own operations. At the start of 1962 Reuters terminated the arrangement with PA and Extel under which they had distributed commercial news to the British Isles outside central London.

    Comtelburo's overseas managers organized the collection of market information and prices. In Brazil, for example, the main office was at São Paulo, with branch offices in Rio de Janeiro, Santos (the coffee port) and Recife (through which most of Brazil's cotton exports passed). The manager controlled eleven agents countrywide. 'Inland communications are chaotic and occupy a large amount of his time.' Stringers along the coast reported every shipment of coffee or cocoa as it left the country.

    Geiringer resigned in April 1958. He had wanted more resources and

32. Reuter correspondent J. W. Collins, covering the Italo-Abyssinian War 1935.
His three runners, ready to take telegrams to the post office, are lined up behind

33. Samuel Storey, chairman, 1941

34. William Haley, author of the 1941 Reuter Trust deed

35. The Hollywood view of Reuters, 1941

36. Seaghan Maynes, Normandy, 1944

37. D-Day plus six: General Montgomery briefs war correspondents, Normandy, 1944 (Doon Campbell *extreme left*)

38. The British press: Playing-card issued to German troops, 1942

39. *right* Cecil Fleetwood-May, pioneer of wireless and commercial services, 1951

40. *below* Hellschreiber in use: Manila, Philippines, 1950s

41. Monitoring the Balkans: Green End Listening Station, 1962

42. 85 Fleet Street: The Lutyens building, 1951

43. Christopher Chancellor with Walton Cole—and the Baron, 1951

44. John Burgess (chairman 1959–68), and Cole, 1960

45. John Ransom with Stockmaster, *c.*1966

46. Fred Taylor with Videomaster, 1971

47. Gerald Long with Monitor, 1979

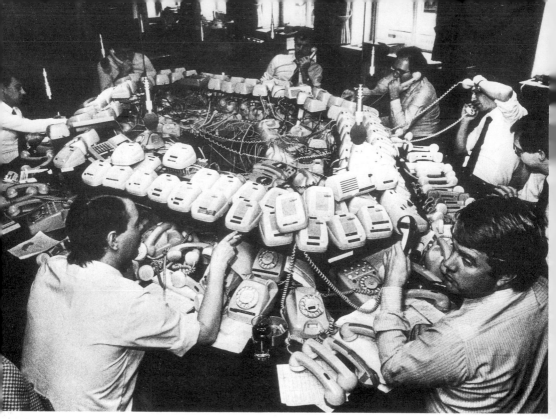

48. A Frankfurt dealing-room before Monitor

49. Dealing-room with Reuter terminals, Canadian Imperial Bank of Commerce, London, 1987

50. Advanced Reuter Terminal (ART), 1986

51. William Barnetson, chairman 1968–79

52. The 1984 flotation: Nigel Judah, Denis Hamilton (chairman 1979–85), Glen Renfrew, and Michael Nelson at the London Stock Exchange

53. Christopher Hogg (chairman 1985–) and Peter Job (managing director 1991–)

54. The editorial team: Sid Mason and Geoffrey Imeson, 1951

55. London editorial: Japan and Pacific desk, *c.*1952

56. Harold King and General de Gaulle

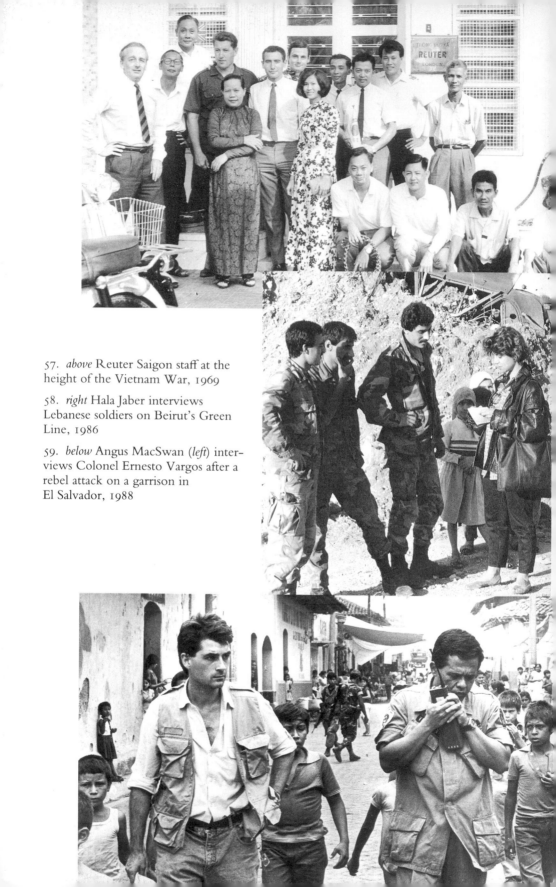

57. *above* Reuter Saigon staff at the height of the Vietnam War, 1969

58. *right* Hala Jaber interviews Lebanese soldiers on Beirut's Green Line, 1986

59. *below* Angus MacSwan (*left*) interviews Colonel Ernesto Vargos after a rebel attack on a garrison in El Salvador, 1988

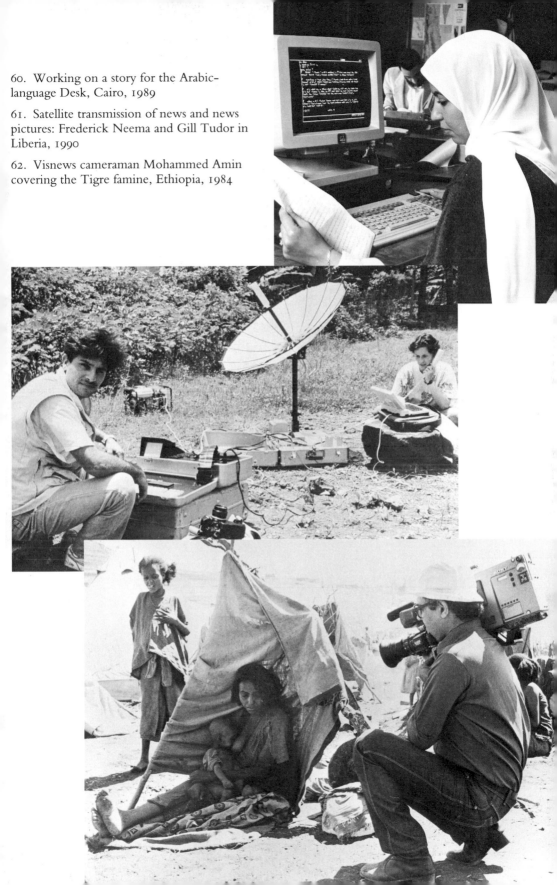

60. Working on a story for the Arabic-language Desk, Cairo, 1989

61. Satellite transmission of news and news pictures: Frederick Neema and Gill Tudor in Liberia, 1990

62. Visnews cameraman Mohammed Amin covering the Tigre famine, Ethiopia, 1984

63. The Berlin Wall comes down, 1989: Reuter news picture

more authority, and his relationship with Chancellor had become increasingly uncomfortable. In particular, Geiringer had asked for a separate Comtelburo communications network. This would have begun to give the commercial services equality with the general-news services. Such boldness brought Geiringer into conflict with Cole, who saw him as a possible rival as Chancellor's successor.

Geiringer's lasting contribution was that he had understood the need to recruit and train university graduates to become the managers and correspondents of the economic services of the future. When markets and technology presented great opportunities in the 1960s, Reuters was unique in possessing a corps of young men who understood the business of fast economic information and who were capable of identifying and exploiting those opportunities.

Reuters had recruited its first graduate trainees for the editorial department from Cambridge University in 1947. Chancellor told the 1948 Royal Commission on the Press that when he and Cole took over they had been 'startled by the haphazard method of recruitment'. Recruitment was gradually extended to include Oxford and other universities. Fluency in at least one language other than English was usually expected, plus a willingness to learn further languages as needed. Some old hands, who had themselves begun in the hard school of provincial journalism, viewed the new graduates with disdain. Not all stayed for long: by 1960 forty-four university trainees had been accepted since 1947, but twenty-three had left. Reuters could not match the salaries offered by the London newspapers or by the American agencies.

VI

Chancellor gave up as general manager in June 1959 at the age of fifty-five. He had long believed that executives, such as himself, who had reached the top comparatively young, should not remain until retirement, but should seek a change. He went on to become chairman briefly of Odhams Press, and subsequently chairman and chief executive of the Bowater Paper Corporation.

Chancellor had been strengthened in his determination to leave Reuters by dissatisfaction with the Reuter board during the 1950s. The NPA in particular seemed to be no longer much interested in Reuters. One episode had especially discouraged Chancellor, as he explained in a memorandum written at the time of his resignation (19 February 1959):

I know that my own enthusiasm and belief in the future of Reuters suffered a setback when one director (Lord Burnham) vetoed a scheme whereby the PA and Reuters jointly could have entered the television field by performing the functions now performed by ITN. I felt at the time, and still feel, that this was an opportunity that should not have been thrown away.

Chancellor's proposal that Reuters should supply news to the new British commercial television network had been made in 1954. After joining the Reuter board in June of that year, Burnham of the *Daily Telegraph* had immediately begun to argue that Reuters ought not to venture into preparing television news programmes. It should seek only to supply news in the usual way. Burnham gave fear of financial loss as his initial reason. He later began to argue that if Reuters became directly identified with news appearing on commercial television screens, 'the Reuter board would be constantly under criticism and attack'.

At the same board meeting (12 January 1955) John Burgess, a director from the PA, expressed strong disappointment that Reuters had lost 'a great opportunity'. Burgess, the chairman of Cumberland Newspapers, was well regarded for his good sense and good humour. This became particularly important when the Reuter board began to look for a successor to Chancellor in 1959. Chancellor himself wrote in his resignation memorandum: 'I do not have to stress the desirability, indeed the inevitability, of Mr Cole's appointment.' Yet, added Chancellor, Cole would need 'the support, and at times the control and guidance' of a reliable part-time chairman. Either Laurence Scott of the *Manchester Guardian* or Burgess would be able tactfully to manage Cole, who had great energy and 'remarkable intelligence', but who in Chancellor's view did not possess all the qualities necessary for sole charge of Reuters:

> I cannot see him acting as the focal point of a board without a Chairman. I am not sure how firm a grip he would keep on the general finances of the Company, and I think occasions would arise when his judgment might falter unless he had someone to consult. He is a bad administrator in the sense that he refuses to delegate. He will now have to organise himself quite differently, and he will need someone who is both sympathetic and strong to help him in this process.

Chancellor's advice was taken by the Reuter board. Scott was too busy to take on the chairmanship. So on 1 July 1959, at the same time as Cole became general manager, Burgess was appointed non-executive chairman of Reuters for three years. Cole was deeply upset at being given a minder. He seems to have discovered that the move had been suggested by Chancellor. He did not blame Burgess, but he never forgave Chancellor.

Happily, John Burgess (1912–87) proved well able to fulfil the chairman's role designated for him. Although he looked like a simple fresh-faced country gentleman, he was much more than he appeared. He was obviously upright, both in bearing and in mind. This was to make him a good figurehead for Reuters. But as well as an engaging presence, Burgess possessed a clear mind and a mind of his own. This enabled him to respond quickly and constructively to ideas put to him. Burgess's responsiveness was to prove of great benefit to Reuters during the nine years of his chairmanship.

VII

Soon after becoming chairman, Burgess began to recognize that Reuters would only progress in the face of increasing worldwide competition if—instead of aiming at little more than balancing the books—it committed itself to earning a sufficiently large annual surplus to permit significant investment in development and innovation.

On 7 October 1959 Burgess told the board of his regret that Reuters had been so often driven to making disruptive economies. He added:

> In order that the editorial machine should work smoothly, it is my opinion that Reuters should always operate on a substantial surplus. This should be a cushion for the unexpected and unpredictable expenditure, but, if this should not be required, the surplus should be placed to reserve for capital expenditure and for financing new services during their early non-productive life.

Burgess admitted that the partners in Reuters might feel aggrieved 'at having to subsidise more than is immediately necessary and then see half of the excess going in taxes'. But such thinking, argued Burgess, would be short-sighted: 'it is in the interests of the owners that their agency should be run efficiently.'

As part of their campaign to persuade a reluctant Reuter board to take long views, financial and otherwise, Burgess and Cole submitted a steady stream of reports and proposals. Cole revelled in pie-charts, diagrams, and maps. For example, in November 1960 the board was shown 'Communication costs at a glance' (Fig. 13), and in September 1962, how the revenue of 12,706,787 for 1961 had been earned and spent (Fig. 14). Reuters was spending nearly £600,000 a year on communications, compared with editorial costs of £376,300.

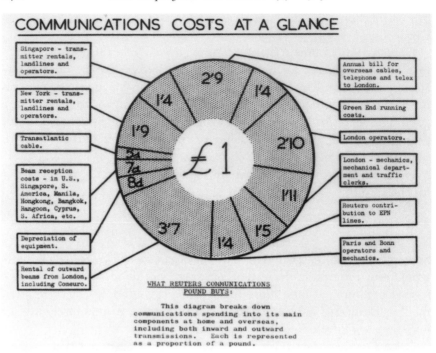

FIG. 13. 'Communications costs at a glance', November 1960

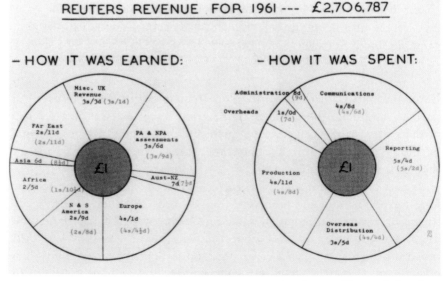

FIG. 14. How Reuters revenue for 1961 was earned and spent (figures in brackets show values in 1960)

The biggest single user of news from Reuters was the British Broadcasting Corporation. In 1960 the BBC's main news subscription was worth £101,250. No other subscriptions approached six figures: the next three were Kyodo (£48,750), DPA (£40,820), and the Arab News Agency (£29,800). Long-time subscribers such as the *New York Times*, *France-Soir*, the *Chicago Tribune*, and the main European national news agencies each contributed sums varying from £20,000 to £29,000.

Since 1944 the arrangement had been that the BBC paid a basic subscription equal to 22.5 per cent of the total PA and NPA assessments. Both the BBC and Reuters accepted that they stood in a special relationship. Indeed, in 1941 the British Government had encouraged the idea of the BBC entering into the Reuter partnership. But the Reuter board, aware of the close relationship between the Government and the BBC, had been unresponsive.

At intervals the BBC complained about the increasing sums which it was required to pay under the 22.5 per cent formula. A BBC deputation led by Sir Ian Jacob, the director-general, met the Reuter board on 9 October 1957. Harry Lindley, the Reuter chairman for the meeting, emphasized that the board wanted the BBC to feel that it was 'not just a client and customer but some way to being a partner'. Jacob answered that if the BBC were ever to become merely a customer, it would expect to pay less; but it had decided 'that it was right under the present circumstances to continue to support Reuters as a British institution'. The two sides agreed that in future the BBC should have access to all essential documents and accounts, and that the director-general should be free to attend Reuter board meetings 'whenever he felt that there was some reason for doing so'. Contact on a daily basis was maintained from November 1955 by two liaison editors from the BBC working on the London editorial floor. In his resignation memorandum Chancellor remarked that 'sooner or later' the BBC's claim to a share in the ownership would have to be met. It never was.

VIII

In 1960 the Arab News Agency's £29,800 was the fourth-highest overseas subscription paid to Reuters. The payment was valuable, but compromising. The ANA was covertly subsidized by the British Government; Reuters knew it to be so. None the less, in 1954 it had handed over to the ANA the distribution of its general and commercial news throughout most of the Middle East. Reuters continued with its own news-gathering organization, but the ANA supplied commercial reports from the area.

The ANA had been started during the Second World War in 1941. At that time Reuters regarded it as an unfair competitor, and the board was warned at intervals about its activities. After the war Chancellor complained on 8 January 1946 to Ernest Bevin, the British foreign secretary, about 'sham "news agencies"' in the Middle East and elsewhere: 'I feel there are cleaner and indeed more effective ways of presenting the British case abroad.' Official overseas publicity services, suggested Chancellor, 'can run in parallel with Reuters'.

Reuters did not relish having to compete with the ANA. Chancellor told the board on 26 June 1951 that he saw little hope of extending the Reuter presence in the Middle East. The costs of teleprinter equipment for additional services would be heavy, and they would require translation into Arabic, an expensive extra. In 1953 Cole was sent to explore the possibility of a hand-over of Reuter distribution to a projected new Egyptian national news agency, but the project collapsed. 'It was in this vacuum', recollected by Cole in 1961, 'that I entered into negotiations with ANA.'

Reuter trading profit from the area had been little more than £1,000 for 1953, and was falling. Cole negotiated an agreement with the ANA in the next year. This guaranteed an annual profit to Reuters of £28,500 for seven years. In return, the ANA was granted the exclusive right to distribute a Reuter-originated world-news file throughout the Arab world. The ANA promised to pay Reuters one-third of any new commercial revenues which it collected. And it bought up the assets of Reuters in Egypt.

Such terms had proved irresistible. The board discussed the ANA offer on 14 July 1954. Chancellor described it as financially 'very attractive'. 'The objection to the contract was the fact that the Arab News Agency was known to be subsidised by the British Government.' In discussion, Laurence Scott argued that the question of serving Government-subsidized organizations had arisen before: 'and the view had always been taken that Reuters was prepared to serve any organisation regardless of its politics so long as the purchaser did not tamper with the service.'

The difference in this case, which Scott apparently did not address, was that the ANA was to become much more than a purchaser of a service. It was to take over the function of news distribution from Reuters, and in an important part of the world. Never before had Reuters sold distribution rights for more than one country to any agency. At the same time the ANA's financial dependence upon the British Government was to remain concealed. Therefore, not only was Reuters knowingly accepting British Government money to help conduct its business and to balance its books, it was also entering into a pretence of knowing nothing about the official origins of the money which it was agreeing to accept. The board none the less empowered Chancellor to sign the contract.

During the Suez crisis the ANA was expelled from Egypt. Its head-quarters were moved from Cairo to Beirut. Looking back in March 1961, Cole defended the relationship in the light of experience. There had been, he noted, no complaints about the distribution of the Reuter ser-vice, and the ANA had scrupulously credited Reuter news. 'Our position has been revitalised throughout the territory.' Reuters was now 'almost indispensable' to any newspaper of standing and to broadcasting stations throughout the Arab world. Cole, in other words, was judging the con-nection entirely by its results, not by its implications.

IX

Burgess told the 1960 annual general meeting that 'the whole of West Africa is alive and tingling'. Reuters, he said, was planning a service of news to and from Black Africa 'in the great tradition of the past'. Reuters could not have responded to this challenge without help from the British Government. Murray of the Foreign Office had told Burgess on 12 November 1959: 'We want more news—more Reuter news—into Africa.' Cole warned Murray on 16 June 1960 that an intensive survey had revealed that 'deficit development' expenditure of about £50,000 would be needed to introduce services into West and Central Africa, including in particular a French-language service. Reuters did not ask for a subsidy as such, but for a large increase in British Government and Central Office of Information (COI) subscriptions for delivery of news services to their offices and agencies. Much of this extra money would then be available to finance expansion into Africa. From 1 April 1961 the block subscription on behalf of British Government overseas departments was raised to £70,000 per annum plus £22,120 for the COI, with delivery charges paid for at cost. This total amounted to an increase of £60,199, which was about half of what Reuters had asked for.

With this financial support Reuters launched into Black Africa, both English- and French-speaking. The venture was entrusted to Patrick Crosse. In just five busy years he spread the name of Reuters across the continent. This notable achievement owed much to Crosse's diplomatic skill. His patrician manner—quietly strong while courteously sympathetic—served him well in dealing with African politicians and newspapermen, who would have resented being patronized but who yet needed guidance. Crosse had joined Reuters in India in 1936, where Moloney, his uncle, was manager. He had served as a war correspondent, was captured, and spent three years as a prisoner of war.

Crosse realized that the news needs of each country would have to be met individually. At the same time each country would expect to receive a good service of news from the rest of Africa as well as from the wider world. Reuters had enjoyed an early success in Nigeria, where Cole had negotiated long-term contracts in 1956 with the Federal Government (£9,000) and three leading newspapers. The policy there, and everywhere, was to work with Governments as the only sure points, and to assist the desire of most African States to establish their own national news agencies. Cole reminded the board in May 1960 that 'Reuters as a matter of principle and of policy does not itself attempt to be a domestic news agency.'

By 1965 Reuters had made news contracts in thirty-five independent African States. The only exceptions were The Gambia, Rwanda, and Burundi. In February 1965 Long, by now general manager, attributed the success of Reuters in Africa to its continental dimension: 'It is through the Reuter report that African countries have news of one another.' He emphasized that news contracts with the African Governments required them to preserve the integrity and identity of the Reuter news service when issuing it internally. The name of Reuters now reached into French-speaking Africa, once the preserve of Havas or AFP.

By 1965 Africa had twenty-four correspondents, plus fifty stringers. Five years earlier there had been just three staff correspondents to cover the whole continent. Reporting costs in the mid-1960s totalled about £215,000 annually. This allowed a clear surplus of revenue over expenditure: annual revenue was £175,000 from English-speaking Africa, £121,000 from French-speaking Africa. Reuters served 132 media clients. Unfortunately, regretted Long, too many of them paid their subscriptions only in arrears.

X

A conference of top managers and senior departmental executives had decided in October 1960 that Reuters should plan for the eventual direct distribution of its news services to West European countries. Traditional ties with national news agencies were to be relaxed. This contrasted with Chancellor's attitude towards the European agencies: he had been ready to settle for sure contracts and small returns, emphasizing shared interests and a common concept of press freedom.

Cole reported to the board on 14 December 1960 that he had successfully resisted a plan by Daniel Rylandt of Belga, who acted as leader of the 39 Group, to allow only uniform subscription increases for the European agencies and to refuse individual negotiations with Reuters. Gerald Long, the assistant general manager for Europe, told Cole on 20 July 1962 that the revenue from commercial-news delivery to the smaller western European countries was 'derisory', bearing in mind that they were advanced economies with high volumes of foreign trade.

Michael Nelson, the new young manager of Comtelburo, argued on 29 October 1962 that Reuters ought to run its own commercial service in Belgium because of 'the growing need to make services on the European level, and the importance of Brussels in this'. Glen Renfrew, another young Comtelburo specialist, was sent to assess the Belgian situation. His report, dated 7 December, confirmed that profits could be doubled with direct Reuter management. The whole situation, said Renfrew, was typical of what he had also found in other countries— badly produced services, no selling, no effort to persuade customers to take more services.

Against this background, Long proposed and Cole agreed that the Belga subscription for general news should be increased by 20 per cent, and that the running of the commercial services in Belgium should be taken over by Reuters. Rylandt was shocked; but he found that the new realism in Reuters could not be gainsaid. Rylandt was described by Cole in December 1962 as 'capricious'. 'It is imperative that we stand up to Mr Rylandt. Belgium is a test case for us.'

Cole was in poor health, and left Long to conduct the detailed negotiations in Brussels. On 25 January 1963 Rylandt flew to London to continue the discussions. Fog delayed his arrival. Cole, feeling unwell, lay down for a rest on a sofa in his office. When his secretary came to rouse him, she found that he had died from a heart attack.

Cole's death made no difference to the Belga negotiations. He was succeeded as general manager by Long, who insisted upon the 20 per cent increase in the general-news subscription and upon selling Reuter commercial services directly. Belga tried and failed to develop a commercial service of its own, based upon the AFP economic service.

XI

On 19 October 1962 a wall-plaque had been unveiled at the Aachen inn where Julius Reuter had conducted his pigeon service in 1850. Pigeons were released to race to Brussels as part of three days of celebrations in memory of the founder. The board had met in Aachen that same morning, its very first meeting outside London. Cole was in an expansive mood. ' "Stand still", he exclaimed at a luncheon for West European newspapermen, 'was a phrase unknown to Paul Julius Reuter. It is also unknown for us who follow him in the space age.'

TWELVE

Making the New Reuters
1963–1981

The Coming of the Reuter Monitor

I

D URING the twenty years after Cole's death in 1963 Reuters was transformed. Its aspiration to high principles of conduct in the collection and distribution of news remained the same; but the nature of its involvement with news was greatly changed.

As a happy result, by the 1980s Reuters was making annual profits running first into tens and then into hundreds of millions of pounds. Ninety per cent was coming from services delivered by computer to traders in the financial and commodities markets. Scores of economic journalists were recruited into Reuters; at their side came thousands of technical, marketing, and sales personnel. The general-news services to the media continued to operate, and even expanded. Here was a novel mixture—a recipe for much public success, and for some private tension. Here was a new Reuters.

How long could the old Reuters have survived after 1963? Money was the key. A modest annual working surplus could never have financed a successful transformation of Reuters. For that, millions of pounds in long-term investment was needed, and needed quickly. The man who convinced Burgess and the board of the need was Gerald Long, Cole's successor as general manager. When Long resigned in 1981, his contribution was summed up by Sir Denis Hamilton, the chairman:

> Mr. Long's two decades as Chief Executive of Reuters have been of historical importance to the Company. He has maintained and developed the traditional highest standards of integrity and reporting of Reuters as the largest world news service. He has now, after a period of incredible risk taking and technical innovation, built it up into the greatest international

service of financial and business information, provided for almost every country in the world.

This high praise, although almost routine in such circumstances, was sufficiently deserved. While others were the creative forces, it was Long who oversaw the making of the new Reuters.

Long's appointment as general manager in 1963 came as a surprise to many. At thirty-nine he was the youngest of the internal candidates, all of whom were assistant general managers. The others were Patrick Crosse, Stuart Underhill, and Doon Campbell. The only outside candidate was Michael King, the son of Cecil King, chairman of the *Daily Mirror* group and a former Reuter director. King, who had worked for Reuters as a diplomatic correspondent, had apparently applied for the job. When asked at interview how he would propose to raise more money, he replied that, since the newspapers would not pay more, the money would have to come from the British Government.

Among those consulted by Burgess was Chancellor, who had written in 1959 that Long would be a strong candidate for the top job in the future. Support from so well-informed a quarter obviously carried weight, but it was not allowed to be conclusive in itself. Burgess played the leading part in deciding in favour of Long. The chairman never doubted in later years that he had made the right choice, even though he was to find Long less easy to work with than Cole. In 1973 Long joined the board as managing director.

He had been born in 1923, the son of a York postman. While serving in the British army in postwar Germany, he became involved in setting up newspapers under British military control. He was recruited by Reuters in 1948 straight from Cambridge University, where he read modern languages. Long spoke both French and German like a native. He had a rare, because equal, liking for French and German literature, music, art, and (not least) food and drink. After spells in Paris—where he won over an initially hostile Harold King—and Ankara, Long was appointed chief representative in Germany in 1956. Cole began to ask for his opinions, and to take him on tours. In 1960 he was made assistant general manager for Europe in London.

Long's personality was intriguing. He had a Yorkshire forthrightness, which those unused to the north of England were likely to take for brusqueness. Yet he could also be engaging. His face provided a striking canvass for either humour. His hair was short-cropped, his eye steady, his gesture firm, his voice slow but decisive. It all depended upon the play of expression around the full moustache, sharp chin, and thrusting eye-brows. He could be amiable or he could be fierce. He was rarely neutral, even when he was silent, which he sometimes was. You were left in no doubt about Long's mood.

All discovered themselves at odds with him sooner or later, even his protégés. The answer was not to let him slip into bullying. He enjoyed an equal exchange, and he accepted contradiction if it was well informed and obviously offered for the good of Reuters. His concern for the company was undoubted, and his knowledge of its history was considerable. Long set out to become the second founder of Reuters. He wanted to make it an aggressive and profitable organization, such as it had been in Julius Reuter's prime. Long rightly believed this to be necessary if Reuters was to be sure of survival. He also wanted to gain acceptance for Reuters as a truly international organization. In representing Reuters throughout the world, he liked to emphasize that he did not speak for a 'British' institution.

Long encouraged a very strong sense of the specialness of Reuters. This built up morale. He was entirely undeterred by charges of arrogance about his own or the company's attitude. Cole had drawn all lines of communication within the top management towards himself, suspicious of direct discussion between senior staff. Long, by contrast, had no fear of cabals. He revelled in free-wheeling discussions.

One of the questions asked in these discussions was how best to develop the economic services without causing tension with the general-news journalists. No soothing answer was found. Nevertheless, prompted by Nelson, Long quickly decided that Reuters must invest urgently in projects and equipment for the economic services. This was a crucial decision for Reuters.

II

Long realized that Reuters needed to modernize its handling both of its finances and of its people. Straight away from 1963, he began to seek better methods of controlling costs. He also introduced a comprehensive policy for staff relations. Both moves were long overdue.

In 1963 the financial position of Reuters was, as so often before, precarious. There were to be losses in 1964 and again in 1967. The British newspaper proprietors, who were the senior partners in Reuters, were themselves hard pressed. Television was now competing strongly for advertising revenue. The assessments paid by the NPA, PA, AAP, and NZPA were falling rapidly as a proportion of Reuter turnover.

Against this background, Long introduced careful planning in the use of the limited resources available. Planning, in Long's definition, was more than a matter of making economies, although there were still to be economy drives at intervals. He pressed for as much investment as possible. The nineteen main contracts running in 1965, each worth £20,000 or more per year, totalled £684,525. Reuters could not risk losing any of them. Long wanted to escape from such dependence. By the time of his resignation in 1981 Reuters had certainly done so. Major new products were on offer which had already begun to make large profits and were destined to make much larger.

Reuters drew about 70 per cent of its revenue from outside the British Isles, its headquarters territory. It was unique in this regard among news agencies—quite unlike AP or UPI, with their strong home bases, or AFP, which was Government-subsidized, or Tass, which was an official agency. AP revenue for 1964 had exceeded £19 million, well over five times the Reuter figure; AP made a profit on the year of £186,792: Reuters made a loss of £57,092; AP could afford to spend £2,678,571 on foreign news coverage: Reuters £1,256,000, less than half. Reuters needed to find the financial strength appropriate to an organization committed by its agreement of trust to being 'the leading world news agency'.

In July 1971 Long defined for the board what he regarded as the company's objectives:

> Reuters central purpose is to achieve the highest standards of excellence in the provision of news services, and information and communications systems to subscribers throughout the world. To maintain this purpose Reuters must be profitable, since profit is the condition of Reuters existence and the touchstone of Reuters efficiency. The use of profit is to develop Reuters services and to benefit Reuters shareholders and staff.

He repeated this statement more than once in later years.

Long recognized the need for profitability, but he was not himself a businessman. He came to depend heavily upon the financial expertise of Nigel Judah, the secretary and chief accountant of Reuters since 1960. Judah had joined the company as an accountant in 1955. Chancellor and Cole promoted him rapidly, and for thirty years he was destined to serve near the top, trusted by successive chief executives. His contacts in the financial world enabled him to secure large foreign loans for Reuters. His style was always softly courteous.

By the mid-1960s Long had decided that insufficient surplus was being generated internally. A key document from Judah, dated 24 June 1966, concluded that the company needed a minimum capital injection of £250,000. He suggested that the owners might themselves put up this fresh capital by subscribing for additional stock; but they refused to do so. The alternative was to borrow. When the directors expressed reluctance, Long made his determination clear. He was supported by Burgess. Faintheartedly, the board agreed to borrow.

A loan of $430,000 was raised in October 1966 from Morgan Guaranty Trust. A second loan of 4,500,000 Swiss francs (£375,000) in August 1967 came from Crédit Suisse of Zurich. This loan was for ten years at 6.75 per cent, subject to a guarantee from the company's bankers, the Bank of Scotland. The Reuter reserves were pledged by way of further guarantee; they were worth approximately £350,000.

The Reuter board was told by Long in June 1967 that the Swiss loan was needed for both immediate and longer-term purposes. Immediately:

(1) To buy a computerized message-switching system for handling the news services more effectively;
(2) To fund a United Kingdom overdraft;
(3) To buy Agence Cosmographique; this was appropriate in order to exploit the now strong position of the economic services in the highly profitable Swiss market.

By 1972 investment in new equipment was totalling £1,217,954 for the year. This heavy expenditure was partly financed out of cash flow, and partly by an unsecured loan of $864,000 at 5.5 per cent over five years from Morgan Guaranty, in association with the Export/Import Bank of Washington. Judah had been pleased to recommend this bank. Such a loan had to be spent exclusively upon the purchase of equipment manufactured in the United States for export; this presented no problem since Reuters wanted to buy there in any case. At the end of 1973 outstanding borrowing from all sources totalled £1,400 230, only 14 per cent secured.

Turnover was now growing fast. It passed £10 million in 1970 and reached £50 million by 1977. In that year sixteen countries each recorded a turnover in excess of £500,000. Nine were in Europe, plus the United States, Canada, Hong Kong, Japan, Singapore, Brazil, and South Africa. In other words, although Reuters maintained a presence nearly everywhere, its prosperity depended upon the Westernized capitalist world. Its economic services were particularly designed to serve that world.

In 1965 proper budgeting was introduced for the first time into Reuters. Annual forecasting was introduced from 1973, and from 1976 a yearly 'budget and plan' document was produced. At first five-year planning was attempted, but from 1982 this was reduced to three years in order to concentrate attention upon achieving early benefits.

The effects of devaluation led Reuters in 1967 to abandon its traditional policy of expressing its major contracts in sterling. S. G. Warburg, the merchant bank, advised that the company should have as much of its income as possible expressed or paid in the hardest currencies, particularly in Swiss francs.

Long was interested in the visual as well as in the financial. In 1965 he called in a leading designer, Alan Fletcher of Pentagram, to devise a Reuter logo for use on stationery, buildings, vehicles, and elsewhere. The result was a distinctive presentation of the word 'Reuters', picked out in dots, a design inspired by teleprinter tape.

III

Reuters was a labour-intensive organization. Staff costs during the 1960s amounted to about half of total budget. Staff numbers were growing steadily, especially overseas. The total first reached 2,000 in 1976:

TABLE 12.1. Worldwide staff numbers, 1964 and 1976

	Head Office	Overseas	Total
1964	699	653	1,352
1976	893	1,143	2,036

Long was keen to introduce a comprehensive policy for staff. He handed over this side to Brian Stockwell, who was made staff manager at the end of 1963. Stockwell was a quiet, popular man, responsive without being weak. His father, Tom Stockwell, had spent a lifetime in Reuters. Brian joined in 1938, and acquired wide experience as a journalist and manager in London and overseas. The fact that all members of staff had access to him illustrated how the company was still comparatively small and London-centred.

Stockwell began by negotiating the introduction of graded salary structures for all employees. This suited both management and trade unions. By July 1966 Long was telling the board that Stockwell had 'regained in most of our dealings with the unions the initiative which previously lay permanently with them'. He had organized recruitment and training programmes, and had brought staff wastage 'within bearable limits'.

The trade unions within Reuters during this period were active, but they were much more reasonable than those within the Fleet Street newspaper offices. Reuters met no blanket resistance to the introduction of new technology. A crucial success for Stockwell was a 1966 agreement for the joint manning of computer installations. These jobs had been claimed by two unions, and the agreement provided for recruitment turn by turn for all new computer staff, except engineers and technicians. Demarcation disputes, which might have wrecked the new ventures so vital to Reuters, were thereby avoided.

During the 1970s the London press telegraphists were worried at the prospect of visual display units (VDUs) being introduced into news-rooms. Kevin Garry, who was in charge of staff relations from 1974, told a meeting of the telegraphists on 19 March 1975 that 'anybody in the Company, whatever union card he held, should be able to use VDUs'. In October and November 1974 national officials and Reuter union repre-sentatives visited Reuters New York at company expense to study video editing in operation. This had been introduced there at the start of the year. Garry hinted that, if London refused to follow New York, the whole Fleet Street editorial operation might be moved outside the United Kingdom. Agreement was reached on 2 July 1975. The telegraphists abandoned their right to exclusive control of the transmis-sion of news to line, and in return Reuters offered retraining and rede-ployment without redundancies, plus phased pay supplements. In the event, the introduction of video editing into London was delayed for technical reasons until the end of 1979. Although the telegraphists had conceded the right of London journalists to input news directly, the jour-nalists demanded extra payment for doing so. Eventually £625 a year was conceded.

Labour problems were to be found during these years not only inside Reuters, but also within the British Post Office and in the electricity-supply industry. Strikes in these areas, or a strike within the London tech-nical centre of Reuters itself, could have cut off the computerized economic services. Customers for price information needed it second by second, and Reuters knew that disruption of these economic services would have been even more damaging than disruption of the general-news services. This was one reason for the decision in 1979 to establish a second technical centre at Geneva. Switzerland enjoyed good industrial relations as well as good communications. The centre opened in May 1982.

IV

Communications technology was developing very fast during the 1960s. A circular on 'Reuters Communications' from the statistical unit in 1965 began arrestingly. 'By the time you read this note some of the information may well be out of date. . . . Reuters watches all new developments, and as soon as they are practicable technically and commercially, uses them to further the basic aim of giving "the world's news to the world".'

Long had been put in charge of communications development by Cole, and he continued to take a close interest after he became general manager. In a note for the board in February 1968 he explained how Reuters had recently concentrated upon exploiting the advantages of 'bulk working' in international communications. Wherever possible, it had bought high-capacity circuits 'so to speak wholesale' from the communications authorities. This process had begun in March 1963, when Reuters leased a voice circuit across the Atlantic and bought terminal equipment to divide the circuit into twenty-two teleprinter channels. The capital cost of equipment was a modest £5,000, while the lease cost £80,000 a year.

During the 1950s Reuters had worked the transatlantic route exclusively by radio. But radio was liable to interruption, and communication by physical link came back into favour when coaxial cables were developed. Miniaturization techniques allowed the insertion of electronic repeaters into such cables at frequent intervals. In August 1960 Reuters began to lease a circuit in a new transatlantic coaxial cable for nine hours each day. Within two years it had entirely abandoned the use of radio across the Atlantic.

Reuters was able to operate these circuits with a new independence. It was no longer just another ordinary customer of the national telecommunications authorities. It lobbied extensively to reduce official constraints upon how it conducted its business. By the early 1970s Long was able to claim that Reuters was operating the largest and most technically advanced news and information network in the world. This network had two main arteries: one crossed the Atlantic and Pacific (Tatpac); the other (Europlex) linked the main cities of the Continent to each other and to London. In June 1964 Reuters leased eighteen channels in the new round-the-world Commonwealth cable to Sydney via Canada. Within six years Tatpac had become fully operational. It joined London to Singapore and Tokyo through Montreal, Sydney, and Hong Kong. The complementary Europlex system became operational in the autumn of

1967 after difficult negotiations with the European telecommunications authorities. Europlex connected London, Paris, Geneva, Frankfurt, The Hague, and Brussels in an eighty-eight-channel ring. This was fed by data-spurs and leased teleprinter lines from other major European cities.

Cables had made a comeback, but satellites were already demonstrating that the communications technology of the future would be looking upwards into space. Reuters was among the earliest users of the experimental Telstar satellite. On 19 July 1962 New York transmitted by Telstar to London the first Reuter news report by satellite. Early Bird, the first working communications satellite, was launched on 6 April 1965.

V

At the London heart of the Reuter news service network was a message-storing and switching system known as ADX (Automatic Data Exchange), introduced in July 1968. Reuters was the pioneer in using such techniques in the news field. ADX could process up to three million words daily. It made possible the editing of English-language regional services from one central position, the World Desk, rather than from numerous regional desks. Only the French and Western Hemisphere Desks survived. They did so, the quip said, because they each handled a foreign language—French and American English. The World Desk had been formed in 1964 in place of the old Central Desk, whose output had been dominated by the needs of the British newspapers. The World Desk was more outward-looking.

During the mid-1960s Reuter news services were reaching nearly 6,500 daily newspapers in 112 countries. These papers claimed an aggregate daily circulation of 276,479,000 copies. Reuter news was also supplied to networks said to serve 393,678,000 radios and 177,184,000 television sets.

A new General News Division (GND), started in July 1967, represented a major initiative by Long—not only in structural but also in psychological terms. It was intended to reinforce the position of the general-news services in comparison with the rapidly growing economic side. Long was enthusiastic for the further development of the economic services; but he was himself a former general-news journalist, and he hoped that the new structure would help general news to hold its own within Reuters by enabling it to make money. In 1962 trading revenue from general news had still been everywhere ahead of the revenue from economic services. By 1970 it was far behind in Europe, and also in North America:

TABLE 12.2. Comparison of trading revenue
figures for general-news and economic services,
1962 and 1970 (£000)

	1962		1970	
	GND	Comtelburo	GND	RES
Europe	342.2	246.3	644.5	2,962.3
Africa	167.6	71.9	503.6	367.5
N. America	209.0	91.7	566.6	694.2
Asia	257.0	37.2	614.3	492.3
TOTAL	975.8	447.1	2,329.0	4,516.5

Down the years different titles had been used for the commercial services in different parts of the world—'Comtelburo', 'Comtel Reuter',
'Reuters Economic Services' (RES). From April 1966 this last title, hitherto confined to Australia, was adopted everywhere. The Reuter name
was now clearly linked to all non-media services.

RES revenue overtook that from GND in 1968. Could general news
ever make a comeback? Long was encouraged to believe so by a young
journalist who had trained under him in Germany. This was Brian
Horton, a New Zealander with a family background in journalism, who
had joined Reuters in 1957. In October 1968 Horton was made editor-
in-chief and an assistant general manager, and put in charge of GND.

GND had been designated a profit centre alongside RES. This gave
GND responsibility not only for the collection and distribution of its
news, and for controlling its own costs, but also for the sale of media
products throughout the world. In other words, GND and RES were set
to operate in parallel. Each employed their separate staffs in London, and
each ran their own newsrooms. In most Reuter offices throughout the
world there were two editors and two budgets. In October 1969 GND
had 276 staff in London (including 130 journalists), while RES had 233
staff (48 journalists).

Horton cut GND numbers in London to 213 by 1973. As a result, he
was able to contain news-service costs. But he could not generate more
revenue by greatly increasing the price of news from Reuters, because
AP, UPI, and AFP were already charging their overseas subscribers far
less. In 1968 the general-news loss on the year was about £100,000.
Inflation and rising communications costs magnified the problem so that
by 1978 the annual loss on general news was £7 million.

Horton's critics within Reuters contended that he had been at best
foolish and at worst arrogant to believe that he could make money out of

news. The whole history of Reuters demonstrated otherwise. In the executive committee Nelson, Horton's counterpart, was openly critical. Long remained convinced that the GND initiative had been worth attempting; but he now reluctantly recognized that Nelson was nearly indispensable, whereas Horton was not. Long had also come to realize that to reveal so plainly the large losses being made on general news was bad public relations.

At the end of 1973 the experiment of making GND a profit centre was abandoned. In its place came Reuters World Service (RWS). This was now designated a cost centre; RES remained a profit centre. RES possessed its own editorial network, although it relied on RWS for general reporting. Reuters Media Services (RMS) and Reuters North America (RNA) became other profit centres. The strength of RES within the new Reuters had now been recognized. Horton resigned.

VI

The three rivals of Long for the top job in 1963—Crosse, Underhill, and Campbell—had all left Reuters within ten years. Two younger men, Nelson and Renfrew, were rising fast within the company throughout the 1960s. While Long planned broadly and dealt with the board, these two were foremost among the builders of the new Reuters.

Michael Nelson was born in 1929, the son of a carpenter. Geiringer recruited him for Comtelburo in 1952 as a graduate trainee from Oxford University; his first overseas posting was to Thailand in 1954. He soon became known for his purposefulness. Underhill, who was instrumental in getting Nelson made manager of Comtelburo in 1962, recollected years later 'a slight, red-haired young man, thoughtful in manner', but with 'the toughness, cheek and adaptability of an English sparrow'. Throughout his career Nelson was to be precise, hard-working, acute, strong-minded, usually good-humoured, and sometimes humorous. This strong combination served him well as a manager and negotiator for Reuters.

During the 1960s and 1970s Nelson oversaw the introduction of a succession of computerized and other products for the distribution of economic information. These were to earn great profits for Reuters. Nelson did not himself create these products, although he sometimes suggested improvements. Rather, he carefully evaluated the possibilities, and gave steady support to just a few initiatives. He was being bold and cautious at the same time. He knew that the company was too poor to make expensive mistakes.

Nelson was a good spokesman for his growing band of economic journalists. He insisted upon proper recognition for himself and for his staff, and by the late 1970s, with the demise of GND, he had gone far towards achieving this. In 1976 he became general manager in succession to Stockwell, and a joint deputy managing director. He was put in charge of company planning, and of the business management and trading of Reuters apart from North America. He also became the medium of communication with middle management. By this date many in the company regarded him as the obvious successor to Long.

Also appointed joint deputy managing director in 1976 was Glen Renfrew. Born in 1928, Renfrew had joined Comtelburo in 1952, a few weeks before Nelson. They were destined eventually to compete for the top job. Whereas Nelson was soon recognized as a coming man, Renfrew's start had been slower. He was the tenth child of an Australian coalminer, who left the pit to become a lay preacher. Renfrew revealed a talent for languages, becoming fluent in French, German, and Italian. After graduating from Sydney University, he travelled round Europe. He walked into 85 Fleet Street and asked for a job. His potential was recognized by Geiringer, who appointed him to Comtelburo. More than once, however, during the next few years, he was nearly sacked. Before leaving Australia, he had worked at a construction camp where drinking and fisticuffs ruled, and he later admitted: 'maybe I still had some of the manner of that place.' Yet there was always much more to Renfrew than 'a wild colonial boy'. He was, for example, an enthusiast for literature and the arts. And although his personality was strong, he was not arrogant. He could listen and learn, and he had a clear mind. Helped by a cheery grin and an Australian accent (gradually reduced), he related with people of all sorts. These qualities enabled him to become an outstanding salesman and negotiator for Reuters.

Very importantly, Renfrew became interested in the new communications technology, to such an extent that in evaluating the great developments of the period he was able to hold his own with the specialists. He kept his colleagues aware of what had become possible, and of what further advances might be made. He believed that only by introducing new technology could Reuters hope to protect its existing contracts, attract new business, and make more money. Throughout his career until his retirement as managing director in 1991 he dedicated himself to bringing together fresh products, greater sales, and higher profits.

Between 1955 and 1959 Renfrew was in South Africa, where he ended up as manager for Southern Africa. He was highly successful in developing the economic services. In 1960 he became Comtelburo manager for South-East Asia at Singapore, where again he did what Cole described to the board in July 1960 as 'an outstanding sales development job'. At the beginning of 1963 he was appointed manager for Belgium; this was his first big chance, and he took it. Reuters was breaking its commercial-news connection with Belga, and Brussels was the main centre of the European Economic Community.

In July 1964 Renfrew was made manager of the new computer division of Comtelburo. Here was recognition of his interest in the new technology, but it was left to him to make what he could of the job. He began with just a secretary, a salesman, and three technicians. During the next few years his division was to play a key part in promoting the use of computers by Reuters. His drive and command of languages helped him to get on well with equipment suppliers, potential customers, the stock exchanges, and the regulatory authorities. In 1969 Renfrew was made Nelson's deputy within RES. But not for long. From the start of 1971 he became manager in North America.

VII

Reuters adopted the new information technology not in any spirit of daring, but in a spirit of realism. Long and his colleagues knew that subscribers were always likely to be attracted by fuller and faster services of general and economic news. If Reuters did not exploit the latest technology, subscribers would turn to competitors who were willing to do so.

In July 1965 Long compared the positions of the general news and Comtelburo services. 'Reuters main function in its general-news services is to provide a service, whereas Comtelburo's chief aim is to make money.' Long was here making the same point as Chancellor had made in 1947. Nevertheless, Long's tone in recognizing the dependence of Reuters upon its economic services was not grudging, as Chancellor's had been, but complimentary. He reminded his senior managers on 3 June 1965 that no other firm possessed such a good economic-news network, and such expertise: 'we must make a great effort to ensure that everyone in the organisation realises how much we depend on these services.'

Heavy capital investment was the only way, argued Long, for Reuters to expand its economic services further. On 1 June 1963 the International Financial Printer (IFP) started operation in Brussels, the brainchild of Renfrew. IFP provided bankers and brokers in Europe with high-speed delivery of general and commercial news. This constituted a significant breakthrough. For the first time, businessmen over a wide area could receive news simultaneously. Previously, commercial news and information had been first transmitted to Reuter offices and agents. These had then compiled services, as quickly as they could, for customer distribution by teleprinter, telex, telephone, mail, or messenger. Direct delivery was to be the way of the future, not only (as here) through printers, but especially through new computer-based products.

Long and Nelson knew that old-style teleprinter technology was now under powerful challenge from computer technology. Words need no longer be spelt out on printers: they could be processed by computers. Nelson had become aware of the rapid development of computerized price-quotation products in the United States. Reuters subscribed in New York to Stockmaster, a computerized product from Ultronic Systems Corporation of New Jersey. This was a new firm founded by a group of enterprising engineers from the Radio Corporation of America. With the support of Long, Nelson turned to Ultronic. Robert Sinn, the brilliant and businesslike president of Ultronic, was the pioneer of the coming revolution. His young company was ahead of all others in applying its know-how. Sinn convinced the Reuter management that he was the man to follow. Long explained to the board on 8 April 1964 that the growth of computer technology had 'brought about a revolution in the technique of dealing with the kind of statistical information which is Comtelburo's main stock-in-trade'.

Ultronic, and its American rival Bunker Ramo, had moved into Europe early in 1964 to serve a number of brokerage subscribers in Geneva, London, and Paris. But the prospects for Ultronic on its own in Europe were limited. To provide prices at an acceptable speed, Stockmaster needed to employ a wide communication band; yet the wider the band-width the greater the expense. At this same period Reuters was starting to use twenty-two channels across the Atlantic. The opportunity for a deal became obvious to both sides. A contract with Sinn was signed on 23 April 1964; it was to come into force from 1 July. During the intervening weeks the Ultronic engineers showed their brilliance. They worked out how to apply time-division multiplexing to the handling of the large volume of data to be transmitted across the Atlantic from the master Stockmaster computer. Capacity on the Reuter cable was doubled—from twenty-two to the equivalent of forty-four channels.

The Ultronic system fed ticker-tape signals from stock-exchange and other markets into a master computer at Mount Laurel, New Jersey. This processed the material for feeding by line into slave-memory computers.

One of these was in London, to serve subscribers in European financial centres. Slave memories were connected to the offices of brokers and other subscribers, who each had a small desk unit which gave them access to the latest information on stock prices simply by pressing buttons. The desk unit produced three illuminated digits and looked like an old-fashioned adding-machine (see Plate 45).

This joint-venture agreement made the latest technology available to Reuters at minimum cost and risk. Reuters obtained exclusive rights in Stockmaster outside North America for ten years. This meant a free hand in the United Kingdom, Europe, and elsewhere. Ultronic put up all the capital for equipment, the costs being charged against the project over five years. In return, Reuters also made available the spare capacity in its transatlantic cable channels and its international infrastructure. Net costs and profits were shared equally.

If the risks and costs for Reuters had been proportionate to the opportunity, would the board have taken this chance? Almost certainly not. Reuters was able to begin the transformation of its fortunes upon remarkably easy terms. In January 1969, after five years of operating the joint venture, Long reminded the Reuter board of its good fortune:

> Reuters is attempting to achieve a commercially successful operation without that working capital which for most companies is the prerequisite of development. Ultronic, especially since it has become part of the great electronics complex of General Telephone and Electronics, has capital readily available and is prepared to supply it for joint projects taking Reuters knowhow as our contribution to joint investment. The availability of such a partner has greatly helped Reuters to make the transition from obsolescent teleprinter services to electronic systems, especially those of interrogation and display.

Yet the brilliant start of Stockmaster had been followed by a worrying period of difficulty and loss. Faced with new technology, the monopoly European telecommunications carriers had become obstructive or had imposed tariff surcharges. The carriers claimed that Reuters was seeking itself to function as a carrier because it was transmitting data which were really the property of Ultronic or of the stock or commodity exchanges. The concept of a proprietary database assembled from a number of different sources was yet to be established.

Competition intensified when Telequote, a third American quotation service, intervened in Europe with powerful backing and aggressive pricing. Reuters met this threat by halving the basic Stockmaster subscription from $1,500 to $750 per month. Together with heavy start-up costs, this meant that initial losses were higher than expected. The Reuter loss on the project was about £20,000 for the second half of 1964. Although small in retrospect, this loomed large at the time. The very viability of the joint venture came under question.

These doubts quickly subsided. Stockmaster made a profit for Reuters every year from 1965, reaching as high as £244,000 for 1968. The traditional economic services had sold well enough, but they had been cheap. Stockmaster, by contrast, was able to charge a relatively high subscription rate. Moreover, traditional services often required only a single installation in each subscriber's office. A Stockmaster sale, which might begin with one or two desk units, could readily grow into an installation of twenty or more.

The success of the project meant that the master Stockmaster computer in New Jersey was soon matched by a master in London. This absorbed prices from European stock and commodity exchanges. The network was eventually offering over 10,000 stock or commodity prices at push-button command—at first in fifteen seconds, later in only two seconds.

The demand for Stockmaster became extensive. By April 1969 Ultronic had invested about £880,000 in the project, and Reuters had installed 1,100 desk units in three hundred subscriber offices in ten European countries. Telegraphic circuits, which were difficult to operate, had been replaced by voice-grade channels. Stockmaster soon reached most of the capitalist world, including Hong Kong, Japan, Australia, and South Africa. Reuters now claimed that it was operating a global stock exchange, since material was being fed into the system from all the world's main exchanges. This glossed over the reality that Reuter access to such data long remained uneven. The West German bourses, for example, agreed fairly quickly to distribution of their quotations outside Germany, but they were slower to give approval for distribution of quotations in the German domestic market.

Nevertheless, by the late 1960s the fastest way for a bank in (say) Düsseldorf to inform itself about the quotations on the Düsseldorf exchange was through the Reuter network. Reuters, whose business had long been the moving of international information from one country to another, was now also reaching into domestic markets. This was significant. Two distributors of the Reuter economic services—Jiji of Japan and VWD of west Germany—had each earned more revenue from serving their domestic markets than Reuters was earning from selling its economic services throughout the entire world. This situation was about to change. Whereas Reuters had received only modest fees from offering its traditional economic services for resale by the national agencies, for Stockmaster those agencies were paid only a commission. Most of the revenue went to the joint venture. Moreover, Stockmaster gradually gave RES a presence in many European countries, and this made agency collaboration no longer necessary. In Switzerland, for example, which became the most profitable market for Stockmaster, Reuters bought out Agence Cosmographique, the local distributor, in 1967.

As early as the end of 1965 Stockmaster had become 'the standard tool of the US brokerage industry in Europe'. So wrote Renfrew to Sinn on 5 January 1966. Contrary to the forecast that usage would be limited to the larger American brokers, Stockmaster was now being ordered by the smaller houses. The *Wall Street Journal* of 17 November 1965 quoted comments from brokers describing how Stockmaster had boosted their business. Treasury Secretary Fowler remarked that, thanks to the new information medium, European investment in American stocks had increased significantly and this had benefited the United States balance of payments.

The achievement of Stockmaster and its successors owed much to the expertise of Reuter technical staff, and to a network of field-service representatives. Together they learnt how to create and to maintain the world's first intercontinental real-time information network. Product marketing and selling also became increasingly sophisticated. In 1962 Comtelburo had employed just one salesman, based in London, to push the commercial services. By 1976 RES maintained eight international and forty-seven national sales staff. Reuter salesmen became skilled at demonstrating to potential customers how greatly they needed the new technology, even without needing to understand it. Nelson and his colleagues took care to remember that their products must be simple to operate, highly reliable, and profitable in use.

The prosperity brought by Stockmaster soon changed attitudes within RES and gradually within the company as a whole. Salaries began to improve, starting with the marketing staff. Restrictions upon travel and upon making international telephone calls, which had been severe, were relaxed. Money was spent on product promotion, and frequent demonstration sessions were held in pleasant locations in many parts of the world. Superior accommodation was provided for the computer installations and for the staff involved with them. This was the start of a trend which was eventually to transform the office environment throughout Reuters.

From 2 March 1967 RES ventured upon totally independent reporting out of North America. This marked the ending of a thirty-year association with Dow Jones, the New York financial news agency. Since 1937 Reuters had exchanged its world economic news, delivered in London, for the Dow Jones service of North American financial news, delivered in New York. No payment had been made from either side. Although the agreement made no mention of exclusivity, Reuters had not sold its financial news in North America and Dow Jones had not sold its service in the rest of the world.

In 1965 Dow Jones announced its intention of marketing its ticker in Europe and of ending certain Reuter rights to its material. Dow Jones eventually joined forces with AP, and their Economic Report started on 1 April 1967. Dow Jones withdrew its ticker from the New York office of Reuters, and Reuters withdrew the City ticker from Dow Jones's London office.

Reuters was very worried about the prospective costs and risks of entering into competition with Dow Jones. Fortunately, Ultronic was again willing to put up the money for a joint enterprise—the Reuter Ultronic Report (RUR). This backing transformed a serious difficulty for Reuters into a major opportunity. RES could never have emerged as a complete world player during the next few years if the link with Dow Jones had been maintained. Major customers were becoming increasingly international in their trading, and expected Reuters to serve them throughout the world. RES needed to be free to collect and sell its news and information wherever it wished; and also to be fully independent in the United States, the hub of the international economy.

The Reuter Ultronic Report was launched at the beginning of 1968. It was a United States business wire of prices and related news, delivered to brokers, banks, and news media by 100-word-a-minute teleprinters, or by video display. RUR was competing directly with the Dow Jones tape on its home ground. In May 1969, after intensive lobbying by Reuters, the New York Stock Exchange made it almost obligatory for corporations to file their news to Reuters as well as to Dow Jones. This greatly increased the standing of Reuters. From the start of 1972 Reuters took over the whole enterprise, and renamed it the Reuter Financial Report. By 1974 Reuters had about 700 installations in the United States, compared with an estimated 3,200 for the Dow Jones Economic Report.

The introduction of RUR was significant in technological terms. It was the first Reuter service to be eventually sold to subscribers for display on screen, as an alternative to noisy and space-taking teleprinter delivery.

This facility, known as Videoscan, had been developed by Ultronic at the suggestion of Nelson and Renfrew.

In February 1970 RES introduced Videomaster from Ultronic. With a screen display of seventy-two digits, this was a big improvement upon Stockmaster (see Plate 46). Subscribers could select from over 9,500 world stock and commodity prices, and were offered prompts about related news stories.

In January 1974 Long looked back over the first ten years of the Stockmaster and Videomaster joint venture. He reminded the board that Ultronic had put up almost all the risk capital of £3.4 million. Yet Reuters had received profits totalling some £4 million—£1,321,000 in 1973 alone. Reuters had been well rewarded.

VIII

Stockmaster and the other new products and services of the 1960s and early 1970s had begun the making of the new Reuters. In only a few years it had built up a dominant position in world markets outside North America for the provision of real-time information services. Reuters had established the only intercontinental network capable of operating such services, and it had created a unique database of international financial information. It had also developed an effective technical, marketing, and sales organization. All this had been made possible through the joint venture with Ultronic. By the end of the 1960s, however, Ultronic had lost much of its entrepreneurial zeal, at the same time as Reuters was beginning to feel strong enough to contemplate acting alone. In 1973 came the launch of another major product, this time without any technical or financial help from a partner. This was called the Reuter Monitor Money Rates service.

The introduction of Monitor was a great initiative, and the profits were to be immense. Yet, as with the introduction of Stockmaster, the decision to develop the service was as much defensive as aggressive. Bunker Ramo and Dow Jones in the United States and Telekurs in Switzerland were seeking to leap ahead into a new field. In December 1971 the American companies announced a joint venture to develop a computerized financial-news retrieval service. Fortunately, Reuters was already preparing a similar product.

In this process, an important contribution was being made by a unique Reuter character, Fred Taylor (1920–76). Taylor had started in Reuters as a messenger in 1934, and for many years he reported London prices for the commercial services. From 1969 he was sales co-ordinator within the United Kingdom sales unit of RES. Taylor was a cockney rough diamond, who insisted upon remaining so. Yet he had developed a wide range of contacts at many levels within the City of London—contacts whom he occasionally met, but whom he more often questioned confidently by telephone. Even Taylor felt uncomfortable, however, when he was invited by one high-powered City contact for a yachting weekend. What to wear? What to do? But Taylor went.

Taylor's knowledge was invaluable, first in shaping the new foreign-exchange service, and then in selling it. The joke was that Monitor was launched on a sea of lunches. These were held chiefly with foreign-exchange managers, many of whom were well acquainted with Taylor. His boss, Alan Jackson, reported on 3 August 1973, soon after the launch of Monitor, that it would have taken much longer to construct the new service but for Taylor's efforts. 'He offers us very lengthy experience coupled with a freshness of approach to problems more often associated with a young graduate rather than a man of over 50.' Sadly, ill health forced him to take early retirement only a year later.

Taylor professed to be suspicious of young graduates. Yet paradoxically, one such graduate, André Villeneuve, was the man who gave shape to Monitor. The idea had already been talked about casually within RES, and others were to play vital parts. But Villeneuve was rightly credited by Nelson with making the crucial proposal. He had joined RES from Oxford University in 1967. The Monitor project gave him the chance to reveal his quality. Villeneuve combined perceptivity of mind and thoroughness of method with charm of manner. In the spring of 1971 he was sent by Nelson on a tour to conduct a survey of the European banking market. The Swiss banks, who were major customers for the Stockmaster/-Videomaster services, had just announced their intention of starting their own Telekurs service in competition with RES. When this was finally launched in 1975, it took its American market data from Bunker Ramo, not from Reuters. How could Reuters meet this prospective competition and loss of revenue? Villeneuve came up with a proposal for a money-rates service, which (he argued) the Swiss and others would find indispensable. He accepted that such a service would be more difficult to conduct than the Stockmaster/Videomaster services. The market for stock and commodity prices had a physical existence, whereas no physical market-place existed for foreign-exchange dealing. But Villeneuve concluded boldly that this absence represented not an insurmountable obstacle but an exciting opportunity.

With the break-up of the Bretton Woods system of fixed exchange rates, dealing in foreign exchange and money was about to expand rapidly. The problem for banks and dealers was how to receive quotations with sufficient speed. Dependence upon telephones and telex was unsatisfactory, since by the time an answer to a request for (say) a bank's dollar/sterling price had been given and transmitted, that price might well have changed. Seconds were important. Villeneuve had the idea of installing computer terminals in the offices of banks and other foreign-exchange markets. Reuters would in this way create an electronic market place. Market-makers (contributors) would be able to insert their foreign-exchange and money rates into the system. At the press of a button, the rates would become available on screen to interested parties (recipients) such as banks and international businesses. Reuters would charge both contributors and recipients for access to this interactive system.

Here was the concept of computerized contributed data. Two companies inside the United States already ran share information services on this basis. But Reuters was to the fore in thinking of bringing contributed data into the field of foreign exchange, a market which functioned between countries and between continents.

How would the London trade unions react to the novel idea of data insertion not by telegraphists in Reuters but by customers? This question was addressed early. David Smee, the staff manager, persuaded the telegraphists that the proposal would not reduce the number of their jobs—and also that if Reuters did not introduce such a product, some rival organization, or the banks themselves, would do so.

On 25 February 1972 John Ransom, the RES development manager, and Villeneuve submitted a detailed proposal to Nelson for what they called 'a Forex system'. They noted that foreign-exchange and money markets had recently developed in line with the growth in world trade and industrial investment across frontiers, now unimpeded by the Bretton Woods fixed parities. 'As a result industrial and commercial entities are forced to devote far closer attention to foreign exchange and money market operations, and stand to gain or lose considerable sums of money on these transactions.' Here was a new opportunity: 'Our proposed service should fill an information gap.' Reuters would provide the equipment, communications, and marketing facilities; market information would be provided by contributors. Ransom and Villeneuve admitted that the London brokers had given them little encouragement. Bankers had been more interested. The service should therefore be designed especially to suit them, starting in London, Western Europe, and North America.

The proposal spelt out the technical aspects in detail. The recommended central system used a software processor, even though a hardware processor might have seemed more likely. A working model using modified Ultronic hardware had been designed and demonstrated by Peter Howse of the technical services department; but a software solution was rightly preferred by Peter Benjamin, the technical services manager, as more flexible for the future. Digital Equipment Corporation (DEC), a world leader in computers, was given the order for desk terminals. Reuters itself was left to develop a suitable keyboard and screen. These were pleasingly designed by Kenneth Grange of Pentagram. The keyboard was manufactured by Honeywell, the screen by KGM Electronics.

On 29 February 1972 Nelson submitted a twelve-page formal proposal to Long. It listed various possible risks. Dealers had never before reported money rates in real time into a central system, and might not co-operate. The banks might decide to run such a service themselves, or the telecommunications authorities might decide that Reuters could not lease circuits because regulations about third-party traffic had not been formulated to take account of contributed data. Ultronic might well claim that the project was an extension of the Stockmaster/Videomaster joint venture: 'we could argue that our Master Agreement with them was anti-trust.' The tone of Nelson's paper was carefully confident. The intention was to launch the service in only ten months' time, on 1 January 1973. But what should it be called? 'Forex', the name so far used, was too limiting, since the service would also include other money rates. Long himself ended the uncertainty with a brilliant choice—'Monitor'. The Roman goddess Juno Moncta had given her name to the word 'money' because of the accident that her temple in Rome had come to house the city's mint.

On 22 June 1972 Long submitted the final proposal to the Reuter board, comparing the promise of Monitor with the performance of Stockmaster and Videomaster. In contrast to the three digits available from Stockmaster, 'Monitor will be part of a Reuter system able to display up to 170 words or 1,100 characters at a time on a television screen from a database capable of expansion to 40 million words. This data will be real-time current information, rarely more than 24 hours old.' Long explained that Monitor would require heavy borrowing, and received permission to secure external finance 'by the best method available'. In the event, a very large Eurocurrency facility of £800,000 was arranged with the Bank of Scotland, repayable over five years. £200,000 was drawn during 1973.

A modular pricing policy was recommended. 'We propose to charge inserting banks per page of information they supply.' The monthly rental for access to one page of data was fixed at £525 for a contributor/recipient, £190 for a recipient only. Each additional page cost £70.

Long and his colleagues realized that Monitor could only hope to succeed if it functioned with very nearly perfect reliability. Partly because of doubts about reliability, and partly because of late supply of equipment, the delayed launch-date of 1 May 1973 was eventually abandoned. Instead, the system became operational gradually. It first ran in London for a full working day (08.30 to 18.00 hours) on 25 June 1973. Thereafter, during thirty-eight working days up to 8 August the system was available for 99.89 per cent of the time. In the first weeks, however, subscriber equipment proved less satisfactory in operation than the central system. The PDP8M mini-computers being used as subscriber processors suffered from assembly faults, which took time to rectify.

In September Long told the board that the Monitor foreign-exchange service had been more widely advertised than any product in Reuter history. Yet at launch there were only fifteen contributor/recipients and fifteen recipients. After three months Barclays, one of the first contributors to be signed up, was expecting the service to collapse. Some banks objected to paying for insertion of their own information. Villeneuve remarked that he had been told: 'without their rates, we had nothing to offer.' Some banks simply did not want to reveal too much. They served corporate customers for whom they had been acting in the markets at more profit to themselves than to the corporations.

Brokers feared that they would lose business if the new service established itself. One admitted as much to Gordon Linacre, a Reuter director, at the 1974 annual lunch. Linacre wrote to Nelson on 21 June:

> I probed [X's] pride; and as a result, his two marriages, his habits (sporting, cultural and sexual) and his pride in his young lions are memories to me as well as him. He fears that Monitor will rob him of his devious livelihood. I hope you can convince his young partners that they can still get fat with Monitor.

Not until 1977 did members of the London Foreign Exchange Brokers Association order the Reuter service.

A serious problem was late delivery of equipment. This left too few contributors or recipients in the system, and so discouraged others from joining. By the start of 1974 111 Monitor customers had been signed up, but 59 were awaiting installation. Installations were progressing at the rate

of only three or four per week. In subsequent years late delivery of
equipment became an irritating consequence of success, as Reuters sought
to buy more equipment than DEC could readily supply.

The forecast capital requirement for 1974 rose to £734,700, compared
with an original forecast of £301,800. Long assured the board in
September 1973 that this was really an encouraging sign. 'The further
outlook is for a much larger market than we had originally envisaged.'
With the service started and with abandonment certain to be highly damaging to the reputation of Reuters, Long was being determinedly optimistic. He also contrived to demonstrate that the amount of capital at risk
was relatively small. Subscribers were required to sign two-year contracts;
yet the capital cost of equipment was covered in about ten months for
recipients and in about half that time for contributors. Subscribers also
paid six months in advance, whereas equipment suppliers gave Reuters
credit.

It was a paradox that high activity in the markets at first almost frustrated the new service. During the Arab–Israeli War of October 1973,
when oil prices shot up dramatically, many contributors found themselves
too busy to think of inserting their rates. Yet the flux in the markets and
intensifying worldwide inflation made a foreign-exchange and money
rates service the more necessary.

The breakthrough came between March and June 1974. Reuters
signed 109 Monitor contracts. By June there were 125 subscribers in the
United Kingdom and 121 in the rest of Europe; 52 were contributors/
recipients and 194 were recipients only. Two years later these last two
totals had reached 175 and 896 respectively. The Monitor range was
extended to bonds (1975), equities (1978), commodities (1978), and
United States Government securities (1978). By 1980 the system was
reaching round the world, and was averaging 136,800 page updates each
day from contributors and 840,000 page requests.

In August 1975 a money-news retrieval facility, promised from the
start, was at last made available. A series of headline pages could be called
up, with extra details on offer if wanted. Long told the board in June
1975 that this gave 'uniqueness to the content of Reuter Monitor', and so
made competition more difficult. A particular strength was Monitor's
expandability, its ability to carry add-on facilities. By the time of the
tenth anniversary in 1983 forty-seven distinct local and international
Reuter Monitor services were on offer.

One problem of success was that large amounts of capital were becoming locked up in the value of standing equipment. This was threatening

to block further progress; the answer was found by Judah. Under agreements made in 1975, some Reuter-owned equipment was leased back, while other equipment became leasable directly. Leaseback continued until 1982.

In the first five years, up to June 1978, Monitor generated gross revenue of well over £30 million, and operating profit of over £11.5 million. This compared with an original forecast of just over £1.1 million. By 1983 operating profit after ten years totalled £100 million. Here was a remarkable success, which transformed the face and fortunes of Reuters. Company turnover in 1983 was fourteen times that of 1973.

Opportunities for currency speculation were, of course, increased in the new situation. But the Monitor Money Rates service did not itself encourage speculation. By making so much contributed data available worldwide, Monitor was simply creating a purer market. How players then conducted themselves remained their own responsibility. An article in the *Harvard Business Review* in 1979 noticed with satisfaction that the Reuter Monitor Money Rates service was enabling quotations to be obtained simultaneously from twenty-five world money markets. Bankers, brokers, and treasurers of international businesses could now take advantage of varying rates as never before. 'In the broadest sense,' noted the article, 'we have for the first time a genuine international economy in which prices and money values are known in real time in every part of the globe.'

IX

The possibility of venturing into a computerized dealing service had been considered when the Money Rates service was under discussion before 1973. A cautious step-by-step approach was eventually decided upon—with dealing by dialogue accepted as a next stage, and possibly beyond that 'matching', the automatic consummation of deals on the basis of requirements stated by subscribers. The paper of 25 February 1972 from Ransom and Villeneuve, detailing what became the Monitor Money Rates system, had explained why they were not then recommending an early advance into dealing. 'Many banks want the rates they put on the screen to be indicative only; they do not wish to feel any obligation to trade at the rates they screen.' Also, noted Ransom and Villeneuve, a dealing system would be very demanding technically, and would take longer to create than a money-rates system. This indeed proved to be the case.

Once again Villeneuve pointed the way. He prepared a twenty-page 'Reuter Monitor Dealing Feasibility Study', dated 18 April 1975. He reported that a simulated dealing facility had been demonstrated to thirty-seven Reuter customers in the United Kingdom and western Europe. Thirty-one had shown interest, and enquiries in North America had revealed a similar interest there. Most subscribers to Monitor Money Rates regarded dealing as a logical progression: 'Our presentation stressed that the objective involved no change in current market practice. Personal contact, a sensitive subject amongst dealers, would not be undermined by the proposals. Dealers would continue to use the telephone. There was no attempt to create a matching system.'

Villeneuve emphasized that the lasting commitment of the banks to the proposed service needed to be ensured. He suggested offering them close involvement, either through equity participation, or through some less formal association. This would prevent them from setting up a dealing service of their own. Nelson was cool about the equity proposal, and Renfrew hostile, feeling that it would unnecessarily complicate the development of the project.

In a paper dated 1 May 1975 Nelson recommended that a dealing project should be promoted, but that it should be financed 'as we did with the Reuter Monitor'. Once again there was a mixture of aggressive and defensive motivation. The motives, he said, were not simply profit but also protection of existing revenue. 'We believe that if a successful dealing system were established by another organisation it might make the Reuter Monitor redundant.' Nelson emphasized what he saw as the novelty of the proposal:

> A dealing system is different from Reuters present business. It is information handling, but makes Reuters an instrument in the execution of a transaction which we have never been before. At least one senior executive believes that we should not do it because it will affect our relationships with our sources since we shall become a part of the actual trading operation.

In December 1974 Long secured board authorization to study the establishment of 'a money dealing system'. He knew that such a system had already been started on a small scale by Tafex in the United States. It failed soon afterwards.

The name of David Ure became closely associated with the dealing project. Ure had joined RES in 1968 as a graduate trainee from Oxford University. He was a thoughtful Scot, deliberately recruited by Nelson as different from the usual run of RES graduate recruits, whose social graces (Nelson had begun to suspect) sometimes exceeded their business intelligence. Ure trained on the financial desk in Brussels, returning there in mid-1970 as RES manager. Long noticed Ure's high intelligence and wry sense of humour. He became product planning manager in 1974, and at the beginning of 1977 he was made dealing project manager. The dealing project was the great hope of the company for future profit. Yet success was far from certain. Ure persevered in the face of technical difficulties and trade-union awkwardness. His reports were never misleadingly optimistic.

In May 1976 Long was given board approval to spend £69,000 on development work. Not until 13 July 1977, only after clearance had been given by the European telecommunications authorities (PPTs), did Long request and receive final endorsement for the dealing project to go ahead. He was authorized to spend £2,563,000 during 1977–9. There had been serious doubt whether the coordinating Comité Européen des Postes et Télécommunications would allow Reuters to operate a dealing service at all. After intensive representations the committee had finally agreed in March to allow Reuters to lease circuits, with charges levied at a higher rate related to the volume of traffic. This was a remarkable breakthrough by Reuters because it broke new ground in relations with the PTTs, and it did so at a time when such a breakthrough was vital for future progress. Instead of having one point broadcasting to all points, the dealing service was designed to place two people in communication with each other. The PTTs had feared that this innovation would threaten their revenues.

Long explained that the new service would widen the revenue base. The now lucrative Money Rates service remained vulnerable because it depended upon quite a small number of contributors. He admitted that there was opposition to the dealing project from foreign-exchange brokers, who feared loss of business. On the other hand, 'a strong body of opinion in European banks . . . trusts Reuters'. This opinion, continued Long, 'believes our well-accepted reputation for neutrality and reliability makes us a suitable medium for essential information exchange'.

A succession of promised launch-dates was to come and go throughout 1979 and 1980. Technical difficulties were made the harder to solve because of problems with the workforce, which was split into disharmonious elements. Over a hundred people became involved—far too many for systematic progress. The development of a software multiplexing system (SWM) for the data-communications network was in the hands of a Reuter team; the development of the dealing equipment was in the hands of consultants. On 3 July 1978 Ure had ventured to put a price upon failure. Abandonment at once would leave Reuters with a loss of just over £1 million; if the project collapsed at launch the loss would be trebled; if the service stopped six months after launch, assuming only fifty initial orders, the loss would be £3,745,000.

Reuters pressed ahead with enlisting foundation subscribers. Long reported to the board in December 1979 that 146 contracts had been secured worldwide. The projected number at launch was 160. No more were wanted at first, because subscribers needed to be trained in the proper use of the service. Villeneuve reminded Nelson on 30 October 1978: 'Dealing is the most sensitive product, in market terms, which Reuters has ever launched. The banks are treating its introduction by Reuters with some suspicion. They are particularly suspicious of the fact that Reuters will have control over the pricing of a product on which they will be heavily dependent.'

Nelson demanded heavy final testing during the last months, in the knowledge that this was not a service which could be left to get better by trial and error. Month after month he found himself telling the board that the service was not yet ready. Huge costs were being carried. About £8 million had been invested in the project—double or treble the company profit for each of the years when it was under development.

The Reuter Money Dealing service went live on 23 February 1981 to 145 subscribers in nine countries. By June there were still only 174 subscribers. The biggest project ever undertaken by Reuters had begun uncertainly. None the less, the availability of the service was extended rapidly—from the United Kingdom, Western Europe, and North America at launch, to Hong Kong, Singapore, and the Middle East in the next year. The breakthrough came after Dealing had reached Bahrain in May 1982. It was now known as the Reuter Monitor Dealing Service.

Bob Etherington was made Dealing market manager in September 1981 with a brief to relaunch the sales presentation throughout the world. He emphasized to potential customers the word 'speed'—how the new product offered the opportunity to conclude deals in two to four seconds, compared with up to ten times as long by existing methods. The Reuter advertisement proclaimed, '30 seconds is a long time in a dealing room'. Support staff were on hand both before and after signing contracts to help dealers overcome their 'techno-fear'. Monitor Dealing was unique. Only through Reuters could dealers communicate with each other at high speed to buy, sell, or lend money through the same screen, taking hard copies of transactions from an associated teleprinter. They still had to work out their own deals, since this was not yet 'matching'; but the new service was a great advance. Charges at launch were $1,500 per month for first terminals, $850 for second, and $500 for third and subsequent terminals.

By the second anniversary in February 1983 the Dealing service had 400 subscribers in twenty-four countries; thirty-seven of the world's top fifty banks were participating; calls through the system were averaging 10,000 per day. A year later calls had doubled again, with peaks of 40,000 in active markets. In May 1984 Renfrew summed up for the board what had become another great achievement. The Dealing service, he wrote, had reached a level of acceptance which made it 'another basic money market tool, like the Reuter Monitor before it, generating its own growth momentum'.

From the 1960s to the 1980s the contribution made by Reuters towards the provision of information to the world business community had been remarkable. Stockmaster had offered computerized stock-market information. Videoscan and Videomaster had introduced screen display. Monitor Money Rates had brought contributed data within a computerized market-place. And finally, Monitor Dealing had drawn Reuters into the very process of trading.

This was an impressive progression, but not an inevitable one. Both Monitor Money Rates and Monitor Dealing might have failed after launch, for both were slow to reach critical mass. They could not have prospered simply because they were technologically advanced. They were based upon careful market research, they were reliable in use, and they were promoted by an energetic sales force. This gave the two products the resilience necessary to achieve ultimate outstanding success.

A Worldwide Presence

I

To achieve his great objectives for Reuters, Long had depended upon the support of successive chairmen of the Reuter board. In 1968 Burgess was succeeded as chairman by William Barnetson (1917–81). Barnetson, created a life peer in 1975, was a Scot who, starting on the *Edinburgh Evening News*, became a busy figure in the world of journalism. From 1966 he was managing director of United Newspapers, then a mainly provincial newspaper group, whose fortunes he revived.

Barnetson persuaded the Reuter board to accept Long's schemes for innovation and borrowing—notably, the Monitor project. Instinctively, he disliked going deeply into debt, and he had said so at the Reuter board before he became chairman. But Long persuaded him that borrowing was necessary to avoid falling behind in the computerized information race. Long humoured Barnetson skilfully: 'he liked a certain kudos, and I liked a free hand and support when needed.'

The extra activity of the 1960s and 1970s required extra working-space. By 1969 Reuter operations in London were spread over seven different buildings, although the main offices and newsrooms remained in Fleet Street. In July 1979 the London technical centre was opened in Great Sutton Street, bringing together computer and communications operations.

Easier communication by telephone and telex and swifter travel by air meant that regional management out of London was possible by the 1960s. Two men were particularly involved: Patrick Crosse was made responsible for Africa and later for Latin America, David Chipp for Asia and the Pacific.

Latin America was an old problem for Reuters. In a 1975 report Peter Job, GND assistant manager for Latin America, surveyed the situation since 1958, the year when Reuters had withdrawn its general-news service. Job noticed that the market was too fragmented and competitive to yield large revenue. AP and UPI supplied radio-photos with their world news, whereas Reuters did not; and AFP offered very low subscriptions without always requiring them to be paid.

The revival of Reuter operations within Latin America had begun in 1963 with the creation of a leased communications network. By 1968 Reuters had twenty-one full-time general-news journalists and managers in the area, plus nine economic journalists and two joint reporters. A Latin American general-news service in English and Spanish was revived from 1 February 1964. This had some twenty-five subscribers by 1966, including the influential *La Prensa* of Buenos Aires. Even so, the Latin American loss for the year was £18,000 and rising. Crosse was appointed in July of that year to transform present 'modest success' into future major achievement.

The return of Reuters to Latin America had been secretly encouraged by the British Government. In 1964 it formed Regional News Services (Latin America) Limited as a front organization. This was a twin of RNS (Mid-East), which collected and distributed Reuter news to the Arab countries. The managing director of both bodies was Tom Little. From

1964 to 1971 RNS paid Reuters generous subscriptions of £25,000 or £30,000 a year, avowedly for mutual assistance in Latin America.

A locally-owned news agency had been talked about for years. The influence of AP and UPI had aroused resentment among both the Governments and newspaper proprietors of Latin America. Crosse decided that Reuters might be able to exploit this resentment by offering to help start an independent agency. Reuters would then hope to shed its local trading loss by handing over its wholesale news distribution; and also to save money by gaining access to the Latin news report. Such was the background to the formation in January 1970 of a Latin American news agency, Agencia Latinoamericana de Información (Latin) SA.

Latin was a co-operative. It began with thirteen newspaper shareholders (*socios*) in seven Latin American countries. The larger shareholders each paid $3,500 per month; others were charged $1,500. In July 1971 Reuters took an 8.5 per cent shareholding, increased in 1973 to 49 per cent, with an option of taking a majority. This increased holding was a way of converting Latin's debt to Reuters into equity. By 1975 Latin owed Reuters an estimated £410,000, not far short of the total company profit for the year.

Crosse was seconded for two years as Latin's first general manager. He was good at negotiating with politicians and newspaper proprietors, less good at day-to-day management. He left Reuters in 1971. Long had been critical of his methods, and was never quite convinced that Reuters was right to join a co-operative rather than to stand on its own. He had told the executive committee on 4 February 1969 that Latin was associated in his mind with 'a defeatist attitude'.

Latin aimed to produce a news service containing half Reuter world news and half Latin American news. This balanced coverage required an initial establishment of seventeen staff correspondents in Latin America and in Washington. Most of these were Reuter-trained. Conversion to satellite communication added to Latin's efficiency, but also to its costs. By 1975 it had about 130 subscribers; these were located throughout Latin America except Cuba, where the Communists pirated the service. The survival of Latin was always doubtful. The newspaper shareholders refused to allow subscription rates to be increased in proportion to rising costs, or even to pay what they had agreed to pay. The Latin trading loss for 1974 was £103,000, and rising.

Yet Reuters could not allow Latin to collapse without damage to its own reputation. Nelson went out in December 1974 to assess the situation. He hoped to attract support from the Latin American Governments. In the end only President Carlos Andrés Pérez of Venezuela proved willing to help financially. In October 1975 his Government signed a contract for Latin to deliver its service to forty-three Venezuelan embassies throughout the world, along with a daily bulletin produced by the Venezuelan Central Office of Information. The contract was worth £680,000 to the end of 1976.

The contract with Venezuela prolonged the life of Latin, but failed to save it. The newspaper proprietors, always politically divided, remained uncertain about their commitment. In November 1977 the Latin and Reuter news-collection operations were merged. In February 1980 the Venezuelan Government contract expired. This removed the last major reason for maintaining the Latin structure, and in May 1981 the agency ceased trading. Henceforward Reuters was to distribute its Spanish services in Latin America under its own name.

II

Like Latin America, North America presented a challenge throughout the 1970s which Reuters actively confronted but did not overcome. In February 1973 Long explained to the board how, with the collapse of the British Empire as the area of chief interest for Reuters, it had turned towards Western Europe and the United States. By 1972 North America was contributing 17.5 per cent of total company revenue (see Table 12.3). But competition was stronger and more deeply entrenched in North America than anywhere else.

TABLE 12.3. Total revenue figures by area, 1964 and 1972 (£000)

	Total world	N. America		Europe (excl. UK)		Rest of world	
		Gross	% of world revenue	Gross	% of world revenue	Gross	% of world revenue
1964	3 583	417	11.6	691	19.3	2 475	69.1
1972	13 827	2 423	17.5	5 162	37.3	6 242	45.1

The long-standing heavy dependence of Reuters upon Dow Jones for American economic news, on the one hand, and upon AP for general news, on the other, was ended in 1967. From that year Reuters began fully independent reporting out of North America. This double break was one of Long's key initiatives. When he took over in 1963, Reuters in North America was still operating under the constraints of contracts signed a generation earlier. Out of total press revenue from the United States of £207,000 per annum, £42,857 came from the *New York Times* subscription, £21,428 from the *Chicago Tribune* subscription, and £14,600 from the *Chicago Tribune* Press Service. The connection with the *Tribune* syndicate service, undertaken with justifiable satisfaction in 1945, had come to seem restrictive by the 1960s.

The supply of news from North America was equally unsatisfactory. Under the 1947 agreement with AP, Reuters received AP's 'A-wire' service of American news in exchange for the PA service of British news. As the importance of news from Britain declined, this arrangement had begun to look unequal to the Americans. Long recognized that AP would sooner or later demand payment of a differential. Yet at the same time the A-wire service from AP had become inadequate for Reuters; AP's service for newspapers in the United States was much fuller.

Long warned the board on 26 May 1965 that this dependence upon AP for news was now threatening Reuters. 'It is a sword hanging over our heads by a string and no one knows just how thick the string is.' Long described Wes Gallagher, the general manager of AP, as 'dour and tough and no friend of Reuters': 'the only safe course is to begin now to build up a news collection network in the United States which will enable us as soon as possible to become independent.'

In September 1966 Gallagher gave notice that AP would require payment of a differential from the following September: 'we're trading elephants for apples.' At first he would not reveal how much he wanted, but he eventually demanded $200,000 per annum. This was, as Long recollected years later, 'a fortune for us at that time'. Underhill spent three months in the United States assessing the situation. He concluded that AP would break the relationship sooner or later, even if Reuters paid up now. And he estimated that Reuters could produce its own independent report for $225,000 a year—in other words, for not much more than AP was now demanding for its inadequate service.

Gallagher would not reduce his demand; Long would have settled for (say) $100,000. It turned out to be a blessing in disguise for Reuters that AP stuck to its price. Gallagher simply did not believe that Reuters would be able to compete successfully in reporting North American news. The Americans failed to take into account that Reuters would not be in pursuit of every small-town story. Its customers outside the United States wanted only selected news—news about events likely to affect their own countries, plus a leavening of scandal and gossip about prominent people in American politics and entertainment.

Long pressed a reluctant Reuter board into authorizing the creation of an independent news file out of North America. The directors remained fearful of the risk and expense. They would have much preferred either to settle with AP, or to enter into an alliance with its rival, UPI. But Long was insistent. He knew that Reuters had already been building up its staff to improve the quality of American news output. In 1965 there had still been only sixty-four full-time Reuter staff in the whole of the United States and Canada. Five additional correspondents were then sent to New York, two to Washington, and one to Chicago. By January 1968, after the break with AP, 105 full-time staff were in post.

Reporting of economic news independently of Dow Jones began on 1 April 1967. Reporting of general news independently of AP followed on 7 September; the AP printer in the New York office went dead at midnight. The executive who planned the new economic-service coverage and who had started the expansion of RES in North America was Cyril Smith, who had earlier been Comtelburo news editor in London. The independent general-news report was organized by Julian Bates, a journalist with long experience in the Far East and elsewhere. Renfrew took charge of North America in January 1971. He ordered the integration of the general-news and economic services. There was to be one news-collecting team, and one marketing and sales force, though with general-news and economic-news specialists within each group. In September the Western Hemisphere desk moved from London to New York.

From the start of 1968 the arrangement with the *Chicago Tribune* Press Service was ended. Henceforward Reuters was free to sell its news anywhere in the United States. The *New York Times*, the *Chicago Tribune*, and the *Washington Post* were long-established customers, but Reuters needed subscriptions from more than a few prestigious names. The newspaper client-base was to drop to as low as sixteen during the 1970s, before recovering to nearly 100 papers during the 1980s.

By 1980 Reuters had four addresses in New York, plus offices in Washington and six other American cities. New York was the head office, and Washington filed its news through New York editorial, a cause of continuing complaint. The practice was described by Ian Macdowall, the chief news editor, on 23 October 1979 after a visit to North America, as 'an essentially political decision by RNA that Washington should not have direct contact with head office'. Reuters North America had been set up in 1973. The Washington bureau had only 27 staff in 1974 against AP's 130 and UPI's 100, and Reuters was still treated as a second-class agency by the White House and State Department. This meant that its correspondents were not given equal access with the American agencies to the president or the secretary of state. From the late 1970s, however, the performance of the Washington bureau took on a new sharpness as greater resources became available. Reuters at last began to achieve a sufficiently strong presence in the political news capital of the Western world.

Renfrew divided RNA into five profit centres—brokerage, banking, media, cable, and Canada. The first four corresponded to specific markets at which different Reuter services were aimed. These services, and the technology to develop them further, were Renfrew's particular interest. But shortage of money and also the restrictions about North American involvement which were built into the joint venture with Ultronic, precluded an early attack upon the basic computer-information markets. Renfrew looked instead to openings on the fringe, where competition was likely to be less intense.

The American market was still at this period overwhelmingly domestic in its interests, and this necessarily limited the demand for international information from Reuters. Paradoxically, however, this bias proved to be advantageous, because it kept the attention of the American information-providers focused on their home market. During Renfrew's first year as manager his enthusiasm for cable technology resulted in the creation of Reuters News View, which offered two channels—one of general news, and the other of financial and sports news. The Reuter teleprinter multi-plexing network retained sufficient spare capacity to accommodate a textual signal which was just fast enough to look acceptable on television screens. Reuters could not have afforded a separate network. News View was an immediate success.

III

What would follow Stockmaster and Videomaster? Here was a crucial question for the new Reuters. London's answer was the Reuter Monitor Money Rates service. But Renfrew in New York began to search for a cheaper and even bolder product. He launched a technical development programme, which became centred upon a subsidiary company formed in March 1973—Information Dissemination and Retrieval Inc. (IDR) of Farmingdale, Long Island. IDR set out to develop a computerized data system of advanced performance. The aim was for data to be delivered by coaxial cable for display on television screens at more than 400,000 words per minute; transmission by cable was to be continuous. At the push of a button, subscribers were to be enabled to use keyboards to 'grab' material as it flowed by, and to hold it on screen. The 'frame-grabbing' concept—

later changed to 'row-grabbing'—had led Renfrew into discussions with two small American companies. One of them, owned by Robert Nagel, was working on hardware. Nagel became a partner in IDR. He was an enthusiast. For a time, he carried Renfrew along with him. After a legal action brought by Nagel in 1977 but settled out of court, he returned his IDR shares in return for $180,000 paid to him by Reuters. According to Nagel's evidence, Renfrew had told him in 1973 that he was 'by far the most brilliant technical person he had ever met'.

Reuters had put systems together before, and had written software for them; but this project called for hardware to be made by Reuters itself—and made, moreover, for a revolutionary system. By the end of 1974 a prototype row-grabbing system was on offer to business houses in New York, via Manhattan Cable Television. Long told a press demonstration optimistically that in about a year Reuters would be able to put out news and information cheaply, even upon family television screens. Row-grabbing technology came to employ a mixture of satellite, cable, micro-wave, and phone-line relay. Unfortunately, the exciting prospect offered by row-grabbing proved to be difficult to translate into a widely available and reliable service. In addition, row-grabbing needed wide-band com-munication, which was chiefly available in North America. A study by Ure and the technical department in London advised against attempting to introduce it into Europe. It did not cross the Atlantic.

During the years 1973–83 IDR lost well over $1 million, mainly because of its work upon row-grabbing. But IDR also became involved in other activities. From 1977 it gradually became the main supplier to Reuters of terminals for use as cheap alternatives to DEC models for the Monitor services, both in North America and elsewhere. After a slow start the Monitor Money Rates service operated successfully in North America, using telephone lines rather than cable for delivery.

In 1973 Renfrew promised that RNA would seek to earn profits. But when? He took full responsibility not only for revenue growth but also for cost control—insisting that all costs arising within RNA should be charged to RNA. Inevitably this made his search for profitability much harder. In March 1978 he had to admit that 'while escalating losses have been avoided, we have not been able to make any progress towards the RNA definition of area profitability'. The loss for 1977 reached almost $2 million. During the second half of 1980 RNA finally recorded overall profitability. For 1981–2 RNA's improved position showed in the annual trading-area profit figures:

TABLE 12.4. Annual trading-area profit figures,
1980–1982 (£000)

	1980	1981	1982
Reuters Europe	4 519	9 498	16 331
Reuters Asia	5 423	10 690	16 836
Reuters North America	(83)	2 036	3 909
Reuters Overseas[a]	(865)	(407)	1 758

[a] Middle East, Africa, Latin America

RNA encountered difficulties with its staff as well as with technology. The Newspaper Guild of New York was a union open to all workers in the industry, except printers and typesetters. Its relationship with Reuters became increasingly troubled during the 1960s, as its representation increased. Some union members believed that Renfrew had set out 'to screw the Guild'. Yet in 1971 he decided to accept the Guild's high salary demands in order to secure removal from the agreement of clauses which would have prevented the introduction of automation. In 1974 a ten-day strike by 149 Guild members (out of 195 North American staff) ended with the union settling for salary increases below those initially offered. This was in return for a cost-of-living escalator, which management had originally refused. Reuter executive staff kept all services functioning with help from about twenty non-striking Guild members. NUJ members in London agreed not to handle copy from New York.

A strike was narrowly averted in 1977, but RNA management was prepared for a confrontation in 1980. In that year a new salary structure was offered which reflected market rates, rather than the above-market rates demanded by the Guild. Management knew that the Guild was in serious financial trouble. Jim Bell, the Reuter unit chairman, even began to recommend a switch of allegiance to the American Communications Association (ACA), which was an affiliate of the notorious International Brotherhood of Teamsters. Bell contended that Reuter staff would be better represented by a vigorous union rather than by an almost bankrupt one. The prospect of the teamsters moving into Reuters horrified the management—at headquarters in London as well as in New York.

On 1 November 1979 the ACA filed a petition with the National Labor Relations Board for an election to be held at Reuters to ask staff whether they wanted representation by the Guild or the ACA, or by neither. The Reuter management urged staff to vote 'neither'. On 14 December the ACA suddenly withdrew from the contest. This meant that the Guild retained its place within Reuters, since there was now no opportunity for staff to vote 'neither'.

Negotiations dragged on throughout the first half of 1980. One ingenious union demand was for a staff holiday on Julius Reuter's birthday. On 3 July Reuters terminated the old contract unilaterally, posting new conditions of employment and implementing pay increases. These ranged from 5 per cent for lower job categories to 8.5 per cent for the highest.

In response, the Guild called a strike from noon on 24 July. Telegraphic circuits out of New York and video-editing installations broke down; but the strike proved to be ineffective, even though the Guild received transatlantic support. For the first time in the history of Reuters, journalists in London came out on strike; their sympathy action lasted for eight days. Some clerical and administrative staff joined them briefly. Attempts to spread the strike to continental Europe failed, and editorial operations in both New York and London were maintained by executives. Over a quarter of Guild members remained at work. After twenty-five days, the Guild accepted terms less good than those originally on offer.

IV

Australia continued to generate both problems and opportunities for Reuters. Some top managers, including Long, regretted privately that Reuters had ever allowed the Australian Associated Press into the partnership in 1947. The Australians, for their part, emphasized how they had injected much-needed capital into the company in 1947; how closely they had worked with Reuters in the Pacific area; and how greatly they were contributing to the expansion of the economic services. They claimed optimistically that by the 1970s—but for the partnership constraint—the AAP would have been offering strong competition to Reuters in the Far East.

Reuters had been seeking modification of the partnership agreement for several years, but AAP had been reluctant. In particular, Reuters wanted complete editorial control of news from the Pacific area. An informal committee of the 'A' and 'B' Reuter stockholders was formed in April 1965, deliberately excluding the Australian and New Zealander 'C' stockholders. This committee viewed with equanimity the prospect of the Australians and New Zealanders leaving the partnership. Burgess even mentioned the possibility of inducing them to quit 'by making the present Agreement unworkable'.

The Australians and New Zealanders were receiving a one-third rebate of their assessments; the total AAP rebate for 1965 was £33,956. The concession had been intended chiefly to cover office expenses in London and New York. The 'A' and 'B' directors argued that the rebate had ceased to be justified now that the Australians had reduced their staff in London and no longer kept anyone in New York. The new cable gave the AAP easy access to the full Reuter file for sub-editing in Sydney.

Conveniently, the rebate arrangement had been found to be *ultra vires*. This legal opinion was revealed at a meeting of representatives of all the stockholders in London on 8 June 1965. Rupert Henderson, one of the makers of the 1947 agreement, and Duncan Hooper, managing editor of AAP, were present. The discussions were long and often heated, with Henderson contending that the Reuter management was anti-AAP, and that it was 'no part of their task to lay down policy.'

The 1947 agreement spoke of the 'paramount interest' of Australia in the Pacific area. Long insisted that Reuters now had at least an equal interest in news from this increasingly important part of the world. He refused to believe that the Australians were especially expert in Pacific affairs, or more acceptable in Asia than the British. Although in practice the Australian right to appoint correspondents had often gone by default because of lack of suitable candidates, Long did not like the principle involved. He complained in June 1965 that the idea of qualification by nationality was 'entirely out of place in Reuters'.

AAP and NZPA finally accepted major changes to the 1947 agreement. The new arrangement was spelt out in a letter of 10 August 1965 from Henderson to Burgess. The assessment rebate was replaced by a payment which recognized 'the additional financial burden falling on AAP and NZPA by reason of their mode of operation'. New terms for running the economic services were also agreed. The Australians and New Zealanders were to be entitled to nominate 'not fewer' than four correspondents in the Pacific area, but editorial control was to be exercised from London. This crucial concession was cosmetically qualified by the creation of a Pacific board, whose functions were deliberately not spelt out in detail. Burgess told Long on 5 November 1965: 'We don't want Frank Packer to say that rule so and so has not been obeyed by the pommy bastards!' Packer, one of the dominant figures in AAP, was a long-time director of Reuters. The Pacific board was never allowed to exercise much influence, and it faded away during the 1980s.

The 1965 agreement had left the AAP responsible for the news service for Reuters out of Australia and New Zealand. Macdowall, the chief news editor, reported tartly to the editor-in-chief on 27 June 1973: 'The presentation of the AAP file is occasionally satisfactory and more frequently deplorable.' In 1974 two correspondents were sent to Sydney, one for general news and one for economic services. They received a cool welcome. Finally, in 1977 Reuters assumed main responsibility for both the RWS and RES files from Australia.

V

Reuters was also moving away during these years from too much dependence upon the European news agencies. Long was particularly interested in Western Europe. After the Second World War it became the main revenue-earning area for Reuters, producing over half the total by the 1970s. In a note for the executive committee (undated, but probably 1970) Long described his aspirations for Europe. It was 'time for us to pull the disjointed elements of our European activity together into a coherent policy'. He asked how the reputation of Reuters as 'a neutral collector and supplier' stood in the eyes of the European media, RES customers, and European Governments. 'We have in Europe, as elsewhere, tended to increase our acceptability by co-operating with a national partner.' But was this policy, hitherto unavoidable because of financial weakness, still the best for Reuters? The Europeans, Long argued, must now come to accept the right of Reuters to distribute directly whenever it wanted to. 'We must establish Reuters reputation as a news agency whose domestic area is Europe.'

Long assured the board in October 1977 that RWS and RES reporting teams were co-operating well in all the European bureaux, but particularly in Brussels, where the nature of the EEC report required close editorial liaison. None the less, Germany—not Belgium—had been made the European focal point for Reuters.

In Germany, as in the United States, Reuters finished up standing on its own in the provision both of general and of economic news. And as in the United States, the bold decisions were taken with a mixture of reluctance and enthusiasm. A German-language news service, edited in Bonn for distribution to the German press, radio, and television, was launched in December 1971. This followed the ending of the relationship with DPA, the German agency. The initiative for the break came not from Reuters, but from DPA; yet Reuters was glad to go its own way. Long's contempt for DPA in general, and in particular for its general manager, Wolfgang Weynen, was strong. He believed that DPA was using Reuters largely as a tip-off service, crediting its stories as little as possible. This had caused the virtual disappearance of the Reuter name from the West German press. Long also argued that the revenue from the DPA connection was inadequate as a subscription from the entire West German press.

Long reported in April 1971 that DPA had been told of this growing dissatisfaction. Weynen said that he still wished to renew the contract, so Reuters had offered terms. Yet on 2 July a letter from Weynen arrived in London saying that DPA had decided to accept another offer. Reuters knew this to be from UPI. Relations were so bad that Weynen had not told Long of his decision even though they had met in Frankfurt on the same day. Long believed that Weynen had treated the Reuter offer only as a target for UPI to beat: 'I conclude that he never intended to renew the contract with Reuters.'

Manfred Pagel, who had joined Reuters in 1961 as a local correspondent in Bonn, became the German-service editor. German by birth and American by education, he seemed well suited to handle the challenge. Yet the service was slow to take off, partly because its charges were high, partly because of uncertainty about its objectives. Was it seeking to provide a secondary service for the German market, which meant that it was in competition with AP and AFP, who also provided domestic German news? Or was it aiming to match DPA in its home territory? The latter was too ambitious: how best then to beat the other agencies? By the late 1970s Reuters had realized that a service of foreign news plus domestic highlights, adequate for broadcast subscribers, would offer only weak competition to AP and AFP. The Reuter domestic report was therefore expanded to attract more subscribers from the German press. Even so, during the 1980s about 60 per cent of German media revenue still came from radio and television stations.

The decision to break with VWD, the German economic-news agency, was influenced by its lack of enterprise. Reuter economic services were distributed through VWD, and Reuters had access to the VWD economic report. But VWD was slow to start teleprinter services, and when Reuters introduced Stockmaster in 1964, VWD refused to participate in a joint company. Nationalistic protectionism coloured VWD attitudes; all sales interviews for Stockmaster had to include a VWD representative. A new five-year contract between Reuters and VWD was signed in 1973, which at last gave RES a free hand in selling and running its computerized services. But in October 1977 Long was still describing the relationship as 'uneasy'.

The breakdown came at the end of the following year. Reuters refused to continue paying commission to VWD on RES computerized services, while VWD wished to reduce its subscription for Reuter news services. Long explained to the Reuter board in June 1978 why he viewed the break with equanimity. 'In major European countries we must operate retrieval services independently of agencies because of the need for international coordination and because such services are too important to our existence and our future to confide them to an outside agent.' In 1980 the one-third shareholding of Reuters in VWD was sold back to the company itself for DM1.4 million. A nationalistic article in *Die Zeit* on 11 December complained that Reuters had always exploited VWD, and had now abandoned it when there was no more to gain: 'these British gentlemen crucified their German partners.'

Against this background, RES began independent reporting in West Germany from 1 January 1979. The number of RES journalists was increased from three to seven, and part of the economic-reporting operation was transferred from Frankfurt to Bonn to facilitate liaison in producing the German-language service.

Reuters sought to be strong in France as well as in Germany. The entrenched position of the subsidized AFP made this difficult. The French-language service, produced by Reuters in London, was offered in France, Belgium, and Switzerland. From 1972 Reuters worked with the second-largest French agency, Agence Centrale de Presse (ACP) of Marseilles. The ACP file mixed international news from Reuters with its own domestic news. The connection proved to be less advantageous than had been hoped. The added play given to the Reuter service in provincial France was limited, and the financial benefit was negligible.

The French- and German-language services were part of a plan to extend the Reuter presence in western Europe. Presence had become more important than profit in the collection and distribution of general news throughout the Continent. Long told the board in October 1977 that media services to Europe now contributed only 9 per cent of profits.

VI

During the 1970s Reuters made notable progress in the Far East. Rapid growth began in Singapore, Malaysia, and Hong Kong. Gordon Hanson, manager for South-East Asia, exploited the fact that colonial and former colonial territories, with their strong entrepreneurial spirit, contained large numbers of potential customers for RES teleprinters and for the

Monitor services. A particular opportunity for Reuters was provided when Singapore set out to develop an Asian dollar market, which soon became very large.

Elsewhere in Asia, nationalistic susceptibilities caused difficulties. China and India insisted upon Reuters working through their national agencies, while Japan, Korea, and Taiwan could be penetrated only through licensing agreements. In June 1969 Long informed the board that revenue from Japan was approaching £300,000 per annum, third only to revenue from the United Kingdom and from Switzerland. Reuters worked with three Japanese partners—Kyodo, the national news agency; the *Asahi Shimbun*, the country's leading newspaper (which in 1969 had just passed ten million for its combined morning and evening circulations); and Jiji Press, the economic-news agency. In addition, from 1971 Reuters held a small share in Quotation Information Center (QUICK), who distributed computerised services for Reuters.

Long remarked in 1969 that relations with both Kyodo and *Asahi Shimbun* were extremely good, less good with Jiji. Its president Saiji Hasegawa was 'an old-fashioned Japanese nationalist', who denounced dependence upon foreign news sources as 'news colonialism'. He had refused to join with Reuters in introducing computerized economic services into Japan. The Japanese media liked to limit their dependence upon the international news agencies by using all of them a little and none of them very much. In 1968 there were 262 Reuter staff in Asia. The largest offices were in Singapore (75), Hong Kong (60), and Tokyo (24). The Tokyo office had been transformed by Kevin Garry, chief correspondent 1964–7. Garry set out to encourage a strong sense of loyalty to Reuters. He explained his methods to Campbell on 20 June 1964:

> I found a very demoralised staff here when I arrived a month ago . . . The general idea seemed to be that they were the 'coolies' for the foreign staff . . . I try to talk a lot about the news to the Japanese staff, and seemingly for the first time, explain why we can or cannot do such and such a thing . . . I am trying to make life more fun for them—sending them out on their own for small stories instead of relying on Kyodo (which is unreliable) or telephone calls. This costs us nothing but gives them experience, makes them feel responsible for the success of Reuters.

Japan, China, and the Indian subcontinent were managed from London until 1978. Singapore ran South-East Asia until 1976, when regional headquarters moved to Hong Kong. This transfer was pushed through by RES against the wishes of the general-news staff.

During the years of decolonization, Reuters was active in many parts of the world helping to launch news agencies for newly independent and Third World countries; it provided editorial and technical training and assistance. The Ghana News Agency, started in 1957, was an early example. By 1978 Reuters had given help—free, excluding hardware costs—to as many as thirty-four agencies. This involvement was not entirely altruistic. The benefits expected from Latin have already been indicated. The new national agencies began with close trading links to Reuters.

In 1980 Unesco published a report of a committee under the chairmanship of Sean MacBride, a former Irish foreign minister, entitled *Many Voices, One World*. Some Third World politicians and journalists were demanding the creation of a 'new information order'. Western and capitalist news agencies, such as Reuters and AP, were alleged to be maintaining a stranglehold over the coverage of news. Their files were said to be shaped by Western interests—in both senses of the word. Only bad news from the Third World—disorder, corruption, famine—was said to receive much notice.

At the 1979 annual meeting of the International Press Institute Long spoke out strongly against attempts to control the flow of international news. He had taken the lead in campaigning against such interference. He suggested that much of the clamour was coming from countries with authoritarian regimes which censored their domestic news output: 'an international flow of information is only achieved by those countries which have a very well developed internal flow . . . you cannot have repression at home and enlightenment abroad.' The clamour against the international agencies eventually diminished.

VII

Relations with the British Government remained closer during the 1960s and 1970s than Reuters liked publicly to admit. By 1960 payments under the 1945 Radcliffe–Chancellor agreement were overdue for revision. Reuters was spending over three times as much on transmission costs in 1960 as in 1945—£271,219 compared with £84,200. Yet Government payments had increased by only £2,500 during that period, and Cole complained that the amounts had become 'derisory and frankly do not bear scrutiny on any commercial basis'.

Reuters was eager to establish at least the appearance of a commercial basis. Burgess assured the board in February 1961 that Reuters would negotiate with the British Government only for services rendered. It

would not accept a block payment by way of grant-in-aid; 'and no payment was to be made by the Government to Reuters which could not be
thoroughly justified, nor should any strings be attached in any way to any
payment'.

This sounded high-minded enough. Yet the negotiations were kept as
quiet as possible both by Reuters and by the Foreign Office. All correspondence took the form of personal letters. Such official business,
Burgess explained on 9 July 1963 to Leslie Glass of the Foreign Office
Information Research Department, was handled within Reuters only by
the chairman, general manager, and secretary: 'the files were kept separately.' Glass answered that his department was the only one in the
Foreign Office with a separate registry, 'and whose files did not go into
the archives'. Burgess expressed himself 'glad to hear this'. One reason
given for this secrecy was that knowledge of enlarged official payments to
Reuters might lead its customers to expect lower subscriptions.

At a meeting on 12 November 1959 Murray, the permanent under-
secretary, had assured Burgess that the Foreign Office did not seek to
involve itself in the running of Reuters, or to influence its editorial policy, or to act contrary to the Reuter trust principles. But it did want 'a
strong and expanding Reuters'. Notably, it wanted Reuters strong in such
areas as newly independent Black Africa, where news services were
bound to be uneconomic. In support of this objective, explained Murray,
the Foreign Office might pay 'a major subscription'. Was 'major' then the
same as 'commercial'? Not entirely, explained Murray: 'of course it must
not be totally out of line on a commercial basis for what is provided in
the way of services—it would enable Reuters to undertake certain development programmes in areas where there can be no entry within the
limits of reasonable economic trading.'

Words and expectations were not always in phase during the subsequent discussions. Thus Cole emphasized to Murray on 16 June 1960 that
he was expecting only 'fair and adequate commercial rates of subscription' from the overseas departments of the British Government. Yet in
the same letter he was welcoming Foreign Office interest in expanded
Reuter coverage of both Black Africa and Latin America. Deficit development expenditure in Africa, he told Murray, would approach £50,000
for the next twelve months.

How might this desirable but uneconomic activity be best supported
by the British Government? Not by open subsidy. Instead, support could
be channelled through generous Government subscriptions to Reuters for
the delivery of its services to official recipients—Government offices,

agencies, embassies, and the like. On 21 February 1961 the Foreign Office offered £70,000 from its overseas departments and £22,120 from the Central Office of Information. Reuters accepted this offer, but only for one year. For long-running subscriptions it wanted even higher payments.

The Government offer expressly indicated that some of the money on offer was intended to sustain or to start non-viable services. 'Her Majesty's Government also note your Board's determination to continue to implement the paragraph in your Trust Deed stating: "That no effort shall be spared to expand, develop and adapt the business of Reuters in order to maintain in every event its position as the leading world news agency."' This was piquant indeed. The Trust Agreement—intended to proclaim the independence of Reuters—was being quoted by the Foreign Office in a paragraph relating to payments which amounted to subsidies.

By 1967 the Foreign Office was paying £123,480 per annum on behalf of the overseas departments, and £40,000 on behalf of the COI. Judah told Long on 7 July that the contract with the Foreign Office was regarded by both sides 'as a normal commercial one'. Consequently, the negotiations had been lengthy. The Treasury required a detailed analysis of Reuter cost increases to justify a claim for increased subscriptions. The Treasury was certainly being careful; but the original 1961 payments, now being periodically increased in line with rising costs, had contained an element of subsidy. That element was still being protected. In 1975, for example, the subscription from the Foreign and Commonwealth Office (FCO) and COI was increased from £239,000 to £387,000. The Government accepted that Reuters had suffered a 40 per cent rise in world reporting and production costs during the previous two years.

The readiness of Reuters to accept British Government help so long as it was not explicit was strikingly illustrated by the continuing connection with the Arab News Agency. The ANA, which was subsidized through large subscriptions from the Foreign Office Information Research Department and the BBC, had collected and distributed news for Reuters in the Middle East since 1954. Not until 1969 was the connection ended, and then on still compromising terms.

Upon becoming general manager in 1963, Long had seemed content to continue what he described to the board in June as 'our very satisfactory association with this organisation'. In that same year the Arab News Agency changed its name to Regional News Services (Mid-East) Limited. Even when arguing at the end of 1968 for the resumption of direct Reuter operations in the Middle East, Long did so entirely on commercial grounds. Shahe Guebenlian, the sales manager for Africa, had conducted a survey which showed that the Reuter annual trading surplus from the region was over £50,000. Yet, he argued, it could have been more. RNS concentrated too much upon general news, and this was restricting potentially profitable expansion for the economic services in the Middle East.

An important and revealing meeting took place on 18 November 1968 between Horton and Judah for Reuters and Nigel Clive, head of the Foreign and Commonwealth Office Information Research Department. They met to discuss how Reuters might best resume direct operations in the Middle East. Horton and Judah emphasized that, although Reuters wanted to end the connection with RNS, it did not want to lose the benefit of Government money.

The agreed record (marked 'secret' on every page) explained that Reuters had not yet been able to work out the extent, or the annual incidence, of the necessary direct subsidy, 'diminishing at the end of five years to nil'. In the next paragraph the word 'subvention' took the place of 'subsidy'. Was this a belated attempt at delicacy in choice of word? Yet the substitution scarcely softened the indelicacy of what was being requested. 'Reuters representatives hoped that all the necessary subvention could be channelled to them through the External Services of the BBC.' These services were themselves funded by the Foreign Office. The idea for this manœuvre came from Charles Curran, director-general of the BBC.

In discussion of this request, 'it was noted that RNS (ME) would become widely known as "bought out" by Reuters, and there might be dangers in its continuing to pay a large sum to Reuters for no apparent reason'. Horton and Judah outlined the recent Reuter successes in Africa, the Far East, and the United States. 'Reuters were backing themselves, and were asking HMG to back them, to achieve a similar success in both the Middle East and Latin America.' The British Foreign and Commonwealth Office was happy to respond. On 2 April 1969 Sir Denis Greenhill, the permanent under-secretary, assured Barnetson of FCO satisfaction. It wanted 'strong and independent' Reuter operations in the Middle East: 'this will be of value to British interests.'

Reuters resumed direct distribution in the Middle East from 1 July 1969. The BBC External Services' subscription to Reuters was increased from £20,000 for 1968 to £80,000 for 1969 and 1970, £90,000 for 1971, and £100,000 for 1972. These payments rose as RNS operations were run down. Formally, the BBC was paying for rights 'in such Reuter regional services as are available in London which the BBC may from time to time require'. The BBC did indeed use Reuter material in its external services, and this had been fairly reflected in the £20,000 subscription for 1968. But the much higher payments from 1969 onwards amounted to a concealed subsidy.

Twenty years later Judah emphasized that, whatever may have been the intention in earlier periods, these payments were not now intended by the FCO to influence the handling of news by Reuters. Because of this, successive postwar general mangers had convinced themselves that acceptance did not contravene the commitment to independence made in the 1941 Trust Agreement. Nevertheless, in the *Oxford English Dictionary* sense of the word the money certainly constituted a subsidy: 'financial aid furnished by a state or public corporation in furtherance of an undertaking or the upkeep of a thing.'

Why was so much care taken to conceal the content of the negotiations with the British Government? Mainly because, argued Judah in retrospect, outsiders might well have taken them as evidence that the British Government did indeed exert an influence over the news from Reuters. Looking back in later years, Long was to admit much greater unease than Judah that such a close relationship with the British Government had continued under his management into the 1970s—when Reuters was proclaiming louder than ever that it was not at the service of the British or of any other Government.

In 1976 Nelson prepared a paper for Long, dated 19 January, about Reuter contracts with Governments, including the British Government. Nelson argued that the percentage of income derived from Governments in countries where international news agencies had their headquarters ought not to exceed 2 per cent of revenue. This was the exact percentage received by Reuters from the British Government at that date (see Table 12.5). Nelson calculated that AP and UPI derived respectively 2.2 and 1.6 per cent of their income from the United States Government.

The generous payments to Reuters from the BBC were adjusted during 1973-5 in line with rising reporting costs and currency fluctuations. But from 1976—paradoxically because of British Government pressure upon the BBC to cut expenditure—full adjustment ceased. Finally, from 19 May 1980 the BBC ended the External Service contract with Reuters entirely. Payment was then running at the rate of £250,000 per annum.

Into the 1980s Reuters was still officially regarded as qualifying for moral support from the British Government, even though it no longer needed financial backing. This supportive attitude was maintained despite

TABLE 12.5. Contracts with the British Government: Subscriptions paid to Reuters, 1965–1975 (£000)

	1965	1970	1975
FCO/COI	134.0	118.0	386.8
COI special traffic	—	—	12.7
BBC external service	20.0	80.0	156.1
INRAR[a]	45.0	—	—
Miscellaneous	2.7	4.0	6.6
Total	201.7b	302.0c	562.2d

[a] International News Rights and Royalties Ltd.—subsidized by the British Government
[b] 5% of total Reuter revenue of £4,051,000.
[c] 2.9% of total Reuter revenue of £10,491,000.
[d] 1.9% of total Reuter revenue of £29,921,000.

full awareness that Reuters was now more than ever determined to present its news without regard to any particular national interest. Indeed, at the time of the flotation of Reuters as a public company in 1984, the joint permanent secretary to the Department of Trade and Industry (Sir Anthony Rawlinson) went so far as to welcome such 'integrity', even while lobbying for Reuters with the insurance companies on grounds of 'public interest'. He wrote on 5 January 1984:

> The Secretary of State is of opinion that, as has been recognised in the past, Reuters is an undertaking involving special considerations of public interest, and that because of this factor it is desirable both that adequate safeguards should continue to sustain the integrity of the news service, and that the proposed share issue should be made in London, with substantial subscription by British institutions.

Was this attitude on the part of the British Government paradoxical? Or did it reflect a shrewd perception that the presence in London of a great supranational news and information organization benefited the host country?

In 1986 payments from the British Government were finally put on an unquestionably commercial basis. In that year the annual British Foreign and Commonwealth Office subscription was drastically reduced from £296,000 to £20,000. The old payment was a survival from the days of subsidy; now the British Government was keen to make economies. The FCO had received offers from AP and other agencies to supply services for under £10,000 per annum. Sir Antony Acland, the permanent under-secretary, wrote to Renfrew on 6 February emphasizing FCO readiness to continue to take the Reuter services, but not at the old price; the FCO was willing to pay £20,000. Significantly, the head of the FCO News

Department remarked during the negotiations that Reuter offices overseas now seemed to keep their distance from the British embassies. Renfrew accepted the FCO proposal for a cut to £20,000 with unusual but deliberate readiness, only insisting that the subscription should rise to £40,000 over three years. The amount received had long since ceased to be important in revenue terms, but that was not why Renfrew had acted. He wanted to remove a shadow cast by the past, to eliminate a last residue from the days when there had been a special relationship between Reuters and the British Government.

Early in 1976 Reuters had been embarrassed by leaks from the proceedings of a United States Congressional Committee on intelligence activities. William Colby, director of the Central Intelligence Agency, was said to have testified that a number of Reuter correspondents had worked for the CIA, manipulating news. Colby held a press conference on 26 January at which he denied that the CIA had ever tried to influence Reuter news reports. Despite this denial, the allegation resurfaced at intervals.

In 1981 a BBC programme investigating intelligence activities included a former CIA officer. He spoke of 'the general assumption of my colleagues that a Reuters journalist is more likely than not to be tied in with British intelligence in some way'. A number of such journalists have revealed how at various times in various places—especially in Europe during the cold war—approaches were made to them by British embassy or other officials to undertake casual intelligence gathering.

VIII

The question of the cost, priority, and status of general-news collection was an issue which received much attention during the 1970s. In all previous decades the general-news journalists had regarded themselves—and had generally been accepted—as superior to those who worked in the economic services. This attitude was becoming harder to sustain as Reuters began to prosper because of the increasing profits made by the latter.

The General News Division had to bear the steeply rising costs of running a world reporting network at a time when revenue was increasing only slowly. Reuters Economic Services, on the other hand, benefited from healthy revenue growth upon a relatively small cost base. Capital was going into the Reuter Monitor services ahead of investment in improvements likely to save time and increase efficiency in the handling of news. The resignation of Horton as editor-in-chief of GND at the end of 1973 was a clear sign that the general-news side had lost the initiative within Reuters. Having ceased to be the top dogs, many general-news journalists began to fear that they were becoming the underdogs.

Part of the problem was the old one that the general-news services did not pay for themselves. In 1978 the British newspaper proprietors, the chief owners of Reuters through the NPA and PA, were actually paying smaller assessments in money terms than they had paid in 1965. The total assessment for 1978 was £619,900: to have maintained its 1965 value, it ought to have been four times as large.

During the late 1970s Long began to argue that instead of aiming at profitability, the general-news services for the world's media and business must seek cost-effectiveness and quality. How best to achieve this purpose became the subject of a major inquiry within Reuters during the late 1970s. Known as the media study, it was conducted by Michael Neale, who was appointed media development manager in May 1977. Neale was an experienced journalist, who had been bureau chief in both South Vietnam and Japan.

From January 1978 Michael Reupke became editor-in-chief. He came to the post from being manager for Latin America, after previous experience as a correspondent in Africa and West Germany. Long greatly respected his cool judgement, his attachment to principle, and his courtesy to all. Editor-in-chief was an old title, but this was a new post in the sense that Reupke was made responsible for all editorial operations. He oversaw the collection and distribution of news both for the media markets and for the economic services.

In February 1979 Reupke called a meeting of Reuter senior editors at the Royal Automobile Club in London to prepare them for the changes which he had in mind. He wanted to overcome the siege mentality which had grown up among many general-news journalists. He also wanted to remove grievances to be found among the economic journalists. They felt themselves to be still undervalued, working endless hours unnoticed in London. They feared that they were unlikely to become bureau chiefs overseas.

Reupke—born in Germany but educated in Britain—also wanted to 'de-Londonize' attitudes. In the field, the impression prevailed that Fleet Street editorial was unaware of operational needs and that the ultimate test of quality seemed to be whether or not the London papers had printed a Reuter story. As part of the media study, a reconstruction had rearranged the figures to reveal what was called the 'GND gap'. These were losses which would have shown if GND had continued to exist after 1973. They were now concealed, but the reconstruction found them to be huge and accelerating, reaching over £5.4 million by 1977. The forecast was for a gap of well over £12 million by 1983: this prospect was obviously unacceptable.

The most important structural change resulting from the recommendations of the media study was the merging of the existing RWS and RES editorials into one all-embracing new Reuters World Service. The logic for doing this was clear, but the psychology of the situation was delicate. The merger therefore took some time for Reupke to push through. Nelson, now less of a partisan for the economic services than in earlier days, accepted the change, although with hesitation. He was influenced by Reupke's proposal that Pagel, the RES editor, should be made editor of the combined service.

The merger became effective from 1 January 1980. The new RWS was designated a cost centre; the North American operation was still separate. Reupke had warned that Reuters would need to be careful not to dissipate the specialist knowledge which RES had built up. This did not happen; instead, there were quite other problems. The promotion of Pagel was seen by some as a victory for RES. Hans Ouwerkerk, manager for Asia based in Hong Kong, wrote to Reupke on 21 November 1980 expressing the fears of some journalists in Asia that Reuters was 'progressively opting out of the news-gathering business'. Morale—which is nearly always said to be lower than it has ever been—was duly said to be lower than it had ever been. A few senior general-news correspondents decided to quit. Yet the reporting of general news by Reuters was being strengthened, not weakened. Reupke might have been more strident in saying so.

A second major structural change resulted in 1982 from the media-study analysis. Editorial responsibility began to be shared between London, Hong Kong, and New York for eight hours each per day. Traditionally, editorial direction had been in the hands of a team of journalists located in London, operating twenty-four hours daily seven days a week. The new arrangement was intended to reduce tension by promoting greater responsiveness to regional needs. From 17 October, for the period of the Hong Kong day and of the London night, the responsibility of the London desk was devolved to Hong Kong; New York was brought in later. To give Hong Kong the status which such devolution of responsibility demanded, Reupke assigned Macdowall, a skilful and experienced journalist, as the new editor for the Far Eastern time zone.

IX

Writing in the budget and plan for 1981 about the years of his leadership, Long was able to claim a logical, although not inevitable, progression for Reuter market strategy since 1963. That strategy, he explained, had been:

(1) to employ American technology in order to expand in Europe, and then to spread computerized retrieval services throughout the markets of the world;
(2) to spend profits earned by the new services in Europe to help build a stronger base in the United States;
(3) to use that United States base to produce technologically advanced services employing cable television.

This progression was clearer in retrospect than at the time. It had certainly not been easy to sustain, and the third objective—centred upon row-grabbing—had scarcely been attained. The whole movement might well have faltered, if Long had not been persistent and if he had not been fortunate in his senior colleagues.

The breakthrough into computerized information-retrieval services need not have been led by Reuters. The lead might well have come from a new company such as Telerate, based in the United States. Reuters in 1963 was an old company, reputable but not known for its daring. Yet by the time of Long's resignation in 1981 the success of the new Reuters was becoming apparent to all. The quadrupling of profits in that year, and their more than doubling again in 1982, signalled a novel prosperity. Interviewed in 1989, Nelson described the realization that the company had at last achieved financial ease as his most rewarding moment in Reuters.

Nelson was to be well rewarded financially as well as emotionally for his contribution. Long was not to be so fortunate. He resigned as managing director from 1 March 1981. His departure came suddenly. He had accepted an offer to become managing director of Times Newspapers from Rupert Murdoch, its new owner. Long had completed his main work at Reuters by the mid-1970s, and had latterly shown signs of becoming bored. This left his eccentricities in greater prominence. His tendency to lapse from acceptable forthrightness into unacceptable rudeness intensified, and his fascination with good food and drink became intrusive. When managers were required to organize Long's almost royal overseas tours down to the last restaurant they felt driven (in the words of Ure, who was one of them) by 'an electricity of terror'. Cole had struck his own kind of terror during such tours, but he had also done much business. Long did less, either on tour or in London. 'It is the right moment for me to go and it will benefit the company.'

This was true. Yet by leaving when he did, Long missed the chance to become a millionaire—as his colleagues Renfrew, Nelson, and Judah soon did when, at Renfrew's insistence, they were allowed to acquire shares on easy terms in the now booming company. In the opinion of one *New Statesman* reviewer, writing on 17 May 1985, this made Long the 'tragic hero' of the new Reuters. Both noun and adjective were perhaps too strong: but even so the extent of the exaggeration will remain a matter of opinion.

THIRTEEN

Going Public

1981–1984

I

G ERALD LONG was succeeded as managing director not by
Nelson, as many in the company had expected, but by Renfrew.
At a meeting of senior staff in London, called to hear the news,
Long left no doubt that he had recommended Renfrew as his successor.
Renfrew's knowledge of communications technology—'the lifeblood of
Reuters'—was, claimed Long, unequalled outside the ranks of the special-
ists. This, Long believed, had made Renfrew especially well qualified for
the top job. Nearly two years later, Long explained his thinking more
fully in a letter to Rupert Murdoch on 18 November 1982:

> I had prepared the succession for Renfrew for many years, against the pas-
> sive opposition of Barnetson, who thought Nelson would be safer. I
> thought he would be too safe, that, like me, he had given Reuters all he
> had to give, whereas Renfrew still had development potential, chiefly
> through his knowledge of computerised business services and his creative
> command of technology.

Long told Murdoch that he had previously wanted Renfrew to take
charge of all Reuter communications, but that he had been unwilling to
do so—partly because of his involvement in North America, partly
because he did not want 'the fight with Nelson that would have ensued'.
Opinions about Renfrew within Reuters differed sharply, and continued
to do so throughout the 1980s. His critics questioned whether his
undoubted technological enthusiasm had been matched by sound judgement. In North America he had concentrated during the 1970s upon
developing broad-band and satellite technology for row-grabbing services, aiming to blast out data to cheap terminals. Reuter Monitor Money
Rates and Reuter Monitor Dealing had been developed under Nelson's
control in London and had interested Renfrew much less. Yet these
expensive interactive products were the ones which were to make huge

profits for Reuters. Renfrew's defenders answered that his pursuit of new technology had greatly improved the image of Reuters in North America, and had also prepared for the successful introduction of small-dish satellites in the 1980s.

Long's farewell remarks in 1981 gave the impression that he had virtu-ally nominated his own successor. This was not so. Long could do no more than recommend Renfrew strongly to Sir Denis Hamilton, the chairman of Reuters. A selection subcommittee was appointed consisting of Hamilton and two other directors, Alan Hare of the *Financial Times* and Christopher Dicks of the *Huddersfield Examiner* group. The subcom-mittee looked no further than the obvious candidates, Renfrew and Nelson. At interview, as Dicks recollected some years later, Renfrew came over as 'the hungrier of the two', full of ideas for the future.

Renfrew was felt to have the right combination of personality and experience. He had even contrived during 1980 to steer RNA at last into profitability. The directors, some of them doubtful about the heightened involvement of Reuters in North America, were relieved and impressed by this. Conversely, the Reuter Dealing project, with which Nelson was associated, had been repeatedly delayed. It was still not launched when Long announced his departure.

II

Renfrew was able to tell the board in November 1981 that profits for the third quarter 'left previous records far behind'. At £6,472,200 they were six times more than budget, and ten times more than in the same quarter of the previous year. During Long's last years as managing director Renfrew had advocated a determined push into large profitability. Long had not disciplined Reuters to take full financial advantage of its increas-ingly strong product and market position, even though he had himself overseen the establishment of that position. Renfrew knew that the potential for a profit explosion was there, and as soon as he took over he began vigorously to fuel such an explosion. He brought new revenue down to the bottom line as never before. The year 1982—his first full year in charge—was much better than 1981 for profit growth. Although revenue for the year increased by rather less than in 1981 (£41 million compared with nearly £49 million), 1982 pre-tax profit rose by some £20 million against just over £12 million in the previous year. This meant that nearly half of all new revenue was now being brought down to the bottom line: in 1981 little more than a quarter of new revenue had shown through in this way. The 1981 percentage was again to be surpassed in 1983, 1984, 1988, and 1989.

Renfrew had become deeply impressed during the years of the joint venture with Ultronic by the American emphasis upon profitability and upon the need to show an adequate return on capital. Revenue targets and financial forecasting, first introduced by Renfrew for the joint venture, had eventually spread to the whole company. As managing director he was to lay great stress upon the setting of targets. He was also to emphasize strongly that profitability depended not only upon adding to revenue but also upon restraining costs even when revenue was booming. Equipment costs were reduced, notably by extending the use of cheaper IDR terminals. And the appetite of the technical staff for ever more resources was curbed. During the 1970s this had diminished the benefits of increased revenue. For 1980, profit before tax as a percentage of revenue was only 4.3 per cent; Renfrew told management on 1 July 1981 that this was 'not good enough to guarantee the security of the company'. The percentage rose to 12 per cent in 1981, and to 23.7 per cent for 1984. Renfrew had asked for 15 per cent by that year.

He had reported in November 1981 that RWS costs for the previous September were equivalent to only 14.4 per cent of revenue. This was the lowest such proportion on record, and was (Renfrew suggested) 'far below the level at which the costs of the news service might be seen as an excessive burden'. He wanted to emphasize how much the new regime valued the contribution of the journalists to Reuters. A management circular on 1 July 1981 announced that 'the primary objective' was to achieve the highest possible standards in the news services. Renfrew rightly believed that the editorial dimension to the work of Reuters gave it a distinctiveness and an authority which set it apart from its computer-service competitors which depended solely upon technology.

The highest standards for Renfrew meant having the biggest as well as the best. He launched a drive to open new reporting bureaux. On 16 November 1983 he reminded Lord Matthews, a Reuter trustee, that editorial spending had risen by 85 per cent since 1981. Reuters already had 'many more *international* bureaux than any other agency'. Renfrew compared the numbers of journalists posted outside the countries of their respective headquarters by the main agencies. At the end of 1984 Reuters had 514 such journalists; AP and Dow-Jones only 346, AFP 310. The hundredth bureau was opened in Oman in October 1984.

Reuter staff numbers reached 3,865 by 1984: 2,085 in Europe, 817 in North America, 675 in the Middle East, Asia, and Australia, and 288 in

Latin America. In the United Kingdom, however, Renfrew pushed through large staff reductions. He came fresh from his victory in the 1980 New York strike. General enabling agreements were negotiated with the Reuter unions; these agreements introduced changes in working conditions, including the abolition of demarcations. Between 1980 and June 1983 the number of London editorial staff, journalists and non-journalists, fell from 387 to 271. Renfrew told the board briskly in November 1981 that the journalists 'now seem to have accepted that it is better to negotiate the future than to have it imposed on them'.

From June 1982 the importance of general news to the economic services was illustrated and exploited by the introduction of news summaries on Monitor screens. A Reuter picture service was started at the beginning of 1985 following the acquisition of the UPI news-picture service outside the United States. Reuter representatives, particularly in Asia and Latin America, had for years complained about the lack of a picture service to complement textual news.

In 1960 Reuters had bought shares in Visnews, the television news film agency. The holding was increased from 11 per cent to 33 per cent in 1968, the same as the BBC's. By 1983 Visnews employed 350 staff in London, plus a further 50 overseas; it was able to draw upon the Reuter network of offices and communications worldwide. Nevertheless, Reuters felt Visnews to be under-capitalized and over-bureaucratized. Long had at one stage wanted to pull out entirely; Renfrew and Nelson were keener, and in October 1985 Reuters took a 55 per cent shareholding. From the first, Visnews had been committed to objectivity. The motto of its photographers was said to be 'We don't take sides, we just take pictures.'

Renfrew believed strongly in decentralization. He was determined to appoint able young area managers and to give them their heads. He later explained why in the *Financial Weekly* of 25 September 1986:

> we restructured the management of Reuters into profit centres and gave our best executives bottom-line responsibility for geographical areas. We decentralised. For a long time I knew we needed geographical profit centres, because previously a lot of our costs were managed centrally. We did not combine responsibility for revenue growth and cost control with the same executive. That's basically wrong.

In other words, Renfrew was establishing everywhere the same combination of responsibility which he had insisted upon assuming when he was manager of RNA.

From 1 May 1981 two new profit centres—Reuters Europe (RE),

including the United Kingdom and Ireland, and Reuters Overseas (RO)—were established alongside the existing Reuters North America. The central management of both RE and RO was placed in London. André Villeneuve became manager of Reuters Europe, and Peter Job manager of Reuters Overseas. Renfrew continued to manage RNA.

The decentralization process was completed when from the beginning of 1983 Reuters Overseas was split up. RO remained the profit centre for Africa and Latin America. A new Reuters Asia (RA) profit centre was created to cover Asia, Australia, and New Zealand; Job became its manager, based in Hong Kong. Villeneuve was transferred to become manager of Reuters North America. Ure succeeded him as manager of RE, after two years as European marketing manager. These were the rising stars within Reuters.

Job at forty was the oldest of the group. Eight years later he was to succeed Renfrew as managing director. He had joined Reuters in 1963 as a graduate in French and German from Oxford University. He had steadily acquired all-round experience in journalism, marketing, and management—mainly in Asia and Latin America.

III

Reuters in West Germany, which had taken on a new dynamism in the 1970s, continued in the same spirit into the 1980s. In December 1980 Ingo Hertel, who had been the first German journalist hired for the new German-language service in 1971, was appointed editor of a German-language retrieval service for economic news. This was targeted at securities markets within German-speaking Europe. Reuters Europe was the most developed trading area: it had the largest turnover and made the largest contribution to profits:

TABLE 13.1. Turnover figures for 1983 by area (£000)

	RE	RA	RO	RNA
Turnover	122,133	62,822	16,985	39,827
Contribution to profit	33,585	24,360	2,204	226

Reuters North America was expanding steadily. A big new technical centre was opened in November 1982 at Hauppage, Long Island, forty miles from New York City. Yet by the end of 1983 RNA had fallen back into loss. Two American companies, Quotron and Telerate, were posing problems for Reuters. Quotron held over half the United States market for financial-information video systems. Telerate had the advantage of direct access to one of the big Wall Street brokers (Cantor Fitzgerald), which acted as a market-making intermediary for United States Government securities. This made Telerate a unique source for bond-price movements.

Reuters Asia was one of the fastest-growing areas during the 1980s, with more than half its revenue coming from the Monitor Money Rates service. Revenue grew dramatically from £5.7 million in 1978 to over £240 million in 1989. In Japan the Monitor services were distributed through QUICK, but the distribution agreement was allowed to run out in May 1984. The received wisdom had been that foreign organizations always needed a partner to succeed in Japan. Job, the RA manager, had concluded that Japan had sufficiently liberalized its attitude to make this no longer necessary. He assured Nelson on 30 August 1983 that the connection with QUICK had become an impediment. 'I do not mean that there are no non-tariff barriers, though many of them exist only in the minds of foreigners. There are such barriers. Ours has long ago been identified. It is KDD.' Kokusai Denshin Denwa was the Japanese telecommunications agency. It had delayed the introduction of Monitor Money Rates into Japan until 1979; Reuter Monitor Dealing was to be delayed until 1986.

In October 1985 Reuters had introduced its first internal-news product for Japan. The Reuters Japan Financial Service combined news and financial-market reports with real-time foreign-exchange and money market rates. A new editorial desk in Tokyo provided the news content. The new service took its place within the expanding range of non-English-language services from Reuters—Arabic, French, German, and Spanish.

IV

Reuters was operating one of the largest private communications networks in the world. The five primary computer-data centres were located in London, Hong Kong, New York, Frankfurt, and Geneva. The latest innovation had been direct satellite delivery by small dishes (SDS). Introduced from October 1982, it was placed by Nelson in the sequence of major Reuter innovations—following upon the International Financial Printer, Stockmaster, and the Reuter Monitor Money Rates and Dealing services. SDS offered economies in equipment and transmission, while still allowing subscribers fast access to data. It began in the United States, and was extended in 1984 to Central America. Market data, textual news, and news pictures could all be received on the same satellite signal.

Renfrew was fascinated by this technology. He was also strongly motivated by a desire to make money—for Reuters, and for his family. Upon becoming managing director, he quickly addressed the question of how to allow senior executives a stake in the company through a share-option scheme. Judah had been pressing for some such provision for years, but Long had always procrastinated. Renfrew by contrast was convinced that most people wanted to earn ever more money, and that this motivation could be harnessed to persuade them to work purposefully. During the early 1980s he therefore promoted various schemes which offered a stake in the company upon favourable terms—first to top executives, led by himself; then to other executives; and then to all members of staff. 'It's human nature, it's just good business to give those responsible for success a share in that success. Then you get more success.'

In 1981 a new class of non-voting 'E' shares was introduced. The first beneficiaries were Renfrew, Nelson, and Judah. They ended up with 545, 361, and 306 'E' shares respectively. Such provision for senior executives was becoming widespread among British companies, but Judah and his two colleagues were to be especially fortunate: their holdings soon made them into sterling millionaires. They were each allowed to buy one year's salary-worth of shares. Reuters in effect loaned them 90 per cent of the share valuation by issuing the shares 10 per cent paid, with the balance to be paid up only on disposal. The shares were initially priced at £147. The company was valued on a price/earnings multiple of four: this was very low, but it was decided by the Inland Revenue Capital Office, which estimated the worth of the shares in open trading. When a dividend was paid by Reuters in November 1982, the first for many years, the multiple rose to eight. Subsequently it trebled again. As the company was bound to buy any 'E' shares which a holder wished to sell at current valuation, there was a safe market. For these various reasons the shareholdings of Renfrew, Nelson, and Judah became extremely valuable. By September 1983, only two years after first issue, the 'E' shares were valued at £6,450 per share.

The 'E' share scheme was made available in stages to 124 other senior executives. The more senior got sixty-seven shares; recipients were selected from all parts of the company, but complaints were later heard that only sixteen editorial staff had been included. Some middle-ranking executives, who were offered 'E' shares in 1983, were already participating in an incentive cash bonus scheme which had been launched at the beginning of 1982. Bonuses were related to achievement of profit targets. Renfrew told the board in July 1983 that the bonus scheme had become 'an important factor in the steep and sustained growth of company profits'. Garry, assistant general manager in charge of staff policy, wanted a bonus scheme for all employees. His motives were mixed. He argued on 8 November 1983 that it would encourage loyalty towards Reuters. 'It would help us to reduce loyalty to unions', and it would cut salary increases by 1 or 2 per cent per year.

Renfrew admitted in September 1983 that there was 'a sense of growing division between those staff who had benefits and those who did not'. To counter this, a share-savings scheme was introduced in June 1984, after the public flotation of Reuters. This scheme did not contain any element of reward and was open to all staff who chose to join. Staff acquired non-transferable options to buy 'B' shares through saving for five years. Three principal schemes were devised, to suit employees in different parts of the world. Out of 3,342 eligible staff, 1,600 joined the scheme—a very high participation ratio. In addition, an employee and pensioner share offer was made at the time of the flotation in 1984. Three million 'B' shares were made available at only 75p each; 3,335 staff bought 2,353,450 shares.

Reuters could now afford to pay Renfrew, Nelson, and Judah the full market rate. New service contracts for the three men were drawn up at the time of the flotation in 1984. Renfrew's paid him £36,000 in respect of his duties within the United Kingdom and $148,000 in respect of duties elsewhere. On 1 June 1984 Sir Denis Hamilton wrote to Christopher Hogg, soon to be his successor as Reuter chairman, about the three top executives:

> I was convinced that our competitors would be poaching this year, and I have no regrets that already their expectations have gone to the stratosphere! But they made it all a success, Glen more than his predecessor Gerry Long, who went to The Times in 1981 and is crying his eyes out now, and taking the credit for what Glen and Mike Nelson fashioned . . . I am a great believer in motivating your leaders and technical experts—the human factor I learned as a CO on the D-day beaches 40 years ago . . . I am always open to serious argument based on facts, rather than the envy which fills the souls of some of our Board colleagues.

V

The flotation of Reuters as a public company in 1984 was described by *Time* magazine on 11 June as a saga that had almost everything: 'high-risk corporate strategies and fierce boardroom battles, missing heirs and angry workers, high technology and hard news.' There were four sets of interested parties:

(1) the British, Irish, Australian, and New Zealand newspaper publishers who collectively owned Reuters, and amongst whom the British publishers wanted to take out some of the millions to which they now found themselves entitled;
(2) the three executive directors (Renfrew, Nelson, and Judah), who owned 'E' shares;
(3) the trustees, who were the guardians of Reuters;
(4) the staff, who depended upon Reuters for their livelihoods.

The man charged with presiding over the discussions on whether to float Reuters as a public company was Sir Denis Hamilton (1918–88), Barnetson's successor as chairman. Hostile critics said that he was a man who had advanced in the newspaper industry beyond his abilities, chiefly by seeming to be 'a nice chap'. He had started as a reporter for Kemsley Newspapers in the north-east of England before the Second World War. He had a 'good war' and eventually commanded a battalion, something to which he often referred. He was always conventionally well dressed, and enjoyed his contacts with the great and the good. Hamilton was famous for his long silences, thoughtful without being a deep thinker. His greatest contribution was made as editor of the *Sunday Times* from 1961 to 1967; he was editor-in-chief of Times Newspapers from 1967 to 1981. He had many cultural interests outside Fleet Street, and was knighted for his services to the arts in 1976.

Hamilton joined the Reuter board in 1967, becoming chairman in 1979. By the time of the flotation advancing illness meant that he could work only intermittently. He concentrated upon ensuring that the principles of the Reuter trust agreement were not forgotten, either in making the decision to go public or in planning the accompanying corporate reorganization. Hamilton deserves credit for helping to ensure that the Reuter trust arrangements emerged greatly strengthened under the new public company. But he certainly did not play the dominant part in the flotation process claimed in his posthumous memoirs, *Editor-in-Chief*, published in 1989.

The Offer for Sale of shares in the new Reuters Holdings PLC in June 1984 explained why Reuters had become a public company. This prospectus adroitly linked the recent changes with the maintenance of the Reuter trust principles:

The guarantee of independence and integrity provided by the Reuter Trust Agreement has been a key factor in Reuters business. In 1983 the Directors of Reuters Limited decided that, by means of a corporate reorganisation, Reuters could obtain access to the public capital markets and thereby more readily achieve its business objectives and enable existing shareholders to realise part of their investment, while preserving the Reuter Trust Principles.

Why did Reuters not go public sooner? During 1977–8 Long had aired a scheme to float a new company—'Newco'—to handle all Reuter activities except the media services. But the prospective financial gain was not yet great enough to be likely to tempt the cautious PA stockholders. What changed the situation in the eyes of the Reuter owners, first of all in the NPA and then in the PA, was the dramatic growth in Reuter profits during the early 1980s. First, these quadrupled between 1980 and 1981, and then they more than doubled again for 1982. Reuters even began to declare dividends: £1.9 million for 1981, £5.8 million for 1982.

Here was clear evidence to the four partners in Reuters that their holdings had taken on a vastly greater value. The NPA representative directors began to be much more interested, and at the same time the PA representatives began to be much more guarded in what they told the PA board. The PA and NPA remained, however, very different bodies—in terms of the personalities connected with them, and also in terms of status. PA was a legal entity and a co-operative, and its members usually maintained a common front. The NPA, on the other hand, was no more than an organization which represented the national newspaper groups in labour negotiations and for a few other common purposes. Its members remained fierce rivals in the newspaper market-place. This commercial rivalry was sometimes reflected in personality clashes at NPA council meetings.

These tensions became the more serious when the possibility of a public flotation for Reuters made it necessary for the NPA to establish the precise holdings in Reuters attributable to each member newspaper group. Down the years the groups had tried to minimize the size of their payments towards the Reuter assessment. With the prospect of a flotation, however, each group now wanted to lay claim to as many shares in Reuters as possible. This led to prolonged wrangling within the NPA.

The PA had its own problem of finding owners for 1,800 derelict shares. Having been worth nothing for over a hundred years because the company had never paid a dividend, these shares were now worth millions. In January 1985 the PA launched a national advertising campaign to find the heirs of the original owners. Predictably, this led to a field-day for genealogists and lawyers. Some heirs were never found:

TABLE 13.2. Total shareholdings in Reuters, May 1983

	%	Stock	'E' shares
PA	40.8	37,500 ('A')	2,085
NPA	40.8	37,500 ('B')	2,085
AAP	13.6	12,500 ('C')	695
NZPA	2.7	2,639 ('C')	139
Executives	2.1	—	1,993

VI

The chief players among the directors and trustees during the discussion and implementation of the flotation of Reuters were:

Directors	*Trustees*
Rupert Murdoch (NPA)	Lord Matthews
Ian Irvine (NPA)	Lord Hartwell
Peter Gibbings (NPA/PA)	Lord Rothermere
Mick Shields (NPA)	
Richard Winfrey (PA)	
Lyle Turnbull (AAP)	

Rupert Murdoch was the best-known newspaperman involved. He had joined the Reuter board in 1979 as an NPA representative—not (as was sometimes assumed) as a representative of AAP, in which at that time he had only a minor shareholding. The majority share-owners—the *Melbourne Herald* and *Weekly Times*, and the John Fairfax Company, owners of the *Sydney Morning Herald*—regarded him with suspicion. His contact with Reuters went back to his teens, when his father, Sir Keith Murdoch, had been active in bringing AAP into the Reuter partnership.

Branching out from Australia, Murdoch had gained control of the *News of the World*, the *Sun*, and (in 1981) *The Times*. These established London titles, now owned by News International, brought Murdoch the prospect of a shareholding in Reuters worth up to £100 million. How much did this financial prospect influence his attitude during the flotation discussions? Murdoch's care for Reuters was thought by many to be genuine, strongly influenced by the memory of his father. But did such care rule out the possibility—perhaps even increase the possibility—that he might have aspirations to take control? The suggestion was often heard that he wanted to own Reuters. Perhaps Murdoch was doing no more than keeping an open mind. Des Anderson, a senior accountant with the *Melbourne Herald*, reported back to Australia on 5 October 1983: 'Murdoch stated that he is leaving his options open with Reuters, but the concern is that he has a master plan to take control of Reuters shortly after it is floated.' Certainly, Murdoch took a close interest throughout the prolonged flotation discussions and he rarely missed board meetings.

Ian Irvine was an accountant who became managing director of Fleet Holdings in January 1982. He knew that Fleet, which owned the *Daily Express*, was vulnerable. It needed assets to show in its books, and he quickly realized that Fleet's shareholding in Reuters might be valued at £100 million if the company were publicly floated. In retrospect, Irvine was to argue that such awareness was not greed—that Fleet was less interested in getting money out of Reuters than in obtaining an authentic valuation for its holding. Although Fleet Holdings took about £5.7 million from the flotation, it still retained three-quarters of its 'B' shareholding. Irvine became an NPA representative director of Reuters at the beginning of 1984.

The chairman of Fleet Holdings was Lord Matthews, a self-made businessman and only recently a newspaper proprietor. He was a trustee of Reuters. Briefed by Irvine, Matthews was to play an active early part in pressing for Reuters to go public. The chairman of Associated Newspapers was Lord Rothermere, another Reuter trustee. He represented the third generation of the Harmsworth newspaper family. Rothermere's *Daily Mail* was in fierce competition with Matthews's *Daily Express*. At meetings of both the NPA council and of the Reuter trustees he clashed with Matthews over the flotation.

Lord Hartwell came from the Berry newspaper family, being a son of Lord Camrose. He was chairman and editor-in-chief of the *Daily Telegraph*. Like Matthews and Rothermere, he served both as a member of the NPA council and as a trustee of Reuters. 'Of all the proprietors,' remarked another NPA council member, 'it was Hartwell who insisted on preserving Reuters' virginity.' Nevertheless, he became persuaded that a careful flotation need not infringe the Reuter trust principles.

Another member of the NPA council who played an important part was Peter Gibbings, who was also on the PA board. He was chairman of the *Guardian* and *Manchester Evening News* group. Gibbings and Mick Shields, the managing director of Associated Newspapers, were said by Irvine to be the only players, apart from Matthews and himself, who fully understood the financial complexities. Gibbings became an NPA director of Reuters at the beginning of 1984.

Richard Winfrey was managing director of East Midland Allied Press. He became a PA director of Reuters in 1981, and was chairman of the PA during 1982–4. With Hamilton ill, he was made chairman of an unofficial working party of Reuter shareholders. Winfrey worked with great diplomatic skill to achieve agreement over the mechanics of the flotation.

Lyle Turnbull had served as the AAP director on the Reuter board since 1974. He felt a deep respect for the Reuter tradition. During the flotation discussions, he feared that many NPA members did not share the same respect. He therefore campaigned forcefully in defence of the trust principles.

VII

Who first thought of pressing for Reuters to go public? The idea seems to have grown in several minds at much the same time. An article by Maggie Brown in the *Guardian* on 10 June 1982 gave the first informed account in the press of how the owners of Reuters were realizing how they might gain access to large sums of money. Flotation was being canvassed by Gibbings and by Alan Hare, the chairman and chief executive of the *Financial Times*, and an NPA director of Reuters. Hare knew that PA support would be vital, and he sent a letter which was discussed at a special PA board meeting on 10 August. At a further PA board meeting on 9 September Gibbings spoke in favour of flotation.

In a letter of 23 July 1982 to Dicks, who was acting as Reuter chairman while Hamilton was away ill, Hare argued in favour of Reuters going public so long as the trust principles were maintained. After talking to Murdoch and Renfrew, he claimed that neither was 'adverse to the idea'. However, at a Reuter board meeting on 8 September, which Hare was unable to attend, Renfrew gave the idea only minimum encouragement. Hare emphasized that the company already possessed plenty of development capital. He did concede that 'realising their investment' was a matter for the shareholders. But he drew attention to the trust principle that Reuters should 'at no time pass into the hands of any one interest, group or faction'.

Hare had circulated a study of the position and prospects of Reuters, 'which Lazards have done off their own bat'. It was dated 19 July. This declared that the long history, excellent profit record, and 'exciting potential' of Reuters meant that there would be no difficulty in obtaining a listing on the London Stock Exchange. Hare wanted Lazards to be authorized to explore the matter further. Ian Fraser of Lazards (once a

Reuter correspondent) lobbied NPA members. But Renfrew told Winfrey on 3 November that he would always oppose any merchant bank 'digging into Reuters', except under the control of management. Hare said that he had expected Murdoch to contact the Australians. In view of Murdoch's poor relations with the AAP board, Max Suich of John Fairfax, an AAP board member, commented that the idea was 'quite comical'. Murdoch, for his part, complained to Dicks on 20 September about the 'atmosphere of conspiracy' which was developing: 'all these discussions should be conducted openly at the board table.' Judah told Renfrew on 28 September that Hare was now admitting 'that he had presented the case very badly'.

Matthews and Irvine had their own reasons for wanting a flotation. The annual general meeting of Fleet Holdings was fixed for 13 October. Institutional shareholders needed to be persuaded to hold on to their Fleet shares. Matthews began to talk to journalists about the golden prospects for Reuters. Fleet revealed in September that it had received a Reuter dividend. In his speech as chairman at the Fleet annual meeting Matthews said nothing about Reuters, but one of the first questions from the floor concerned Fleet's Reuter shareholding. Matthews afterwards claimed that he was not expecting the question. But he was ready with an encouraging reply which received wide publicity in the press. 'Their profits are rising fairly dramatically. For many years we've been helping to prop them up. Now suddenly there is a new look about them. In the end it will mean a market quotation.' In another answer, Matthews added that he had been 'chivvying' Reuters towards a market quotation. 'I would imagine there would be two classes of shares. There would still have to be control. It could happen this year.'

Next morning, the *Wall Street Journal* duly noticed that Fleet Holdings, 'whose newspapers posted losses last year', would find its stake in Reuters a valuable asset. The *Journal* added that Murdoch was joining Matthews in moves towards flotation. This was not correct. Brian Horton, formerly of Reuters and now on Murdoch's staff, phoned Matthews to say that Murdoch was 'very irritated' by what Matthews had said: 'he felt the whole affair should be allowed to simmer down now.' Immediately after Matthews had spoken, Nelson had tried to dampen expectations by issuing a statement that Reuters had 'not authorised any action', nor any inquiry.

Matthews had spoken of possible developments before the end of the year. Rothermere let it be known within the NPA that he was opposed in principle to any public issue of Reuter shares. Most other NPA members, however, were keen for a flotation. And how long would it be before the members of the PA decided that they needed the money? Several provincial newspapers were in financial trouble, and most of them wanted to introduce new printing technology. Winfrey admitted to Renfrew on 3 November that pressure upon the PA board would probably increase. Winfrey also wondered if 'it might be best to find some way of letting the NPA members have what they appear to want, and do it quickly rather than wait for pressure for action to build up'.

The staff of Reuters was growing understandably concerned about these manœuvres and rumours. The Reuter NUJ sent a letter to *The Times* on 19 November, but it was not published. The letter expressed the fear that the independence of Reuters was being threatened, and asked for a strengthening of the powers of the Reuter trustees.

The Reuter board met on 8 December. Turnbull there told his NPA and PA colleagues plainly that the AAP and NZPA had been 'somewhat disturbed' by the persistent talk of a flotation. The Australians saw definite advantages in the present arrangements, which ensured the independence of Reuters, and were not themselves looking for any capital gain. They would be satisfied to receive increasing dividends. In response to this firm line, the Reuter board agreed to the publication of an announcement to staff and to the press. This declared that no proposal had been considered 'for any kind of change in Reuters ownership'. This was of course true—up to that point. The announcement also reaffirmed the commitment of the board to the Reuter trust principles.

Turnbull was not so naïve as to believe that this would be the end of the matter. In a memorandum for his fellow AAP directors written on 23 December 1982, he noted that the NPA's members wanted the question of going public to be raised again. Murdoch, in particular, had asked for further consideration, apparently having changed his attitude.

VIII

By the spring of 1983, calls for action were once more being heard. The *Financial Times* of 9 March quoted Irvine as saying that if Reuters wanted to compete internationally, 'it is going to have to establish a much broader base for raising finance'. Renfrew replied tartly in a letter, published on 12 March, that Reuters had been competing with success internationally for 132 years. 'It is financing its heavy capital investment programme entirely from its own resources and still has surplus cash balances.'

On 24 March *The Times* looked at 'the extraordinary rise and sudden desirability of Reuters'. The article noted that the members of the NPA were squabbling over their respective stakes. An NPA council meeting on 26 April, according to leaks reaching Winfrey, was 'very stormy'. The members could not agree how to split the 1982 Reuter dividend.

The Reuter board met on 18 May 1983 in New York. Renfrew now submitted a management proposal for the issue of non-voting but marketable shares in Reuters. He admitted that two months earlier he had disagreed publicly with suggestions that the company needed to attract outside capital in order to compete internationally. But his appetite had been whetted by the 'impressive' success of recent Datastream and Telerate stock issues. Extra capital would enable Reuters to make major acquisitions. Telerate had gone public on a remarkable price/earnings ratio of 54: 'and is now in a stronger surplus cash position and better placed to make strategic investments than we are.' At a price/earnings ratio between 25 and 40, continued Renfrew, an issue of 10 per cent of total Reuter stock would be worth between £125 million and £200 million.

Meanwhile, another proposal had been prepared for Matthews and Irvine to present to the NPA. This allowed NPA members to hold marketable ordinary Reuter shares directly; but it sought to protect the independence of Reuters through reserve powers attached to 'special voting shares'. These would carry the right to appoint 'special Reuters directors', who were to possess 'the absolute power to veto' any proposal contrary to the principles of the Reuter trust. Ownership of the special shares would be through the NPA, PA, and AAP. But the ordinary shares would be vested in a new company—Reuters Holdings—and would be held by members separately.

Hartwell, an NPA council member speaking as a Reuter trustee, quickly dismissed the proposal. So also did Renfrew, when proposing the bonus share scheme to the May board meeting. He described the proposed system of two boards—and of two classes of directors within the Reuter board with different voting powers—as 'objectionable and probably unworkable'. Renfrew argued that it would also weaken the trust safeguards. If, for example, the directors appointed by Reuters Holdings chose to cut back the news-reporting network for short-term financial reasons, the special voting directors 'would only have an ill-defined power of veto and could not force the Reuter Board to take positive action'. These were unanswerable objections.

At the board meeting on 18 May Winfrey admitted that the PA membership was interested in raising capital from Reuters, even though the PA board had not yet agreed to this. Turnbull of the AAP also now revealed himself ready to accept some change. He supported Renfrew's proposal for a bonus share issue. He was pleased to find that the NPA view, as relayed by Hare and Murdoch, 'did accept that any change in the capital structure would be done only within the intentions of the Reuter Trust'. Discussion at the board had run on without much shape until Murdoch exclaimed 'equity is *for ever*'. He meant by this that if Reuters went public, the resulting equity would have to be serviced by a dividend, and that 'City' considerations would influence policy. He contrasted this unfavourably with the existing private-company status of Reuters, under which it was possible to take decisions which might depress immediate profitability for the sake of longer-term benefits.

The board agreed to make a final decision at its September meeting. A general order to staff on 14 July announced that Reuters had commissioned Binder Hamlyn, its auditors, to produce a report, 'following a management proposal that it should issue stock'. Staff were also told that the board had 'decided to study ways of enabling existing shareholders to put a value on their stock in Reuters'.

The press now had no doubts that the outcome would be a public flotation. 'Reuters set to go public', announced *The Times* on 26 May. 'Reuters is set for £1bn market float', proclaimed the *Sunday Times* on 12 June. Both Winfrey for the PA and Hamilton for Reuters issued statements denying that there was any commitment to go public. Hamilton's denial appeared on 10 June, the day of the meeting of the Reuter trustees and of the annual general meeting. At the trustees' meeting Matthews tried to gather support for an initiative. He was opposed by Rothermere, Hartwell, and others:

> Matthews: As Trustees we would not be opposed to a public flotation in some formal manner provided the safeguards of the Trust were there, and you suggested obviously that proposals have to be put forward. But by whom? Would it be improper for a Trustee to put them forward, or would we look to management to initiate that proposal, or otherwise we remain silent on it? There is a distinct feeling that, while everyone is rather shy of saying too much about it, I have a feeling that no one would be really opposed to it because obviously there is substantial money involved . . .
>
> Rothermere: I think the Trustees only come into this at a considerable remove. Their fundamental duty is not to the shareholders and their profits but to uphold the objectives of the trust, and I don't think in that connection that this Board of Trustees should take the initiative in anything. We should be fully informed, and we should contemplate and

make our decision on whatever is put before us to ensure that it is in
accord with the Reuter Trust . . .

Matthews: I would also suggest we have a responsibility not only for the
Trust but for the shareholders as a whole. It is implied.

Rothermere: I don't think so.

Matthews: That is my view, that it is our duty to look after the trust and
the shareholders.

Rothermere: I think that is the duty of the directors.

Arguments continued within the NPA council about the points system
used to establish the assessments payable on behalf of each paper to Reuters.
The more points each group could claim the more valulable would be its
holding if Reuters went public. Dailies received six points, London
evenings three points, Sundays one point. These weightings had been
devised to reflect the use likely to be made of the Reuter news service by
each category of paper. But there were some anomalies, which now gave
room for argument: the *Sporting Life*, for example, had been counted as a
daily, whereas the *Financial Times* counted only as a Sunday.

IX

A meeting of the board of the AAP on 30 June 1983 considered the position by that date. The AAP board expressed its willingness to support
action, but with important qualifications:

> The board agrees in principle to a bonus issue of Reuter shares and to a
> public issue of non-voting shares provided AAP ownership rights are
> retained at not less than the present level, and provided also that the issued
> non-voting stock could not be converted to voting stock nor could it
> diminish the control of the management of Reuters by the present owner-
> ship, in order that all the provisions of the Reuter Trust are preserved.

This resolution was read out to the Reuter board on 13 July.

The two possible courses of action endorsed by the AAP—a bonus
issue and a public issue—were discussed throughout the summer of 1983.
At the 13 July board Renfrew expressed concern that the bonus-share
proposal for the benefit of the shareholders seemed to be overshadowing
the management proposal to issue shares to build up a capital fund. He
was assured by Dicks and Hamilton that the management's wishes were
regarded by 'everybody' as 'the first priority'.

During August 1983 two Australian representatives, Des Anderson and
Max Suich, were in London for consultations. The AAP and PA decided
to work together, and to present 'a united front on matters of control'.

Both also needed to overcome major tax difficulties before selling any part of their holdings in Reuters. However, at a meeting of the Fairfax board on 15 September Suich was still far from certain that a flotation would prove to be possible. Although the shareholders had agreed in principle, two serious obstacles remained, said Suich. 'One was the disputation at board level, and the other was whether Mr Renfrew would leave. There was no one adequate to take his place.' The fear was that Renfrew would cash in his 'E' shares and run.

The likely introduction of non-voting shares, devised to allow the existing owners of Reuters to retain control, had brought a further difficulty. The British Insurance Association Investment Protection Committee and the National Association of Pension Funds let Reuters know that they were firmly opposed to the issue of equity capital without voting rights. They represented such major investors as Prudential Insurance, the largest sub-underwriter of United Kingdom issues.

Warburgs had previously advised that non-voting shares would be acceptable to the market. Now, revealed Renfrew to the crucial Reuter board meeting on 14 September, they admitted that there would be opposition from the institutions. None the less, management had instructed Warburgs to estimate the market available for non-voting shares. 'Non-voting shares', insisted Renfrew, 'represent the simplest way of raising money without changing the principles of the Reuter trust agreement.' Warburgs had concluded that there would be a market for non-voting shares of up to £200 million in the United Kingdom, and of up to $300 million in the United States.

In general, Warburgs had been encouraging. They concluded in a report for the Reuter board in September 1983 on the prospects for a flotation:

(1) that Reuters could be valued at between £1,000 million and £1,500 million, and would be attractive to a broad section of investors in both the United Kingdom and United States;

(2) that a tax structure was designable which would avoid double taxation for the PA;

(3) 'A flotation of the company is compatible with safeguards for control of Reuters.'

Protection against taxation difficulties would require the creation of a holding company above the existing Reuters Limited. This would necessitate the reinstatement of the Reuter Trust Agreement in relation to the new company.

Murdoch had other ideas. He revealed them to the very meeting of the Reuter board on 14 September which heard these Warburg proposals. He suggested that Reuters should be split into two companies. Reuters Limited would continue to sell the general-news services on the existing basis:

> Into a new company would be put the business services, the economic services, the whole revenue flow and the whole costs which today produce the profit Reuters had overall. The continuing subsidy of the news services would be provided for by simply licensing the name Reuters to the new company which had an identical management and the same staff.

The idea of some such split was, of course, not new. Long had wanted it in his time as managing director, and had now recommended it to Murdoch.

The Reuter management, which had shown early reluctance to support the idea of a flotation, came down very firmly against this suggestion. A management paper, dated 21 September, dismissed the idea of separation as being based upon two false assumptions: firstly, that there was a clear separation between services sold to the media and those sold to business subscribers; and secondly, that 'guarantees of independency and integrity' were only needed to protect general news and not economic news. Both assumptions were not merely wrong but dangerous.

At Murdoch's suggestion, a working party was set up to consider four options:

(1) a financial restructuring 'to separate editorial activities from trading activities';

(2) 'An issue of marketable non-voting shares';

(3) 'An issue of marketable shares with restricted voting rights, with the existing owners retaining 30 per cent of Reuters equity';

(4) 'An issue of marketable shares with restricted voting rights, with the existing owners retaining a minimal equity interest.'

A first meeting of the working party on 20 September had to take the form of a mere discussion between interested parties and advisers. Some NPA members had objected to their interests being represented by others. The meeting was attended by Irvine and Shields from the NPA, Winfrey from the PA, Anderson from the AAP, and Renfrew and Judah from Reuters; Hamilton was in the chair. Advisers were present from Warburgs and Binder Hamlyn. The meeting quickly concluded that the first option, Murdoch's separation scheme, was not practicable. Renfrew spoke against it emphatically, describing it as 'disaster for the company':

Reuters could not be divided simply between news services and business services. The meeting also decided against option 2, an issue of non-voting shares. Such an approach was thought likely to limit substantially the number of shares which could be sold, and would reduce their price.

The meeting therefore concentrated upon options 3 and 4. Hamilton described option 3—an issue of marketable shares with restricted voting rights, and with the existing owners retaining 30 per cent of equity—as 'a half-way house'. This formula was designed to preserve as far as possible the form of the present arrangements, by keeping 'A', 'B', and 'C' shares and by entrenching the appointment of 'A', 'B', and 'C' directors.

Option 4—an issue of marketable shares with restricted voting rights, with the existing owners retaining a minimal equity interest—involved the replacement of the existing control structure by a special share, 'the master share'. All the rest of the shares would be voting ordinary shares, and would be listed. The master share would carry the right in defined circumstances to cast sufficient votes on a poll at a general meeting to pass any ordinary resolution and to defeat any ordinary or special resolution. The master share would be held by the Reuter trustees, and a revised agreement of trust would set out the circumstances in which they would be able to wield it.

The NPA, as a body, was still unable to offer a united reaction to any proposals. The PA was capable of doing so. At its board meeting on 13 October it came out strongly in favour of combining the idea of the master share with that of weighted voting.

Although a practicable scheme was now beginning to emerge in private, outside observers still feared that the reputation of Reuters was about to be sacrificed simply to satisfy the greed of the press barons. This was the fear of many veteran Reuter figures, notably Malcolm Graham (a director in 1941), Burgess (the former chairman), and Chancellor (the former general manager). During the summer they had variously expressed their concerns by letter and in person to Hamilton and Renfrew. Chancellor proved very difficult to calm. Hamilton wrote to Burgess on 11 October 1983 about 'the wanderings, in every sense, of Christopher Chancellor'. Sadly, Chancellor's mind was growing enfeebled, but his contacts were extensive. Not least, his son Alexander—himself a former Reuter correspondent—was editor of the *Spectator*, the respected London weekly. The issue for 22 October contained a three-page article written by Alex Chancellor and Geoffrey Robinson, a barrister. It was entitled 'Reuters: The Price of Greed'. This article surveyed the history of Reuters as a general-news agency, and noticed how the Reuter Trust had been formed in 1941 for its protection. Unfortunately, claimed the article, the great profits now being earned by the Monitor services had become a danger to the integrity of Reuters.

Nelson and Judah read the article and invited Alex Chancellor to lunch. One of their purposes was to explain that the three executive directors had no personal interest in pushing for a flotation, since their 'E' shares had a high value whether or not Reuters went public. They would not countenance a reorganization of the company which did not respect the Reuter Trust principles. Alex Chancellor was persuaded of the integrity of Renfrew, Nelson, and Judah; but in a paragraph on 5 November he still spelt out what their holdings would be worth if Reuters went public at £1,000 million—respectively £5,450,000, £3,610, 000, and £3,060,000. Paragraphs about Reuters appeared in the *Spectator* each week throughout November.

During the summer of 1983 Gibbings had used his overlapping position within both the NPA and the PA to try to find a way forward towards a flotation, which he himself had favoured from the start. He had called informal meetings at his office. One such meeting on 25 October brought together Hare, Irvine, and Shields from the NPA and Dicks, Winfrey, and Donald Anderson from PA. It proved very fruitful in giving firm shape to detailed proposals which were accepted in the final scheme. The note of the meeting included the following points:

> The structure of the new company should be kept simple and as near to the existing one as possible.

> There should be commercial reasons for a possible flotation, because 'the Revenue did not take kindly to artificially created schemes'.

> The present shareholders should retain the lowest possible economic interest consistent with retaining control. The PA suggested a 25 per cent interest with a 3–1 multiple. The NPA suggestion of 30 per cent was too high.

> The NPA members should control their shares individually, but under cover of a shareholders' agreement. The PA, AAP, and NZPA should hold their control shares under a separate agreement.

> If voting control by present shareholders dropped below 50 per cent then a 'Master Share, controlled by Trustees', should operate in certain specified circumstances.

> No one shareholder to hold more than 15 per cent.

> The new board to comprise up to fourteen members—three PA; three NPA; two AAP; three Reuter executives; three outside directors.

The note concluded with the reminder: 'Agreed integrity of Trust re independence vital.'

At the Reuter board on 9 November Murdoch described weighted voting shares as an attempt to sell and yet to keep control:

> He thought it was a case of wanting to have one's cake and eat it, and really the decision ought to be whether one kept it as an entirely private company. He thought it 'a classic case of great British hypocrisy', at which Turnbull interjected that he thought 'it was more international than that'.

Murdoch emphasized that he was speaking personally, and not for the NPA. He would not press the point, as he was a director appointed to represent the NPA, which had now agreed to a flotation on the proposed terms. Hare, another director from the NPA, afterwards described Murdoch's last-minute reservations as 'pure theatre', intended to demonstrate that he was not a greedy press baron. Perhaps. But Murdoch had a point.

After Murdoch had made his point, the discussion proceeded. The flotation was not called off, but the AAP continued to act as a brake. As regards possible reductions in holdings, Turnbull finally conceded that a reduction from 25 to 20 per cent of the equity could take place with only 75 per cent of the present shareholders approving; but he insisted that for anything below 20 per cent approval would have to be unanimous. Three classes of shares were now envisaged. Ordinary 'B' shares in the new company were initially to form 25 per cent of the equity. 'A' shares were to have 4 votes per share. No person or group was to own more than 15 per cent of any shares. The master share was to be held by a separate company, with the Reuter trustees as directors. The board also agreed that the company should itself raise $100 million at the time of the flotation. This would create the capital fund wanted by management.

X

Hartwell now resolved the problem of the division of share interest in Reuters between the NPA members. He produced an analysis of the competing claims for the NPA Council. His paper of 8 November amounted to a piece of *reductio ad absurdum*. It recommended adoption of a neutral plan put forward by John Le Page, the NPA director. This was now accepted.

A press release after the Reuter board meeting on 9 November confirmed—what had already become public knowledge—that the Reuter Trust Agreement was in fact no more than a shareholders' agreement: the owners could repudiate it. Renfrew sought to reassure his staff and the public by emphasizing that the changes being envisaged would ensure that 'the principles of the present Trust Agreement would be maintained'.

The NUJ at Reuters responded by passing a resolution on 1 December which called upon the owners to strengthen the trust 'in terms which would imply legal obligations'. The journalists were well aware that not all the NPA shareholders respected the Trust constraints. Des Anderson reported on 5 October:

> Fleet openly expresses the view that the Reuters Trust is no more than a shareholders' agreement based upon old-fashioned ideals which do not have a place in the commercial world of today. Fleet say that such things as Trusts and restrictions should not exist, as market forces will come into play and dictate the policy and future of Reuters.

James Callaghan, the former British prime minister, had been told by Christopher Chancellor about his fears for Reuters. Callaghan was interviewed on BBC Television on 10 November, and on BBC Radio the next day. He argued that if the Trust—created in 1941 after the House of Commons had discussed the future of Reuters—was not really a Trust at all, the Commons should again look into Reuters.

Even now, a flotation was not quite certain. The shareholders' working party met on 17 November and 6 December, under Winfrey's chairmanship. No AAP representatives were present, which was a pity. The AAP was becoming increasingly concerned at what it regarded as attempts by the various NPA groups to weaken the control mechanism exercised through the 'A' shares. The Australians insisted upon tight restrictions upon 'A' share ownership and sale, to provide a control element in addition to that operating through the trustees—'belt and braces'.

The working party met again on 13 December, with Turnbull of the AAP present. In his report back to Australia on 20 December Turnbull described the meeting as 'difficult':

> Both the NPA and PA representatives there (and their nine advisers from Warburgs and Rothschilds) sought to persuade me to change the AAP position so that there could be a less restricted float.
>
> Specifically, they sought to change the previous decisions that we should maintain a minimum equity in Reuters after the minimum 3-year locked-in period; they also sought relaxation of other essential elements of the scheme, the consequence of which I thought would make inevitable our future loss of control of the company.
>
> I denied their final claim that we were using a minority shareholder's

veto to block the proper future development of the company. I told them this was humbug and the opposite of the truth; in fact, only AAP seemed to be interested in the purposes of the Trust and in a long-term commitment to Reuters.

Both the NPA and PA sought the right to drop below a 20 per cent equity in Reuters after three years with only a simple majority of shareholders agreeing; our position was that we should not go below 20 per cent (with a weighted vote ratio) unless with the unanimous consent of all shareholders. In the end, when things got blunt, I said their choice was whether they wanted to get the benefits of 80 per cent of something, or 100 per cent of nothing.

The transcript notes of the meeting confirmed the sharpness of some of the exchanges. Irvine charged Turnbull with advocating controls which would act against one of the Reuter Trust principles, the commitment to develop the business:

> Turnbull: You have got it back to front. I don't believe it is your intention to preserve the integrity, the trust of Reuters.
> Irvine: You have not answered the question.
> Turnbull: You are saying we are exercising a veto. We are just saying we wish to preserve the present.

The Reuter board meeting on 14 December proved to be even more contentious, although the formal minutes spoke only of 'full discussion'. Turnbull telexed an account of the proceedings back to Australia:

> An eight-hour meeting after much argument today agreed in principle to float Reuters in London and New York along lines of the scheme approved by us, that is weighted voting, media-controlled board plus founder share and trustee system. Murdoch tried to upset whole plan by arguing for an abandonment of the weighted voting system on grounds that Warburgs advice was that it would reduce market value of the float in London. We therefore had to argue all over again the principles already decided at yesterday's committee meeting.
>
> I said that we would not agree to a float except on our terms, and that in any case there was no time left to go back to square one and produce a new scheme if they wanted to get their money out next year. This was finally conceded.

In the background to these disputes about structure were doubts about the prospects for a flotation. Warburgs and Rothschilds, reported Turnbull, had told the board 'that our scheme was not popular in the City', and that there would be difficulty selling a scheme which relied heavily upon weighted voting and a controlled board membership.

In addition, there were differences about the future policy of the new company. Turnbull reported that Murdoch and Renfrew had 'clashed repeatedly' over this at the board of 14 December. According to Turnbull, Murdoch had argued against further investment in hardware, and also against acquisitions. He wanted Reuters to confine itself to the provision of services. The top executives, reported Turnbull, had told him privately that they were 'very grateful to us for the preservation of what they regard as the proper future control of the company'.

After the board meeting of 14 December, a press release and a general order to staff announced that the board had decided to seek a public flotation of Reuters, 'and to submit a plan to the Reuter trustees for their comments'. It was noticed that the trustees were not being asked for their 'approval'. Two days later Renfrew had to issue another general order. 'I do want to assure staff, yet again, that preservation of the principles of the Reuter Trust Agreement has been the paramount consideration in all the discussions.'

Renfrew then launched into an attack upon recent press comment, and also upon those who were seeking to bring the British Government and parliament into the matter. Any connection with the Government or legislature of any country, wrote Renfrew, was 'simply not consistent with Reuters principles of independence'. This was confusing the wish of the British authorities to be reassured about the future independence of Reuters with a desire to interfere in that independence. In fact, the former ruled out the latter.

The benevolence of the interest being shown by the British Government was revealed early in January 1984. The Department of Trade and Industry tried to persuade the leading investment institutions to waive in the special case of Reuters their opposition to non-voting or weighted shares. On 5 January the permanent under-secretary, Sir Anthony Rawlinson, asked David Walker, the executive director of the Bank of England, to use his influence 'on grounds of public interest'. Walker was authorized to copy Rawlinson's letter to the chairmen of the relevant City of London institutions. The National Association of Pension Funds on 9 January and the British Insurance Association on 20 January both refused to give way. The chairman of the BIA suggested that the master-share safeguard would be sufficient to protect Reuters, without need for weighted 'A' shares.

At the Reuter board meeting on 11 January 1984 the mechanics of flotation were discussed, including the feasibility of a joint offering in London and New York. It would be the first initial public offering made simultaneously in the two cities. David Scholey of Warburgs explained that this was desirable to demonstrate how much Reuters was a world-wide company. Scholey also said that it would be desirable to add some non-press directors to the Reuter board. Murdoch asked him what sort of persons and Scholey suggested that they might be bankers. 'We don't want to fill this board with a lot of City stiffs', answered Murdoch.

The House of Commons discussed the position of Reuters on 27 January, upon a motion from a Labour back-bencher, Austin Mitchell. The board had authorized the briefing of Kenneth Baker, the minister for information technology; Nelson talked to him. As in 1941, only a handful of members were present in the Commons; but the fact that the debate had taken place at all was a useful expression of concern for the maintenance of the Reuter trust principles by the new company. One Member of Parliament, Nicholas Soames, Churchill's grandson, still spoke of Reuters in the old vein as 'a splendid British institution'; but Mitchell's opening remarks had recognized its international role. He asked for Government intervention to protect not British interests but 'the public interest worldwide'. In reply, the minister reconciled the different emphases by describing Reuters as 'a national asset' because it was a successful international company with its headquarters in Britain. And it was the more an asset, continued Baker, because it was unconnected with the British Government. He declared himself satisfied that the board and trustees of Reuters would preserve its independence after flotation.

At meetings of the Winfrey working party on 25 January and 7 February 1984 Irvine returned to the attack on the 'A' share restrictions because they would affect market value. Winfrey reminded the meeting on 7 February that the 'A' shares had been devised to reconcile the wish of the British owners to raise money with their wish to retain control. Des Anderson told the meeting forcefully that the AAP had already compromised over the percentage of equity to be retained by the holders of 'A' shares. 'Originally we suggested 51% for ever and a day. We have come now to 25% and 20%. We are certainly not prepared to go below that, and that is final.' And so it was.

The trustees had not become involved in the prolonged discussions of ways and means. They waited to be asked for their reaction to a particular scheme. Although their powers had been shown to depend only upon a shareholders' agreement, their moral authority remained strong. In particular, they were in a good position to comment upon any proposed new trust agreement. Hartwell was particularly active in collecting opinion. At a meeting on 21 February the Reuter trustees accepted the new trustee structure devised by the Reuter board. This centred upon the creation of a Founders Share held by a Founders Share Company. A deed of mutual covenant, agreed by the owners, was to convey to the Founders Share Company the right to enforce procedures for the preservation of the Reuter Trust principles. The 1941 statement of principles, as revised in 1953, was to be reaffirmed with updating amendments. The trustees were assured that the new trust would be given sufficient powers:

1) If any single Reuter Trustee believes that an interest group or faction has obtained or is seeking to obtain or maintain control of Reuters, then a majority of the Reuter trustees can ensure that the Founders Share rights are exercised to ensure compliance with the Reuter Trust Principles.

2) If any attempt is made to vary the protective powers vested in the Founders Share, then any two Reuter Trustees can ensure that the Founders share rights in the holding company are exercised to prevent this.

The necessary deed of mutual covenant was entered into by the owners on 9 May.

At their meeting on 21 February the Reuter trustees had expressed 'enormous satisfaction' with the proposed reorganization of the ownership of Reuters. This had involved considerable legal manœuvring. The taxation difficulties which had threatened PA and AAP were circumvented, and the NPA was enabled to participate as a legal entity through a new body, NPA Nominees. A new public limited company, Reuters Holdings, acquired Reuters Limited. Reuters Holdings was initially given four classes of share capital:

(1) 'A' ordinary shares, representing 25 per cent of the equity, entitling holders to four votes on most matters and producing a voting majority for 'A' shareholders, with restrictions on share transfer;

(2) 'B' ordinary shares, representing 75 per cent of the equity, with one vote per share;

(3) one Founders Share, with a minimal economic interest but with overriding voting rights in defined circumstances;

(4) 'E' shares.

Three or four 'independent' 'D' trustees were to be added to the existing 'A', 'B', and 'C' trustees. These independent trustees were to have no connection with Reuters, and no financial interest in the newspaper industries of the United Kingdom, Ireland, Australia, or New Zealand likely to affect their independence. The 'D' trustees eventually appointed were Kingman Brewster, a former United States ambassador to the United Kingdom and a distinguished academic lawyer; John Freeman, chairman of London Weekend Television, once a Labour junior minister and subsequently ambassador to the United States; Kenneth Morgan, director of the Press Council, an experienced journalist; and Lord McGregor, Professor of Social Institutions at London University and chairman of the Royal Commission on the Press 1975–7.

Critics such as Callaghan and the Chancellors now expressed themselves satisfied. 'As an exercise in having one's cake and eating it,' conceded the *Spectator* on 3 March, 'the restructuring of the company is to be admired.' In a private letter to Christopher Chancellor on 8 March, Hamilton summed up soothingly:

> I would have preferred that the structure of Reuters had been left alone, and we could have gone on building up reserves sufficient to develop our businesses still further . . . Anyhow, as we both know, people new to journalism see it as a heaven-sent opportunity to line their own pockets and develop their rather fragile businesses. The only real sympathy I have for some of our Fleet Street friends is that they have been plundered by the unions and at last they will get something back, though I fear the printers will grab what they can, as they always have done. Michael Hartwell has been magnificent throughout all this, and I must tell you that Rupert Murdoch, himself, has played a constructive and statesmanlike role in memory of his father.

XI

The offer of 'B' shares to the public took further time and discussion. Uncertainty persisted up to the last minute about just how many 'B' shares each owner would be prepared to offer for sale. This uncertainty caused friction at a meeting of Winfrey's working party on 12 March. When Des Anderson suggested that every shareholder would be a seller, Winfrey answered that this would not be the case:

Anderson: If we are going to have a cat and mouse game as to who is going to sell and who is not, I think our stand could well be that we won't sell any shares.

Winfrey: A float gives value to the shareholding.

Anderson: It should be equal. The purpose was to benefit the company. If those commercial reasons for the company are not there and it is only an exercise to benefit certain shareholders, we ought to know . . . If we are going to find the large shareholders are not going to sell, then we can say 'the float's off'.

Irvine: The shareholders in the NPA have said that they would prefer not to sell shares. In order to establish a market they will be willing to sell shares.

Reuters Holdings was registered as a public limited company on 11 April 1984, and held its first board meeting on that day. A new board was constituted, with Hamilton—as chairman of the old Reuters Limited—appointed chairman also of the new company. At a board meeting on 8 May three new 'B' directors were appointed. These 'outside' directors were intended to introduce high-powered and international business experience into the direction of the new public company. The old board had decided that they should be drawn from the United Kingdom, continental Europe, and the United States. The individuals appointed were Christopher Hogg, chairman and chief executive of Courtaulds, Pehr Gyllenhammer, chairman of Volvo, and Walter Wriston, chairman of Citicorp.

The same board meeting on 8 May discussed the size of the 'B' share offering (106.8 million shares), the likely valuation of the company (£708–£920 million), the minimum tender price (180p), and the consequences of a joint flotation in London and New York. Joint flotation prevented the usual fixed-price share offer. Instead, there had to be an auction by tender through Warburgs and Rothschilds. The suggested valuation range was considerably less than earlier estimates of £1,000 million or more: the institutional boycott had lowered the figure by perhaps £100 million. The valuation at sale was £770 million.

Applications by tender had to be received by 1 June 1984, and trading in Reuter shares began on 4 June. The seventy-two-page prospectus was one of the largest ever issued. It was advertised in full over nine pages in four British national newspapers. 'Road-show' presentations by senior management were made in London and Edinburgh, and in cities across the United States and Europe. Up to 70 per cent of shares were thought likely to be sold to institutions. In the event, the response in the United States was less than expected, partly because share prices there had recently collapsed. Investors in New York were offered 49.8 million 'B' shares, but subscribed for only 39 million. The shortfall was made up in London, where investors took up 67.8 million against an originally planned 57 million.

The choice of a striking-price had been a final matter of sharp contention. It was set too low. Despite the boycott by financial institutions, the British market could have absorbed the whole issue at over 200p per share. But in order to suit the reluctant American market, Merrill Lynch and Morgan Stanley, who were handling the New York offering, insisted upon a figure of 196p. The London *Times* commented on 5 June that the experiment of making simultaneous offerings was 'unlikely to be repeated in a hurry'.

Murdoch's News International finally decided not to offer any 'B' shares for sale, perhaps for tax reasons. Proceeds from the flotation of

TABLE 13.3. The main sellers of Reuter shares and their approximate proceeds

	£m.	% of total
International Thomson	20.7	13.6
Associated Newspapers	14.9	9.8
Reed International (including Mirror Group)	11.7	7.7
United Newspapers	9.5	6.3
Daily Telegraph	6.7	4.4
S. Pearson (including *Financial Times*)	6.4	4.2
Fleet Holdings	5.7	3.8
Westminster Press	5.4	3.6
Eastern Counties Newspapers	5.4	3.6
Guardian and *Manchester Evening News*	5.1	3.4

[a] The total proceeds for all newspaper groups amounted to £152m. The table assumes capital gains tax deducted at 15%.
Source: UK Press Gazette, 11 June 1984.

Reuters helped to finance the removal to new premises and the modernization of several British national and provincial newspapers. In this connection, however, the value of retained shareholdings mattered at least as much as money taken out. Their Reuter shareholdings now enabled several newspapers to borrow heavily: for example, within a year the *Daily Telegraph* had raised £110 million for two new printing works.

On the afternoon of 5 June Judah, Hamilton, Renfrew, and Nelson appeared on the floor of the London Stock Exchange—all looking suitably confident (see Plate 52). The atmosphere turned out to be low-key—despite the previous questioning in parliament and by the press, and even though the issue was oversubscribed 2.7 times in the United Kingdom. The trading-floor remained open after hours, and the price rose to 218p. But there was no great excitement. Reuters itself raised £53 million through the sale of new shares. This cash, plus marketable paper, was now available to finance acquisitions.

XII

Not everyone was convinced that the flotation was right. Eleven months after the event *The Price of Truth: The Story of the Reuters Millions* was published, promising 'a story of greed and intrigue surrounding Fleet Street and of how a small group of men broke a solemn undertaking in their efforts to unlock a treasure house'. It was written by John Lawrenson, who had worked for Reuters between 1955 and 1971, and Lionel Barber, a young financial journalist.

How valid was the charge that the owners of Reuters had broken their solemn undertaking? Under the Trust Agreement, the NPA, PA, and AAP newspaper groups had been committed to treating their ownership 'in the nature of a trust rather than as an investment'. These were high-sounding words, which were omitted from the restatement of Reuter Trust principles at the time of the flotation. Was this significant? Was it a tacit confession of guilt by the owners—about the money which they had just made, and about the money which they intended to continue to make?

Not at all. Firstly, Reuters had now been floated publicly. Within the new public company, these same newspaper groups—in their role as controlling 'A' shareholders—had accepted an obligation to the ordinary 'B' shareholders to seek profits. In such circumstances, the 1941 form of words was obviously inappropriate.

Secondly, even though the 1941 form of words had still been operative when the owners cashed in, they had a good defence against any charge of breach of faith. Their defence turned upon the wording of the limitation imposed upon them. Had the owners of the old private company really been excluded from seeking in any circumstances to make money out of Reuters? The question had not arisen for forty years because there had been little money to make. The language of the Trust Agreement had been chosen by Haley in 1941 with deliberation: he was a careful writer. He chose to describe the commitment of the owners as 'in the nature of a trust rather than as an investment'. He did not write 'in the nature of a trust *and not* [or *and never*] as an investment'. In other words, Haley imposed a qualified and not a total negative. The chosen formulation at least left open the possibility of the owners treating Reuters as an investment, so long as they did not infringe the Trust principles.

In 1984 the owners were able fairly to claim that in the process of taking money out of Reuters they had actually made the Trust much stronger. Its authority was no longer founded simply upon a shareholders' agreement. Moreover, in order further to protect the company they had introduced weighted 'A' shares, even at the expense of reducing the market value of their own holdings.

All this was explained well enough by Lawrenson and Barber, despite the strong language of their dust-jacket. The temptation to satisfy greed through breach of faith had certainly existed during 1982–4—for some more than others: it had been successfully resisted. The high-principled among the owners had coached the less principled. Greed had been scaled down to merely hearty appetite.

FOURTEEN

The World's News

1945–1989

I

AT the coming of peace in 1945, the reputation of Reuters as a news agency stood high. In the succeeding decades the task of Chancellor, Cole, Imeson, Mason, and their successors was to maintain and to develop that reputation. 'Now the hard work begins,' exclaimed Cole. By this he meant that reporting the Second World War had been comparatively easy: the issues were clear, and despite difficulties of censorship and travel, news editing was straightforward. The problems of peacetime would be more complex.

One problem was how to handle ideology, not least at 85 Fleet Street itself. Derek Jameson has written about the small left-wing cell on the editorial floor at 85 Fleet Street in the late 1940s, of which he was himself briefly a member. If Reuters had ever been forced publicly to admit the existence of this group, the agency's name for objectivity would have been tarnished. The left-wingers numbered perhaps a dozen, of whom only three or four were Communist Party members; the rest were fellow-travellers. Their leader was Lawrence Kirwan, one of the duty editors. The purge came after Frances Wheeler, one of the group, was found to have omitted an important reference to the Cold War in a speech by President Truman. Was this omission politically motivated? According to Jameson, the left-wingers had always been careful not to let their politics influence their news handling; others in Reuters thought differently. Called to explain herself, Wheeler revealed all about the cell. There were no sackings, but the main figures were removed from positions of responsibility, and gradually left Reuters. Several reappeared working for Tass and other Communist news organizations. The obligation of all Reuter staff to maintain political non-commitment was emphasized by Chancellor in a letter to Kirwan, dated 24 June 1950. 'Working for Reuters', wrote Chancellor, involved its staff 'in a form of self-discipline and self-abnegation. Those of you who feel strongly on political matters must be doubly careful in the position of trust which working for Reuters involves.'

Reuter correspondents in the field were receiving between £1,000 and £1,500 during the mid-1950s. This was a decidedly modest salary for a demanding job. They were a mixed bunch whose talents varied. Some had good contacts; some possessed a nose for news; some could write well. Not even the best commanded all three qualities in equal measure. But all aspired to objectivity in their reporting. Long explained to Lord Nicholas Gordon Lennox of the British Foreign and Commonwealth Office on 8 December 1980 why objectivity did not mean neutrality: 'What we seek is not so much neutrality in the sense of evenhandedness between different sides in a conflict, but rather the absence of emotion in vocabulary, so that events may be judged dispassionately, at least a far as the account of them is concerned.' Objectivity (as here defined) allowed room for interpretation, so long as it helped to explain a story and did so without bias.

Reuters was chary of using words, especially adjectives, which might be read as implying a value-judgement. This was well illustrated during the brief career in Reuters (1961–5) of Frederick Forsyth, who went on to become the author of *The Day of the Jackal* and other best-selling political thrillers. The qualities of imagination and language which were to make his novels so gripping had scarcely recommended Forsyth to his superiors in Reuters. 'He views the world around him in rather unreal terms like a spectator at the cinema identifying himself with the larger-than-life characters and incidents depicted on the screen.' Such was an assessment of Forsyth written on 22 April 1964 by David Sells, chief correspondent in Bonn. A few days later, when Forsyth filed that 'East Berlin seethed with East German troops in the small hours of today', Campbell sent back a reprimand about use of the verb 'seethed'. Forsyth had not realized that this military activity was merely in preparation for the annual May Day parade. Nor had he understood that his report was likely to cause alarm 'at deadline time in America'.

Successive Reuter style guides always emphasized the importance of sourcing. No story was complete without it; moreover, it provided protection for Reuters. When Hermann Goering committed suicide in his cell in 1946, just before he was to be executed as a Nazi war criminal, Reuters put out an incorrect report that all eleven criminals—by implication including Goering—had been hanged. The source was given as DANA (Deutsche Allgemeine Nachrichten-Agentur), the American-zone news service, but with the prudent addition 'So far the report is unconfirmed.' The British national newspapers headlined the news without qualification, and then unfairly blamed Reuters when the unexpected truth became known. Of course, mistakes were bound to occur, usually because of human error, and hoaxes were an ever-present danger.

The 1988 *International Style Guide* addressed the key question: 'What is news?' Its short answer was that what Reuter reported became news by the very fact of being reported: 'we give it the Reuter hallmark and it rises above the status of a mere report to that of news.' In the postwar years correspondents were expected to satisfy an educated British readership. Cole told the 1948 Royal Commission on the Press that 'our criterion' was what suited *The Times*, the *Manchester Guardian*, the *Glasgow Herald*, and the *Scotsman*. The assumption was that the more popular papers would edit Reuter material to the requirements of their readers. By the mid-1960s, however, Reuters was no longer reporting with the British press particularly in mind. It was aiming to produce an internationally acceptable file, with world regional and national variations.

II

Censorship presented Reuter correspondents in many countries with continuous difficulties about what and how to report. Such difficulties were not confined to the Communist bloc. On occasion even the Western democracies were prepared to interfere. During the Korean and French Indo-China wars of the 1950s Western military censorship was very tight. It was rather less so during the Vietnam War a decade later.

A round-up from the Reuter statistical department on 16 June 1965 noted that relatively few countries operated formal censorship in peacetime, 'in the sense of officials blue-pencilling press matter'. Only eleven countries attempted this for outgoing stories. A further eighteen had imposed restrictions on filing copy in certain emergencies. And thirty-six countries had adopted 'responsibility censorship'. This allowed the authorities to take action against correspondents who had filed copy which was not liked. Despite these impediments, Reuters preferred to maintain a presence under censorship rather than no presence. Long remarked in a BBC broadcast on 23 May 1968 that 'any honest reporting is better than no reporting'.

Conditions were particularly difficult for Reuters in Moscow. 'Blind' censorship became the Soviet practice during the early years of the cold war. Correspondents were required to submit their copy through the central telegraph office, and they were not told what cuts had been made. Any hint of shortcomings was disliked. Partly in exasperation and partly for reasons of economy, Reuters had withdrawn its full-time correspondent, Don Dallas, from Moscow at the beginning of 1950. The cost of maintaining one correspondent in the Soviet capital soared by 50 per cent after the 1949 devaluation of the pound sterling. The press rate from Moscow was as much as 5*d.* per word, compared with only 1*d.* from Australia. Nearly all the news that Dallas was allowed to send had already been picked up by Radio House from monitoring of Soviet or East European broadcasts. Dallas was replaced by an American working part-time.

Radio House enjoyed many successes, but it failed badly over the death of Stalin. At 01.03 on 6 March 1953 a dictation-speed broadcast from Moscow for Soviet provincial newspapers announced the dictator's death.

FIG. 15. Cartoon by Reuter correspondent Adrienne Farrell, 1946

Unfortunately, Radio House was not listening to that channel. Exchange Telegraph heard the broadcast, and issued the news at 01.09. The first Reuter snap came only at 01.14 via New York:

NEW YORK RADIO STATIONS REPORTED TONIGHT THAT STALIN WAS DEAD.

Weak as this was, it was the only way for Reuters to break the news. Six minutes later came a snap from Oslo, where the Norwegian news agency had heard the Moscow broadcast. Reuters still had nothing of its own. The editorial report for the month admitted 'our worst defeat for many years'.

After Stalin's death Reuters sent Sidney Weiland to Moscow. He was the only British correspondent in the Soviet capital at that period. His nickname within Reuters was 'sizzling Sid', because of his energy. The one-man Moscow assignment certainly needed both energy and stamina. The censorship continued, although correspondents were now given a copy of their stories to show what had been cut. When Weiland included pointed comments in one air-mail feature about Soviet economic plans on 6 January 1956, most of his remarks were censored. For example, the words italicized in the following sentence were struck out: 'In many cases, this has meant a readjustment of piecework rates *so that workers must now work harder and produce more in order to get the same wages which they took home before the change.*' Weiland served two terms as Moscow correspondent, 1953–6 and 1964–7. He gleaned much information from the Soviet press, subscribing to the few papers available to foreigners from the Soviet republics. These were scanned by a translator, who was supplied by the Soviet authorities. Correspondents obtained early copies of *Pravda* and *Izvestia* at the central telegraph office, usually after midnight.

On 11 February 1956 Weiland was invited with Richard Hughes of the *Sunday Times*, and representatives of Tass and *Pravda*, to witness the reappearance in public of Guy Burgess and Donald Maclean, the British diplomats who had defected five years earlier. In a Moscow hotel room the two men handed over a statement, and talked in a desultory fashion. But they were not allowed to be properly interviewed.

Only a month later Weiland secured an outstanding success. On 16 March 1956 the Moscow office reported a remarkable speech denouncing Stalin, delivered on 25 February by Nikita Khrushchev, the Soviet leader, to the 20th Communist Party Congress. Weiland had first heard of the denunciation on 11 March in a whispered conversation with a friendly Communist journalist at a Finnish Embassy reception. The journalist had given merely a brief outline of the speech, but enough to indicate its importance. Khrushchev had called Stalin a mass murderer and a military incompetent. Weiland wrote a cleverly guarded brief first report which slipped past the censors. Minutes later all cables about the speech were barred.

Weiland's colleague, John Rettie, obtained a much fuller version from an acquaintance. For four days the censors blocked all attempts to get this out. Fortunately, Rettie was due for leave. At about 2 a.m. on 16 March Weiland and Rettie went for a walk in the street to talk over the details of the speech. Rettie kept as much as possible in his head. He then flew to Stockholm, from where he telephoned a long outline to London. In an attempt to protect Rettie's position when he returned to Moscow, the report was published under a Bonn dateline as coming from 'reliable Communist sources':

BONN, MARCH 16–NIKITA KHRUSHCHEV HAS BITTERLY ACCUSED STALIN OF RESPONSIBILITY FOR MASSACRE AND TORTURE DURING HIS 30 YEARS AS RUSSIA'S LEADER, ACCORDING TO REPORTS FROM RELIABLE COMMUNIST SOURCES REACHING HERE TODAY.

THESE REPORTS SAID KHRUSHCHEV CHARGED STALIN WITH CRIMES NEVER BEFORE MENTIONED IN THE SOVIET UNION . . .

MR KRUSHCHEV IS SAID TO HAVE PAINTED A VIVID PICTURE TO THE DELEGATES OF THE REGIME OF 'SUSPICION, FEAR AND TERROR' THROUGH WHICH STALIN RULED, ESPECIALLY IN HIS LAST YEARS.

EVEN OTHER TOP LEADERS WERE SUBJECT TO THIS REGIME, INCLUDING MR KHRUSHCHEV HIMSELF.

HE IS REPORTED TO HAVE HELD STALIN RESPONSIBLE FOR SOVIET FAILURE IN THE EARLY STAGES OF LAST WAR BOTH BY IGNORING WARNINGS BY SIR WINSTON CHURCHILL AND BY 'WEAKENING' THE COUNTRY'S MORALE AND ECONOMY IN THE GREAT PRE–WAR PURGES.

THESE REPORTS SAID THE DECISION TO THROW OPEN THE TERRIBLE SECRETS OF THE STALIN ERA WAS REACHED BECAUSE IT WAS FELT TO BE THE ONLY WAY OF BREAKING THE MAGIC OF THE 'STALIN CULT' WHICH HAS GRIPPED THE SOVIET CITIZENS FOR 30 YEARS . . .

The full text of this speech did not reach the West for over two months.

In April 1964 Reuters mistakenly reported Khrushchev's own death, attributing the news to DPA citing Tass. In fact Tass had published no such report, and Reuters had held the story until other agencies had used it. Campbell regarded the Reuter report as an avoidable mistake, not excused by the inclusion of a source. He issued an emphatic note on 'Fact and Rumour' on 16 April 1964:

For Reuters to lend its name to this report was sufficient guarantee for many subscribers to accept it as fact, even though pinned to another agency . . . Rumours and unconfirmed reports can cause financial collapse, panics, riots and revolution . . . The credit does not go to an agency which first reports a rumour.

It goes to the agency which can first report the FACT.

'Blue pencil' censorship out of the Soviet Union had been abandoned in 1961, when the authorities allowed direct lines to be installed in foreign news-agency offices. But the subsequent 'responsibility censorship' was still oppressive. In February 1968 Adam Kellett-Long, the chief correspondent in Moscow, was warned against publishing stories based upon contacts with private citizens. The most serious instance of harassment occurred, however, in June 1974. A Soviet official told the chief correspondent that a Soviet citizen claimed to have had homosexual relations with two Reuter correspondents; the claim was an invention. On 30 July 1975 Long took the unprecedented step of addressing a letter to the Soviet foreign minister, Andrei Gromyko, asking him to put a stop to the harassment of foreign correspondents working in Moscow. He received no reply.

III

The Cuban missile crisis of 1962 saw the cold war nearly end in real war. The White House praised Reuters for providing the first version of Khrushchev's crucial message of 27 October proposing a 'deal'. This reached President Kennedy via his Reuter printer. The report had come from a Reuter radio listener at Green End, who scribbled down the text in Russian while a colleague looked over his shoulder and dictated a rough English translation down an open telephone line to the Central Desk at 85 Fleet Street. A copytaster polished the English, and then dictated to an operator teleprinting directly into the circuit.

In the previous year the cold war had taken on a physical expression with the erection of the Berlin Wall. The story broke on 13 August 1961. Kellett-Long, the correspondent in East Berlin, had received a tip-off from a member of the East German hierarchy that something was going to happen that weekend. But what? Rumours had been circulating for several days about drastic action to stop the exodus of East Germans to the West via Berlin. Kellett-Long had reported these rumours to London with a report starting 'Berlin is holding its breath . . .' He was beginning to wonder whether he had overdone the story when at about 1 a.m. he received an anonymous phone-call in German. A man's voice simply said: 'I strongly advise you not to go to bed tonight,' and then rang off. Soon afterwards the East German agency teleprinter rattled out a Warsaw Pact communiqué from Moscow urging 'effective control' round West Berlin. Kellett-Long decided to hurry out to see what was meant by 'effective control'. He thus became the first reporter to discover that the Brandenburg Gate crossing-point to the West was closed. The wall was about to go up.

Reuters was eight minutes ahead with the news:

THE EAST–WEST BERLIN BORDER WAS CLOSED EARLY TODAY

This was a major beat not only because Kellett-Long gave the first news, but because he was able follow up with a widely-published eyewitness account:

> The first that the sleeping East Berliners knew of the moves was when the wailing sirens of speeding police cars and the rumble of lorries filled with troops woke them up.
>
> It happened a few minutes after 12.30 a.m. GMT, when the East German news agency ADN [Allgemeiner Deutscher Nachrichtendienst] began publishing the restriction announcements.
>
> The streets were filled with lorry-loads of troops, police cars and motor-cyclists. Lights flicked on and people watched from their windows as I drove to the main border crossing point at the Brandenburg Gate.
>
> There I found steel barricades blocking the West-bound roads and a police cordon around the gate itself.
>
> When I tried to drive through a policeman stopped me and said: 'You are not allowed to go through.' Later I tried to approach another border point but a police cordon stopped me before the border was in sight.
>
> Black-uniformed railway police, some still buttoning their uniforms, were running towards the stations to control trains which now stop at the border.
>
> The East German radio began broadcasting the government communiqués at 2 a.m. GMT and repeated them throughout the night. The woman announcer opened the morning programme with the words: 'A fine good morning to all our listeners.' The radio then played a record of 'Basin Street Blues'.
>
> At one sector border crossing point the police and 'factory fighting group' men slowly pushed the crowd off the road, and it split into two groups on either pavement. The crowd of about 200 was slowly pushed back until it was 600 yards from the border.
>
> Violent arguments developed among the crowd, with Communist speakers apparently outnumbered. But the atmosphere was not so tense as

it could have been. People were laughing at each other's arguments. It might have been Hyde Park on a Sunday afternoon but for the police and 'fighting groups'.

Eleven years earlier John Peet, the Reuter correspondent in West Berlin, had sent to 85 Fleet Street the news of his own flight to the Communist world. On 12 June 1950 he suddenly announced that he 'could no longer serve the Anglo-American warmongers'. Peet, who had joined Reuters just after the Second World War, came from a Quaker family, and had served in the International Brigade during the Spanish Civil War. His background was thus both pacifist and left-wing. But until his flight his reporting had always been objective. At a press conference in East Berlin Peet said that the last straw for him had been 'lying and warmongering reports in the Western press of the great Whitsun Peace demonstration in Berlin'. He was also disturbed about the prospect of a West German army being created with encouragement from the Western powers. Peet's colleagues in Reuters were completely taken by surprise, as was British intelligence in Berlin.

Reuters published a full account of the press conference, and continued to report the story until it faded. The danger was that Reuters might be accused by the Americans of being lax in appointing such a man as a correspondent, especially to Berlin. Fortunately, Cole happened to be in the United States. On 15 June he was able to reassure Chancellor: 'it was a twelve-hour wonder, and we did ourselves a lot of good in unpleasant circumstances by frankly handling the story.' Peet had committed no offence in English law, and he paid occasional visits to the West until his death in 1988.

IV

The civil war between the Nationalists and the Communists in China after 1945 was fully covered by Reuters. Graham Jenkins, one of the first AAP-Reuter correspondents, was arrested by the Nationalists in 1949 and sentenced to death, but then released. For two years from 1956 David Chipp was one of only two Western correspondents based in China. Direct Reuter coverage was particularly welcomed by United States subscribers, since American journalists were not allowed to open offices in China for another twenty years.

Chipp's successor, Jack Gee, stayed for only a few months in 1958. Chancellor reported to the board that Gee had 'given offence', and suggested three reasons for acquiescing in the Chinese demand for Gee's

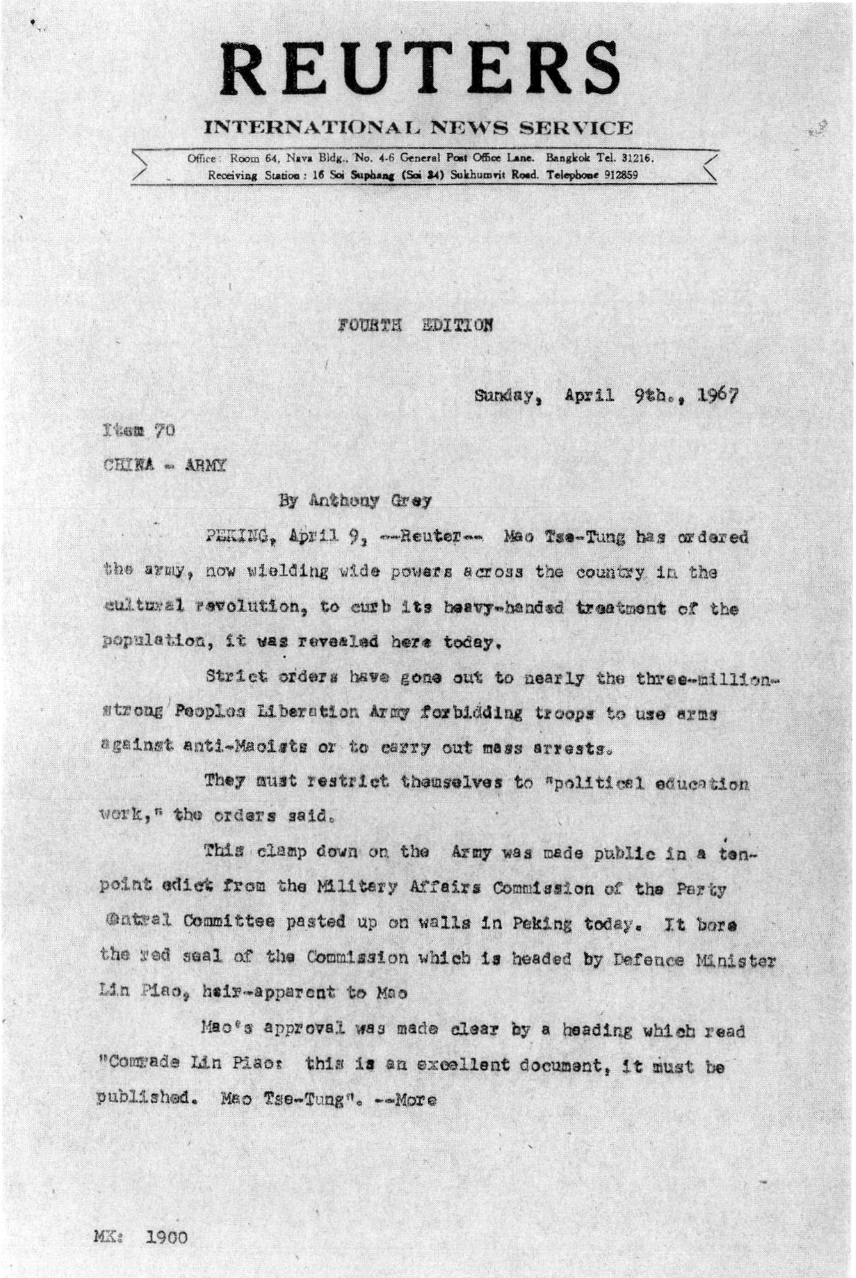

REUTERS

INTERNATIONAL NEWS SERVICE

Office: Room 64, Nava Bldg., No. 4-6 General Post Office Lane. Bangkok Tel. 31216.
Receiving Station : 16 Soi Suphang (Soi 34) Sukhumvit Road. Telephone 912859

FOURTH EDITION

Sunday, April 9th., 1967

Item 70

CHINA - ARMY

By Anthony Grey

PEKING, April 9, --Reuter-- Mao Tse-Tung has ordered the army, now wielding wide powers across the country in the cultural revolution, to curb its heavy-handed treatment of the population, it was revealed here today.

Strict orders have gone out to nearly the three-million-strong Peoples Liberation Army forbidding troops to use arms against anti-Maoists or to carry out mass arrests.

They must restrict themselves to "political education work," the orders said.

This clamp down on the Army was made public in a ten-point edict from the Military Affairs Commission of the Party Central Committee pasted up on walls in Peking today. It bore the red seal of the Commission which is headed by Defence Minister Lin Piao, heir-apparent to Mao

Mao's approval was made clear by a heading which read "Comrade Lin Piao: this is an excellent document, it must be published. Mao Tse-Tung". --More

MK: 1900

FIG. 16. Reuter report, Peking, 9 April 1967

withdrawal. Firstly, concern for his safety; secondly, the importance of maintaining Reuter representation in Peking; and thirdly, 'our £20,000 a year contract with Hsinhua'. In short, a soft response had been deliberately chosen. Ronald Farquhar was sent in Gee's place. After his own return from China, Farquhar heard that one of his Chinese translators had been arrested. He wrote to Mason urging that Reuters should protest, even if to no purpose. 'Reuters didn't gain any face with the Chinese by pulling Jack out without demur as soon as they were asked to.'

The position of Reuter correspondents in Peking had obviously been delicate. It became dangerous soon after Anthony Grey took over as Reuter correspondent in March 1967. In July he was put under house arrest in retaliation for the arrest and imprisonment of eleven Chinese Communist journalists after riots in Hong Kong. He was confined until October 1969—a total of 806 days. On one occasion he was attacked at his house by Red Guards, and for a time he was held in a tiny room.

The Chinese Government presumably believed that action against Grey would force the British and Hong Kong Governments to free the rioters quickly, but this did not happen. The prison sentences for ten of the Communist journalists were completed in September 1969; the eleventh was released at the same time. This enabled the Chinese to release Grey on 4 October 1969 without loss of face. He had kept a secret diary, and this formed the basis for his book, *Hostage in Peking*, published in 1970.

The Peking office was reopened by James Pringle in September 1971. He was accompanied by a second correspondent, partly to improve coverage and partly to provide moral support. The Chinese authorities still insisted upon regarding Reuters as a semi-official organization. Their attitude, Long told the board in July 1977, was likely to fluctuate with shifts in Sino-British relations. Another Grey incident could not be entirely ruled out. Indeed, in April 1976 Peter Griffiths, a later correspondent, was manhandled, briefly arrested, and fiercely interrogated. The Chinese authorities objected to his interviewing people in Tiananmen Square during riots following the death of Premier Chou En-lai. In the 1970s, however, after the *rapprochement* with the United States, the number of foreign correspondents in Peking grew from about 30 in 1971 to about 150. Vergil Berger, who had preceded Grey in Peking, returned in 1987 as chief correspondent to conduct a much-enlarged news operation. One thing remained unchanged, however. There had never been any formal censorship, but correspondents were still called for 'little chats' when the authorities did not like what they had written.

V

The world was not at peace after 1945. Five Reuter staff correspondents were killed on duty during the next thirty years. Derek Pearcey was blown up in a jeep while covering the Korean War in 1951. Bruce Pigott and Ronald Laramy were shot dead during a Vietcong ambush in Saigon in 1968. Najmul Hasan was killed by a land-mine in 1983 while covering the Iran–Iraq War. Photographer Willie Vicoy was fatally wounded during an ambush by Philippine Communist guerrillas in 1986.

The best correspondents did not pretend to be brave, but were often in danger. In September 1960 Sandy Gall, the Reuter correspondent in the Congo during the civil war, was detained and nearly shot as a Belgian spy. In July 1988 Helen Womack, a Moscow correspondent, described for *Reuters World* her feelings while covering the Soviet withdrawal from Afghanistan:

> Exhausted, ravenous, filthy, thirsty and dying for the toilet on the non-stop eight-hour trip through scorching heat and dust, I had little room for thoughts of mortality. But on a later trip by military aircraft to the Soviet border, when I was well fed, watered and rested, I broke down for fear of Stinger missiles.

The experience of Bernd Debusmann, chief correspondent in the Middle East, was particularly testing. In April 1975 he was expelled from Addis Ababa for refusing to reveal his sources regarding a report of the execution of five Ethiopian army officers. After five hours of questioning, the interrogating officer remarked: 'Our prisons are not very pleasant.' Fingering a gun he added pointedly: 'You know, accidents can happen.' In September of the following year Debusmann was wounded by gunfire while visiting Beirut's commercial sector. Most seriously of all, in June 1980 he was shot by a gunman firing from a passing car. This was presumably an attempt at censorship by terror. The general rule everywhere has always been that Reuter correspondents should never risk their lives for the sake of a story. But in practice some stories simply cannot be ignored.

VI

A succession of wars in Asia demanded much attention. The Korean War of 1950-3 was reported less effectively by Reuters than it would have liked. It could not afford the same blanket coverage as the American agencies, and it was often beaten on timings.

For thirty years from the end of the war in the Pacific until the Vietcong capture of Saigon in 1975, Indo-China—Laos, Cambodia, and Vietnam—provided a continuing story, and Reuters assigned many of its best reporters to cover it. By 1967 the Saigon office had grown to a staff of three or four London-based correspondents, plus two or more from Singapore and several local reporters. One locally engaged correspondent, Pham Xuan An, admitted in later years that, as well as working with Reuters and later becoming a correspondent for *Time* magazine, he was an intelligence double agent. He worked for the CIA but even more for the Vietcong. He claimed that he never fed Reuters with false reports: 'if I had I would have been sacked, and no one else was paying me.'

Reporting out of Vietnam was costing Reuters as much as £40,000 a year by 1970. But, as in the Korean War, AP and UPI were able to command much greater resources. Each maintained at least three times as many correspondents on the ground. Reuters was able to earn good revenue, however, by carrying newspapers' own dispatches as special traffic on its recently improved telecommunications link to Singapore.

Pringle served two spells in Saigon (1966–8, 1970–1), but the strain of the assignment meant that most correspondents stayed for only about a year. During the 1968 Tet offensive Saigon was under attack, and the Reuter office itself became exposed. It was located in a house midway between two prime Vietcong targets, the presidential palace and the United States Embassy.

One report from Vietnam by John MacLennan was communicated in full to the Reuter board:

> Hue, Feb. 7 REUTER—Black smoke coiled hundreds of feet above this ancient fortress today as jets pounded North Vietnamese forces within the citadel with 500 pound bombs.
>
> After eight days of tough house-to-house fighting North Vietnamese soldiers still hold half of the mile-square (2.5 sq km) fortress and government troops measure their progress foot by painful foot.
>
> The American and government jets, flying above the mist and drizzle which has shrouded the city for the last few days, used radar bombing techniques to strike at North Vietnamese soldiers entrenched on the citadel walls and around the Imperial Palace. Government artillery in the citadel fires almost constantly at the communist soldiers clinging stubbornly to their positions in the citadel.
>
> In the government-controlled half of the citadel civilians fled the fighting carrying babies, bags of rice and cooking pots.
>
> They crouched to avoid sniper and machine-gun fire as they filed past the lily-covered ponds of the Imperial gardens and dived for cover when-

ever they heard the flat, vicious crack of a Chinese-made AK-47 rifle.

Snipers were using hideouts such as the tops of palm trees which grow all over the citadel, ornamental stone bridges connecting island gardens in the ponds, and tiny pagodas covered in peeling red and yellow paint.

A wounded man used a golf club as a crutch while his whimpering dog, also wounded, hobbled along behind him.

In 1975, when the American evacuation had become inevitable, all Reuter staff with British or American passports were withdrawn. Bernard Edinger, a Frenchman, was flown in to cover the final stages. He qualified for protection from the French Embassy in Saigon, which remained open. Edinger filed the first story under the new Communist regime.

VII

Reuters was to the fore in reporting the decolonization of both the British and French Empires. Doon Campbell was in India to cover the coming of independence on 15 August 1947, and its effects. 'I saw more violence and slaughter in Delhi in the next few weeks', he wrote in his unpublished reminiscences, 'than I had seen in Europe at war.' In these circumstances Campbell instructed the Reuter staff to be more than usually careful not to circulate rumours or to use emotional language; hard-sourced statistics were to be preferred. Twice daily Campbell travelled round Delhi to make a count of the corpses, starting at the very doors of his hotel.

During this period Campbell was to experience a particularly bad example of something which all reporters fear—'bright' but inaccurate rewriting of copy by a sub-editor thousands of miles away in London. Lord Mountbatten, the governor-general, told a press conference that a news agency, 'one that prided itself upon its international reputation for accuracy', had sent a lurid report about Old Delhi being engulfed in blood and flame, when in reality the violence had been on a relatively small scale.

Campbell was horrified to be shown the report by one of Mountbatten's staff, attributed to Reuters in the *Chicago Tribune* and several other American papers. He had sent nothing of the sort, and he cabled Cole asking for a denial that it was a Reuter story. But unfortunately the story had indeed been issued by the North American desk. A sub-editor, deciding that Campbell's copy was pedestrian, had lifted a report from a London newspaper and filed it as a Reuter dispatch without giving the source. The sub was sacked. Cole sent a fulsome apology to the Indian authorities. Campbell, who had been at risk of expulsion, was allowed to stay.

He was still in India when Mahatma Gandhi was assassinated on 30 January 1948. P. R. Roy, a keen young Indian reporter, had asked Campbell's permission to cover a prayer meeting in Delhi to be attended by Gandhi. Roy was told to telephone only 'hot' news. At 5.13 p.m. Campbell's desk telephone rang: 'A man has just fired four shots at Mr Gandhi . . . don't know if he's dead . . . worst feared.' Campbell's immediate flash to London read:

MAN FIRED FOUR SHOTS AT GANDHI POINTBLANK RANGE WORST FEARED.

This gave Reuters a beat of seven minutes.

Campbell hurried to the scene, where Roy described what had happened. Campbell took this eyewitness account back to the office, while Roy stayed to wait for further news of Gandhi. Campbell's phone rang: 'Gandhi dead.' Roy was ahead again. In the event, Campbell's flash on Gandhi's death reached Fleet Street just one minute behind a pick-up from All-India Radio, monitored at Radio House. Reuters gained an impressive beat in London, announcing the shooting at 12.12 and Gandhi's death at 12.32: the respective UP and AP timings for the death were 12.46 and 12.47.

VIII

The 1982 Falklands (Malvinas) War between Britain and Argentina was a curiosity—a very late colonial war. As well as being a story unusual in itself, its handling became of particular significance in the history of Reuters. In the nineteenth century such news would have been reported entirely from a British imperial angle. In 1982 Reupke, the editor-in-chief, did not doubt that the file would be objective. When Renfrew asked if Reupke wished to issue a circular similar to that from Chancellor at the time of the Suez conflict (p. 270), Reupke replied that to do so would be an insult to Reuter staff.

At the start of the conflict Reuters made it easier for the Argentinian authorities to allow it to continue to report from Buenos Aires. Most Reuter staff on British passports were quickly transferred to Montevideo in neighbouring Uruguay; non-British staff were flown in as replacements. A full news file was circulated from Montevideo to Latin

American subscribers outside Argentina. The file on the war in Spanish for Argentina was confined to official news from all quarters, often led by Argentinian material but balanced from other sources.

On 6 June 1982 Reupke explained to Ambassador Ros, the Argentinian representative at the United Nations, that Reuters was not a British news agency, and that only a relatively small part of its business was now conducted in the United Kingdom:

> Reuters takes no position, national or otherwise, in any situation or conflict, whether in the war between Iran and Iraq, the conflict between Israel and the Arab states, or the present conflict between Argentina and Britain . . . we have taken care to explain to the world the Argentinian position and the significance of the islands to the Argentinian people. We have in no different manner reported the position of the British Government.

Reuter correspondents, added Reupke, were drawn from forty-eight different nationalities. 'We take pride in that fact.'

The Argentinian authorities at least half accepted these arguments, although they refused to allow a Reuter correspondent to go with their forces. A similar request was made for a Reuter correspondent to accompany the British task force. This request was granted only belatedly, when Leslie Dowd was allowed on the liner *Canberra*, serving as a troop-ship, which sailed ten days behind the first warships.

The British Ministry of Defence had let the Newspaper Publishers Association allocate places for reporters with the task force, and the NPA had not recognized the claims of Reuters. On 5 April Reupke wrote adroitly to the British defence minister, John Nott, explaining that he might find the file from 'the leading international news organisation' damagingly inadequate if Reuters were not allowed to report the British side, particularly for its subscribers in the United States, Latin America, Europe, and elsewhere.

Dowd with the task force became subject to military censorship. But Reuters did not feel bound to take any account of the 'D' Notice system in London. This was an arrangement originating from just before the First World War under which British editors voluntarily agreed to suppress news for the sake of national security or national interest. Reuters emphasized that it was no more concerned with the British national interest than with that of Argentina. When the secretary of the 'D' Notice committee, Rear-Admiral William Ash, telephoned Pagel, the RWS editor, to complain because Reuters had reported the presence of the British fleet near Ascension Island, he was given a short answer 'h asked if Pagel was not concerned about the safety of 'our forces'. Pagel, whose German accent must have been noticed, replied that this was Ash's business and not that of Reuters. 'I'm not British.' Reuters said that it was only prepared to hold back war stories if their release might put lives in danger. This applied to lives on either side. In practice only one report was delayed. But how could Reuters always be sure about the effects of its stories?

Dowd landed with the British troops. His first dispatch was dated 21 May. Perhaps surprisingly, it read as much like a 'British' human interest story as any Reuter report from a Victorian colonial war:

> WITH HEAVILY-ARMED PARATROOPS SPLASHING THROUGH THE ICY WATER AHEAD OF ME, I JUMPED FROM A LANDING CRAFT AND STRUGGLED ASHORE ON THE ISLANDS THAT HAVE BEEN OUR DESTINATION DURING SIX WEEKS AT SEA.
>
> IN SPARKLING SUNSHINE, THE SOLDIERS RUSHED UP THE BEACH AT THIS TINY SETTLEMENT ON THE NORTHWEST OF EAST FALKLAND ISLAND AND ENCOUNTERED NO RESISTANCE FROM ARGENTINE TROOPS IN THE AREA.
>
> FALKLAND ISLANDERS APPEARED RELAXED AS THEY CAME OUT OF HALF A DOZEN BRIGHTLY-PAINTED FARMHOUSES AND OFFERED THE COMMANDOS CIGARETTES AND CUPS OF TEA . . .
>
> MRS JEWETTE BERNSTONE, 35, AND HER FOUR CHILDREN FROM PORT STANLEY, WHO WERE STAYING WITH FARMER RON DICKSON AND HIS WIFE, TOLD ME 'THE ARGENTINES BEHAVED QUITE WELL'
>
> HER 11-YEAR-OLD SON CHRISTIAN ADDED: 'THEY MADE A FUSS OF KIDS ALL THE TIME AND PATTED US ON THE HEAD. I USED TO SHRIVEL UP.'

IX

Harold King was appointed chief correspondent for France after the liberation of Paris in 1944. He remained in charge until his retirement in 1967. He had good contacts in the French political world, but most importantly, he was closer to de Gaulle in and out of power than any other foreign journalist. He also knew all the best restaurants and best wines in Paris. King was given the title of assistant general manager in 1958, still based in Paris. He was made a commander of the Légion d'Honneur in 1971, a rare honour for a foreigner.

His weakness was that he was a poor manager of staff, irascible and demanding, even while sometimes indulgent with a few favourites. Both the favoured and the unfavoured found this climate exhausting. Only the toughest remained unperturbed when King screamed and even foamed at the mouth over alleged misdemeanours.

The fall of the French Fourth Republic in 1958 and the return to power of de Gaulle were stories particularly suited to King's talents. Throughout the crisis he spent up to sixteen hours each day sounding out opinion in the lobby of the national assembly. Once or more a day he met a representative from de Gaulle's private office in Paris.

Long was assigned to Paris to help cover the story. At King's death in 1990 Long claimed that King had never been prejudiced in his reporting, even though strongly prejudiced in his personal opinions. When a young diplomat in the press department of the French Foreign Office once dared to suggest that King should give a particular slant to a report, he was answered with a fierce lecture on the freedom of the press, punctuated by the banging of King's umbrella on the desk. Admittedly, he was inclined to give de Gaulle ample space and his critics less.

The crucial message from de Gaulle, that he was 'prepared to assume the powers of the Republic', reached his Paris office on 17 May 1958. When King arrived there, a hundred journalists were already milling about outside. They were not allowed in, but King was. He found the AFP representative, Jean Mauriac, with a copy of the message in his hand. 'Take it,' said Mauriac generously. King grabbed a phone, and read out the historic words for transmission to London.

King then hurried to the Chamber of Deputies to collect reaction. He cabled London: 'General de Gaulle's record shows that nothing is further from his nature than to lust after a dictatorship. But most of the politicians inside and outside Parliament think that, whatever he declares beforehand, once back in power he will double-cross them by abolishing Parliament.' This was characteristic King. The emphasis favoured de Gaulle, and yet the report included criticism of him.

Two days later, on 19 May, de Gaulle called a press conference. In preparation King rented a bedroom in the hotel where the gathering was to be held. This room became the base for King and two colleagues. His secretary kept the telephone line open by reading continuously from the New Testament. The three Reuter men came in and out in turn to phone through de Gaulle's statement as it unfolded majestically, followed by his answers to questions. Asked whether he would allow the politicians, if they now voted him into power, later to vote him out, de Gaulle answered that 'procedures become very flexible'. 'All is only too clear,' commented one deputy afterwards to King. 'He wants to brush Parliament aside.' Here was an indication of King's standing. Although he was a known admirer of de Gaulle, politicians of all shades were ready to reveal themselves to him.

X

Coverage of the death in a plane crash in 1961 of Dag Hammarskjöld, the United Nations secretary-general, was to test the Reuter creed that certainty and not presumption must be the basis for a news report. Hammarskjöld was flying from Leopoldville to Ndola for talks with the Congolese leader Moise Tshombe. Gerry Ratzin, the correspondent in Leopoldville, had driven to Ndola to cover the talks. Some reporters, using binoculars, had seen a man, whom they presumed to be the secretary-general, leaving an aeroplane at the far side of the heavily guarded airport. They filed the 'arrival'. Prudently, Ratzin did not, because he had not himself identified Hammarskjöld. Unfortunately, London editorial issued a report of the 'arrival' supplied by the South African Press Association. When this came back on the teleprinter to Leopoldville the Reuter correspondent there, Friedel Ungeheuer, who had seen Hammarskjöld off, realized that he could not possibly have reached Ndola so quickly. Ungeheuer cabled his doubts to London. Campbell, the news manager, phoned Ndola and found that indeed the secretary-general had not landed. Reuters immediately issued a correction saying that, contrary to previous reports, Hammarskjöld had not reached Ndola. UPI stuck by the 'arrival' story for another eight hours, and AP for twelve.

Meanwhile, in Ratzin's words:

> the press corps scattered across the (then) Northern Rhodesian copperbelt in search of Hammarskjoeld. After some fruitless searching, I phoned the Government spokesman in Ndola who said the plane with Hammarskjoeld's body had been found. He added that I was the first journalist he had been able to tell, as the rest were out in the bush somewhere.

Ratzin filed the story to London through SAPA, giving Reuters a thirty-eight-minute beat.

XI

The assassination of President John F. Kennedy on 22 November 1963 was described ten days after the event by Heffernan, chief correspondent in Washington, as 'the greatest story we are ever likely to report'.

Kennedy was shot while being driven in a motorcade through Dallas, Texas. No Reuter reporter was there, and early coverage was taken entirely from AP. It continued to supply much of the material put out by Reuters during the drama of the succeeding days. Great efforts were made, however, to keep the file sufficiently distinctive. American television and radio were monitored continuously, and Reuter reporters were busy at the scene and in Washington.

Ralph Harris, the White House correspondent, immediately flew to Dallas, where Lee Harvey Oswald was already being grilled as the chief suspect. In an account for the record, Harris later described the 'fantastic and fiction-like' atmosphere there:

> The most frenzied scene I have ever experienced greeted me on my arrival outside the Homicide Squad Room on the third floor of Police Headquarters. Oswald was being brought in and out for questioning by cigar-smoking detectives wearing ten-gallon hats. Witnesses were besieged and pinned against the wall for interviews before police, armed with revolvers and shotguns, rescued them and took them away.

Harris established himself in a television transmitting-truck parked outside the building, 'keeping one eye on the possibility of trouble from a large ill-tempered crowd outside and the other on the monitors in the truck'. He described his reaction upon seeing Oswald's murder on screen:

> The fatal shot fired by Jack Ruby into Oswald's abdomen at point-blank range in the presence of armed police and reporters had such a stunning impact that the scene froze into a moment of paralysed amazement. Then pandemonium as Oswald dropped to the concrete floor . . .
>
> I ran to a street telephone two blocks away, filed a snap to New York, dashed back to the TV truck, and then back to the phone to fill in some of the details . . . A crowd of about 200 people crowded around me to listen to what I had to say, and as I was talking to New York I could hear some of them shouting, 'He should get a medal' and 'Let's hope he shot him in the eye' (this took place before Oswald died).
>
> I included these remarks in my story, and then turned around to find a small scowling group threatening to express displeasure with what I had filed. It often happens, particularly in the violence-ridden South, that people do not like to be quoted, even anonymously, when they give vent to their feelings. But I was not interfered with, and the next problem was to find transportation to get to the hospital where Oswald was dying.

XII

An exclusive report following the conquest of Mount Everest in 1953 gave Reuters a story headlined throughout the world. The British expedition was under contract to *The Times*, and on 2 June the paper broke the news of Hillary and Tensing reaching the top. But Reuters secured a notable follow-up beat. After a fourteen-day trek leading his own eleven-porter expedition, Peter Jackson, the Reuter Karachi correspondent, reached the Khumbu Glacier, 18,000 feet up. He there obtained the first interviews with Hillary and Tensing and sent his report back by Sherpa messenger on a 200-mile journey over the mountains to Kathmandu. A week later he heard the story broadcast over the radio. His success owed much to the Delhi correspondent Adrienne Farrell, who had played a vital part in organizing the communications. The couple were married a few months later, and for twenty years they were to serve as a successful team for Reuters in India.

Everest was a story of man conquering nature, always fascinating to the public. Space travel provided an even greater challenge. On 12 April 1961 radio monitoring from Green End gave Reuters a two-minute beat in London with the news of the first manned space flight by Yuri Gagarin, the Soviet cosmonaut. Eight years later, filing directly from Houston mission control centre, Reuters was one minute ahead of AP with news of the first landing on the moon.

Sports news was of increasing importance in the postwar Reuter file. Competition was intense, particularly from AFP. The last major sporting event for which Reuters targeted the United Kingdom was probably the Tokyo Olympic Games of 1964, although even then there were full reports for world regional markets. Reporting of the games every four years required detailed planning, with communications usually demanding great attention.

At the 1972 Munich Olympics Reuter reporters assigned to a sports story found themselves covering a news story. Palestinians seized and killed Israeli hostages. Four Reuter reporters were on the perimeter of the Fürstenfeldbruck airbase where the final shoot-out occurred. Although themselves at a distance from the action, they collected good eyewitness accounts. Yet they were beaten in reporting the main point: they failed to notice the Mayor of Munich leaving the base. He was buttonholed by the single AFP reporter, who secured a major beat with the news that all the hostages were dead.

Four Olympics later, coverage of the 1988 Seoul Games cost

£480,000, fifty times as much as Helsinki in 1952. Just under half of this was for news pictures, now an essential feature. Directly attributable revenue was only £80,000. Once again AFP beat everyone on the main story: it was more than an hour ahead with news of drugs being detected in the urine of Ben Johnson, the winner of the 100 metres.

The Reuter *Sports Guide*, first published for internal circulation in 1988, provided a sport-by-sport survey of how to report everything from Alpine skiing to yachting. The *Guide* emphasized that the development of computerized communications meant that Reuters no longer thought only in terms of media outlets. Retrieval figures showed that Monitor subscribers exhibited 'an enormous appetite for sports news [*including sumo wrestling*], provided it is fast, clear and accurate'.

XIII

Both news of business and news for business were demanding increasing attention. In January 1989 an analysis by Reuters of agency play in ten leading world newspapers taking the Reuter service in English revealed that 58 per cent of their business-news content came from Reuters, 21 per cent from AP, and 11 per cent from AFP. For other news, Reuters was only just ahead of AP—36 per cent against 33 per cent. So it was superiority with business news which gave Reuters its competitive edge. Well over half the total news file now consisted of business news.

On the other hand, business subscribers increasingly expected to be supplied with some general news on their screens. A 'question and answer' paper, prepared at the time of the 1984 flotation, pointed out that although only 6 per cent of revenue was derived from press and broadcasting, total revenue earned from all markets by Reuter news was much greater than this.

By the end of the 1980s about two-thirds of the journalists on the United Kingdom editorial reporting staff were primarily economic journalists. Separation of function was not rigid, however. And the same story might require different presentation as economic news or as general news. A most striking instance of this was the 1987 world stock-market crash. It was covered by Reuters minute by minute from financial centres all over the world. On 21 October, when the markets seemed to have settled down, Macdowall, the chief news editor, congratulated the North American staff on its handling of the story. 'Its copy crackled with authority and energy, and was rich in initiative reporting.' He also emphasized the importance of related coverage from Europe and Asia: 'News is indivisible. Each region must guard the backs of the others.' In the United States the Reuter Business Report kept clients abreast with every development:

Wednesday 14 October

0836(EDT): WASHINGTON—The U.S. trade deficit narrowed to $15.68 billion in August from a record $16.47 billion in July, the Commerce Department said Wednesday.

1119(EDT): WASHINGTON—. . . The improvement in the crucial measure of U.S. trade worldwide was less than had been expected by market analysts . . .

The news quickly undermined confidence in U.S. financial markets, sending stocks, bonds and the dollar tumbling.

1319(EDT): LONDON—British share prices ended sharply lower Wednesday after a fall on Wall Street . . .

1320(EDT): NEW YORK—Wall Street stocks plunged Wednesday . . .

1919(EDT): TORONTO—Declines in gold issues combined with fears of rising inflation and interest rates to drag Toronto stocks sharply lower Wednesday.

2043(EDT): MEXICO CITY—The Mexican stock market, which this year has been the world's most bullish, has fallen more than 10 percent in the last two days, brokers said.

Thursday 15 October

0836(EDT): TOKYO—Share prices tumbled from record levels in Tokyo Thursday as investors were shaken by the record overnight point decline on Wall Street, brokers said.

Friday 16 October

1726(EDT): NEW YORK—WALL STREET'S DOW INDEX DROPS 100 POINTS IN BLACK FRIDAY

Monday 19 October

1107(EDT): NEW YORK—Wall Street stocks nosedived again Monday morning in a wave of frantic selling that outdid even Friday's wild plunge.

1443(EDT): CHICAGO—Chaos gripped stock index futures trading pits Monday as prices suffered their largest opening losses in history.

Tuesday 20 October

0819(EDT): LONDON—Share prices took new punishment round the globe . . .

0833(EDT): TOKYO—Tokyo share prices slumped 14.9 percent Tuesday, the index's worst ever one-day decline, as unbridled panic shot through the market . . .

Wednesday 21 October

0938(EDT): SYDNEY—The world share market crash will affect all types of business in Australia, curb affluent lifestyles, and shake up young executives . . .

1120(EDT): PARIS—STOCK TURMOIL FORCES FRANCE TO DELAY PRIVATIZATON PROGRAM

1200(EDT): ZURICH—GOLD MARKET KEEPS COOL AMID GLOBAL STOCK EXCHANGE TURMOIL

1351(EDT): BONN—West Germany called on the United States on Wednesday to play its part in an international accord to coordinate economic policies and stabilize currencies.

1802(EDT): NEW YORK—Tokyo and London investors took their cue from Wall Street's rebound in a global stock market rally Wednesday that broke records in all three financial capitals.

The editorial report for October congratulated itself that economic- and general-news reporting had been 'impeccably integrated', while 'the regions tossed the ball back and forth between them with all the deftness of a pride of circus sealions'. Certainly, there had been truly global coverage.

XIV

The year 1989 was a turning-point in history, notable for the break-up of the Communist empire in Eastern Europe. The collapse of the Communist empire had been foreshadowed and frustrated in Hungary in 1956 and in Czechoslovakia in 1968. During the crushing of the Hungarian uprising, Ronald Farquhar had reported the fighting on the streets of Budapest. He was allowed to use the diplomatic radio at the British embassy after other communication links had been cut. This gave Reuters a series of beats.

In 1968 AP was first with the dramatic news of the Soviet invasion of Czechoslovakia, which put an end to Alexander Dubček's 'Communism with a human face'. But Vincent Buist, the Reuter correspondent in Prague, scored with graphic stories of the tanks rolling into the city:

CROWDS OF CZECHS, MANY OF THEM STUDENTS, ROAMED THROUGH THE STREETS OF THE CAPITAL ON FOOT OR IN LORRIES CHANTING SUP-

PORT FOR PARTY LEADER ALEXANDER DUBCEK, WHO HAD GIVEN THEM
NEW FREEDOMS IN DEFIANCE OF THE KREMLIN, AND HURLING ABUSE
AT SOVIET TROOPS.

SOME PEOPLE SCRAMBLED OVER SOVIET TANKS, ARGUING WITH THE
CREWS. ONE YOUNG GIRL BANGED ON THE BARREL OF A SOVIET PARA-
TROOP LIEUTENANT'S RIFLE AND YELLED: 'GO HOME, DO YOU KNOW
WHERE YOU ARE. YOU ARE IN MY COUNTRY. GO AWAY, YOU IDIOT.'

Buist also obtained an exclusive account, supplied by Czechoslovak contacts, of the abduction of Dubček.

Reuters had been first with the news of the erection of the Berlin Wall
in 1961: it was first again in 1989 with the news that it was to come
down. Such dominance of the continuing story out of East Germany was
the reward for careful groundwork. Since the opening of the Reuter
office in East Berlin thirty years earlier Reuters had maintained close contact with the East German Government through the official agency,
Allgemeiner Deutscher Nachrichtendienst (ADN). From 1987, in antici-
pation of the story to come, Reuters had increased its staff numbers in
eastern Europe, and it assembled some of its best-qualified reporters in
Berlin during the final days. The national angle was fully covered for the
German-language service, while Reuter photographers and Visnews cam-
eramen were present in force.

The event which heralded the crumbling of Communist rule was the
resignation of the Honecker Government on 7 November 1989. Reuters
was nine minutes ahead even of ADN, which found the story hard to
believe. When the wall was opened, Reuters was ahead again in London.
Martin Nesirky followed up with an eyewitness account from West
Berlin on 10 November:

> Hundreds of East Berliners swarmed across checkpoint Charlie and
> West Berliners stood at the Berlin Wall on Friday as a divided city was
> reunited in a tumultuous embrace.
>
> Wide-eyed women clutched their faces, crowds hugged and cheered
> and East German border guards looked on in bewilderment.
>
> At the nearby Friedrichstrasse station crossing, a crowd of West
> Germans crossed to the East and staged a pro-reform protest, chanting:
> 'The Wall is down, the Wall is down.'
>
> At the Brandenburg Gate, two East German girls scaled the Wall,
> helped over into the West by young West Berliners.
>
> The girls telephoned their startled mothers in East Berlin and told them
> they would be home after looking round the shops.

China was the country where the barriers did not come down. To report such a big and difficult story in such a huge country required large resources. About fifty-five staffers from Reuters and thirty from Visnews were involved in covering the demonstrations for democracy in 1989; nineteen were Chinese-speakers. Reuters in Peking patiently followed the story from the first student demonstrations in April until and beyond the Tiananmen Square blood-bath of 3–4 June. The square was watched day and night for both text and pictures. On 3 June at 20.34 (GMT) Guy Dinmore, the chief correspondent in Peking, reported:

> Armoured troops crashed into the heart of Peking early on Sunday killing over 40 civilians and wounding hundreds more who tried to block their way.
>
> In Tiananmen Square, the focus of weeks of pro-democracy demonstrations that humiliated China's ageing leaders, crowds of students and workers huddled waiting for their fate.
>
> Doctors and witnesses at four hospitals said they knew that at least forty-two people had been shot dead and more than 200 wounded. There were unconfirmed accounts of at least 20 more deaths. . . .
>
> 'It's a sheer massacre' a Chinese journalist said.

XV

Reuters was very successful in its reporting of the great events of 1989. Was it none the less unconsciously biased? In the internal editorial magazine, *Highlights*, for April 1990 Dinmore asked some searching questions from Peking, typical of the commendable self-questioning often to be found among Reuter journalists:

> Are we really a 'world information agency' as we rather pompously like to claim? Or, at least in its news coverage, is Reuters still very much a Western-based, Western-looking organisation? Whose views do we express?
>
> Watching events unfold in Eastern Europe, I couldn't help but sense sometimes that elation in our reporting had crossed that hazy boundary into glee . . . It was inevitable that the 'collapse of communism in Eastern Europe' would be portrayed as just that.
>
> But does it, as our and other commentaries often imply, vindicate what is left in the west?

Dinmore then turned to recent coverage of his own territory, China. He described this as 'a sobering experience', apparently suggesting that pro-

Western bias had revealed itself in the form of too much optimism about the outcome, from himself among others:

> The sources we often quoted—diplomats or otherwise—were as much betrayed by their own wishful thinking as we were. Analyses we wrote at the time saying this must be the end of the Deng Xiaoping era were at least premature. I wish I could go back and insert a few more 'But on the other hand . . .'

In the December 1990 number of *Highlights*, Macdowall answered Dinmore's question about pro-Western bias. It was, Macdowall suggested, a matter not of bias but of writing for a market. Most Reuter subscribers were located in Western or Westernized countries. 'If we cater primarily for the West it should not be because of ethnic or cultural bias but because we pay most attention to the needs of those clients who pay us most for our services.' On the other hand, emphasized Macdowall, Reuters did aspire to provide information to the whole world. It must therefore strike a balance between commercial considerations and 'our ethical obligation to provide a news service whose values transcend colour, creed or religion'. Additional national-language services were being introduced during the late 1980s. These variously provided international domestic or economic news; they sought to demonstrate to the countries in question not simply that Reuters was no longer 'British' but also that it was no longer 'foreign'.

Was Dinmore measuring himself and his colleagues against an unattainable standard of perfection? Or against an unsuitable standard of neutrality? Long's warning against 'evenhandedness' was quoted early in the present chapter: the aim was not neutrality but objectivity. And Reuters in 1989 was much more objective in its reporting than in 1939, and very much more objective than in 1889.

FIFTEEN

Retrospect from 1989

I

B Y the late 1980s Reuters was very different from the news agency of earlier times. It had embraced computer technology with great enthusiasm and with great reward. It was operating with much success within a new climate of communication between places and between people.

Reuters had always tried to keep up with the latest innovations, but in the past the effect had been to modernize the company without really changing it. Such had been the consequence, for example, of the introduction of wireless services during the 1920s and 1930s. By contrast, the development of the Reuter Monitor and other services did much more than keep Reuters up to date: these innovations in large part transformed it.

The introduction of computerized services changed Reuters not because of the wonder of the technology—wireless had also been wonderful—but because it meant a change of main market for the organization. It still continued energetically to serve the world's press, radio, and television; but it was now earning most of its money from the global financial industry. In 1989 revenue from media products totalled £78.4 million, whereas revenue from transaction products amounted to £162.7 million and from information products £945.8 million. There were 16,000 customers receiving Reuter news and information worldwide on over 200,000 screens. Only 9 per cent of these customers were in the media; some 60 per cent were finance houses; 25 per cent were business corporations; 6 per cent were Government organizations.

There had been a radical shift in what the majority of its customers received from Reuters: now they chiefly received 'information'. The collapse from the early 1970s of the Bretton Woods system of fixed exchange rates had set in motion a revolution in the markets. Currency values were fluctuating against each other, and dealers wanted to take advantage of slight but rapid changes to make profits. The Monitor Money Rates and other services collected and disseminated the necessary real-time information twenty-four hours a day worldwide. The range of information available came to include foreign-exchange rates, stock-exchange prices, major commodity prices, securities, and options.

Reuters was not just serving individual firms, but was contributing towards the working of the global economy at large. This point was emphasized by Peter Job, the managing director, in a talk to the Royal Institute of International Affairs in 1991 on the influence of Reuters:

> Periodic snapshots of economies at fixed exchange rates had to give way to a moving video . . . It was here that Reuters was the agent of change. Utilising computer technology harnessed to information flow, it was possible to give instant valuations of a country's exchange rate to a broad spectrum of users across the world . . . Using such systems the experts in the banking industry could take a real-time look at national pretensions, and by taking a speculative view of the future, start to use fast information flows to discount what might happen in the following hours, days, weeks or months. I think it is arguable that in this very specialised and highly focused area, we were amongst the first to exploit the freedom to alter and adjust the known values of the world.

In the new climate currency values and other information were often linked to background economic news, which in turn might have a general-news dimension. The oil-price explosion of the 1970s was a striking instance of linkage between commodity-price information and news. Reuters took care that its real-time information and news services were not rigidly separated. Appropriately, it made news stories available on Monitor screens.

In 1989 Walter Wriston, a former chairman of Citicorp and a director of Reuters, described the new situation: 'The world now operates on the information standard, which has replaced Bretton Woods and the gold standard. When the President goes out in the Rose Garden and says something, over 200,000 screens light up in the trading rooms of the world.'

At the same time the media audience for press, radio, and television was extending its interest beyond general news—finding interest even in exchange rates, as their impact upon society and politics became apparent. Stimulated by daily exposure to television, this wider awareness was no longer confined to times of crisis or 'crash', but was becoming continuous. Not just serious newspapers began to offer business pages or sections.

During the 1970s and 1980s the new Reuters had placed itself closely and very profitably in touch with these shifts in expectation among both the world's traders and the world reading, listening, and viewing public. The 1989 annual report summed up carefully yet boldly:

> Reuters is, first and foremost, a news organisation. These days the company's activities extend far beyond those of a conventional news agency, supplying the media with its raw material. And yet the provision of news is central to our worldwide operations.

> Reuters provides customers, whether they be in the media, the financial markets or the corporate world, with an authoritative and accurate picture of a scene that is in a constant state of flux. Aided by the most sophisticated technology available, we aim not only to provide customers with general and specialised news when and as it happens but also to give them the means to process this flood of information.

An independent assessment came from the American *Forbes* magazine (30 October 1989): 'Not long ago Reuters was a poor but proud ward of the British newspaper industry, beset like the rest of Fleet Street by lousy labor relations and lazy management. No more. Reuters has turned itself into nothing less than the world's leading supplier of computerized information.' Mark Wood, the editor-in-chief from 1989, made the point more succinctly: 'Reuters is pacing the world.'

In doing so, in responding vigorously from the 1960s to a new opportunity, Reuters was following the example set by its founder, Julius Reuter, in the 1850s and 1860s. And in the process it was still committed to maintaining the standards which he had set—standards of accuracy, speed, and impartial distribution.

A fourth standard, that of objectivity, had been harder for Reuters to attain during its first hundred years, largely because of the pull of conscious or unconscious British 'patriotism', especially in wartime. Then in 1956 its reporting of the Suez crisis marked a turning-point for Reuters. When Chancellor exhorted his staff not to take sides because British opinion was divided, he appeared to be still assuming that Reuters was 'British'. Yet Reuter reporting from Egypt began to earn a reputation for objectivity of a higher kind. From that period the agency was to be increasingly credited with a supranational perspective.

Chancellor himself can be seen in retrospect as a transitional figure. While serving as Far Eastern manager in China in the 1930s he had been an active representative of the old British imperial order. Yet by the time of his resignation in 1959 he had started to claim that Reuters was 'not an organ for presenting British news'. He had been a protégé of Jones, a lifelong imperialist, and both men accepted offers of British knighthoods. In significant contrast, two later chief executives, Long and Renfrew, made it clear that they would never do so.

II

From 1984 Reuters was a public company. It soon had about 30,000 shareholders worldwide. Fears began to be voiced about their possible influence. Might shareholder insistence upon the making of profits to pay dividends provoke a crisis if Reuters ever ran into serious financial difficulties? Might shareholders demand the pruning or sale of some or all of the media services, if they were losing money?

In answer to these fears, the Reuter management emphasized that the media services were an asset, financially and strategically. Firstly, general news was important to the economic services. Secondly, the economic-news services were highly successful, and their revenue was not included in the media-products total. Finally, the availability of general news on screen, which had been reported and edited with the needs of the economic-services subscribers in mind, gave the company's non-media products an extra competitive dimension.

In the budget and plan for 1985-7 Renfrew recognized the new importance of shareholder expectations. He stated two basic objectives. The second was to secure the longer-term future of the company by 'aggressive development'. But the first was 'to sustain short and medium-term revenue and profit growth rates in line with high shareholder expectations'. After going public, Reuters succeeded in satisfying the first of these objectives while vigorously pursuing the second:

TABLE 15.1. Rise in revenue and
profit figures since flotation in 1984
(£000)

	Revenue	Net profit
1985	434,121	55,360
1989	1,186,910	182,863

'Aggressive development' led to the acquisition of nine companies in North America and the United Kingdom. The aim was to enable Reuters to offer a 'total package' of services. Renfrew assured the board in February 1985 that the purchase of Rich Inc. of Chicago for $58.5 million was justified because of the 'perfect strategic fit'; Rich manufactured trading-room systems. Another acquisition was the purchase of Institutional Network Corporation (Instinet) for just over $100 million in 1987. Instinet ran a computerized equities-trading service. This acquisition ensured that Reuter customers in the securities market would be able to obtain information and deal through one keyboard in the same way as those in the money markets. The perception of Reuters as a force in North America was much enhanced by this decisive intervention.

Prudently, in 1981 Reuters had decided not to buy UPI, the second United States agency, which was on offer upon easy terms. Such an acquisition would have drawn Reuters deeply into the American domestic news market where AP, as a newspaper co-operative, enjoyed unbeatable strength-in-depth.

III

The biggest pessimists within Reuters in the 1980s were (as always) the journalists. Many of those who harked back to the camaraderie of the smaller Reuters of the 1960s even enjoyed remembering their own poverty. Reuters, they complained, had become a business just like any other. The sense of the special nature of Reuters, which had been so powerful a driving force throughout its history—and not least during the initial daring excursion into computerized products—was thought by many long-serving staff to have diminished during the 1980s. The management certainly made it clear that the new public company could not be run on 'family' lines. In a 1989 interview Wood dismissed the 'cradle-to-grave' approach as outdated. 'We can't be both a successful growing organisation and the Civil Service or the BBC.' This did not mean that the management had in fact lost its sense of the specialness of Reuters. There had been no doubt some loss of contact, aggravated by the very rapid increase in staff numbers worldwide resulting especially from the acquisitions. World numbers grew from 3,865 at the end of 1984 to 10,071 five years later. By 1989 the 4,274 technical staff constituted much the largest category, compared with 1,640 in editorial. There were 1,768 in sales and marketing.

Inevitably, the Reuter culture was changing. For over a hundred years that culture had been predominantly 'British'—flourishing not just in London, but in the main Reuter outposts throughout the formal and informal British Empire. The culture had been sustained by the British expatriates who provided most of the senior staff, and it was more or less accepted by the non-British local staff. During the 1980s the British predominance was being reduced, at least in terms of numbers. The 10,071 staff at the end of 1989 were drawn from 160 nationalities, with ten nationalities achieving three-figure totals. The British (3,308) and Americans (2,577) reached four figures.

Was Reuters, then, no longer a British-dominated company? Some said not. The best people, they thought, could rise regardless of nationality. This belief was strong among those who were themselves doing well in the United States. It perhaps reflected the fact that the Americans, as the second-largest group of employees, had the most to gain by playing down the Britishness of Reuters. Staff in continental Europe were much less likely to accept that Reuters had ceased to be British-dominated. If it had changed, said some, it was only because it was now dominated by the Anglo-Saxons together, British and American. Not all Europeans thought this a cause for complaint: many small-country nationals were glad to work for a British or Anglo-Saxon company of such high repute.

Reuters remained male-dominated. A handful of women journalists had played significant parts during the twentieth century, but they had been the exception. Even by 1991 there were comparatively few women in middle- and senior-management positions, only 66 out of 666.

If not British or Anglo-Saxon, then what? About 1980 the idea of moving the headquarters to Geneva was considered and rejected. Job later dismissed such 'pallid internationalism'. He preferred a strong centre in London balanced by strong local organization. This, he suggested, might require the creation of more local subsidiary companies. These gave Reuters greater appeal to local staff, and circumvented the charge that Reuter products were 'foreign'. Most importantly, such a structure also brought tax advantages.

Others in Reuters in the late 1980s were saying that the structure of the company should reflect the fact that it was now product-led internationally. Certainly, one of the strengths of Reuters throughout the 1980s lay in its wide range of products and services. It had become market-sensitive, striving not simply to satisfy expressed customer needs but to anticipate them. To this end, Reuters invested heavily in research and development during the 1980s—£3.2 million in 1980, £59.7 million in 1989.

Julius Reuter in his prime had kept a close eye on the latest developments in communications technology. In the 1860s he had even briefly acquired his own cables as part of his plan to dominate the international news scene. He was frustrated in this, and for nearly a century Reuters claimed virtue for itself in not owning any communication channels. This

demonstrated, so the argument ran, that Reuters was not seeking a monopoly in supplying news. From the 1960s Reuters once more became
deeply involved on its own account in communications. Powerful trading
systems required powerful communications systems. Reuters developed
the world's largest private network. The aim was to lock out competitors
by making comprehensive products available which were tied to Reuter
communications systems. As in Julius Reuter's day, Reuters was aspiring
not simply to compete but to dominate.

Towards the end of the 1980s priority was being given to the
Integrated Data Network (IDN). This was a global 'highway for data',
intended gradually to replace the Monitor system. The aim was compre-
hensiveness and 100 per cent accuracy in databases, plus rapid data-
retrieval times for subscribers (two seconds) and in changing data on
display (one second). The first services on IDN, launched during 1987,
were futuristically named Equities 2000, Commodities 2000, and Energy
2000.

Reuters was able to present its annual revenue figures either by product
or by area. Such double measurement was intended to illustrate the broad
strength of Reuters as an international organization with a growing product range:

TABLE 15.2. *Revenue figures in 1989* (£m.)[a]

	Revenue	% of global revenue
Real-time information	775.8	65
Historical information	40.9	4
Trading-room systems	162.7	14
Transaction products	129.1	11
Media products	78.4	7

[a] The breakdown by area was: REMA—£723.8m.; RA—£249.4m.;
RAM—£234.9m.

IV

The acquisitions had brought some outsiders straight into prominent
positions. Were they all aware of the Reuter Trust principles? A reminder
was thought desirable. 'Integrity, independence and freedom from bias',
explained a 'Code of Conduct', dated 1 November 1988, 'must be
demonstrable daily in the work and activity of all Reuter employees.'

The Reuter Trust had been greatly strengthened at the time of the

flotation in 1984. The powers of the trustees were the strongest of the
defences put in place at that period to protect Reuters against taint or
take-over. A second defence was the limitation of any shareholder to a 15
per cent stake.

In 1988 the effectiveness of this restriction was demonstrated when
Rupert Murdoch increased his holding in AAP, thus bringing his total
number of Reuter 'A' shares to about 23 per cent. He disposed of the
excess 8 per cent under the watchful eyes of the trustees. In 1989 the 'A'
share structure was dismantled. It had been devised in 1984 as a third line
of defence. Each share had been given four votes—as against one vote
per 'B' share—in order to ensure that the newspaper organizations
retained a built-in voting majority. After prolonged discussion among the
interested parties, all the 'A' shares were now converted into ordinary
shares for sale. This meant that the PA and NPA owners of the shares
were finally giving up control of Reuters. The trustees accepted that this
was not dangerous, and was indeed desirable. It made Reuter shares more
marketable by removing the two-tier structure which had provoked
strong objection from some institutional investors in 1984.

The hope was expressed by Hogg, the chairman, and by Renfrew, the
managing director, that in future the Reuter board would function like
that of any other public company, with less sectionalism. The expectation
was also that there would be room for more executive directors. Job,
Ure, and Villeneuve joined the board in 1988; Wood in 1990.

During board discussions on 15 June 1988 Sir Richard Storey—the son
of Samuel Storey, the chairman in 1941—had asked directly if the dis-
mantling of the 'A' shares 'would put the integrity of Reuters at risk'.
Renfrew answered that 'the Founders Share Company was quite capable
of doing its job'. The careful scrutiny of the deal by the trustees, whose
powers derived from their control of the Founders Share, demonstrated
that indeed it was.

A more elusive threat to the good name of Reuters resulted from the
daily appearance of its name on business screens all over the world.
Reuter products had become vital and visible tools of the capitalist system. Had Reuters unwittingly become a tool of the system in a second
sense of the word 'tool'? Had it contributed to the rise of the materialistic
'yuppie' culture of the 1980s? In Sweden and elsewhere the yuppie condition was defined as possession of 'a fat salary, a red Porsche and a
Reuter terminal'.

FIG. 17. The 'yuppie' dimension

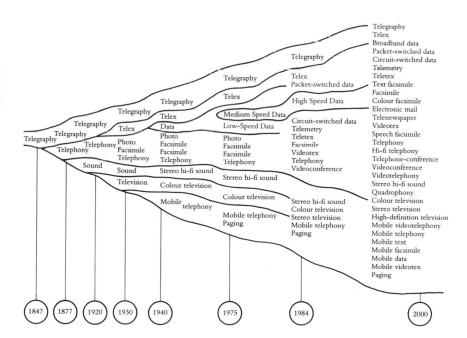

FIG. 18. Telecommunications: Prospects for the year 2000

V

This was blaming Reuters unfairly. Yet undoubtedly the impact of the services supplied by Reuters had become more noticeable and more important than ever before. In Julius Reuter's day the impact had been slower, but it was already apparent. If Reuter were to return at the end of the twentieth century, he would not be surprised by the activities of the company which bears his name. He would be glad to find a continuing commitment to accuracy and speed, and to impartiality in distribution. He would welcome the integration of general and economic news. He would be pleased by the emphasis upon using the latest technology. He would be intrigued to find Reuters so well placed between buyer and seller. He would be glad to find Reuters strong in Germany. He would be interested in its future in Japan. He would be happy that it had at last achieved a truly worldwide presence. Not least, he would be delighted that Reuters was making large profits.

APPENDIX
Comparison of Results 1952–1989 (£000)

Note: All figures are as originally reported in the group accounts of Reuters Limited (1952–83) and Reuters Holdings PLC (1984–89). Figures have not been restated to reflect subsequent events, e.g. changes of accounting policy, legislation, mergers.

	Revenue	% Increase	Profit/(Loss) before tax	% Increase/ (decrease)	Profit/(Loss) before tax as a % of revenue	Profit/(Loss) attributable to ordinary shareholders	% Increase/ (decrease)
1951	1,435.5		2.1			(7.5)	
1952	1,572.9	9.6	31.8	1,430.7	2.0	19.1	355.1
1953	1,667.2	6.0	15.9	(50.0)	1.0	10.5	(44.8)
1954	1,703.8	2.2	0.1	(99.1)	0.0	(10.2)	(197.2)
1955	1,788.6	5.0	11.8	8,346.4	0.7	6.7	165.2
1956	1,934.7	8.2	(19.6)	(265.5)	(1.0)	(18.8)	(381.6)
1957	2,042.2	5.6	38.3	295.9	1.9	27.2	244.9
1958	2,194.3	7.4	3.8	(90.2)	0.2	(6.0)	(122.1)
1959	2,270.3	3.5	35.9	854.8	1.6	18.1	401.2
1960	2,407.3	6.0	(18.5)	(151.6)	(0.8)	(25.8)	(242.5)
1961	2,706.8	12.4	70.9	482.7	2.6	39.6	253.4
1962	2,942.5	8.7	77.6	9.4	2.6	36.7	(7.3)
1963	3,155.8	7.2	53.3	(31.3)	1.7	26.8	(27.0)
1964	3,570.8	13.2	(57.1)	(207.0)	(1.6)	(51.0)	(290.3)
1965	3,992.9	11.8	60.6	206.2	1.5	71.4	239.9
1966	4,330.3	8.5	39.4	(35.0)	0.9	48.1	(32.6)
1967	4,840.0	11.8	(26.5)	(167.2)	(0.5)	(28.3)	(158.3)
1968	6,427.7	32.8	21.3	180.3	0.3	16.5	158.3
1969	8,826.9	37.3	213.7	904.9	2.4	209.6	1,171.5
1970	10,490.7	18.8	208.4	(2.5)	2.0	194.8	(7.1)

	Revenue	% Increase	Profit/(Loss) before tax	% Increase/ (decrease)	Profit/(Loss) before tax as a % of revenue	Profit/(Loss) attributable to ordinary shareholders	% Increase/ (decrease)
1971	11,896.6	13.4	306.5	47.1	2.6	284.9	46.2
1972	13,846.5	16.4	400.0	30.5	2.9	374.9	31.6
1973	17,494.6	26.3	1,023.3	155.8	5.8	798.9	113.1
1974	22,531.8	28.8	784.9	(23.3)	3.5	569.4	(28.7)
1975	29,921.0	32.8	1,124.0	43.2	3.8	1,026.0	80.2
1976	41,921.0	40.1	3,225.0	186.9	7.7	2,954.0	187.9
1977	53,487.0	27.6	3,218.0	(0.2)	6.0	2,892.0	(2.1)
1978	67,712.0	26.6	3,649.0	13.4	5.4	3,167.0	9.5
1979	76,309.0	12.7	3,515.0	(3.7)	4.6	3,100.0	(2.1)
1980	90,095.0	18.1	3,886.0	10.6	4.3	3,246.0	4.7
1981	138,804.0	54.1	16,681.0	329.3	12.0	13,994.0	331.1
1982	179,913.0	29.6	36,730.0	120.2	20.4	33,385.0	138.6
1983	242,630.0	34.9	55,253.0	50.4	22.8	11,907.0	(64.3)
1984	312,990.0	29.0	74,279.0	34.4	23.7	42,610.0	257.9
1985	434,121.0	38.7	93,562.0	26.0	21.6	54,312.0	27.5
1986	620,900.0	43.0	130,077.0	39.0	21.0	80,268.0	47.8
1987	866,875.0	39.6	178,754.0	37.4	20.6	108,831.0	35.6
1988	1,003,249.0	15.7	215,371.0	20.5	21.5	126,054.0	15.8
1989	1,186,910.0	18.3	283,059.0	31.4	23.8	180,634.0	43.3

ACKNOWLEDGEMENTS

In addition to those mentioned in the Preface, the following Reuter staff (and spouses) worldwide, past and present, have helped the History Project (with apologies if any names have been omitted):

Miss S. Abbott; the late Tommy Aldeguer; Mohsin Ali; Margaret Alliston; Anura Amunugama; Gladys Atkins; Gregory Augspurger; Mo Bal; Anthony Barker; C. R. Graham Barrow; Tom Bell; Peter Benjamin; Vergil Berger; Robert Bernecky; Mrs Ursula Bettany; Colin Bickler; Derek Blackman; George Cromarty Bloom; Barbara Bain; Brian Bain; Jan Bradshaw; Phil Bradshaw; the late Jim Broad; Jonathan Broadbent; Nancy Bobrowitz; Annette von Broecker; Daniel Brooksbank; David Brough; Daniel Campbell; Doon Campbell; Ian Capps; Nick Carter; the late Sir Christopher Chancellor; Lady Chancellor; Janiss Chai; H. K. Chang; Tony Cuccia; Melanie Cilliers; Simon Climer; Michael Cooling; Tony Cornish; Correspondence Department, London; Patrick Crosse; David Cutler; Francis Daniel; Dorothy Delman; Gill Denvir; Joan Dixon; Diana Drayton; Sarah Dyer; Eddie Edbrooke; Mike Edbrooke; Bob Elphick; Bob Etherington; Bob Evans; Catrin Evans; Gillian Farnfield; Ronald Farquhar; Jonathan Fenby; Don Ferguson; Reginald Foster; David Friedman; Alfred Geiringer; Ronald Gladman; Ron Golden; Caroline Goudie; Roger Gough; Reg Gratton; Mrs Betty Green; Robert D. Green; Peter Griffiths; Shahe Guebenlian; Andrew Gumbel; Jimmy Hahn; David Harkavy; Ellen Harris; Ralph Harris; Simon Haydon; Rene de Heer; Pat Heffernan; Jim Henry; the late Ingo Hertel; Raymond Hibnick; Sir Christopher Hogg; Peter Holland; the late Duncan Hooper; Allen Horstmanshof; Louise Horstmanshof; Brian Horton; John Hull; Alan Humphreys; Geoffrey Imeson; Adrienne Jackson; Peter Jackson; Derek Jameson; Graham Jenkins; Aleco Joannides; Peter Job; Cynthia Johnson; Ken Jones; the late Nigel Judah; David Keefe; Adam Kellett-Long; Julian Kerr; Ted Kerr; Mike King; Maggie Klein; Joe Laitin; John Lawrenson; Harold Leblang; Michael Littlejohns; Kirsten Lloyd; Anne Long; Gerald Long; Luxemburg office; Charles Lynch; Des Maberley; Ian McCrone; Clare McDermott; the late Ian Macdowall; Henry Manisty; Jill Mann; Patrick Mannix; Gordon Martin; Dean Matthews; Barry May; Seaghan Maynes; Tjet Meijer; Philip Melchior; Howard Meltzer; Vernon Morgan; Trevor Myles; Serge Nabokoff; Michael Neale; Helga Nelson; Michael Nelson; Andrew Nibley; Dorothy Nicholson; Marc Niederhauser; Lesley Ntelbi; Kate O'Brien; Patrick O'Sullivan; Hans Ouwerkerk; Manfred Pagel; E. T. Paine; John Parcell; the late Monty Parrott; Sara Pendlebury; the late Muriel Penn; Phan Xuan An; H. Pickering; Rodney Pinder; Michael Posner; James Pringle; Philip Pullella; Ruth Quail; Jochen

Raffleberg; Michael Rank; John Ransom; Gerry Ratzin; Chris Reddy; Mike Reilly; Scott Rumbold; Daphne Renfrew; Glen Renfrew; Michael Reupke; Syd Rice; Annette Richards; D. Kimpton Rogers; John Rogers; Sue Rowe; Bruce Russell; David Russell; Nat Sager; Chantal Sagot; Feisal Samath; Solange de Santis; Len Santorelli; Anny Schlitz; Bob Schnitzlein; Robert A. Scott; Pat Scott Porter; Felix Sergio; Ian P. Sharp; Peter Sharrock; Richard Shaw; R. Shepard; Phil Siegel; Ranjit Da Silva; Dalton De Silva; Carol Smith; Peter Smith; Stephen Somerville; John Stephens; the late Brian Stockwell; Corinna Stowell; William Swallow; Yasuo Takahashi; John Talbot; Mary Talbot; Phillip Taylor; Christopher Thomas; Brian Timms; T. Tsukazaki; Herbert Ückerman; Stuart Underhill; David Ure; Peter Wade; Heinz Wagner; V. Warketin; Hilary Warren; Sydney Weiland; the late Warren White; Lynn Whiteman; Rachel Whittacker; Howard Whitten; Peter Wisbey; Mark Wood; Nadia Wooldridge; Patrick Worsnip; the late Henry Zaleski; Marika van Zanten; Jeff Zomper.

The author is also grateful for the help of the following:

Aachen Newspaper Museum; Bill Abbey, Institute of Germanic Studies, University of London; Abraham Lincoln Association, Illinois; Letih Adams, Warner Brothers Archives, University of Southern California; Africana Museum, Johannesburg (Helen Haynes and Sandra de Wet); Agence France Presse, Paris; Jonathan Andrews, British Library; Archives Municipales, Valenciennes; Archives de la Préfecture de Police, Paris; Archives de la Ville de Paris; Steve Ashton, Institute of Commonwealth Studies; Melanie Aspey, News International plc; Australian Archives, ACT, Canberra; the Leo Baeck Institute; Robert Baldwin, Royal Observatory, National Maritime Museum; Lady Barnetson; Beincke Library, Yale University; Elaine Benfatto, Kress Library of Business and Economics, Harvard University; Professor Bruno Benfey; Christopher Benfey; Professor O. T. Benfey; Tom Benisch, South African Library, Cape Town; C. Benson, Trinity College, Dublin; L. Berkowitz, Linklaters and Paines; Prem Bhatia; Bibliothèque Historique de la Ville de Paris; Bibliothèque Nationale, Paris; Bibliothèque Royale, Brussels; Bob Boas, S. G. Warburg; David Bowcock, Cumbria Record Office, Carlisle; Peter Boyden, National Army Museum; Sir Theodor Bray; Roger Bridgeman, Science Museum; British Library; Lesley Brits, Kimberley Africana Museum; Michelle Brown, British Library; Deutscher Postmuseum, Frankfurt; Robin Burgess; Lady Burgess; Alan Burnet; Tim Cadogan, Cork County Library; Canadian Pacific Archives; Jane Canovan, Solicitors' Complaints Bureau; Cape Archives Depot, Cape Town; Lee Casey, Australian Associated Press; Madame Caullier, University of Liège; Rudi V. de Ceuster, Agence Belga; Sally Childs-Helton, Indiana Historical Society; Pamela Clark, Royal Archives, Windsor Castle; Clark Spence and Co., Galle; Josephine Coffey, Australian Stock Exchange, Sydney; College of Arms; Wendel Collins, Associated Press; Graeme Conolly, Australian Associated Press; Corporation of London Records Office; Revd John Correira-Alfonso, Bombay; Cory Library,

Rhodes University, Grahamstown; C. Cove-Smith, National Westminster Bank; M. C. F. Cox, Hasly Lightly and Hemsley, Solicitors; Mona Cram, Newfoundland Provincial Resources Centre; E. Crosbie, *Cork Examiner*; Mrs A. Cunningham, William Cullen Library, University of the Witwatersrand, Johannesburg; Jo Currie, Edinburgh University Library; John Curtis, Lloyd's of London; Lakshmi Daniel; Claire Daunton, London Hospital Archives; Stewart Dempster, Press Association Photo Library; Jim Derwin, Maritime Museum, Dun Laoghaire; Christopher Dicks; Grayson Ditchfield; R. Dixon, Stephenson and Harwood, Solicitors; Roger Dixon, Central Library, Belfast; J. W. Dolman, Birch and Co., Solicitors; Graham Dominy, Natal Museum, Pietermaritzburg; Hans J. Dorsch; Barbara Doxat; Eileen Dwyer, *Sydney Morning Herald*; Eamon Dyas, British Library Newspaper Library and News International plc; R. J. Dyke, Standard Chartered Bank; J. R. Elliot, Plymouth Central Library; Alois Engländer; Norman Fairbairn, *Star* Archives, Johannesburg; Shavindra Fernando, Reuter Fellow; Alistair Forbes; B. J. Freedman; Tom Furtado; Sir Peter Gibbings; Leonora Gidlund, New York Municipal Archives; Henry Gilliatt, Bank of England Archives; H. van Gils, South African Press Association, Johannesburg; M. R. Giraud, Bibliothèque de Cessole, Nice; Malcolm Graham; Nadine Graux, Bibliothèque, Verviers; Steve Gray, Law Society, Solicitors' Records Department; Linda Greenlet, *Jewish Chronicle*; Keith Grieves; David Haley; Lady Hamilton; Dorothy Hammerton, Royal Institute of International Affairs; Countess Laurian Anne-Pierre Harcourt; R. H. Harcourt-Williams, Hatfield House archives, Hertfordshire; the Hon. Alan Hare; Kate Harris, Longleat House archives, Wiltshire; Oliver Harris, British Records Association; Lord Hartwell; Joan Hay; Susan Healy, Public Record Office; August Heckscher; Françoise Hildesheimer, Archives Nationales, Paris; Stephen Holder, H. H. Sales Ltd.; André Horgnies; Madame Hoslet, Archives de la Ville de Bruxelles; House of Lords Record Office; Dr Illner, Historisches Archiv, Cologne; Oriental and India Office Collections, British Library; (Richard Bingle, David Blake, Anthony Farrington, Jill Geber, Pat Kattenhorn, Susie Rayner, Tim Thomas); Institute of Historical Research, University of London; Dr Ireland; Aideen M. Ireland, National Archives, Dublin; Irish Railway Records Society, Dublin; Alan Ives; Pierre Jeantet, Agence France Presse; Graeme Jenkins, New Zealand Press Association; Angela Jones; Freddy Joris; M. V. Kamath, Bombay; Christine Kelly, Royal Geographical Society; Serena Kelly, Business Archives Council; Patricia Kemhehan and others, Public Record Office of Northern Ireland; Alison Kenny, Westminster City Libraries; Harold King, jun.; Peter King, Hurstpierpoint College, W. Sussex; Yasuo Kurata; John Laidler, John Rylands Library, Manchester; Professor John Leband, Natal University, Pietermaritzburg; Gwen Lewitt, British Telecom Archives; Liselotte Lenhart; David Linton; Michael Lynch, Institute of Electrical Engineers; Patricia MacCarthy, Cork Archives Institute; Edith H. McCawley, Portland Public Library; Lord MacGregor of Durris; Chrissie Macleod, National Maritime Museum; D. B. Marshall, Young Jones Hair and Co., Solicitors; Marx Memorial

Library; M. M. Massot, Archives de la Ville, Nice; Charles Matyas, New York Municipal Archives; Ralph and Bridget May; Leon Meyer, Hulton Picture Company; Leonard Miall; Middle East Centre, St Antony's College, Oxford; Spencer Minchin, Historical Society of Boputhatswana, Mafeking; Donovan Moldrich, *Times of Ceylon*, Colombo; Jean Morgan, *UK Press Gazette*; Kenneth Morgan; Cormac Murphy, Institute of Irish Studies, Queen's University, Belfast; C. N. N. Nair, Indian Overseas Communications Service, New Delhi; K. N. Narayan; Elizabeth Nathan; National Library of Ireland, Dublin; Nehru Memorial Library, New Delhi; Newcastle upon Tyne Central Library; Newspaper Press Fund; Alexandre Notebaert, Archive du Royaume, Brussels; Liz Ogborn, Bank of England Archives; Peter O'Hara, New Zealand Press Association; Ordnance Survey, Eire; Ted Owers, Baltic Mercantile and Shipping Exchange; Professor Michael Palmer, Department of Communications, Sorbonne, Paris; K. D. Paranavitana, National Archives of Sri Lanka; Jim Parker, Royal Commission on Historical Manuscripts and National Register of Archives; K. Perti, National Archives of India; John Peters, Museum of the Duke of Edinburgh's Royal Regiment, Salisbury; John Phipson, Linklaters and Paines; M. S. de Poorter, Archives départementales des Alpes-Maritimes; Mrs G. Portal; Adrian Porter; Post Office Archives; R. Potts, Tyne and Wear Archives Sergice, Newcastle upon Tyne; Graham Powell, National Library of Australia, Canberra; Public Record Office, Kew; Jack Purdham, Press Association; G. N. S. Raghavan; Gordon Read, National Museums and Galleries on Merseyside, Liverpool; Norman Reddaway; Philip Reed, Imperial War Museum; Audrey Renew, Mafeking Museum; Baroness de Reuter; Eric Rhodes, Press Association; Maureen Richards, Ladysmith Siege Museum; John Rickatson-Hatt; Sue Roach, British Library; Stephen Roberts, Librarian, United States Embassy, London; Lyall Rowe, Australian Associated Press; The Royal Society; Eddy Rutlidge, Australian Archives NSW, Sydney; R. Samways, Greater London Record Office; F. Sartorius; W. Schmitz, Universitätsbibliothek, Cologne; Professor Robert A. Schwarzlose; Hiro Schroff; Anne-Marie Schwirtlich, Australian War Memorial, Canberra; Jon Searle, Garrison Library, Gibraltar; Professor Colin Seymour-Ure, University of Kent; Gerald Shaw, *Cape Times*, Cape Town; Linda Shaw, University of Nottingham Library; Julia Sheppard, Wellcome Institute; Mrs J. Sholto-Douglas; R. F. Shooley-West, Philatelic Collections, British Library; Sally Simpson; Will Simpson; Geoffrey Smith, British Library Newspaper Library; Luc Sonveau; Gavin Souter; South African Post Office Museum, Pretoria (Rita Lombard and J. J. du Toit); Roger Stearn; Professor Jean Stengers; David Stephenson; Professor Gavin Stewart, School of Journalism, Rhodes University, Grahamstown; Sir Richard Storey; Frank Strachan, University of Melbourne Archives; Robin Strathdee, Australian Associated Press; Max Suich, Australian Associated Press; Keith Surridge; Nigel Sutherland; Philip Temple, Survey of London, Royal Commission on Historical Monuments; Anne Thomas, Ohio Historical Society, Columbus; David Thomas, Public Record Office; *Times of India* Archives, New Delhi; A. S. M. du Toit, Natal Archives, Pietermaritzburg;

Transvaal Archives, Pretoria; P. Travers-Laney, Cable and Wireless; Mrs C. Tevelyan-Hall; Dwijendra Tripathi; Heather Tucker, Cheltenham Ladies' College archives; Lyle Turnbull; Peter Turner; University of London Library; P. Unnikrisnan, Press Trust of India, New Delhi; Jean-Pierre Vasseur; Vatican Radio, Rome; Greta Verbeurgt, Archives NMBS, Brussels; Leslie Verry, New Zealand Press Association; Frank van Vree; Miss H. J. C. van der Vyfer, Orange Free State Archives, Bloemfontein; Professor Wesley Wark; Michael Webb, National Maritime Museum and Surrey Record Office; Professor S. Weischenberg; Herr Weise, Rheinisch-Westfälisches Wirtschaftsarchiv, Cologne; R. Wellens, Archives Générales du Royaume, Brussels; Barry Wheeler, Australian Associated Press; David and Clare White; Paul Whittacker; Annesley Wiggins, National Maritime Museum; Glenn Wilkinson; Mrs Betty Williams; Wiltshire Record Office, Trowbridge; K. D. G. Wimalaratne, National Archives of Sri Lanka; Richard Winfrey; J. H. Wolford, Bishoff and Co., Solicitors; Mrs S. Woolgar, Southampton City Records Office; Barbara Worby, South African National Museum of Military History; Gordon Wright, Clare College, Cambridge; Jenny Wright and others, Guildhall Library; Stephen Young; L. Zylbergeld, Archives de la Ville de Bruxelles.

PICTURE ACKNOWLEDGEMENTS

Agence France Presse (Plate 2); Alex (Fig. 17); Bettman Archive, New York (Plate 63); British Library Newspaper Library, London (Fig. 4, Plate 11); Lady Burgess (Plate 44); Canadian International Bank of Commerce (Plate 49); Deutsches Postmuseum, Frankfurt (Plate 4); Financial Times, London (Plate 51); Hulton Picture Company, London (Plates 34, 38); Illustrated London News (Plates 6, 7); Imperial War Museum, London (Plates 21, 37); Gunilla Ingmar, *Monopol pa nyheter* (Uppsala, 1973), 24–5, trans. in Terhi Rantanen, *Foreign News in Imperial Russia* (Helsinki, 1990), 45 (Fig. 6); Liselotte Lenhart (Plate 5); Seaghan Maynes (Plate 36); Mitchell Library, Library of New South Wales, Sydney (Plate 19); National Army Museum, London, courtesy of the Director (Plate 9); National Maritime Museum, London (Fig. 7); *Online Magazine*, Mar. 1990, by permission of Online Inc. (Fig. 18); Postal Museum, Pretoria (Plate 20); Press Association Picture Library, London (Plate 33); Punch Library, London (Fig. 1); Reuters (Frontispiece, Plates 1, 3, 8, 10, 12, 13, 15, 16, 17, 18, 22, 23, 24, 25, 26, 27, 28, 29, 30, 31, 32, 39, 40, 41, 42, 43, 45, 46, 47, 48, 51, 53, 54, 55, 56, 58, 59, 60, 61, Figs. 2, 3, 5, 8, 9, 10, 11, 12, 13, 14, 15, 16); Bob Sacha, New York (Plate 50); Len Santorelli (Plate 57); Transvaal Archives, Pretoria (Plate 14); Turner Entertainment, USA (Plate 35); Visnews, London (Plate 62).

GLOSSARY

beat	News delivered sooner than competitors: 'a beat'.
broadband	Communications channel with a band-width greater than a voice channel and therefore capable of higher-speed data transmission.
cablese	Method of word condensation and combination to save costs of transmission. Latin forms often used: e.g. CUMSPEED, ETBE, POSTDINNER.
copy	Generic term for all news reports and feature articles, general and economic, through from reporters' drafts to issued version.
copytaker	Clerk/telephonist who types copy telephoned through by reporters or other news suppliers.
copytaster	Senior sub-editor who scans incoming copy to decide its news value.
dateline	Place (and often also time) from which a message is sent. Verbal form: 'datelined'.
flash	Signal for highest-priority news of supreme urgency. Conveys the bare fact only, e.g.:
	FLASH
	WASHINGTON: NIXON RESIGNED¯REUTER
kill	A news story already issued but found to be without foundation or even partly inaccurate has to be 'killed'. A substitute version may then follow.
lead	A new opening to a running news story.
multiplexing	Division of a transmission facility into two or more channels. Hence 'time-division multiplexing', allotting a transmission facility to different channels one at a time.
real time	In computer language a system which processes information at the time of input as opposed to storing for processing at a later date. The Reuter Monitor (ch. 12) is a notable example.
representation allowance	Extra payment for personifying 'Reuters', usually for managers or correspondents overseas.
scoop	An exclusive 'beat'.
service message	An instructional or administrative communication to a manager or correspondent.
situationer	A holdable story, suitable for supplementing the immediate news file, containing background and interpretation suitable for feature pages. Sent from overseas by mail.

snap   Signal used to break urgent news just below 'flash' value. Usually of one sentence.

spike   Unusable messages were put on a spike. Hence 'to spike'.

stringer   Part-time correspondent, often a reporter from a local newspaper.

sub-editor Journalist in the newsroom with responsibility for checking, tidying, and if necessary rewriting correspondents' copy.

INDEX

Entries for illustrations are shown in *italics*; *Pl.* indicates one of the plates grouped between pages 128–9 and 272–3; *Fig. (p.)* indicates a figure on that page. Entries for quotations are separately listed—preceded by q.

Farquhar, Ronald 380, 393; q. 380
Farrell, Adrienne 373, *Fig. 15 (p. 373)*, 390
Ferguson, Fergus James 139–40; q. 140
film (Reuter biography) 232–3, *Pl. 35*
Financial News 78
Financial Times 338, 349, 354, q. 352
First World War: role of Reuters 111–31;
    war news 132–46, *Fig. 10 (p. 146)*, 150,
    155, *Pl. 20, Pl. 21*; Reuter memorial 130
flash reports 31, 109, 141, 200–1, 215, 384,
    415
Fleet Holdings 348, 350, 360, 367
Fleet Street, *see* Head Office
Fleetwood-May, Cecil 156–9, 254, *Pl. 39*
Fleming, Ian Lancaster 206–7; q. 206–7
flotation (public company) 331, 337–69,
    Pl. 52
Forbes q. 99
Forcereuter 256
'Forex' 303–4
Forsyth, Frederick 371
Founders Share Co. 364, 404
'frame-grabbing', *see* 'row-grabbing'
France 18, 25, 249, 254, 324, 386–8, *Pl. 56*
Franco-Prussian War 42, 53, 58, 65–6,
    92–4, *Pl. 10*
Frankfurt 51, 94, 255, 291, 342, *Pl. 48*
Fraser, (Sir) Ian 349–50
Freeman, John 365
From Pigeon Post to Wireless (Collins) vi

Gagarin, Yuri 390
Gall, Sandy 381
Gallagher, Wes 315
Gampell, Sydney 160
Gandhi, Devadas 261
Gandhi, Mohandas Karamchand
    (Mahatma) 167, 198, 201, 383–4
Garibaldi, Giuseppe 30
Garry, Kevin 289, 344; q. 325
Gaulle, Charles de, *see* de Gaulle
Gauss, Karl Friedrich 6–7
Gawthrop, Arnold 86–7, 107–8
Gee, Jack 378, 380
Gee, Nina 221
Geiringer, Alfred 254–5, 271–3, 293–4
Geller, Heinrich 11–12
general managers 121, 234, 238, 264, 281
General News Division 283, 291–2, 295,
    332–4, 356, 398, 400
General Strike (1926) 202–3
Geneva 289, 291, 342, 402

George V, King *Pl. 21*
Germany 40, 47, 49–51, 181, 183, 198,
    205, 207, 210, 232, 254–5, 284, 298,
    322–4, 341, 370, 394, 406, *Pl. 4, Pl. 48*;
    First World War 111, 132–6, 138–9,
    141–3, *Pl. 22*; Second World War *Pl.
    38*; Berlin Wall 376–8, 394, *Pl. 63*
Gettysburg Address 37–8
Ghana News Agency 326
Gibbings, (Sir) Peter 347, 349, 358
Gladstone, 1st Visct. 118, 120–1
Glasgow Herald 179, 240
Glenconner, 1st Baron 124
Globereuter 185, 249, 251, 257–8
GND, *see* General News Division
Goebbels, Josef 211, 218–19, 222, 227
Goenka, Ramnath 261
Goering, Hermann 212, 371
Gordon, Gen Charles George 30, 102
Gothic House 215, 252, 275; *see also* Radio
    House
Government (British), *see* British Government
Gower, Dodson & Co 77
Graeco-Turkish War 105–6
Graham, Malcolm 235, 357
Graham-Barrow, Charles Russell 229
Grant, James 21–2; q. 21–2, 52
Green End (monitoring station) 257, 269,
    376, 390, *Pl. 41*; *see also* monitoring
Grey, Anthony *Fig. 16 (p. 379)*, 380
Grey, Sir Edward (later Visct. Grey of
    Fallodon) 134
Griffiths, Frederick John 15–16, 63, 70,
    103; q. 60
Griffiths, Frederick John jun. 16, 130
Griffiths, George 16, 19
Griffiths, Peter 380
Grime, (Sir) Harold 235
Gritzner, Max 10
Guardian 349; *see also Manchester Guardian*
Guebenlian, Shahe 329
Gwynne, Howell Arthur 85, 105–6, *Pl. 14*
Gyllenhammer, Pehr 366

Hahn, Jimmy 267
Hailsham, 1st Visct. 197
Hajduska, Arnold J. 77–8, 114
Haley, (Sir) William John viii, 180, 188–9,
    191–3, 215–16, 239–44, 245, 248–52,
    369, *Pl. 34*; q. 180, 192, 240, 241, 244,
    251
Hamburg 42, 51, 57

Index compiled by David Linton